A

GRAMMAR

OF

THE TIBETAN LANGUAGE.

A

GRAMMAR

OF

THE TIBETAN LANGUAGE,

IN

ENGLISH.

BY

ALEXANDER CSOMA DE KÕRÖS

GYAN

Published by

GYAN

Gyan Publishing House
5, Ansari Road
Daryaganj, New Delhi-110002
Phone: 011-47034999, 9811692060
E-mail: books@gyanbooks.com

Distribution Network
gyanbooks.com
India, USA, Canada, UK, Australia, France

ISBN: 978-81-212-7326-8 (PB)
First Published, 1834

2nd Impression 2023

Printed at: Gyan Press, Delhi.

A GRAMMAR OF THE TIBETAN LANGUAGE
Author: ALEXANDER CSOMA DE KÕRÖS

GRAMMAR

OF

THE TIBETAN LANGUAGE.

BY

ALEXANDER CSOMA DE KŐRÖS.

1834.

A GRAMMAR OF THE TIBETAN LANGUAGE, IN ENGLISH.

PREPARED,

UNDER THE PATRONAGE OF THE GOVERNMENT AND THE AUSPICES OF THE ASIATIC SOCIETY OF BENGAL,

BY

ALEXANDER CSOMA DE KŐRÖS,

SICULO-HUNGARIAN OF TRANSYLVANIA.

Calcutta:

PRINTED AT THE BAPTIST MISSION PRESS, CIRCULAR ROAD.

1834.

༄༅། །བོད་སྐད་ཀྱི་བྱཱ་ཀ་ར་ཎ་ལམ་ཕྲང་སྟོན་པའི་
བསྟན་བཅོས་བཞུགས་སོ། །

(A Byákaraná or grammatical work of the Tibetan Language.)

༄༅། །དཀོན་མཆོག་གསུམ་ལ་ཕྱག་འཚལ་ལོ། །

(Sans. *Namo Ratna Trayáya.* Eng. Reverence to the three Holy Ones.)

༄༅། །བྱཱ་ཀ་ར་ཎའི་ཚུལ་བཞིན་དུ། །
བོད་སྐད་ལེགས་པར་ཤེས་པའི་ཕྱིར། །
མིང་ཚིག་བརྗོད་པ་ཀུན་གྱི་གཞི། །
ཡི་གེའི་སྦྱོར་བ་བཤད་པར་བྱ། །

(For understanding well the Tibetan language, according to grammatical rules, the arrangement of letters, which are the basis of syllables, words, and sentences, is to be explained.)

PREFACE.

THE wide diffusion of the Buddhistic religion in the eastern parts of Asia, having of late greatly excited the attention of European scholars, and it being now ascertained by several distinguished Orientalists, that this faith, professed by so many millions of men in different and distant countries in the East, originated in Central or Gangetic India, it is hoped that a Grammar and Dictionary of the Tibetan language will be favourably received by the learned Public; since, Tibet being considered as the head-quarters of Buddhism in the present age, these elementary works may serve as keys to unlock the immense volumes, (faithful translations of the Sanskrit text) which are still to be found in that country, on the manners, customs, opinions, knowledge, ignorance, superstition, hopes, and fears of great part of Asia, especially of India, in former ages.

There are, in modern times, three predominant religious professions in the world, each counting numerous votaries, and each possessed of a large peculiar literature:—the Christians, the Muhammedans, and the Buddhists. It is not without interest to observe the coincidence of time with respect to the great exertions made by several Princes, for the literary establishment of each of these different religions, in the Latin, the Arabic, and in the Sanskrit languages, in the 8th and 9th century of the Christian Æra: by CHARLES THE GREAT, and his immediate successors, in Germany and France; by the Khalifs AL-MANSUR, HARUN AL-RASHID, and AL-MAMUN, at Bagdad; by the Kings of Magadha, in India; by KHRISRONG DE'HU TSAN, KHRI DE'SRONG TSAN, and RAL-PACHEN, in Tibet: and by the Emperors of the Thang dynasty, in China. But it is to the honour of Christianism to observe that, while learning has been continually declining among the Muhammedans and the Buddhists, Christianity has not only carried its own literature and science to a very advanced period of excellence, but in the true and liberal spirit of real knowledge, it distinguishes itself by its efforts in the present day towards acquiring an intimate acquaintance with the two rival religious systems, and that too, in their original languages. Hence, in the north-western parts of Europe, in Germany, England, France, where a thousand years ago, only the Latin was studied by literary men, there are now found establishments for a critical knowledge both of the Arabic and the Sanskrit literature.

Hence, too, has been founded recently the *Oriental Translation Committee*, composed of the most eminent Orientalists of Europe, from whose labours so much has already been done, and so much more is expected. The students of Tibetan have naturally been the most rare, if they have existed at all, in this learned association. Insulated among inaccessible mountains, the convents of Tibet have remained unregarded and almost unvisited by the scholar and the traveller:—nor was it until within these few years conjectured, that in the undisturbed shelter of this region, in a climate proof against the decay and the destructive influences of tropical plains, were to be found, in complete preservation, the volumes of the Buddhist faith, in their original Sanskrit, as well as in faithful translations, which might be sought in vain on the continent of India. I hope that my sojourn in this inhospitable country, for the express purpose of mastering its language, and examining its literary stores, will not have been time unprofitably spent, and that this Grammar and Dictionary may attest the sincerity of my endeavours to attain the object I had determined to prosecute.

Having in the Preface to my Dictionary expressed my respectful thanks to the British Government of India, for its patronage during my Tibetan studies; and having there gratefully enumerated the kindnesses and good services which I have received from several Gentlemen, it would be superfluous here to repeat my acknowledgments. My selection of the English language, as the medium of introduction of my labours, will sufficiently evince to the learned of Europe, at large, the obligations I consider myself under to that nation. I beg now only to state in a few words, that in the preparation of this grammatical work, I have not observed any strict arrangement of the parts of Grammar, neither have I introduced the definitions of the several parts of speech, nor have I touched upon the analogy which this tongue has to several others ; since the work would thus have been increased to an immense size. But, for brevity's sake, I have enumerated only those articles which I thought to be essentially required for a fundamental knowledge of this yet unknown language. I have gone through all the parts of speech, and have given lists of them as fully as it was in my power to do, together with their derivations and variations, &c., that the learner might at once see and perceive all the constituent parts of the Tibetan language.

Orthography being the most difficult part of this language, in the Syllabic Scheme and in the Dictionary I have endeavoured, with the aid of authentic grammatical works, to express every word in its proper characters. The declension of nouns, and the conjugation of verbs, as in the common Indian dialects, are very simple. A well arranged Dictionary, with a short introduction on the general forms of declensions and conjugations, will be sufficient to conduct the scholar to a perfect knowledge of this language. For further information on the subject and for the contents and arrangement of this Grammar, the work itself may be consulted.

A. CSOMA DE KÖRÖS.

Calcutta, December, 1834.

CONTENTS.

Page.

APPENDIX.

ERRATA AND ADDENDA.

Page.	col.	line.		
1	—	6	*after* "name" *insert* "and power"	
2	—	5	*for* ཞབ་སརྒྱ	*read* ཞབས་རྒྱ
3	—	3	འཇུག	འཕྲུག
4	—	22	ངབྲ	དབྲ
7	—	17	*Swahá*	*Swáhá*
13	2	27	ཕྱ	ཕྱི
18	—	5	ཀ	ཀྱུ
21	—	—	[illegible]	[illegible]
—	—	6	ཀ	ཀཱ
—	—	24	སྒོཔེ	སྒོཔོ
—	—	27	ཕྱོསེ	ཕྱོསོ

Note.—In a few contracted words in this list, instead of ‵ or ′ (as the sign of ཚི, ཚེ, or ཛོ, &c.) *read* ʳ.

Page.	col.	line.		
23	—	6	*for* མངས	*read* མོངས
—	—	27	དཔྱོགས	དཔྱོགས
24	—	4	ཕྱུགས	ཕྱོགས
25	—	1	བརྟོས	བརྟོས
32	—	19	*at the beginning, add* § 63.	
36	—	18	*for* མེལབ	*read* མེལ་བ
42	—	13	སོགསཚོ	སོགས, ཚོ
56	2	2	འཤིག	འཇིག
—	—	20	འབྲབ	འབྲལ
—	—	25	འཆིད	འཆི་མེད
58	1	1	ཚོབ	སྐྱོབ
—	—	5	ཡང་ཏོག	ཡང་མོར
—	2	11	སྲིད་ཅན,	སྲིད་ཅན,
—	—	12	སྲིད་ལྡན	སྲིད་ལྡན
59	—	4	བསྟུལ	བསྟོལ
—	—	16	ཐུས	ཐེས
61	1	17	ཐེམ	ཐོམ
64	—	22	ཨུ—ཏྲེ	ཏྲེ—ཨུ
65	—	20	*for* ན་ནི	*read* ང་ནི
68	—	22	ཀོང་ཅག	ཁོང་ཅག
69	—	9	ངད་ཀྱི	ངེད་ཀྱི
—	—	10	ངརང་དག་གི	ང་རང་དག་གི
—	—	15	ཁྱོད་ར་ང་དག་གི	ཁྱོད་རང་དག་གི
—	—	25	འདེ་ནི	འདི་ནི
—	—	28	ད་ནི	དེ་ནི
—	—	—	དི་ཀོ་ནཉིད	དེ་ཁོ་ན་ཉིད
70	—	26	དང་དག་གིས	གང་དག་གིས
72	—	30	ཕྱེད་པ་པོ	ཕྱེད་པ་པོ
73	—	16	སྤྱའ	སྤྱོའ
75	—	9	དཔ	ད་པ
76	—	19	བཅིད	བཅིད
—	—	23	ཅས	ཅེས
—	—	27	བཤག	བཞིག
77	—	23	འབྲི	དབྲི
79	—	6	གསུང་ཤིག	གསུངས་ཤིག
—	—	12	གཏོད	གཏོང
82	—	22	སྤེལ	སྤེལ
—	—	25	འབྲ་བར་འགྱུར	འབྲལ་ &c.
90	—	5, *also* 7,	རི་ཐོག་པ	རི་ &c.
95	2	22	*after* ནམ་ཡང, *add* ནམས་གྱང	
98	1	11	*for* ཉིམོ་།ཉི་མོར	*read* ཉེ་མོ། ཉེ་མོར
102	2	25	རྫང	རྡུང
—	1	30	ཐང་ན	ཐད་ན
108	—	28	*instead of the dash* —, *read* contractedly.	
110	—	24	རྒྱ་ལཔོ	རྒྱལ་པོ
111	—	29	སྦྱིགས་པམ	སྦྱིགས་པམ
112	—	2	ཁོང་ཁིས	ཁོང་གིས
—	—	8	ཕྱག་མས	ཕྱག་མས
118	1	22	འཛིན་པ	འཛིན་པ

Page.	col.	line.		
122	—	7	*for* བཀྲིག་བ	*read* བཀྲིག་པ
124	2	9	བསྟུབ་བ	བསྟུབ་པ
126	—	3	ཧྲེབི་པ	ཧྲིབ་པ
131	1	29	ཆིར་བ	ཆེར་བ
134	2	24	འདེགས་བ	འདེགས་པ
135	1	26	འཕ་མཔ	འཕམ་པ
137	2	23	ཕིབ་བ	ཕིབ་པ
138	1	9	ཀ་བ	ཀེ་བ
141	1	6	འཁྲུ་བ	འཁྲོ་བ
142	2	23	བཀྲུབ	བཀྲོ་བ
155	—	6	སྐྲངས་བར	སྒྲངས་བར
—	—	8	མེ, for 3 ;	—མེ, for—3 ;
—	—	9	in	is
156	—	28	*add* S. *Phaluka.*	
157	—	27	*after* "a star" *insert* འཁོར་ལོ. hkhor-lo, S. *Chakra*, the circle of the 27 *Nakshatras.*	
158	—	13	*for* ཚེགས	*read* ཚིགས
159	—	15	ཡོད་དན	ཡོན་ཏན
—	—	28	portioned	proportioned
160	—	17	affection	affectation
—	—	19	*Shaddhodana*	*Shuddhodana*
161	—	9	འསབས	འཕགས
162	—	30	shis	she
164	—	30	yས	ནས
165	—	26	ཕྱུར	ཕྱིར
—	—	27	ཕྱིརདང	ཕྱིར་དང
169	—	2	*Svadéshé*	*Sva déshé*

Note. The Remarkable Sayings, No. 16. are attributed to k*Lus grub* (ཀླུ་སྒྲུབ, S. *Nágarjuna,)* a very celebrated ancient sage in India. See བསྟན་ འགྱུར, མདོ, vol. གོ, leaf 165, in the work entitled S. *Niti Shástra, Prajnyá danda*, Tib .ལུགས་ཀྱི་བསྟན་བཅོས་ཤེས་རབ་སྡོང་བུ, an ethical work (entitled) "*The Stem of Wisdom.*" The work of the *Saskya Pandita*, to which they are referred in the text, consists of about 450 Slokas, all of the same kind and tenor of verses as these here quoted from *Nágarjuna.* These verses were found among my extracts from the work quoted in the text, and I did not distinguish the different authors. I take this opportunity of correcting my mistake.

Page.	col.	line.		
—	—	20	*for* རིག་པ	*read* རིག་པར
171	—	21	ཅག་ག	ཅག་གི
—	—	27	འཕྲམ	འབྲུམ
173	—	10	འདོ	འདི
—	—	27	མེམས	སེམས
174	—	26	དི	དེ
175	—	11	དི	དེ
178	—	13	*add:* He made grammatical works, and translated some religious tracts.	
—	—	24	*for* གཙོ་བོ	*read* རྗེ་བོ
179	—	7	གསིལ	གསོལ
180	—	4	ཆོ་སའབྱུང	ཆོས་འབྱུང
—	—	20	ཚིགས	ཚིགས
181	—	4	མཆོ	མཆོ
—	—	23	commanded	commenced.
185	—	28	སས	ནས
187	—	31	142	1427
188	—	12	ཚིས	ཚིས
—	—	13	འབྲུངསདགེ་འཞཅན་	འབྲུངསདགེ་འཅན་
—	—	14	གིས	གྱིས
198	—	7	ཁྲིམས	ཁྲིམས
200	—	28	སྔོནད། པལ	སྔོན། དཔལ
—	—	24	ལུ་གས	ལུགས

A GRAMMAR

OF

THE TIBETAN LANGUAGE.

LETTERS AND THEIR SEVERAL DISTINCTIONS.

§ 1. In the alphabet of the Tibetan language there are thirty simple letters, arranged in eight classes. The forms of them, together with the name of each expressed in Roman characters and Italics, may be represented thus :

1	ཀ ka	ཁ kha	ག ga	ང ṅa
	k	*kh*	*g*	*ng*
2	ཅ cha	ཆ chha	ཇ ja	ཉ nya
	ch	*chh*	*j*	*ny*
3	ཏ ta	ཐ tha	ད da	ན na
	t	*th*	*d*	*n*
4	པ pa	ཕ pha	བ ba	མ ma
	p	*ph*	*b*	*m*
5	ཙ tsa	ཚ tsha	ཛ dsa	ཝ wa
	ts	*tsh*	*ds*	*w*
6	ཞ zha	ཟ za	འ ha	ཡ ya
	zh	*z*	*h*	*y*
7	ར ra	ལ la	ཤ sha	ས sa
	r	*l*	*sh*	*s*
8	ཧ h'a	ཨ á		
	h'	*a*		

§ 2. There are five vowel sounds: *a*, *i*, *u*, *e*, *o*, pronounced according to the general pronunciation in Latin, on the continent of Europe, without any distinction into short and long, but observing a middle sound. The vowel *a*, when sounded after a consonant, is generally inherent; but when otherwise there would be confusion on account of the prefix, it is expressed by འ. The vowels *i*, *u*, *e*, *o*, are expressed by marks put above or below the consonants; thus ི ུ ེ ོ as in ཀི ki, ཀུ ku, ཀེ ké, ཀོ ko. These vowel signs are called ི གི་གུ *gi-gu*, ུ ཞབས་ཀྱུ *zhabs-kyu* ེ འགྲེང་བུ and ོ ན་རོ *na-ro*.

§ 3. There are very few words commencing with any vowel, and those are either of Sanscrit origin, or interjections, or corrupt words. The five vowels, when initial in a syllable or word, are expressed in the following manner: ཨ *a*, ཨི *i*, ཨུ *u*, ཨེ *e*, ཨོ *o*; they may be expressed also by འ *'a*, འི *'i*, འུ *'u*, འེ *'e*, འོ *'o*.

§ 4. The above enumerated consonants and vowels are thus divided with respect to the organs by which they are formed:

ཀ ཁ ག ང འ ཧ ཨ are gutturals.

ཙ ཚ ཛ ཉ ཅ ཆ ཇ
ཞ ཡ ཤ ཨི ཨེ — — } are palatials.

ཏ ཐ ད ན ཟ ལ ས are dentals.

པ ཕ བ མ ཝ ཨུ ཨོ are labials.

ར is liquid and cerebral.

But ང་ ཉ་ ན་ མ, besides what has been stated above, are likewise nasals.

§ 5. The thirty letters of the alphabet are distinguished, according to their accent or sound, by certain genders; thus: ཀ་ ཙ་ ཏ་ པ་ ཅ are called masculine, (ཕོ p,ho;) ཁ་ ཚ་ ཐ་ ཕ་ ཆ་ neuter, (མ་ནིང་ *ma-ning*;) ག་ ཛ་ ད་ བ་ ཇ་ ཞ་ ཟ་ འ་ ཡ་ ཤ་ ས feminine, (མོ *mo*;) ར་ ལ་ ཧ་ low or barren feminine, (མོ་ གཤམ *mo-gsham*;) and the ཨ is said to have no gender.

§ 6. All the thirty letters, in general, may occur as initials, forming the basis of a syllable or word (མིང་ གཞི. *ming-gzhi*). From among the thirty, the following twenty, ཀ་ ཁ། ཅ་ ཆ་ ཇ་ ཉ། ཏ་ ཐ། པ་ ཕ། ཙ་ ཚ་ ཛ་ ཝ། ཞ་ ཟ་ ཡ་ ཤ། ཧ་ ཨ never occur as final letters or after any vowel. The remaining ten, ག་ ང་ ད་ ན་ བ་ མ་ འ་ ར་ ལ་ ས, are the only letters that close any syllable, or follow the vowel, whether inherent or expressed. But these ten letters may likewise stand as initials in a syllable or word.

§ 7. The ten final letters are called affixes, (ཞེས་ འཇུག *zhes-hjug*) from their being affixed to the basis of a syllable. With respect to their sound and use, they are distingnished thus: ག་ ད་ བ་ ས are masculine, (ཕོ *po* ;) ན་ ར་ ལ neuter, (མ་ ནིང་, *ma-ning*,) and ང་ མ་ འ, feminine, (མོ *mo* ;) when the letters ག་ ང་ བ་ མ are followed by ས ; thus: གས་ ངས་ བས་ མས ; or the letters ན་ ར་ ལ by ད, thus ནད་ རད་ ལད, then the ས and ད are called a second affix, ཡང་འཇུག, *yang-hjug*.

§ 8. From among the ten affixes, the following five. ག་ ད་ བ་ མ་ འ, are also called prefixes, སྔོན་ འཇུག, *sn̆on-hjug*, from their being put before the basis of a syllable. They are likewise distinguished thus: ག་ ད་ are called neuter, (མ་ ནིང་ *ma-ning ;)* བ masculine (ཕོ *pho ;)* མ very femenine, (ཤིན་ ཏུ་ མོ *shin-tu-mo* ;) འ feminine, (མོ *mo.)* These prefixes occur in several parts of speech, especially among the verbs. They should always be pronounced, but in common practice are seldom heard. For distinction's sake, they may be represented by the small Roman characters *g*, *d*, *b*, *m*, *h*, when the rest is in Italics or vice versa, and this system will be followed in the present work.

This is all that need be said of the letters of the Tibetan alphabet. We will next procced to the powers of the letters individually, explaining at the same time the plan of writing them in the Roman character.

PRONUNCIATION.

§ 9. 1. Of the thirty simple letters.

ཀ is pronounced like k in king, or c before *a*, *o*, *u*, in call, come, cut; as in ཀ་བ *ka-va*, a pillar; ཀུན kun, all.

ཁ is the same letter aspirated; it may properly be rendered by *kh ;* as in ཁ་ བོ *kha-vo*, the mouth.

ག when simple, is generally sounded like *k* or *q ;* but by some it is pronounced also as *g*. It may always be represented by *g ;* thus in གུར *gur*, a tent; ལག་ པ *lag-pa*, the hand.

ང is the nasal *n* or *ng* in ing. When preceding the vowel in a syllable, it may be rendered by *n̆ ;* after the vowel, by *ng ;* and, when reduplicated by *g ;* thus: ང་རང་ *n̆a-rang*, I myself; རུང་ གམ *rung-gam*, is it convenient? རུང་གོ *rung-go*, it is proper.

ཅ is sounded like *ch* in church ; as in ཅི *chi*, what? It may be represented by *ch*.

ཆ is the same letter aspirated. It may be rendered by *chh ;* as in ཆུ *chhu*, water.

ཇ though by some people is sounded like *ch*, in choose, may always be represented by *j* in just ; as in ཇོ་བོ *jo-vo*, a master, lord ; ཇོ་མོ *jo-mo*, a mistress, lady ; a nun.

ཉ is sounded like *ne* in new ; as in ཉུང་ *nyung*, few, little ; ཉ *nya*, fish. It may properly be represented by *ny*.

ཏ is *t* in tongue ; as in ཏིག་ མེན *tig-men*, a ribband ; ཏིབ་ རིལ *tib-ril*, a tea-pot.

ཐ is the same letter aspirated. It may be rendered by *th ;* as in ཐག་ པ *thag-pa* a rope ; ཐོག་མ *thog-ma*, beginning.

ད when simple, is sounded commonly like *t* in tool ; but by some people it is pronounced also as *d*. It may always properly be represented by *d*, and pronounced accordingly ; as in དད་པ *dad-pa*, faith, belief ; དེ་ རིང་ *de-ring*, to-day.

ན is sounded like *n* in noon ; as in ནོར *nor*, wealth.

པ is like *p* in paper ; as in པར་མ *parma*, a printed work.

ཕ is the same letter aspirated. It may be rendered by *ph*, and pronounced as the *p-h* in up-hill as in ཕ *pha*, father.

བ has three sounds : (*p*, *b*, *v*.) As initial in a word, it is sounded by some like *p ;* as in བོད *pöt* (for Bod), Tibet or a Tibetan. As a prefix, it is silent ; as in བཀའ *kah* (for *bkha*), a precept or command. As an additional syllable, or article after the ང་ འ་ ར་ ལ final letters, or when it has the ད prefix, it is generally pronounced as v ; as in རེ་ བ *ré-va*, hope ; དབང *d,vang*, power. In the two following cases, དབུ and དབོ (*dvu* and *dvo*) the pronunciation is simply as *u* and *o*. With any of the surmounting ར་ ལ་ ས (*r*, *l*, *s*,) or preceding འ *(h)* letters, it is sounded *b*, those letters being then silent. In general it may be represented by *b*.

མ is like *m* in man *;* as in མི *mi*, a man ; མེ *mé*, fire ; ལམ *lam*, way, road.

ཙ is the German *z* or *tz*. It may be rendered by *ts* (as English and French writers use it in foreign names or words) ; as in ཙུག *tsug*, how ? ཙམ *tsam*, how much ? how many ?

ཚ is the same letter aspired. It may be represented by *tsh ;* as in ཚེ *tshé*, life.

ཛ is sounded like the Arabic *dsal* (ذ) or the Italian *z* in mezzo. It may be represented by *ds ;* as in ཛ་ཏི *dsati*, nutmeg. There are no words in Tibetan written by this simple character; but there are many that have it with a མ or འ prefix, which are sounded like the simple ཛ; as in མཛད་པ m*dsad-pa*, to do, make; འཛིན་པ h*dsin-pa*, to seize, take, &c.

The Sanscrit *ch*, *chh*, *j*, *jh*, characters (as they are pronounced in Bengal and by Europeans) are rendered in Tibetan books, by *ts*, *tsh*, *ds*, *dsh*, (ཙ་ ཚ་ ཛ་ ཛྷ,) and pronounced accordingly, as has been explained above. Such is the pronunciation in Cashmir also, and in some parts of the north-west of India. And, as the Tibetan grammarians have observed, it was so anciently in Central India also; though in Bengal the pronunciation has always been the same as it now is, with respect to *ch*, *chh*, *j*, *jh*.

ཝ occurs but in a few words. It is sounded *v* or *w*. བ and ཝ often have the same sound in Tibetan; as in བཱ་ར་ཎ་སཱི and ཝཱ་ར་ཎ་སཱི *Váranási*, Benares. They may be represented thus: བ by *v*, and ཝ by *w*.

ཞ is the French *j*. It may be rendered by *zh*; as in ཞལ *zhal*, the mouth, face.

ཟ is pronounced like *z* in zeal, or *s* in as; as in ཟན *zan*, meat, food.

འ is a soft aspirate, and may be represented by *h* or *a*. Formerly it was added to every syllable ending in a vowel, thus: ཀའ *kah*, ཀིའ *kih*, ཀུའ *kuh*, ཀེའ *keh*, ཀོའ *koh*, instead of the modern ཀ་ ཀི་ ཀུ་ ཀེ་ ཀོ. But now it is left out after the vowel signs, and retained only in those syllables in which the fundamental (or radical) letter is preceded by a prefix, and where there is no closing consonant after the inherent *a*; as in these words: གཟའ g*zah*, a planet; དགའ d*gah*, joy; བཀའ b*kah*, precept; མདའ m*dah*, an arrow; འདའ h*dah*, to pass away. But, when there is a closing consonant, the འ is dropt; as in འདས་པ h*das-pa*, gone away.

ཡ is sounded like *y* in yard, you: as in ཡབ *yab*, father; ཡུམ *yum*, mother, matron.

ར is like *r* in rain; as in རེ་བ *ré-va*, hope; ར་མ *ra-ma*, a she-goat. It is silent when inserted on the top of a letter; as in རྐ r*ka*, pronounced *ka*.

ལ is pronounced like *l* in long; as in ལོ *lo*, a year. It is silent at the top of another letter; as in ལྔ l*ňa*, (*ňa*) five.

ཤ has the sound of *sh* in sheep; as in ཤིང *shing*, wood, a tree.

ས is the *s* in saint; as in སོ་སོ *so-so*, different; སེམས *sems*, the mind, soul. At the top of a letter, as also at the end of a syllable, it is silent, according to common practice.

ཧ is the hard aspirated *h* in heart, horn, as in ཧོར *Hor*, a Turk.

ཨ is sounded like *a* in far, father, as in ཨ་ཆེ *a-chhé*, one's elder sister. The inherent *a* also is not pronounced like the short *u* in up, cup, &c. as in Sanscrit, but it has a middle sound like the French *a* in la, or the English in far, father; as in ལམ *lam*, way, road.

§ 10. Such is the pronunciation of the 30 simple letters. But, besides these, there are many conpound letters, formed either by subjoining one of the following three liquids ཡ་ར་ལ (*y, r, l,*) to another, thus: ཀྱ་ཀྲ་ཀླ; or by placing one of these ར་ལ་ས (*r, l, s,*) on the top of another, thus: རྐ.ལྐ.སྐ, or by both ways at once, thus: རྐྱ་ སྐྱ་ སྐྲ. We proceed now to treat of such compound letters; and first,

§ 11. 2. Of those letters that have a subjoined ཡ, *y*, (ཡ་བཏགས *ya-btags*) written thus: ྱ.

They are seven in number ཀ་ ཁ་ ག་ པ་ ཕ་ བ་ མ, and are represented thus: ཀྱ *kya*, ཁྱ *khya*, གྱ *gya*, པྱ *pya*, ཕྱ *phya*, བྱ *bya*, མྱ *mya*. Their pronunciation is as follows:

ཀྱ is sounded like *t* in tube, or in virtue; as in ཀྱལ་པ *kyal-pa*, idle talk.

ཁྱ is the preceding character aspirated; as in ཁྱི *khyi*, a dog.

གྱ is pronounced like *d* in duke; as in གྱུར་པ *gyur-pa*, he is become, or grown.

པྱ in no word occurs in this simple state. It has either a surmounting ས (thus: སྤྱ *spya*) or a ད prefix, (thus: དཔྱ d*pya*) and then, in each case, it is sounded *ch*, or *sh*; as in སྤྱན *spyan* (*shan* or *chan*) the eye; དཔྱ d*pya* (*sha* or *cha*) tax, tribute.

ཕྱ is pronounced generally *chh*; as in ཕྱུག་པོ *phyug-po*, the rich or rich, (*chhug-po*.) But in Ladak, and in some other parts, it is sounded also like ཕ *ph*; as in ཕྱེ *phye*, meal, flour, pronounced (ཕྱེ *phé*,) as if there were no subjoined *y*, ྱ.

བྱ is pronounced *ch* and *j*; as in བྱེད་པ *byed-pa* (*ched-pa* or *jed-pa*), to do, make.

མྱ is sounded *ny*; as in མྱོང་བ *myong-va* (pronounced *nyong-va*), to taste.

§ 12. 3. Of those letters that have ར subjoined (ར་བཏགས *ra* b*tags*, written thus: ྲ.)

The following fourteen letters ཀ་ ཁ་ ག་ ཏ་ ཐ་ ད་ ན་ པ་ ཕ་ བ་ མ་ ཤ་ ས་ ཧ, subject to this addition, assume the form of ཀྲ *kra*, ཁྲ *khra*, གྲ *gra*, ཏྲ *tra*, ཐྲ *thra*, དྲ *dra*, ནྲ *nra*, པྲ *pra*, ཕྲ *phra*, བྲ *bra*, མྲ *mra*, ཤྲ *shra*, སྲ *sra*, ཧྲ *hra*: and they should also be pronounced accordingly; but, in common practice, they are sounded very obscurely, ཀྲ, ཏྲ, པྲ, are sounded like *ta*; ཁྲ, ཐྲ, ཕྲ, like *tha*; གྲ, དྲ, བྲ, like *'da* or *t'a*, or all the nine like *t*: ཤྲ, སྲ, ཧྲ, are sounded by some people like a cerebral *sh*. As this mode of pronouncing the letters, which have a subjoined *r*, is very uncertain, it is better to write and pronounce them regularly, as in other languages.

§ 13. 4. Of those letters that have a subjoined ལ, *la* (ལ་བཏགས *la* b*tags*) :

The following six letters : ཀ་ག་བ་ཟ་ར་ས, with ལ subjoined, have the form of ཀླ *kla*, གླ *gla*, བླ *bla*, ཟླ *zla*, རླ *rla*, སླ *sla*. All such syllables are pronounced alike, the subjoined *l* alone being uttered, (the upper letters remaining silent, according to common custom,) with the exception of ཟླ *zla*, which is pronounced *da*. But this also sometimes is sounded *la*, as in སྤུན་ཟླ *spun-zla* (*spun-la*), a brother or sister.

Note.—Besides the three subjoined letters above specified, (*y*, *r*, *l*,) there occurs sometimes a small triangle, (called in Tibetan *Vazur*, an angular *v* or *w*, thus : ▵) placed below some letters. In Tibetan words it has no sound, but it is used only for distinction's sake; as in ཚ *tsha*, hot; ཚྭ *tsha*, salt: རྩ r*tsa*, root, vein; རྩྭ r*tsa*, grass, herb. In ཡི་དྭགས the ▵ is added to show that the ད is a radical letter, not a prefix, and to be sounded accordingly. But this ▵ in these and other similar words is not always inserted: many leave it out, the context showing the proper meaning of the word. In Sanscrit words this ▵ is pronounced *o* in Tibet; as in *Bodhisato*, *Sohá*, *Om ! Soti Sidham*, &c. instead of *Bodhisatwa*, *Swahá*, *Om ! Swasti Sidham*.

§ 14. 5. Of those letters that have a surmounting ར, or *r*, inserted at the top.

The following fifteen letters : ཀ་ཀྱ་ག་གྱ་ང་ཇ་ཉ་ཏ་ད་ན་བ་མ་མྱ་ཙ་ཛ, when thus surmounted by ར, have the form of རྐ r*ka*, རྐྱ r*kya*, རྒ r*ga*, རྒྱ r*gya*, རྔ r*na*, རྗ r*ja*, རྙ r*nya*, རྟ r*ta*, རྡ r*da*, རྣ r*na*, རྦ r*ba*, རྨ r*ma*, རྨྱ r*mya*, རྩ r*tsa*, རྫ r*dsa*, and should be pronounced accordingly. But, in general, the ར on the top of a letter is silent, except when it is carried to the preceding syllable, terminating in a vowel; as in རྡོ་རྗེ r*do*-r*jé*, is pronounced *dor-jé*; ཨུ་རྒྱན *u-*r*gyan*, *ur-gyen*; མི་རྣམས *mi-*r*nams* (*mir-nams*), men. The ག་གྱ་ཇ་ད་བ letters are sounded harder, more distinctly, with the inserted ར than in their simple state. རྩ r*tsa*, and རྫ r*dsa* are now sounded also *sa* and *za*, instead of *tsa* and *dsa*.

§ 15. 6. Of those letters that have a surmounting ལ or *l*.

The following ten letters, ཀ་ག་ང་ཅ་ཇ་ཏ་ད་པ་བ་ཧ, when surmounted by ལ, appear in this form ; ལྐ l*ka*, ལྒ l*ga*, ལྔ l*na*, ལྕ l*cha*, ལྗ l*ja*, ལྟ l*ta*, ལྡ l*da*, ལྤ l*pa*, ལྦ l*ba*, ལྷ l*ha*, and they should also be pronounced accordingly. But, in general, the ལ is silent, except in ལྷ, and when the preceding syllable terminates in a vowel, with which it is frequently sounded; as in these words: ཅི་ལྟར (*chi-ltar*) *chil-tar*, how? དགའ་ལྡན (*dgah-ldan*) *gal-dan*, paradise. The ཀ་ ཇ་ད་བ letters, with the surmounting ལ, are sounded harder or more distinctly, than in their simple state.

§ 16. 7. Of those letters that have a surmounting ས (*s*):

The following twenty-two letters: ཀ་ ཀྱ་ ཀྲ་ ག་ གྱ་ གྲ་ ང་ ཉ་ ཏ་ ད་ ན་ ནྲ་ པ་ པྱ་ པྲ་ བ་ བྱ་ བྲ་ མ་ མྱ་ མྲ་ ཙ, when surmounted by ས, have the appearance of སྐ *ska*, སྐྱ *skya*, སྐྲ *skra*, སྒ *sga*, སྒྱ *sgya*, སྒྲ *sgra*, སྔ s ˇ*a*, སྙ *snya*, སྟ *sta*, སྡ *sda*, སྣ *sna*, སྣྲ *snra*, སྤ *spa*, སྤྱ *spya*, སྤྲ *spra*, སྦ *sba*, སྦྱ *sbya*, སྦྲ *sbra*, སྨ *sma*, སྨྱ *smya*, སྨྲ *smra*, སྩ *stsa*, and they should be pronounced accordingly, together with the ས, but it is seldom heard. The letters ཀ་ ཀྱ་ ཀྲ་ ད་ པ་ པྱ་ པྲ are in the present day sounded harder, or more distinctly, than in their simple state. སྐྲ *skr*, and སྤྲ *spr*, in some words, are sounded like *t* or *sh*.

§ 17. According to the instructions of the Tibetan Grammarians, all the three surmounting letters (ར་ལ་ས) should be pronounced, as it were, by uttering a short vowel before them; thus, རྐ *erka*, ལྐ *elka*, སྐ *eska*: (in one syllable.) But this is seldom done. It is however proper, when writing in the Roman character, to express every letter, whether it may easily be pronounced or not; since orthography only can show the true meaning, there being many words according to vulgar pronunciation, of the same sound. Orthography is sufficiently fixed by the great number of printed works in Tibet. Pronunciation is different in different provinces, none of which can be taken for a standard. Grammarians therefore must be consulted.

§ 18. Hitherto it has been shown how such letters should be pronounced that have either of the three subjoined, or of the three surmounting, letters. We now proceed to state the number of the prefixes, and to enumerate the letters to which they are prefixed.

The following five letters ག་ ད་ བ་ མ་ འ་ are called prefixes, སྔོན་འཇུག *sňon-hjug*, from their being put before a basis, or radical letter. They are a sort of prepositive particles, used for modifying the meaning of a word, and for forming the present, past, and future tenses of a verb. They may be prefixed to such letters as are specified below. Therefore

§ 19. 8. Of those letters that have a ག prefix; ག (*ga*) is prefixed to the following eleven simple letters: ཅ་ ཉ་ ཏ་ ད་ ན་ ཙ་ ཞ་ ཟ་ ཡ་ ཤ་ ས, thus; གཅའ་ *gchah*, གཉའ་ *gnyah*,

གཏའ་ *gtah*, གདའ *gdah*, གནའ *gnah*, གཙའ *gtsah*, གཞའ *gzhah*, གཟའ *gzah*, གཡའ *gyah*, གཤའ *gshah*, གསའ *gsah*.

Note.—This ག is prefixed only to eleven simple letters, none of which has either a subjoined or a surmounting letter. All the eleven retain the sound they had without the ག, and the ད after this prefix is sounded distinctly *d*. This ག, as a prefix, is employed in the formation of the present and future tenses of the verbs, besides occurring in many nouns.

§ 20. 9. Of those letters that have a ད prefix.

ད *da* is prefixed to the following fifteen simple and double letters: ཀ་ ཀྱ་ ཀྲ་ ག་ གྱ་ གྲ་ ང་ པ་ པྱ་ པྲ་ བ་ བྱ་ བྲ་ མ་ མྱ་, thus: དཀའ d*kah*, དཀྱ d*kya*, དཀྲ d*kra*, དགའ d*gah*, དགྱ d*gya*, དགྲ d*gra*, དངའ d*nah*, དཔའ d*pah*, དཔྱ d*pya*, དཔྲ d*pra*, དབའ d*vah*, དབྱ d*vya*, དབྲ d*vra*, དམའ b*mah*, དམྱ d*mya*.

Note.—ད is prefixed to letters only of the first and fourth series of the alphabet. They may have, with the exception of ང, also a subjoined *ya* or *ra* (ྱ ྲ) ; but none of them can take a surmounting letter. The ད is also a characteristic letter for the formation of the future tense, in some verbs.

§ 21. 10. Of those letters that have a prefixed བ *b*.

བ *ba* is prefixed to the following forty-four simple, double, and triple letters: ཀ་ ཀྱ་ ཀྲ་ ཀླ་ རྐ་ རྐྱ་ སྐ་ སྐྱ་ སྐྲ་ ག་ གྱ་ གྲ་ རྒ་ རྒྱ་ སྒ་ སྒྱ་ སྒྲ་ ཅ་ རྔ་ སྔ་ ཙ་ རྗ་ ལྕ་ རྙ་ ཏ་ རྟ་ ལྟ་ སྟ་ ད་ རྡ་ ལྡ་ སྡ་ རྣ་ སྣ་ ཙ་ རྩ་ སྩ་ རྫ་ ཞ་ ཟ་ ཟླ་ ཤ་ ས་ སྲ་ སླ་ thus: བཀའ b*kah*, བཀྱ b*kya*, བཀྲ b*kra*, བཀླ b*kla*, བརྐ br*ka*, བརྐྱ br*kya*, བསྐ bs*ka*, བསྐྱ bs*kya*, བསྐྲ bs*kra*, &c. &c.

Note.—This is the only prefix with which the radicals may have also any of the three surmounting letters. This prefix occurs in many words, especially in the preterite and future tenses.

§ 22. 11. Of those letters that have a prefixed མ *m*.

མ *ma* is prefixed to these fifteen simple and double letters: ཁ་ ཁྱ་ ཁྲ་ ག་ གྱ་ གྲ་ ང་ ཆ་ ཇ་ ཉ་ ཐ་ ད་ ན་ ཚ་ ཛ་ thus: མཁའ m*khah*, མཁྱ m*khya*, མཁྲ m*khra*, མགའ m*gah*, མགྱ m*gya*, མགྲ m*gra*, &c. &c.

§ 23. 12. Of those letters that have a prefixed འ *h*.

འ *ha* is prefixed to these nineteen simple and double letters: ཁ་ ཁྱ་ ཁྲ་ ག་ གྱ་ གྲ་ ཆ་ ཇ་ ཐ་ ད་ དྲ་ ཕ་ ཕྱ་ ཕྲ་ བ་ བྱ་ བྲ་ ཚ་ ཛ་, thus: འཁའ h*khah*, འཁྱ h*khya*, འཁྲ h*khra*, &c. [See the Abstract.]

Note.—The five prefixes above specified (ག་ ད་ བ་ མ་ འ), according to common practice, are silent, except when carried to the preceding syllable ending in a vowel; as in སོ་གཅིག *so-gchig*, thirty-one, is sounded as if it were སོག་ཅིག *sog-chig*, བློ་བཟང་ *blo-bzang*, ingenious, by some is pronounced *lob-zang*. རྒྱ་མཚོ *rgya-mtsho*, the sea, *gyam-tsho*; ཡ་མཚན *ya-mtshan*, *yam-tshen*, marvel, &c.

ད and འ are never carried to the foregoing syllable; they are always silent.

The only change in the letters, to which these five characters are prefixed, is with the third letter of each of the five first series of the alphabet, (i. e. with ག་ ཇ་ ད་ བ་ ཛ.) They are sounded now distinctly, without any aspiration, as *g*, *j*, *d*, *b*, *ds*. Though these prefixes occur also with the other parts of speech, yet their general use is among the verbs, for forming and distinguishing the present, preterite, and future tenses.

§ 24. Under the above twelve heads, we have enumerated all the different sorts of letters, that precede the vowel, and form the basis of a syllable or word. Here follow, now, the affixes or those letters that are put after the vowel, whether inherent or expressed, and that close the syllable.

§ 25. 13. Of the affixes or closing letters.

The affixes (རྗེས་འཇུག *rjes-hjug*) are the following ten simple or single, and four double letters: ག *g*, ང *ng*, ད *d*, ན *n*, བ *b*, མ *m*, འ *h*, ར *r*, ལ *l*, ས *s*; and གས *gs*, ངས *ngs*, བས *bs*, མས *ms*. They should always be sounded accordingly, since the Tibetan Grammarians say, that these letters are affixed expressly to render the words sonorous and significant.—

The following are examples of each of the simple affixes, to be sounded as written:

ག in	ནག *nag*,	མིག *mig*,	ལུག *lug*,	རེག *reg*,	ཐོག *thog*.
ང	རང་ *rang*,	མིང་ *ming*,	རུང་ *rung*,	ཐེང་ *theng*,	ཧོང་ *hong*.
ད	ནད *nad*,	ཡིད *yid*,	ལུད *lud*,	མེད *med*,	ཡོད *yod*.
ན	ལན *lan*,	རིན *rin*,	ཀུན *kun*,	ལེན *len*,	དོན *don*.
བ	རབ *rab*,	རིབ *rib*,	ཐུབ *thub*,	ལེབ *leb*,	ཐོབ *thob*.
མ	ལམ *lam*,	རིམ *rim*,	ཡུམ *yum*,	ཟེམ *zem*,	ཟོམ *zom*.
འ	བཀའ b*kah*,	——	——	——	——
ར	མར *mar*,	མིར *mir*,	གུར *gur*,	ཟེར *zer*,	ནོར *nor*.
ལ	བལ *bal*,	རིལ *ril*,	ཡུལ *yul*,	ཤེལ *shel*,	ཡོལ *yol*.
ས	ལས *las*,	རིས *ris*,	ལུས *lus*,	ཤེས *shes*,	གོས *gos*.

The double ones :

གས in	པགས	རིགས	ལུགས	ལེགས	དོགས
	pags	*rigs*	*lugs*	*legs*	*dogs*
ངས	སངས	ལིངས	སྲུངས	རེངས	ཧོངས
	sangs	*lings*	*srungs*	*rengs*	*hongs*
བས	ཐབས	ཆིབས	ཤུབས	ཁེབས	ཧོབས
	thabs	*chhibs*	*shubs*	*khebs*	*hobs*
མས	རམས	རིམས	ཤུམས	སེམས	སོམས
	rams	*rims*	*shums*	*sems*	*soms*

Note.—Besides these, there are yet, according to ancient orthography, three double affixes : ནད *nd* or *nt*, རད *rd* or *rt*, and ལད *ld* or *lt ;* as in གསནད་པ *gsand-pa*, he heard ; གྱུརད་པ *gyurd-pa*, he became ; and གསོལད་པ *gsold-pa*, he begged or requested. Though this mode of writing is the more correct for designing the past tense, yet according to modern practice, the ད is omitted ; and the above words are now written without the ད, thus: གསན་པ, གྱུར་པ and གསོལ་པ.

§ 26. Some of the affixes enumerated above are only obscurely heard ; some are left entirely silent (as the ས in གས, ངས, བས, མས), and some change the preceding vowel.

In Tibet, the final terminations -ས, ུས, ོས, (as, us, os,) are pronounced in three different ways, in different parts of the country. As ལས *las,* work, is sounded *las, la, lé ;* ལུས *lus,* the body, is pronounced *lus, lu, lü,* (ü, the French u ;) ཆོས *chhos,* religion, is pronounced *chhos, chho, chhö,* (ö, the French eu.) And such is the practice with some other letters also, especially with the ག and ད (*g* and *d.*)

The final ིས and ེས terminations are either pronounced accordingly as they are written, or the ས is left silent. As in རིས, which is pronounced either *ris* or *ri ;* and in ཤེས is sounded either *shes* or *shé*. And this is the case with some other letters also, especially with the ག and ད (*g, d*). Such is the practice with the affixes. It is proper to write and pronounce them regularly, as has been exhibited above.

§ 27. In the following abstract, from Nos. 1 to 209, is exhibited, how the basis of every word in the Tibetan language, together with the inherent *a*, should be written and pronounced ; and in continuation from Nos. 210 to 226, the affixes or letters following the vowel, are enumerated, together with their names and powers. The abstract, in this form, contains only the radical letters with the inherent *a*; but, if to these roots be added the four vowel signs ི, ུ, ེ, ོ, (*i*, *u*, *e*, *o*,) spelt in the ordinary manner: (viz. ཀ་ ཀི་ ཀུ་ ཀེ་ ཀོ or བཀའ་ བཀི་ བཀུ་ བཀེ་ བཀོ) followed by such affixes, as may be required, then this abstract will comprehend every word of the Tibetan language.

§ 28. The several columns of the abstract contain respectively; I. General number of letters in the whole scheme. II. Particular number of each class of letters. III. Roots in Tibetan, with the inherent *a*. IV. The same in Roman character. V. Power of those roots without any vowel taken grammatically. VI. Ditto vulgarly.

Abstract of the Orthography and Orthoepy of the Tibetan Language.

§ 29. 1. The thirty simple letters of the alphabet:

I	II	III	IV	V	VI	I	II	III	IV	V	VI
1		ཀ	*ka*	*k*	—	16		མ	*ma*	*m*	—
2		ཁ	*kha*	*kh*	—	17		ཙ	*tsa*	*ts*	—
3		ག	*ga*	*g*	*k* or *q*	18		ཚ	*tsha*	*tsh*	—
4		ང	*ňa*	*ň,ng*	—	19		ཛ	*dsa*	*ds* or *dz*	
5		ཅ	*cha*	*ch*	—	20		ཝ	*wa*	*w*	*v*
6		ཆ	*chha*	*chh*	—	21		ཞ	*zha*	*zh*	french j
7		ཇ	*ja*	*j*	*ch*	22		ཟ	*za*	*z*	—
8		ཉ	*nya*	*ny*	—	23		འ	*ha*	*h*	—
9		ཏ	*ta*	*t*	—	24		ཡ	*ya*	*y*	—
10		ཐ	*tha*	*th*	—	25		ར	*ra*	*r*	—
11		ད	*da*	*d*	*t*	26		ལ	*la*	*l*	—
12		ན	*na*	*n*	—	27		ཤ	*sha*	*sh*	—
13		པ	*pa*	*p*	—	28		ས	*sa*	*s*	—
14		ཕ	*pha*	*ph*	—	29		ཧ	*h'a*	*h'*	—
15		བ	*ba*	*b*	*p, v*	30		ཨ	*á*	*a*	—

Note					
	1 ཀ *ka*	ཁ *kha*	ག *ga*	=	ཀ or *k*
	2 ཅ *cha*	ཆ *chha*	ཇ *ja*	=	ཅ or *ch*
	3 ཏ *ta*	ཐ *tha*	ད *da*	=	ཏ or *t*
	4 པ *pa*	ཕ *pha*	བ *ba*	=	པ or *p*
	5 ཙ *tsa*	ཚ *tsha*	ཛ *dsa*	=	ཙ or *ts*

That is, the three first letters of each of the five series of the Tibetan alphabet, have nearly the same sound, according to the common pronunciation in Tibet, when heard by a stranger or foreigner whose ear cannot distinguish immediately the sharp or flat, aspirated and hard, letters. But it is expedient for the learner to write and pronounce them accordingly; since by this means only can a fundamental and correct knowledge of the Tibetan language be obtained.

§ 30. 2. The seven letters having a subjoined ཡ, *y*.

I	II	III	IV	V	VI	I	II	III	IV	V	VI
31	1	ཀྱ	*kya*	*ky*	- -	35	5	ཕྱ	*phya*	*phy*	= *chh*
32	2	ཁྱ	*khya*	*khy*	—	36	6	བྱ	*bya*	*by*	*ch*, *j*
33	3	གྱ	*gya*	*gy*	—	37	7	མྱ	*mya*	*my*	*ny*
34	4	པྱ	*pya*	*py*	*sh* or *ch*						

§ 31. 3. The fourteen letters having a subjoined ར, (*r* or ྲ).

I	II	III	IV	V	VI	I	II	III	IV	V	VI
38	1	ཀྲ	*kra*	*kr*	= *t'*	45	8	པྲ	*pra*	*pr*	= *t'*
39	2	ཁྲ	*khra*	*khr*	*t'h*	46	9	ཕྲ	*phra*	*phr*	*t'h*
40	3	གྲ	*gra*	*gr*	*d'* or *t'*	47	10	བྲ	*bra*	*br*	*'d*
41	4	ཏྲ	*tra*	*tr*	*t'*	48	11	མྲ	*mra*	*mr*	—
42	5	ཐྲ	*thra*	*thr*	*t'h*	49	12	ཤྲ	*shra*	*shr*	*s'h*
43	6	དྲ	*dra*	*dr*	*'d*	50	13	སྲ	*sra*	*sr*	*s'h*
44	7	ནྲ	*nra*	*nr*	—	51	14	ཧྲ	*h'ra*	*h'r*	*s'h*

§ 32. 4. The six letters with a subjoined ལ, *l*.

I	II	III	IV	V	VI	I	II	III	IV	V	VI
52	1	ཀླ	*kla*	*kl*	= *l*	55	4	ཟླ	*zla*	*zl*	= *d* or *l*
53	2	གླ	*gla*	*gl*	*l*	56	5	རླ	*rla*	*rl*	*l*
54	3	བླ	*bla*	*bl*	*l*	57	6	སླ	*sla*	*sl*	*l*

§ 33. 5. The fifteen letters having a surmounting ར, r.

I	II	III	IV	V	VI	I	II	III	IV	V	VI
58	1	རྐ	r*ka*	r*k*	= *k*	66	9	རྡ	r*da*	r*d*	= *d*
59	2	རྐྱ	r*kya*	r*ky*	*ky*	67	10	རྣ	r*na*	r*n*	*n*
60	3	རྒ	r*ga*	r*g*	*g*	68	11	རྦ	r*ba*	r*b*	*b*
61	4	རྒྱ	r*gya*	r*gy*	*gy*	69	12	རྨ	r*ma*	r*m*	*m*
62	5	རྔ	r*ňa*	r*ň*	*ň*	70	13	རྨྱ	r*mya*	r*my*	*my* or *ny*
63	6	རྗ	r*ja*	r*j*	*j* or *zh*	71	14	རྩ	r*tsa*	r*ts*	*ts* or *s*
64	7	རྙ	r*nya*	r*ny*	*ny*	72	15	རྫ	r*dsa*	r*ds*	*ds* or *z*
65	8	རྟ	r*ta*	r*t*	*t*						

§ 34. 6. The ten letters having a surmounting ལ, l.

I	II	III	IV	V	VI	I	II	III	IV	V	VI
73	1	ལྐ	*lka*	lk	= *k*	78	6	ལྟ	*lta*	lt	= *t*
74	2	ལྒ	*lga*	lg	*g*	79	7	ལྡ	*lda*	ld	*d*
75	3	ལྔ	*lňa*	lň	*ň*	80	8	ལྤ	*lpa*	lp	*p*
76	4	ལྕ	*lcha*	lch	*ch*	81	9	ལྦ	*lba*	lb	*b*
77	5	ལྗ	*lja*	lj	*j*	82	10	ལྷ	*lha*	lh	*l'*

§ 35. 7. The twenty-two letters with a surmounting ས, s.

I	II	III	IV	V	VI	I	II	III	IV	V	VI
83	1	སྐ	*ska*	sk	= *k*	94	12	སྣྲ	*snra*	snr	= *nr*
84	2	སྐྱ	*skya*	sky	*ky*	95	13	སྤ	*spa*	sp	*p*
85	3	སྐྲ	*skra*	skr	*kr* (*t,s'h*)	96	14	སྤྱ	*spya*	spy	*py sh* or *ch*
86	4	སྒ	*sga*	sg	*g*	97	15	སྤྲ	*spra*	spr	*pr, t'*
87	5	སྒྱ	*sgya*	sgy	*gy*	98	16	སྦ	*sba*	sb	*b*
88	6	སྒྲ	*sgra*	sgr	*gr 'd*	99	17	སྦྱ	*sbya*	sby	*by, j* or *zh*
89	7	སྔ	*sňa*	sň	*ň*	100	18	སྦྲ	*sbra*	sbr	*br* or *'d*
90	8	སྙ	*snya*	sny	*ny*	101	19	སྨ	*sma*	sm	*m*
91	9	སྟ	*sta*	st	*t*	102	20	སྨྱ	*smya*	smy	*my* or *ny*
92	10	སྡ	*sda*	sd	*d*	103	21	སྨྲ	*smra*	smr	*mr*
93	11	སྣ	*sna*	sn	*n*	104	22	སྩ	*stsa*	stsa	*s*

§ 36 8. The eleven simple letters preceded by a ག, g.

I	II	III	IV	V	VI	I	II	III	IV	V	VI
105	1	གཅའ	*gchah*	gch	= *ch*	111	7	གཞའ	*gzhah*	gzh	= *zh*
106	2	གཉའ	*gnyah*	gny	*ny*	112	8	གཟའ	*gzah*	gz	*z*
107	3	གཏའ	*gtah*	gt	*t*	113	9	གཡའ	*gyah*	gy	*y*
108	4	གདའ	*gdah*	gd	*d*	114	10	གཤའ	*gshah*	gsh	*sh*
109	5	གནའ	*gnah*	gn	*n*	115	11	གསའ	*gsah*	gs	*s*
110	6	གཙའ	*gtsah*	gts	*ts*						

§ 37. 9. The fifteen simple and double letters having a ད d, prefix.

I	II	III	IV	V	VI	I	II	III	IV	V	VI
116	1	དཀའ	*dkah*	dk	= *k*	121	6	དགྲ	*dgra*	dgr	*gr d'* or
117	2	དཀྱ	*dkya*	dky	*ky*	122	7	དངའ	*dňah*	dň	*ň*
118	3	དཀྲ	*dkra*	dkr	*kr t'*	123	8	དཔའ	*dpah*	dp	*p*
119	4	དགའ	*dgah*	dg	*g*	124	9	དཔྱ	*dpya*	dpy	*py, sh* or *ch*
120	5	དགྱ	*dgya*	dgy	*gy*	125	10	དཔྲ	*dpra*	dpr	*pr* or *t'*

I	II	III	IV	V	VI	I	II	III	IV	V	VI
126	11	དཝའ	*dvah*	d*v*	*v* { དབུ = *u*, དབོ *o*	128	13	དྲ	d*vra*	d*vr*	*vr*
						129	14	དམའ	d*mah*	d*m*	*m*
127	12	དྱ	d*vya*	d*vy*	*vy* or *y*	130	15	དམྱ	d*mya*	d*my*	*my*, *ny*

§ 38. 10. The forty-five simple, double, and triple letters having a བ, or b prefix.

131	1	བཀའ	b*kah*	b*k* =	*k*	154	24	བཏའ	b*tah*	b*t* =	*t*
132	2	བཀྱ	b*kya*	b*ky*	*ky*	155	25	བརྟ	b*rta*	b*rt*	*t*
133	3	བཀྲ	b*kra*	b*kr*	*kr*, *t'*	156	26	བལྟ	b*lta*	b*lt*	*t*
134	4	བཀླ	b*kla*	b*kl*	*kl* or *l*	157	27	བསྟ	b*sta*	b*st*	*t*
135	5	བརྐ	b*rka*	b*rk*	*k*	158	28	བདའ	b*dah*	b*d*	*d*
136	6	བརྐྱ	b*rkya*	b*rky*	*ky*	159	29	བརྡ	b*rda*	b*rd*	*d*
137	7	བསྐ	b*ska*	b*sk*	*k*	160	30	བལྡ	b*lda*	b*ld*	*d*
138	8	བསྐྱ	b*skya*	b*sky*	*ky*	161	31	བསྡ	b*sda*	b*sd*	*d*
139	9	བསྐྲ	b*skra*	b*skr*	*kr*, *t'*(*sh*)	162	32	བརྣ	b*rna*	b*rn*	*n*
140	10	བགའ	b*gah*	b*g*	*g*	163	33	བསྣ	b*sna*	b*sn*	*n*
141	11	བགྱ	b*gya*	b*gy*	*gy*	164	34	བཙའ	b*tsah*	b*ts*	*ts*
142	12	བགྲ	b*gra*	b*gr*	*gr*, *d'*	165	35	བརྩ	b*rtsa*	b*rts*	*ts*, *s*
143	13	བརྒ	b*rga*	b*rg*	*g*	166	36	བསྩ	b*stsa*	b*sts*	*s*
144	14	བརྒྱ	b*rgya*	b*rgy*	*gy*	167	37	བརྫ	b*rdsa*	b*rds*	*z*
145	15	བསྒ	b*sga*	b*sg*	*g*	168	38	བཞའ	b*zhah*	b*zh*	*zh*
146	16	བསྒྱ	b*sgya*	b*sgy*	*gy*	169	39	བཟའ	b*zah*	b*z*	*z*
147	17	བསྒྲ	b*sgra*	b*sgr*	*gr*, *'d*	170	40	བཟླ	b*zla*	b*zl*	*d*
148	18	བརྔ	b*rňa*	b*rň*	*ň*	171	41	བརླ	b*rla*	b*rl*	*l*
149	19	བསྔ	b*sňa*	b*sň*	*ň*	172	42	བཤའ	b*shah*	b*sh*	*sh*
150	20	བཅའ	b*chah*	b*ch*	*ch*	173	43	བསའ	b*sah*	b*s*	*s*
151	21	བརྗ	b*rja*	b*rj*	*j* or *zh*	174	44	བསྲ	b*sra*	b*sr*	*sr*, *s'h*
152	22	བརྙ	b*rnya*	b*rny*	*ny*	175	45	སླ	b*sla*	b*sl*	*l*
153	23	བསྙ	b*snya*	b*sny*	*ny*						

§ 39. 11. The fifteen simple and double letters having a མ, m, prefix.

176	1	མཁའ	m*khah*	m*kh* =	*kh*	179	4	མགའ	m*gah*	m*g* =	*g*
177	2	མཁྱ	m*khya*	m*khy*	*khy*	180	5	མགྱ	m*gya*	m*gy*	*gy*
178	3	མཁྲ	m*khra*	m*khr*	*khr*, *t'h*	181	6	མགྲ	m*gra*	m*gr*	*gr*, *'d*

I	II	III	IV	V	VI	I	II	III	IV	V	VI
182	7	མངའ	*mñah*	mñ	*ñ*	187	12	མདའ	*mdah*	md	= *d*
183	8	མཆའ	*mchhah*	mchh	= *chh*	188	13	མནའ	*mnah*	mn	*n*
184	9	མཇའ	*mjah*	mj	*j*	189	14	མཚའ	*mtshah*	mtsh	*tsh*
185	10	མཉའ	*mnyah*	mny	*ny*	190	15	མཛའ	*mdsah*	mds	*ds*
186	11	མཐའ	*mthah*	mth	*th*						

§ 40. 12. The nineteen simple and double letters having a འ, h, prefix.

191	1	འཁའ	*hkhah*	hkh	= *kh*	201	11	འདྲ	*hdra*	hdr	= *dr, 'd*
192	2	འཁྱ	*hkhya*	hkhy	*khy*	202	12	འཕའ	*hphah*	hph	*ph*
193	3	འཁྲ	*hkhra*	hkhr	*khr, t'h*	203	13	འཕྱ	*hphya*	hphy	*phy, chh*
194	4	འགའ	*hgah*	hg	*g*	204	14	འཕྲ	*hphra*	hphr	*phr, t'h*
195	5	འགྱ	*hgya*	hgy	*gy*	205	15	འབའ	*hbah*	hb	*b*
196	6	འགྲ	*hgra*	hgr	*gr, d'*	206	16	འབྱ	*hbya*	hby	*by, j*
197	7	འཆའ	*hchhah*	hchh	*chh*	207	17	འབྲ	*hbra*	hbr	*br, 'd*
198	8	འཇའ	*hjah*	hj	*j*	208	18	འཚའ	*htshah*	htsh	*tsh*
199	9	འཐའ	*hthah*	hth	*th*	209	19	འཛའ	*hdsa*	hds	*ds*
200	10	འདའ	*hdah*	hd	*d*						

§ 41. 13. The ten simple and four double affixes.

210	1	ག	*ga*	*g*	= *k* or *q*	217	8	ར	*ra*	= *r*	
211	2	ང	*ña*	*ñg*		218	9	ལ	*la*	*l*	
212	3	ད	*da*	*d*	*t*	219	10	ས	*sa*	*s mute*	
213	4	ན	*na*	*n*		220	11	གས	*gs*	the *s* is	
214	5	བ	*ba*	*b*	*p*	221	12	ངས	*ngs*	*mute*	
215	6	མ	*ma*	*m*		222	13	བས	*bs*	*in all*	
226	7	འ	*ha*	—*h*		223	14	མས	*ms*	*these*	

To which may be added the following:

224	15	ནད	*nd* or *nt*		226	17	ལད·	*ld* or *lt*	
225	16	རད	*rd* or *rt*						

OBSERVATIONS.

1. In the above abstract of the orthography and orthoëpy (of this language) forming 209 combinations, classed under 12 heads, is exhibited the basis of every word in the Tibetan language.

2. Many of these syllables, as they now stand, are significant words; others become so by the addition of any of the affixes (enumerated under the 13th head).

3. In all these syllables the vowel *a* is inherent, and must be pronounced with the same tone, as in 'far' or 'father' in English. It must be remembered that every syllable in the Tibetan language, where there is no apparent vowel sign, must be pronounced with the inherent *a*; as in ང *ṅa*; རང *rang*; ལགས *lags*; བསམས bs*ams*, &c.

4. This inherent *a* is visible, and expressed by the letter འ, in such syllables, as have a prefix before the simple radical (or fundamental) letter, and when there follows no consonant closing the syllable. But when the radical or fundamental letter is a compound one, or when there follows a consonant (or two consonants) after the radix, the *a* vowel is inherent, and must always be pronounced. It is visible in syllables like the following words:

གཏའ k*tah*, pawn, pledge, bail.	མདའ m*dah*, an arrow.
དགའ d*gah*, joy, pleasure.	འགའ h*gah*, some, any.
བཀའ b*kah*, a precept, commandment.	

and inherent in such syllables or words as follow:

དགྲ d*gra*, an enemy.	བཀས b*kas*, split or cleft asunder.
བསྐ bs*ka*, bitter (taste).	མདངས m*dangs*, the forehead; yesterday.
འདྲ h*dra*, like, similar.	
དགར d*gar*, a separating.	འགྲམ h*gram*, the jaw, &c.

5. All words or syllables, in this tongue, having the inherent or visible *a* (འ) are written and pronounced as has been explained. Those that have any of the four vowels (i, u, e, o.) marked thus: ◌ི, ◌ུ, ◌ེ, ◌ོ, are formed of the same 209 syllables, as have been already exhibited in alphabetical order, by adding the vowel signs. Thus the whole may be formed into a syllabic scheme, to which if the affixes (enumerated under the 13th head) be added as may be required, every word in the Tibetan language will then be comprehended in this scheme.

The whole may be spelt in the same manner, as here is exhibited with the first syllable of each of the 12 heads: as,

1	ཀ *ka*	ཀི *ki*	ཀུ *ku*	ཀེ *ké*	ཀོ *ko*
2	ཀྱ *kya*	ཀྱི *kyi*	ཀྱུ *kyu*	ཀྱེ *kyé*	ཀྱོ *kyo*
3	ཀྲ *kra*	ཀྲི *kri*	ཀྲུ *kru*	ཀྲེ *kré*	ཀྲོ *kro*
4	ཀླ *kla*	ཀླི *kli*	ཀླུ *klu*	ཀླེ *klé*	ཀློ *klo*
5	རྐ r*ka*	རྐི r*ki*	རྐུ r*ku*	རྐེ r*ké*	རྐོ r*ko*
6	ལྐ l*ka*	ལྐི l*ki*	ལྐུ l*ku*	ལྐེ l*ké*	ལྐོ l*ko*
7	སྐ s*ka*	སྐི s*ki*	སྐུ s*ku*	སྐེ s*ké*	སྐོ s*ko*
8	གཅའ g*chah*	གཅི g*chi*	གཅུ g*chu*	གཅེ g*ché*	གཅོ g*cho*
9	དཀའ d*kah*	དཀི d*ki*	དཀུ d*ku*	དཀེ d*ké*	དཀོ d*ko*
10	བཀའ b*kah*	བཀི b*ki*	བཀུ b*ku*	བཀེ b*ké*	བཀོ b*ko*
11	མཁའ m*khah*	མཁི m*khi*	མཁུ m*khu*	མཁེ m*khé*	མཁོ m*kho*
12	འཁའ h*khah*	འཁི h*khi*	འཁུ h*khu*	འཁེ h*khé*	འཁོ h*kho*

6. With respect to the affixes (enumerated under the 13th head, from the 210th to 226th number) it must be remarked, that these are the only letters of the Tibetan alphabet that close a syllable, or follow any vowel; they likewise enjoy the office of initials: but thatthe 20 other letters of the alphabet, (as ཀ་ ཁ། ཅ་ ཆ་ ཇ་ ཉ། ཏ་ ཐ། པ་ ཕ། ཙ་ ཚ་ ཛ་ ཝ། ཞ་ ཟ་ ཡ། ཤ། ཧ་ ཨ།) never close the syllable, or never are put after any vowel, but only occur as initial letters.

§ 42. The following is an Abstract exhibiting those simple and compound letters that have a similar sound, according to the common practice in Tibet.

ཀ *ka*	ཀ་ རྐ་ ལྐ་ སྐ་ དཀའ་ བཀའ་ བརྐ་ བསྐ	= ཀ =	*ka*
	ཀྱ་ རྐྱ -- སྐྱ དཀྱ བཀྱ བརྐྱ་ བསྐྱ	ཀྱ	*kya*
	ཀྲ སྐྲ་ དཀྲ་ བཀྲ་ བསྐྲ (ཏ་ ཊ་ པྲ་ དཔྲ་ སྤྲ་)	ཀྲ	*t'a*
	ཀླ བཀླ (ཀླ་ གླ་ བླ་* རླ་ སླ་ བརླ་ ཟླ་ ལ)	ལ	*la*
ཁ *kha*	ཁ་ མཁའ་ འཁའ	ཁ	*kha*
	ཁྱ་ མཁྱ་ འཁྱ	ཁྱ	*khya*
	ཁྲ་ མཁྲ་ འཁྲ (ཕྲ་ ཐྲ་ འཕྲ)	ཁྲ	*t'ha*
ག *ga*	ག when simple, in general		*ka* or *qa*
	ག་ རྒ་ ལྒ་ སྒ་ དགའ་ བགའ བརྒ་ བསྒ་མགའ་ འགའ་ རྒ		*ga*
	གྱ་ རྒྱ་ སྒྱ་ དགྱ་ བགྱ་ བརྒྱ་ བསྒྱ་ མགྱ་ འགྱ		*gya*
	གྲ་ སྒྲ་ དགྲ་ བགྲ་ བསྒྲ་ མགྲ་ འགྲ (ཌ་དྲ)		*d'a*

* Pronounced both *la* and *da*.

	ཀླ (see གླ and ཟླ)	=	= *la*
ང *ña*	ང་ ངེ་ ལྔ་ སྔ་ དངའ་ བངེ་ བསྔ	ང	*ña*
ཅ *cha*	ཅ་ ལྕ་ གཅའ་ བཅའ་ (དབྱ་ སྦྱ)	ཅ	*cha*
ཆ *chha*	ཆ་ མཆའ་ འཆའ (ཕྱ་ འཕྱ)	ཆ	*chha*
ཇ *ja*	when simple, commonly ..	..	*c'ha*
	ཇ་ རྗེ་ ལྗ་ མཇའ་ འཇའ བྱ་འབྱ་ སྦྱ ..	..	*ja*
ཉ *nya*	ཉ་ ཉེ་ རྙ་ གཉའ་ བཉེ་ བརྙ མྱ་ མྱོ་ སྨྱ་དམྱ	ཉ	*nya*
ཏ *ta*	ཏ་ ཏེ་ ལྟ་ རྟ་ གཏའ་ བཏའ 'བཏེ་ བལྟ་ བརྟ'	ཏ	*ta*
	ཊ (see ཏྲ)	..	*t'a*
ཐ *tha*	ཐ་ མཐའ་ འཐའ་	ཐ	*tha*
ད *da*	ད when simple, commonly	ད	*ta*
	ད་ དེ་ ལྡ་ རྡ་ གདའ་ བདའ་ མདའ་ འདའ་ བདེ་ བལྡ་ བརྡ་ ལྡེ་ ཟླ } ..		*da*
	ཌ་ འཌ (see དྲ) ..	..	*d'a*
ན *na*	ན་ ནེ་ སྣ་ གནའ་ བནེ་ བསྣ་ མནའ	ན	*na*
	ནྲ་ སྣྲ	..	*nra*
པ *pa*	པ་ སྤ་ ལྤ་ དཔའ (བ)	པ	*pa*
	པྲ (see ཏྲ)	..	*t'a*
	དཔྱ་ སྤྱ = *sh* or *ch*, see ཅ and ཤ	..	
ཕ *pha*	ཕ་ འཕའ	..	*pha*
	ཕྱ་ འཕྱ (see ཆ)	..	*chha*
	ཕྲ་ འཕྲ (see ཁྲ)	..	*t'ha*
བ *ba*	when simple in the beginning	..	*pa*
	བ་ བེ་ ལྦ་ རྦ་ འབའ་ སྦ ..	..	*ba*
	བ་ དབའ་ ཝ	..	*va*
	for བྱ see ཇ ; བྲ see དྲ ; བླ see ཀླ and ཟླ	..	
མ *ma*	མ་ མེ་ རྨ་ དམའ་	..	*ma*
	མྱ་ མྱོ་ སྨྱ་ དམྱ (see ཉ) ..	..	*nya*
	མྲ་ སྨྲ	..	*mra*
ཙ *tsa*	ཙ་ བཙའ་ གཙའ (རྩ་ སྩ་ བརྩ *s*) ..	..	*sta*
ཚ *tsha*	ཚ་ མཚའ་ འཚའ	..	*tsha*
ཛ *dsa*	ཛ་ མཛའ་ འཛའ་ རྫ	..	*dsa (ja)*

ཝ *wa*	ཝ་ དམའ་ བ	..	..	..	*va* or *wa*
ཞ *zha*	ཞ་ གཞའ་ བཞའ (ཞི་ཞུ)	..	..	..	*zha*
ཟ *za*	ཟ་ གཟའ་ བཟའ (ཟི་ བཟི)		..	..	*za*
	ཟླ see ད and ལ	..	..	..	
འ *ha*	འ་ ཨ	..	..	..	*a*
ཡ *ya*	ཡ་ གཡའ. (དབྱ)	..	..	..	*ya*
ར *ra*	ར	..	..	..	*ra*
ལ *la*	ལ (ཟླ་ བླ་ རླ་ སླ་ ཀླ་ བསླབ་ སྦལ་སླུ)	..		..	*la*
ཤ *sha*	ཤ་ གཤའ་ བཤའ (དཔྱ་ཤུ)	..	..	..	*sh*
	ཤྲ (ཤྲ་ ཤྲ *s'h*	..	..	..	*s'hra*
ས *sa*	ས་ གསའ་ བསའ་ (སུ་བསྒྲ་སྦུ)		..	..	*sa*
ཧ *h'a*	ཧ	..	..	..	*h'a*
ཨ *a*	ཨ་ འ	..	..	..	*a*

From this extensive catalogue, the student of this language will perceive, what a great difference there is in writing and pronouncing words (according to common practice), and how essential it is to know the words in their proper characters, to be able to judge of their true meaning.

Alphabetical scheme of the Sanskrit language, when written in Tibetan characters.

§ 43. The Tibetans having early adapted their own characters (formed in imitation of the Nagari letters), to write the Sanskrit, the student of the Tibetan language should be acquainted with this scheme also, that he may distinguish the two different languages, and read the Sanskrit accordingly.

Here follows a scheme of the Sanskrit Alphabet, as it is generally known to Europeans, both in Nagari and Roman characters, rendered by their equivalents in Tibetan.

Vowels.

Sans.	अ *a*	आ *ā*	इ *i*	ई *ī*	उ *u*	ऊ *ū*	ऋ *ri*	ॠ *rī*	ऌ *li*	ॡ *lī*
Tib.	ཨ	ཨཱ	ཨི	ཨཱི	ཨུ	ཨཱུ	རྀ	རཱྀ	ལྀ	ལཱྀ

Sans.	ए *e*	ऐ *ai*	ओ *o*	औ *au*	अं *ang*	अः *ah*
Tib.	ཨེ	ཨཻ	ཨོ	ཨཽ	ཨཾ	ཨཿ

Consonants.

ཀ *k* ཁ *kh* ག *g* གྷ *gh* ང *ng;* ཙ *ts* ཚ *tsh* ཛ *ds* ཛྷ *dsh* ཉ *ny;* ཊ *t'* ཋ *t'h*
for क *k* ख *kh* ग *g* घ *gh* ङ *ng;* च *ch* छ *chh* ज *j* झ *jh* ञ *ny;* ट *t'* ठ *t'h*
ཌ *d'* ཌྷ *d'h* ཎ *n';* ཏ *t* ཐ *th* ད *d* དྷ *dh* ན *n;* པ *p* ཕ *ph* བ *b* བྷ *bh* མ *m;* ཡ *y* ར *r* ལ *l*
ड *d'* ढ *d'h* ण *n';* त *t* थ *th* द *d* ध *dh* न n; प *p* फ *ph* ब *b* भ *bh* म *m;* य *y* र *r* ल *l*
ཝ *v* or *w* ཤ *sh* ཥ *s'* ས *s* ཧ *h,* ཀྵ *ksh,* ཛྙ *jňyá.*
व *v* or *w* श *sh* ष *s'* स *s* ह *h,* क्ष *ksh,* ज्ञ *jňyá.*

The Sanscrit Vowels are joined to the Consonants, thus:

ཀ *kă* ཀཱ *kā* ཀི *kĭ* ཀཱི *kī* ཀུ *kŭ* ཀཱུ *kū* ཀྲྀ *krĭ* ཀཷ *krī* ཀེ *ké* ཀཻ *kai* ཀོ *ko* ཀཽ *kau* ཀཾ *kang* ཀཿ *kah* and so on with all the thirty-four consonants.

The *y r l w* are subjoined thus: ཀྱ *ky* ཀྲ *kr* ཀླ *kl* ཀྭ *kw,* and so on with the rest.

The nasal *ň* is expressed variously by *ň*, *ny, ń*, *n*, *m*, accordingly as it is followed by letters of different classes (with respect to the organs). One letter is placed above another (or is doubled) thus: ཀྐ k*k* ཁྑ k*hkh* གྒ g*g* གྒྷ g*hgh* ངྔ ňň, &c. The surmounting *r* is placed thus: རྦ r*b*, རྨ r*m*, རྐ r*k*, རྒ r*g* ། སརྦ མངྒལཾ *Sarva mangalam.*

§ 44. A list of contracted words, to show the manner in which such contractions may be made in writing (especially in the small characters), and how such words should be pronounced entirely:

ཀེུན for ཀུན་མཁྱེན, all-knowing.
ཀེུས — ཀུན་ཤེས, omniscient.
ཀིུགས — ཀུན་གཟིགས, all-seeing.
ཀུནྶ — ཀུན་ནས, from every place.
ཀོུབེ — ཀུན་རྫོབ, entirely vain, not real.
ཀིུས — ཀུན་དཀྲིས, misery, natural corruption.
ཁམསུཾ — ཁམས་གསུམ, the three regions or worlds.
ཕྱོསེ — ཕྱར་ཚོས, the cheek.
ཁྱོུག — ཁྱུ་མཆོག, the chief of any herd or flock; a bull, ram, &c. a Buddha.
ཞིང — ཞེན་རིང་, extension and length.
ཞེད — ཞེན་མེད, without extent.

ཁྲོད for ཁྲུམ་སྟོད, name of a star or constellation.
གྟོག — གུར་ཏོག, a tent's top, or upper part.
གྱིག — གྱུར་ཅིག, be it, let it be, may it be.
གྲིན — གྲུ་འཛིན, a harbour, port, haven.
གྲོན — གྲུ་ཡོན, a boatman's fee.
གྲི — གྲུ་བཞི, quadrangular; a square.
གྲོབ — གྲུབ་ཐོབ, one that has found the supreme perfection, a sage, a saint.
གྲོར — གྲོང་ཁྱེར, a town, a city.
གླེམ — གླེགས་བམ, a volume, a book.
གཙལ — གཙ་གལ, importance, matter.
གཏིང — གཏུན་ཤིང་, a pestle.
གཏྨོ — གཏུམ་མོ, fierce, cruel.
གདྟེན — གདུང་རྟེན, a shrine where relics are deposited.
གདྫིན — གདུང་འཛིན, ditto.
གདུབུ — གདུབ་བུ, a bracelet, a ring ; an ornament.
གཙྟོར — གཙུག་ཏོར, a head-band ; an excrescence on the head.
གཞོག — གཞུ་ཐོག, an arched roof.
གཞོམས — གཞུ་འདོམས, a fathom, two yards.
གཞོནུ — གཞོན་ནུ, young, a young man.
གཟིང — གཟུ་ཤིང་, a lever, a bar.
གཟོ — གཟུ་བོ, straight, upright.
གཟུགིན་འདུག — གཟུག་གིན་འདུག, it aches, it is in pain.
གཟེུར — གཟུག་ཟེར or གཟེར, pain, dolour.
གཟུགསྐུ — གཟུགས་སྐུ, the image of a BUDDHA, &c.
གཟུགསྦུག — གཟུགས་སྦུག, a handsome body.
གཟེུད — གཟུགས་མེད, incorporeal.
གསུབ — གསུང་རབ, chief precept; sacred scriptures.
དྐྱིག — དམར་སྐྱིག, faint red colour ; a garb of ditto.
ཆེས — ཆ་ཤེས, a part, portion.
ཆྐྱིལ — ཆུ་དཀྱིལ, the middle of a river, &c.

ཆོད for ཆུ་སྣོད, a vessel for water.

ཆྲིན — ཆུ་སྲིན, a crocodile, a dolphin.

ཆྲོལ — ཆོ་འཕྲུལ, a miraculous change of one's self, &c.

ཉྴི — ཉི་ཤུ, twenty.

ཉིང — ཉིན་གུང, mid-day, noon.

ཉོཾངས — ཉོན་མོངས, misery, sin.

ཏིངཛིན — ཏིང་འཛིན deep meditation, ecstasy.

ཐཾ་པ — ཐམ་པ, entire, integral.

ཐཾད — ཐམས་ཅད, all, the whole.

ཐྒེ or ཐྒེགས— ཐུགས་རྗེ, generosity, liberality.

ཐྒེ or ཐྒེགས— ཐུགས་བརྩེ, mercy, love, affection.

ཐྲིན — ཐུན་བཞི, the four watches of night.

དེཞིནེ་པ — དེ-བཞིན་གཤེགས་པ, a *Tathágata*.

ཅསུ — ཅས་སུ, in the time of, at the time of, &c.

དྲོང — དྲང་སྲོང, an hermit, a *rishi*.

དྲིག — དྲུང་ཡིག, a clerk, secretary, amanuensis.

དཀོལ — དཀར་ཡོལ, porcelain, China-ware.

དཀོག — དཀོན་མཆོག, God.

དཀོར — དཀོར་ནོར, wealth, riches, treasure.

དཀྱོར — དཀྱིལ་འཁོར, a circle, mandal.

དཀྱིག — དཀྱང་ཐིག, the meridian line.

དགེན — དགེ་འདུན, the clergy, priesthood.

དགློང — དགེ་སློང, a priest, monk, friar.

དགླུགས — དགེ་ལུགས, virtuous manners.

དངྲུབ — དངོས་གྲུབ, natural, real.

དཔལྡན — དཔལ་ལྡན, noble, illustrious.

དཔུཚོགས — དཔུང་ཚོགས, assembled troops; an army.

དབྱུག — དབང་ཕྱུག, *Ishwara*, Jupiter.

དབོད — དབུ་ཐོད, a turban; a crown.

དམོན — དམག་དཔོན, a general.

དམུང — དམག་དཔུང, a troop of soldiers or warriors.

ནམཁའ for ནམ་མཁའ, the void space above, heaven.
ནྦྱོགས — ནུབ་ཕྱོགས, the western quarter of the world.
ནྦོར — ནོར་བུ a gem.
ཕྩུགས — ཕུན་ཚོགས, perfect, best.
ཕྱལོ — ཕྱག་འཚལ་ལོ, reverence be to, or I adore, &c.
ཕྲིས — ཕྲིན་ལས, affair, business, commission.
བྴིང — བུད་ཤིང་, fuel, wood for fire.
བྨེད — བུད་མེད, the female sex, a woman.
བྦོང — བོང་བུ, an ass.
བྱྩོགས — བྱ་ཚོགས, a flock of birds.
བྱྥོགས — བྱང་ཕྱོགས, the northern quarter.
བྩུབ — བྱང་ཆུབ, a Bodhisatwa.
བྱོང — བྱོལ་སོང, a beast, a quadruped.
བྲེམ — བྲམ་ཟེ, a brahman.
བློུན — བླུན་པོ, a fool, idiot.
བློས — བློ་གྲོས, prudence, understanding.
བློན — བློན་པོ, an officer, magistrate.
བཀྲིས — བཀྲ་ཤིས, blessings ; glory.
བཅིུག — བཅུ་གཅིག, eleven.
བཅིུས — བཅུ་གཉིས, twelve.
བཅུམ — བཅུ་གསུམ, thirteen.
བཅིུ — བཅུ་བཞི, fourteen.
བཅུག — བཅུ་དྲུག, sixteen.
བཅུན — བཅུ་བདུན, seventeen.
བཅོྒྱད — བཅོ་བརྒྱད, eighteen.
བཅོཾན — བཅོམ་ལྡན, BHAGAVAN.
བཅོཾནས — བཅོམ་ལྡན་འདས, Ditto.
བསྐུར — བསྙེན་བཀུར, respect, reverence ; civility, politeness.
བདེགས — བདེ་གཤེགས, a Sugata, BUDDHA.
བདྩོད — བདུད་རྩི, the food of immortality, nectar.
བདྤོས — བདུག་སྤོས, any odoriferous incense.
བསྡུལ — སྡུག་བསྔལ, distress, misery, affliction.

བརྩོས for བརྩོན་འགྲུས, industry, diligent application.
བསོདྣམས — བསོད་ནམས, moral merit, happiness.
བསྙོཾདས — བསོད་སྙོམས, alms.
དམིར — མིག་དམར, the planet Mars.
མྟེགས — མུ་སྟེགས, a *Tirthika*, a Hindu, not *Buddhist*.
མྒེ — མུ་གེ, famine.
མྟིག — མུ་ཏིག, a pearl.
མྨེན — མུ་མེན, name of a precious stone.
མྟོག — མེ་ཏོག, a flower.
མློང — མེ་ལོང, a mirror, a looking glass.
མྱན — མྱ་ངན, misery.
མཁའགྲོ — མཁའ འགྲོ, walking in the void space above, a *D'ákiní*.
མཆོྟེན — མཆོད་རྟེན, a holy shrine, fane, a *Chaitya*.
མཉོད — མཉན་ཡོད, name of a city (S. *Shravasti*).
མཐོབ — མཐའ་འཁོབ a barbarous country.
མཐྱིན — མཐར་ཕྱིན, perfect, arrived at perfection, emancipated.
མཐོུང — མཐུན་མོང, common.
མཐེོང — མཐེ་བོང, the thumb.
མཐོིས — མཐོ་རིས, *Swerga*, paradise.
མཚིད — མཚན་ཉིད, criterion, definition by its criteria.
ཙྡན — ཙན་དན, sandal wood.
ཚུྡན — ཚུལ་ལྡན, regular.
ཚིུམས — ཚུལ་ཁྲིམས, morality ; good morals.
འོེར — འོད་ཟེར, a beam of light.
འོདཀར — འོད་དཀར, white brightness.
ཡིེ — ཡི་གེ, letter, a letter or epistle.
ཡིནམ — ཡིན་ནམ, is it ?
ཡནག — ཡན་ལག, a number, limb ; part.
ཡེས — ཡེ་ཤེས, fore-knowledge, wisdom.
ཡོྟན — ཡོན་ཏན, good quality.
རིཆེ — རིན་ཆེན, of great value, precious metal.

རྡོལ for རོང་ཡུལ, a country having many defiles.
རྒྱོ — རྒྱ་མཚོ, the sea, ocean.
རྒྱོལ — རྒྱལ་པོ, a prince, king.
རྒུམ — རྒུན་འབྲུམ, grapes.
རྗེཙུན — རྗེ་བཙུན the reverend, a title.
རྡོརྗེ — རྡོ་རྗེ, a *Vajra*, thunderbolt, diamond.
རྣེསཾ — རྣམ་ཤེས, cognition, knowledge.
རྣངྶ — རྣམ་གྲངས, enumeration, specification.
རྣསཾ — རྣམས, the plural sign.
རྫུལ — རྫུ་འཕྲུལ, a miraculous change ; juggle.
རྫུས — རྫུས་སྐྱེས, born in a miraculous or supernatural manner.
ལེགྦྱར — ལེགས་སྦྱར, elegant or fine composition ; Sanscrit.
ལོངསྤྱོད — ལོངས་སྤྱོད, wealth, substance.
ལོངྐུ — ལོངས་སྐུ, an emanated person (of the divinity).
ལྕར — ལྕགས, iron, fetters.
ལྕགྒྲོག — ལྕགས་སྒྲོག, chains or fetters of iron, for the feet of a malefactor.
ཤེབ — ཤེས་རབ, wit, understanding.
ཤེྱས — ཤེས་བྱ, what is to be known, science, learning.
སརྒྱས — སངས་རྒྱས, the most perfect Being, a Buddha.
སེངྒེ — སེང་གེ, a lion.
སེསཾ or སེམྶ — སེམས, the soul.
སེཾན — སེམས་ཅན, animal being.
སེཾདཔའ — སེམས་དཔའ, a valiant soul, a saint.
སོ༹བ — སོ་སོ་བ, different, various.
སོ༹ར — སོ་སོར, asunder, differently.
སོསཾ་ཤིག — སོམས་ཤིག, let him mind or reflect on.
སློན — སློབ་དཔོན, a teaching master, professor.
སློད — སློབ་འདོད, one desirous of learning.
སྡིན — སྡིག་སྦྲིན, a scorpion.
སྣོགས — སྣ་ཚོགས, all sort of, various.
སྡུབ — སྡིགས་མཛུབ, a menacing finger.

སྤྱས་གཟིགས for སྤྱན་རས་གཟིགས, Chan-ras *g*zigs (vulg. Chenrézi,) (S. *Avalokiteswara.*)

སྦྲིང — སྦྲང་རྩི, honey.

ལྷིག — ལྷན་ཅིག, together, in company with.

ལྷྱས — ལྷན་རྒྱས, a colleague in an office (that uses the same seal with his colleague).

ལྷྱོགས — ལྷོ་ཕྱོགས, the southern quarter or corner.

ABBREVIATION OF NAMES OR WORDS.

དཔོན་སློབ — སློབ་དཔོན་དང་སློབ་མ, the master and the pupil.

ལོ་པཎ — ལོ་ཙཱ་བ་དང་པཎྜི་ཏ, *Lotsáva* (interpreter, translator) and pandit.

ས་པཎ — ས་སྐྱ་པཎྜིཏ, *Sa-skya pandita*, (a celebrated poet, learned man, and LAMA, in Tibet, in the 13th century.)

རྒྱལ་བློན — རྒྱལ་པོ་དང་བློན་པོ, the king and the officers (or ministers).

བློན་འབངས — བློན་པོ་དང་འབངས་འཁོར, the officers and the subjects, or people.

སྣང་མུན — སྣང་བ་དང་མུན་པ, light and darkness.

ཉིན་མཚན — ཉིན་མོ་དང་མཚན་མོ, day and night.

ས་གནམ — ས་གཞི་དང་གནམ་ག, earth and heaven.

ཁྱོ་ཤུག — ཁྱོ་དང་ཆུང་མ, husband and wife.

ཡབ་སྲས — ཡབ་དང་སྲས, the father and his child.

མ་སྲས — མ་དང་སྲས, the mother and her child.

ཚ་ཞང — ཚ་བོ་དང་ཞང་པོ, a grandchild (or nephew) and maternal uncle.

མེས་དཔོན — མེས་པོ་དང་ཚ་བོ, grandfather and grandchild.

བཅད་ལྷུག — ཚིགས་བཅད་དང་ལྷུག་མ, verse and prose.

བཀའ་བསྟན — བཀའ་དང་བསྟན་བཅོས, the Kah-gyur and Stan-gyur, (S. *Veda* and *Shastra.*)

རྒྱ་བོད — རྒྱ་གར་དང་བོད, India and Tibet.

or རྒྱ་ནག་དང་བོད, China and Tibet.

དགེ་སྡིག — དགེ་བ་དང་སྡིག་པ, virtue and vice.

བསག་སྦྱང — ཚོགས་བསགས་པ་དང་སྡིག་པ་སྦྱངབ, the acquiring of virtue and purification of sins (or confession).

བླ་སློབ — བླ་མ་དང་སློབ་མ, the LAMA (or Guru) and his disciple.

འགྲོ་སྡོད for འགྲོ་བ་དང་སྡོད་པ, going and sitting (or remaining, tarrying).
ཚེ་བསོད — ཚེ་དང་བསོད་ནམས, life and moral merit.
གསོན་གཤིན — གསོན་པོ་དང་གཤིན་པོ, the living and the dead.
བྲིས་པར — བྲིས་མ་དང་པར་མ, a written book or manuscript, and a printed book.
སྣག་སྨྱུག — སྣག་ཚ་དང་སྨྱུ་གུ, ink and pen.
སྣག་ཤོག — སྣག་ཚ་དང་ཤོག་བུ, ink and paper.
ཡབ་སྲས — ཡབ་དང་སྲས or བླ་མ་དང་སློབ་མ, father and son, or the master and the pupil.
འཁོར་འདས — འཁོར་བ་དང་མྱང་འདས, rotatory migration (or worldly existence) and deliverance from pain (or from bodily existence).

Such is the method which the Tibetans observe in contracting syllables or abbreviating words.

§ 45. SOME ADVENTITIOUS PARTICLES.

There occur frequently among the parts of speech some adventitious particles, many of which are of like meaning, differing only in orthography, on account of the final letter of the preceding word. Some of them require a short explanation in this place.

§ 46. ཀ་ ཁ་ ག:—All these three denote a sort of definitive article. They are used thus:

ཀ after ག་ ད་ བ་ ས ; as in དྲུག་ཀ all the six; དཔྱིད་ཀ the spring season; ནུབ་ཀ the west or the very evening ; གཉིས་ཀ both, or all the two.

ཁ after ན་ར་ལ ; as in སྟོན་ཁ the autumn ; དབྱར་ཁ the summer season ; རྒྱལ་ཁ the gaining the field, the being victorious. These (and other words of the same nature) occur either thus: སྟོནད་ཀ, དབྱརད་ཀ, and རྒྱལད་ཀ, according to ancient orthography, or without the ད as above given.

ག after ང་ མ་ འ, or any vowel; as in ལོང་ག the gut or the entrails; གསུམ་ག all the three; རི་ག the mountain, hill ; གཉི་ག both. But they are frequently confounded.

§ 47. ཀྱང་ འང་ ཡང་, are conjunctions ; too, also ; though, although ; ཀྱང་ is used after ག་ ད་ བ་ས; as in འདུག་ཀྱང་ though there is (or be) ; ཁྱེད་ཀྱང་ thou also ; ཐོབ་ཀྱང་ though he finds ; ཤེས་ཀྱང་ although he knows.

འང is used after any vowel ; as in ངའང I also ; ཅིའང whatever ; འགྲོའང though he go or goes.

ཡང is used after ང་ན་མ་འ་ར་ལ, as well as after any vowel; as in གང་ཡང, whichsoever; རིན་ཡང, the very price; ནམ་ཡང, never; ང་ཡང, I also; མར་ཡང, butter also; ཡུལ་ཡང་མི་འདུག, inhabited place even is not to be found there (or there is even no village).

§ 48. ཀྱི། གི། གྱི། འི or ཡི are genitive signs, denoting 's, of, or pertaining, belonging, relating to.

ཀྱི is used after ད་ བ་ ས; as in བོད་ཀྱི of Tibet; ནུབ་ཀྱི of the west, western; སེམས་ཀྱི of the soul or the soul's, &c.

གི is used after ག་ ང་; as in བདག་གི of me, mine; ཤིང་གི of a wood.

གྱི occurs after ན་ མ་ ར་ ལ; as in རིན་གྱི, of the price; ལམ་གྱི, of the road; གསེར་གྱི, of gold; ཡུལ་གྱི of a country; མིའི or མི་ཡི of a man, a man's, human.

§ 49. ཀྱིན། གིན། གྱིན། འིན or ཡིན correspond to the English participial termination *-ing*. Put after the root of a verb, they form, with the auxiliary འདུག, the continuative indicative present; as in བྱེད་གྱིན་འདུག, he is doing; ཀློག་གིན་འདུག, he is reading; སྟོན་གྱིན་འདུག, he is showing or teaching; འགྲོའིན, or འགྲོ་ཡིན་འདུག, he is going. They are used after the same letters respectively, as have been enumerated above for ཀྱི.

§ 50. ཀྱིས། གིས། གྱིས། འིས, (or instead of it, -ས), and ཡིས, are the signs of the instrumental case, signifying, by, with; as in ཁྱོད་ཀྱིས, by thee; བདག་གིས, by me; གསེར་གྱིས, with or by gold; མེས or མེ་ཡིས, with or by fire. They are used after the same letters as said above of ཀྱི &c. ཀྱིན &c.

§ 51. གམ་ ངམ་ དམ་ ནམ་ བམ་ མམ་ འམ་ རམ་ ལམ་ སམ and ཏམ are all of the same power, and are formed of the preceding word, by reduplicating its final letter, and affixing the མ. They are interrogative signs, or express a doubt; whether? whether or not? The term ཏམ is used only in the perfect tense after ན་ ར་ ལ (for ནད་ རད་ ལད): as for example: འདུག་གམ, is there? སོང་ངམ, is gone? ཡོད་དམ, is there? ཡིན་ནམ, is it? ཐོབ་བམ, have you found? ང་འགྲོའམ, shall I go? or whether I go? གསེར་རམ་དངུལ, whether is it gold or silver? དངུལ་ལམ་ཟངས, silver or copper? ཤེས་སམ, do you know? གསན་ཏམ (for གསནད་ཏམ), have you heard? ཁྱེར་ཏམ (for ཁྱེརད་ཏམ), has he carried away? གསོལ་ཏམ (for གསོལད་ཏམ), has he begged or asked?

§ 52. གོ་ ངོ་ དོ་ ནོ་ བོ་ མོ་ འོ་ རོ་ ལོ་ སོ and ཏོ are likewise all of the same power, and are formed of the preceding word, by reduplicating its final letter, and adding the *o* vowel sign (ོ). They have the power of the substantive verb, am, art, is, are;

or of do, have. They are frequently used with the present, perfect, and future tenses. The term ཏོ ought to be used only in the perfect tense, after ན་ ར་ ལ (for ནད་ རད་ ལད་) : for example: འཚམ་མོ, is, there is; སོང་ངོ, is gone; རིང་ངོ, it is long; ཡོད་དོ, there is; ཡིན་ནོ, it is; ཐོབ་བོ, has found; ལམ་མོ, it is a road; མིའོ, it is a man; ང་འགྲོའོ, I go, or am going; I will go; འགྱུར་རོ, it will become; གསོལ་ལོ, I beg, I request, &c.; ལེགས་སོ, it is well, well! གསན་ཏོ (for གསནད་ཏོ), I have heard; གྱུར་ཏོ (for གྱུརད་ཏོ), he has become; གསོལ་ཏོ (for གསོལད་ཏོ), he has begged or requested.

§ 53. ཅིག་ ཞིག་ ཤིག, after a substantive denote the indefinite article: a, an, any. After the imperative, conjunctive present, or hortative mood, they may be rendered in English by, let, may.

ཅིག is used after ག་ ད་ བ (and sometimes after the inherent *a*) thus: ལུག་ཅིག, a sheep; སྣོད་ཅིག, a vessel; ནུབ་ཅིག, an evening, a night; ཁ་ཅིག, some, somebody. And again, in verbs: ཀློག་ཅིག, read, let him read, he may read; ཤོད་ཅིག, explain, tell, let him explain; སྒྲུབ་ཅིག, make ready, prepare, let him prepare, &c.

ཞིག is used after ང་ ན་ མ་ འ་ ར་ ལ thus: ཁང་ཞིག, a house; ལན་ཞིག, an answer; ལམ་ཞིག, a road; འགའ་ཞིག, anybody; མི་ཞིག, a man; མཁར་ཞིག, a fort or castle; ཤེལ་ཞིག, a crystal. And again, with verbs, thus: གསོན་ཞིག (for གསོནད་ཅིག), hear, let him hear; ཤམ་ཞིག, let him die, perish; མ་སྨྲ་ཞིག, say not, let him not say; སྐོར་ཞིག (for སྐོརད་ཅིག), turn round, let him turn; གསོལ་ཞིག (གསོལད་ཅིག), beg, ask of him, let him beg.

ཤིག is used after ས thus: གོས་ཤིག, a garment; སེམས་ཤིག, let him mind.

§ 54. ཅིང་ ཞིང་ ཤིང express the participial termination *ing* in English, and are a sort of statistical adverb. They are used after such letters as has been stated above for ཅིག་ ཞིག་ ཤིག. Examples: ཀློག་ཅིང་, reading; བཀླགས་ཤིང, having read over or perused; སྨྲ་ཞིང, speaking or saying; སྨྲས་ཤིང་, having spoken or said.

§ 55. ཅེ་འམ། ཞེ་འམ། ཤེ་འམ thus, or
ཅེ་འོ། ཞེ་འོ། ཤེ་འོ, thus so, thus says he, &c.
ཅེས། ཞེས། ཤེས, so, thus;
} or a sort of adverbs. Example: འདི་སྐད་ཅེས་སྨྲས་སོ, he said so.

ཅེ་ན། ཞེ་ན། ཤེ་ན, conjunction for: indeed, I pray, pray; as in ཅི་བྱེད་ཅེ་ན, what do you, I pray; ཅི་ཕྱིར་ཞེ་ན, why I pray you; སུས་ གསུངས་ཤེ་ན, pray by whom was it ordered, (or said,) commanded.

In all the particles, thus enumerated, the ཅ is used after ག་ ད་ བ; the ཞ after

ང་ ན་ མ་ འ་ ར་ ལ ; and the ཤ་ after ས་, in the same manner as we have seen above, in ཅིག ཞིག ཤིག.

§ 56. ཏུ་ དུ་ རུ or ར་ སུ are dative, adverbial, infinitive future, and gerund signs, signifying: to, for, &c.

ཏུ is used after ག་བ and ན་ར་ལ (for ནད་ རད་ ལད); as in ཀློག་ཏུ, for reading, or to be read; རྒྱབ་ཏུ back, towards the back or behind; ཀུན་ཏུ (for ཀུནད་ཏུ) everywhere.

དུ is used after ང་ ད་ ན་ མ་ ར་ ལ ; as in གང་དུ whither, to what place? བོད་དུ, to Tibet; ལམ་དུ, in answer to ལམ་དུ་འགྲོ་བ, going on a journey; ཤར་དུ, to the east; རྒྱ་གར་དུ, into India; བཀའ་ཕུལ་དུ གསོལ, I beg to commend me, &c.

རུ or ར after འ or any vowel, thus: ནམ་མཁའ་རུ or ནམ་མཁར་ འཕུར་བ, flying to heaven, (or into the air above;) འདི་རུ or འདིར hither; དེ་རུ or དེར thither.

སུ is used after ས, thus: གཡས་སུ, to the right (hand or side); ནུབ་ཕྱོགས་སུ, to, towards, on at, the western quarter or corner of the world.

§ 57. ཏེ་ དེ་ སྟེ joined to the participle present, or verbal root, form a sort of statistical adverb; as འདུག་སྟེ, sitting, or in a sitting posture; in like manner with the perfect participle, as སྨྲས་ཏེ, having said. The ཏེ is used after ན་ར་ལ་ས; the དེ after ད, and the སྟེ after ག་ ང་ བ་ མ་ འ. Examples: གསན་ཏེ, hearing; འཁུར་ཏེ, carrying; ཉལ་ཏེ, lying (on the ground): སེམས་ཏེ, meditating; ཡོད་དེ, being; རྒྱུག་སྟེ, running; འཆེང་སྟེ, standing erect; སློབ.སྟེ, teaching; སྙེམ་སྟེ, imagining; སྨྲ་སྟེ, saying.

§ 58. པ / བ } are participial, adjective, verbal noun, and substantive terminations, or a sort of article.

པ is used after ག་ ད་ ན་ བ་ མ་ ས ; as in ཀློག་པ, reading; ཡོད་པ, being; སྟོན་པ, showing; སློབ་པ, teaching; སྡོམ་པ, restraining; ཤེས་པ, knowing.

བ is used after ང་ འ་ ར་ ལ ; as in འོང་བ, coming; འདའ་བ, passing away; འགྲོ་བ, going; འགྱུར་བ, changing; འབུལ་བ, offering, presenting. But in many substantives (not verbal) the པ is used after every consonant; as in ལྗང་པ,a valley; མཐའ་པ,onedwelling on the boundary of a country; ཤར་པ, one of the east; ཡུལ་པ, a country man, villager.

§ 59. པར / བར } are dative, adverbial, and infinitive signs, signifying: to, for, &c. They are used respectively after the letters before stated. Examples: ལག་པར, into the hand; མགྱོགས་པར, speedily; ཀློག,པར, to read; རྣ་བར, into the ear; གསལ་བར, clearly; འོང་བར, to come.

§ 60. ཕས } pron. vulg. *pé* { are comparative signs, signifying: than, more than; and
བས } *vé* { the pluperfect participle also is sometimes formed by these particles added to the perfect participle. Examples: ཁྱོད་ཕས་ང་ནག་པོ་ཡིན, I am more black than thou (or you); ང་བས་ཁྱོད་དཀར་པོ་ཡིན, thou art more white than I; ཞེས་སྨྲས་ཕས, after having said thus, or thus having said; ཕྱག་ཏུ་ཕུལ་བས, after having given into his hand (or presented to him). The terms ཕས and བས also are used with the same distinction (with respect to the preceding final letter) as before stated.

§ 61. པོ } express the definite article '*the.*' པོ is used, in general, after consonants, and
བོ } བོ after vowels. But in verbal nouns that denote an agent, the པ may be used after a vowel also; as in འགྲོ་པོ (for འགྲོ་བ་པོ) the, or a, walker. Examples of the པོ being used after consonants: མིག་པོ, the eye; ཤིང་པོ, the tree or wood; མེད་པོ, the indigent, poor; མཁན་པོ, the master, teacher; ཟབ་པོ, deep or the deep; ལམ་པོ, the road, way; ཡུར་པོ, the canal; ཡུལ་པོ, the country, inhabited place.

བོ after vowels is used thus: ཁ་བོ the mouth; རི་བོ the mountain; ཆུ་བོ the water or river; མེ་བོ the fire; མགོ་བོ the head.

§ 62. འོན་ཀྱང་། འོན་ཡང་། འོན་དང་། *conjunction*—though, although. In all these, the terms ཀྱང་། ཡང་། དང་ may be used indiscriminately.

SPECIMENS OF THE RESPECTFUL LANGUAGE.

The Tibetans employ different words from those in common use (especially for denoting the several parts of the body, meat, drink, clothes or garments, furniture, equipage, and various actions of men) when speaking respectfully to, of, or before superiors; and such terms frequently occur in their books also. To give an idea of them, here follow some specimens of the respectful language (ཞེ་སའི་སྐད་ *zhé-sahi skad*) together with the common or vulgar idiom མཉམ་གཏམ, *mnyam gtam* (speech used to equals.)

Respectful term.	*Common term.*	*Respectful term.*	*Common term.*
ཡབ, father, ..	ཕ	སྐུ་གཟུགས, the body, ..	གཟུགས (པོ)
ཡུམ, mother, ..	མ	སྐུ་ལུས, ditto, ..	ལུས་པོ
སྲས, son, ...	བུ	སྐུ་སྟོད, the upper part or trunk of the body, ..	ལུས་སྟོད
སྲས་མོ, daughter, ..	བུ་མོ	སྐུ་སྨད, the lower part of ditto,	ལུས་སྨད
མཚན, name, ...	མིང་	སྐུ་རྒྱབ, the back of ditto,	རྒྱབ
སྐུ, person, the body, ..	གཟུགས (པོ)		

སྐུ་བྲང་, the breast, ... བྲང་
སྐུ་ལྟོ, the belly, ... ལྟོ་བ
སྐུ་ཤ, the flesh of the body,.. ཤ
སྐུ་མཚལ, the blood of ditto,.. ཁྲག
སྐུ་གདུང་, the bone, relics, .. རུས་པ
སྐུ་ཚེ, one's life or age, .. ཚེ
སྐུ་མཁར, a great man's residence or castle, ... མཁར

and in like manner many other words denoting parts of the body, or having relation to a great personage, may be formed respectfully, by prefixing the particle སྐུ, *sku.*

The following are other specimens of the respectful form of expression:

དབུ, the head, ... མགོ
དབུ་སྐྲ, the hair of the head, .. སྐྲ
དབུ་ཞྭ, a hat or cap, ... ཞྭ་མོ
དབུ་ཐོད, a turban, a crown, .. ཐོད
དབུ་མཛད, a president, a headman, ... འགོ་པ
དབུ་ཅན, a capital letter,.. .. མགོ་ཅན
དབུ་མེད, a small character, .. མགོ་མེད
དབུ་ཆེན, a headman, a master,.. འགོ་པ་ཆེན་པོ
དབུ་ཆུང, a mate, ... འགོ་པ་ཆུང་བ
ཞལ་གདོང, the face, ... བདོང།-པ
ཞལ, the mouth, ... ཁ
ཞལ་ལྤགས, the lip, ... ཁ་ལྤགས
ཞལ་ཚྭས, ཞལ་ཟས, } meat, food, .. ཟས or ཁ་ཟས
ཞལ་སྐོམ, drink, ... སྐོམ
ཞལ་བཟེད, a spittle-box, .. མཆིལ་སྣོད
ཞལ་ཆེམས, testament, last will, ཁ་ཆེམས
ཞལ་གདམས, advice, counsel, .. གདམས།-པ
ཚེམས, the tooth, ... སོ
ཚེམས་ཤིང, a tooth-pick, .. སོ་ཤིང
ལྗགས, the tongue, ... ལྕེ
ལྗགས་ཆབ, spittle, ... མཆིལ་མ
ལྗགས་ཀྱི་མཆིལ་མ, ditto, ... ditto.

ལྗགས་རྩེ, the tip of the tongue, ལྕེ་རྩེ
ལྗགས་རྩ, the root of ditto, .. ལྕེ་རྩ
ཤངས, the nose, ... སྣ
ཤངས་སྣ, ditto, ... ditto.
ཤངས་རྩེ, the tip of the nose, .. སྣ་རྩེ
ཤངས་ཁུང, the nostrils, .. སྣ་ཁུང
སྤྱན, the eye, ... མིག
སྤྱན་འབྲས, the apple or ball of the eye, ... མིག་འབྲས
སྤྱན་གཤོག, the eye-lash, .. མིག་གཤོག
སྤྱན་ལྤིབས, the eye-lid, .. མིག་ལྤགས
སྙན, the ear, ... རྣ་བ
སྙན་ཁུང, the ear-hole, ... རྣ་ཁུང
སྙན་ཤལ, the flap of the ear, .. རྣ་ཤལ
སྙན་གསན, hearing with the ear, རྣ་ཐོས
ཕྱག, the hand, ... ལག།-པ
ཕྱག་གཡས, the right-hand, .. ལག་གཡས
ཕྱག་གཡོན, the left-hand, .. ལག.གཡོན
ཕྱག་ངར, the wrist of the hand, ལག་ངར
ཕྱག་དཔུང, the arm of ditto, .. དཔུང་པ
ཕྱག་སོར, the finger of ditto,.. ལག་སོར, སོར་མོ
ཕྱག་མཛུབ, the forefinger, .. མཛུབ་མོ
ཕྱག་སེན, the nails of the finger, སེན་མོ
ཕྱག་བྲིས, hand-writing, .. ལག་བྲིས

ཕྱག་དཔེ, a book, manual, .. དཔེ་ཀ་དཔེ

ཕྱག་ན་རྡོ་རྗེ, *Vajra Páni*, .. ལག་ན་རྡོ་རྗེ

ཕྱག་འཕྱི, a handkerchief, a napkin, ... ལག་འཕྱི

ཕྱག་ཤུབས, a glove for the hand, ... ལག་ཤུབས

ཕྱག་འཁར, a walking stick, .. འཁར་བ

ཕྱག་ཏུ་འབུལ་བ, to give into his hand, ... ལག་པར་གཏོང་བ

ཞབས, the foot, ... རྐང་པ

ཞབས་སོར, the toe, ... རྐང་སོར

ཞབས་སེན, the nail of a toe, .. རྐང་སེན

ཞབས་མཐིལ, the sole of the foot, རྐང་མཐིལ

ཞབས་ཤུབས, stockings, .. རྐང་ཤུབས

ཞབས་ལྷམ, a shoe, boot, .. ལྷམ

ཞབས་རྟིང, the heel, ... རྟིང་པ

ཞབས་རྗེས, a foot-step, track, .. རྐང་རྗེས

ཞབས་རྟེན, a foot-stool, .. རྐང་རྟེན

ཞབས་བསིལ, water for washing the feet, ... རྐང་ཆུ

ཞབས་འཆག་པ, to walk on foot, རྐང་པས་འགྲོ་བ or འཆག་པ

ཞབས་ལ་འདུད་པ, to bow down to, or at one's feet, .. རྐང་པ་ལ་འདུད་པ

ཐུགས, the heart, the mind, .. སྙིང

ཐུགས་རྗེ, mercy, generosity, .. སྙིང་རྗེ

ཐུགས་རྗེ་ཅན, generous, .. སྙིང་རྗེ་ཅན

ཐུགས་བརྩེ་བ, affection, love, .. སྙིང་བརྩེ་བ

ཐུགས་སྡུག, heart-pleasing, .. སྙིང་སྡུག

ཐུགས་དགའ་བ, of a joyful heart, glad, ... སྙིང་དགའ་བ

ཐུགས་འདོད, heart's wish, desire, wish, ... འདོད་པ

ཐུགས་ཚིམ, contented heart or mind, content, satisfied, .. སྙིང་ཚིམ

ཐུགས་སུན, tedious, irksome, .. སུན་པོ

མནལ, sleep, repose, ... གཉིད

མནལ་བ, sleeping, ... གཉིད་ལོག་པ

མནལ་གཟིམས་པ, ditto, .. ditto.

མནལ་བར་མཛད་པ, ditto, .. ditto.

མནལ་ལམ, a dream, ... རྨི་ལམ

མནལ་ལམ་གཟིགས་པ, to dream, རྨི་ལམ་རྨི་བ or རྨི་ལམ་མཐོང་བ

མནལ་ལྟས, token or sign of a dream, ... རྨི་ལྟས

ཕྲིན་ལས, affair, business, commission, ... ལས།ལས་ཀ

ཕྲིན་ཡིག, a letter, an epistle, .. ཡི་གེ

ཆབ, water, any liquid thing, ཆུ

སྤྱན་ཆབ, the tears of the eye, .. མཆི་མ

ཞལ་ཆབ, spittle, ... མཆིལ་མ

གསང་ཆབ, urine, ... གཅིན

ཆབ་སེར, bilious moisture, the bile, ... ཆུ་སེར

ཆབ་ཁྲུང, the necessary or privy, ... ཕྱགས་ས

ཆབ་སྒོ, the door or gate, .. སྒོ

ཆབ་ཤོག, a diploma, ... བཀའ་ཤོག

ཆབ་ཚོད, an hour, a clock, watch, ... ཆུ་ཚོད

ཆིབས, a horse, a carriage, .. རྟ་བཞོན་པ

ཆིབས་ར, a stable for horses, .. རྟ་ར

ཆིབས་ཆག, grain for horses, .. རྟ་ཆག

ཆིབས་ཆས, horse furniture, .. རྟ་ཆས

ཆིབས་སྒ, a saddle for a horse, ... རྟ་སྒ

ཆིབས་སྲབ, a bridle, ... སྲབ

ཆིབས་ལ་བཅིབ་པ, to mount a horse, ... རྟ་ལ་བཞོན་པ

ཆིབས་ལས་གཞོལ་བ, to alight from a horse, to dismount, .. རྟ་ལས་འབབ་པ

ན་བཟའ, a garment, dress, .. གོས

ན་བཟའ་གསོལ་བ, to put on a garment, to dress one's self, ... གོས་གོན་པ

སྙུན, disease, sickness, .. ནད

སྙུན་ཅན, diseased, sick, .. ནད་ཅན

སྙུན་གཞི, the cause of disease,.. ནད་གཞི

སྙུན་མི་མངའ་བ, not to be sick,.. ནད་མེད་པ

སྙུན་ལས་སྒྲོལ་བ, recovered from sickness, ... ནད་ལས་གྲོལ་བ

ཞུགས, fire, ... མེ

ཞུགས་ལ་བཞེན་པ, to burn in fire, ... མེ་ལ་བསྲེག་པ

སྤུར or པུར, a corpse, a dead body, ... རོ

སྤུར་ཁང, a burial place, a small building in which a corpse is burned or buried, a vault, a grave, .. རོ་ཁང

སྤུར་སྒམ, a coffin, ... རོ་སྒམ,

སྤུར་ཤིང, wood for burning a dead body, ... རོ་ཤིང

སྤུར་བཞུ་བ, to burn a dead body, ... རོ་བསྲེག་པ

དགུང་ལོ, a year, one's year, or age, ... ལོ

དགུང་ཟླ, a month, ... ཟླ

དགུང་ཞག, a day, ... ཞག

སྙམ, flesh, ... ཤ

བཞེས, meal, meat, dinner, .. ཟན

གསང་མ, ditto, ... ditto.

གཟུགས་ཚོད, ditto, ... ditto.

བཞེས་གསོལ་བ, to dine, eat, .. ཟན་ཟ་བ

བཞེས་མི་གསོལ་བ, not to dine, .. ཟན་མི་ཟ་བ

བཞུགས,
མཆིས,
མངའ,
གདའ,
ལགས,
འཚལ,
མངའ་མེད

are substantive verbs signifying, am, art, is, are, there is, there are; I have, I do, &c. .. འདུག ཡིན ཡོད གནས

མཛད་པ, to do, make, &c. is used of, and to, superiors, བྱེད་པ

བགྱིད་པ, to do, make, &c. is used when speaking of one's self or of others, before a great personage, ... བྱེད་པ

Both these verbs are frequently added to common ones, to make them more complete and respectful: as

འབྲི་བར་མཛད་པ, to write, describe, ... འབྲི་བ or འབྲི་བར་བྱེད་པ

འབྲི་བར་བགྱིད་པ, to write, describe, འབྲི་བ or འབྲིབར་བྱེད་པ

གནང་བར་མཛད་པ, to grant, permit, ... གནང་བ

བལྟམས་པ, born, ... སྐྱེས་པའམ་བཙས་པ

སྐུ་བལྟམས་པ, ditto, .. ditto.

འཁྲུངས་པ, ditto, .. ditto.

གཞེས་པ, to exist, live, .. འཚོ་བ

འགྲོངས་པ, to die, decease, .. འཆི་བའམ་ཤི་བ

གཤེགས་པ, ditto, deceased, .. འཆམ་པའམ་ཆམ་པ

བདེ་བར་གཤེགས་པ, ditto, .. ditto.

གནམ་དུ་གཤེགས་པ, ditto, .. ditto.

ཞི་བར་གཤེགས་པ, ditto, .. ditto.

ཞིང་ལ་ཕེབ་པ, ditto, .. ditto.

སྐུ་ནོངས་པ, ditto, .. ditto.

བགྲེ་བ, to grow old, རྒས་པར་འགྱུར་བ

གསུང་བ, མོལ་བ, བཀའ་སྩོལ་བ, } to command, order, say, tell, ཟེར་བ སྨྲ་བ

གསན་པ, to hear, hearken to, .. ཉན་པ

གསན་པ, to hear, perceive, .. ཐོས་པ

བཞུགས་པ, to sit; to be, .. འདུག་པ

བཞེངས་པ, to stand erect, .. འགྲེང་བ

མནལ་བ, to lie, lean to, .. ཉལ་བ

འཆག་པ, to walk, .. འགྲུལ་བ

བཞུད་པ, to depart, .. འདོང་བ

གཤེགས་པ, to go away, to go, འགྲོ་བའམ་སོང་བ

འབྱོན་པ, to come, arrive, .. འོང་བ

ཕེབ་པ, to arrive, .. སླེབ་པ

བསྐྲུན་པ, to generate, beget, .. བསྐྱེད་པ

སྩོལ་བ, to give, .. གཏོང་བ

གནང་བ, to grant, give, .. གཏོང་བ

བསྣམས་པ, to take, put on, .. ལེན་པའམ་ཐང་བའམ་གོན་པ

བཞེས་པ, to accept of, .. བླང་བ

བཀའ་མཆིད་མཛད་པ, to discourse, གླེང་བ

དགོངས་འགྲེལ, a commentary, .. འགྲེལ་པ

གཟིགས་པ, to see, to look on, regard, ... བལྟ་བའམ་མཐོང་བ

མཁྱེན་པ, to know, understand, ཤེས་པའམ་རིག་པ

གཟིམ་པ, to sleep, to rest, .. ཉལ་བའམ་གཉིད་ལོག་པ

མཉེལ་བ, to be tired, .. ངལ་བ

སྐུ་ངལ་བ, ditto, .. ditto.

སྐྲགས་པ, to fear, be afraid, .. འཇིགས་པ

ཤུམ་པ, to weep, .. ངུ་བ

སྤྱན་འདྲེན་པ, to invite, call, .. འབོད་པ

སྤྱན་དྲང་བ, ditto, .. ditto.

སྤྱན་དྲངས་པ, invited, called, .. བོས་པ

སྤྱན་མ་དྲངས་པ, uninvited, .. མ་བོས་པ

སྤྱན་མ་དྲངས་པར, without being invited, ... མ་བོས་པར

ཞུ་བ, to beg, ask, request, .. འདྲི་བ

གསོལ་བ, ditto, .. ditto.

ཞུས་པ, begged, asked, .. དྲིས་པ

གསོལ་པ, ditto, .. ditto.

འབུལ་བ, to offer, present, give, ... གཏོང་བ

ཕུལ་བ, offered, presented, given, ... བཏང་བ

དཕུལ་བར་བྱ་བ, to be offered, &c. .. .. གཏང་བར་བྱ་བ

Parts of Speech.

§ 64. The parts of speech will be treated in the following order: article, noun, (including substantives, adjectives, and numerals,) pronoun, verb and participle, adverb, postposition, (which occupies the place of the preposition in the Occidental languages,) conjunction, and interjection.

Of the Article.

§ 65. The particles below enumerated, put after any noun, as an additional syllable or syllables, may be considered as articles either definite, or indefinite, denoting the very person or thing; male or female; or as a sort of emphatic particles. They are frequently dropt, especially in composition, and in short and indefinite expressions.

§ 66. Enumeration of several additive particles, used as a kind of article, illustrated by examples.

	Articles.	*Examples.*
1	པ	ལག་པ, a, or the, hand; ཀློག་པ, reading.
2	བ	ཀ་བ, a, or the, pillar; འོང་བ, coming.
3	མ	ཐ་མ, the end, བླ་མ; a superior.
4	པོ	ལམ་པོ, the way or road; བྱེད་པོ, the maker.
5	བོ	ཆུ་བོ, the water or river; མི་བོ, the man.
6	མོ	མ་མོ, the mother; བ་མོ, a or the cow.
7	པ་པ	དགོན་པ་པ, a man residing in a monastery.
8	པ་མ	དགོན་པ་མ, a female person ditto.
9	པ་པོ	བྱེད་པ་པོ, a, or the, doer, maker.
10	པ་མོ	བྱེད་པ་མོ, a, or the, female ditto.
11	བ་པ	འགྲོ་བ་པ, } the, or a, goer, walker.
12	བ་པོ	འགྲོ་བ་པོ, } the, or a, goer, walker.
13	བ་མ	འགྲོ་བ་མ, } the, or a, goer, walker.
14	བ་མོ	འགྲོ་བ་མོ, } the, or a, goer, walker.
15	ཀ	དཔྱིད་ཀ, the spring season.
16	ཁ	དབྱར་ཁ, the summer.
17	ག	རི་ག, the hill or mountain; གནམ་ག, the heaven.

18 ང སྒོ་ང, the, or an, egg.

19 གེ སེང་གེ, the, or a, lion.

20 ངེ ཏིང་ངེ, deep, or the deep.

21 ཞེ མི་ཞེ, the man.

(*Note.*—Amongst the double particles (from 7 to 14) the last པ and མ, པོ and མོ, are properly articles, denoting the male and female person; the first, པ and བ, being a sort of adjective, or participial termination, that is generally dropt in composition.)

§ 67. The following particles གུ, ངུ, ནུ, བུ, འུ, likewise are a sort of articles either definite or indefinite; or diminutive signs; as in ཕྲུ་གུ, the, or a, little child; ཆུང་ངུ, the small or little; གཞོན་ནུ, the, or a, young man; ཕད་བུ, the, or a, little sack; མིའུ, the, or a, little man, a dwarf.

§ 68. The indefinite article, properly so called, is expressed by either of these particles ཅིག, ཞིག, ཤིག, put after the noun respectively according to its final letter; they signify, a, an, any, some; as in ལུག་ཅིག, a sheep; མི་ཞིག, a man; སུ་ཞིག, any one, some body; གོས་ཤིག, a garment.

Of the Noun.

§ 69. Many of the Tibetan nouns, whether substantive or adjective, appear very frequently as monosyllabic words; and often a single letter, with the inherent a, constitutes a whole or entire word; as in the following instances; ཀ, a pillar: ཁ, snow or the mouth; ང, I; ཆ, part, portion; ཇ, tea; ཉ, fish; ཐ, end; ད, now; ན, sick; ཕ, father; བ, a cow; མ, mother; ཚ, hot; ཚྭ, salt; ཝ, fox; ཞྭ, a cap; ཟ, he eats; ཡ, upper; ར, a goat; རྭ, a horn; ལ, a passage over a mountain; ཀྭ, a kind of garment; ཤ, flesh; ས, earth, ground, soil.

§ 70. In many instances, a single letter, with either of the four vowel signs, makes an entire word, the article being dropt; as ཀོ, leather; ཁུ, juice, sap; uncle; གོ, armour; shield; ངོ, nature; the face; ཅི what? ཆུ, water; ཇོ, master, lord; ཉི, sun; ཐུ, principal, chief; དེ, that; ཕོ, male; མི, man; མོ, female; ཚེ life; ཞོ, curds; འོ, milk; kiss; རི, a hill; རོ, a corpse; ལི, mixed metal or bell-metal; ཤི, death, dead; སུ, who? སོ, the tooth.

§ 71. But the greater part of monosyllabic words have two or more consonants with the inherent *a*, or the expressed vowel signs; as in ལག, hand; རྐང, foot; བཟང,

good ; ངན, bad ; དཀར, white ; གཟུགས body ; སེམས, soul ; སྟོབས, strength. All such words become dissyllabic as soon as they assume any of the above enumerated articles ; as ཀ་བ, the pillar ; ཁ་བོ, the mouth ; ཁ་བ, snow, &c. ; ཀོ་བ, dressed leather ; ཁུ་བོ, uncle ; མ་མོ, the mother, &c. ; བཟང་པོ, the good ; སྟོབས་པོ, the strength. These and other similar words occur more frequently without any article.

There are many compound nouns and consequently polysyllabic words, some of which consist of many syllables ; as བཅོམ་ལྡན་འདས, Bchom-ldan-hdas, S. Bhagaván : དེ་བཞིན་གཤེགས་པ, *Dé-bzhín-gshegs-pa,* S. Tathágata ; ཁ་ན་མ་ཐོ་བ་མེད་པ, *kha-na-ma-tho-va-med-pa,* sinless.

Of the Gender.

§ 72. With respect to gender in nouns : for things in general, there is no distinction. Several nouns are found with either article indifferently applied ; as ཐིགས་པོ, a large drop ; ཐིགས་པ or ཐིགས་མ, a drop ; ཐིགས་བུ, a small drop.

The terminations, པོ and བོ, are a sort of definite articles or emphatic particles, denoting a person or thing especially or in an eminent degree ; as ལུས་པོ, the body ; མི་བོ, the man. With some nouns, པོ and བོ, as articles, denote the male, and མོ, the female ; as རྒྱལ་པོ, the or a king, prince ; རྒྱལ་མོ, the or a queen, princess ; ནུ་བོ a younger brother ; ནུ་མོ, a younger sister.

With respect to animals, the gender is expressed either by different names, or by distinct articles ; as ཕོ for the male, and མོ for the female, which may precede or follow the primitive noun ; as གཡག, the male *bos grunniens* or yak of Tibet ; འབྲི་མོ, the female of ditto. They may be expressed also thus: ཕོ་གཡག, a male: and མོ་གཡག, a female yak ; རྟ, a horse ; རྒོད་མ, a mare: or རྟ་ཕོ or ཕོ་རྟ, a horse ; རྟ་མ or མོ་རྟ, a female horse: ཕག, a swine ; ཕོ་ཕག or ཕག་ཕོ, a male hog ; མོ་ཕག or ཕག་མོ, a female hog or sow ; བྱ, a bird, fowl ; བྱ་ཕོ, the cock ; བྱ་མོ, the hen ; ཁྱི, a dog ; ཁྱི་ཕོ a male dog ; ཁྱི་མོ, a female dog, a bitch. The un-castrated male of quadrupeds is frequently expressed by ཕ, preceding the noun, thus : ཕ་གླང, a bull ; a not castrated elephant ; ཕ་གཡག, a bull yak, or not castrated yak ; ཕ་རྟ, a stallion ; ཕ་ཕག, a boar.

The terminations, མ or མོ, denote a female, or any thing of an ambiguous gender ; as ར་མ, a she-goat ; སྒོ་མོ, a door ; ཐིགས་མ, a drop. The བུ and ཙུ are diminutive signs, and denote a quality or thing in a small degree.

པ and བ are common terminations to participles and adjectives, both for male and female, and for nouns denoting a thing in a middle or indefinite sense; as ནུས་པ, one being able; འགྲོ་བ, one walking; མཁས་པ, a wise man; མཛེས་མ, a beautiful female person. But all such nouns may be taken substantively also, as: the being able, a walking; or in a general sense; as: the wise, the beautiful.

§ 73. There are some nouns that are taken both adjectively, and substantively, and which have but one termination, in མ: as སྔ་མ, prior, former, antecedent; ཕྱི་མ, posterior, latter, an inferior; འོག་མ, lower; གོང་མ, (or བླ་མ) upper, superior, a superior; ནང་མ, inner, inward; ཕྱི་མ, outer, outward.

§ 74. By the addition of པ (sometimes of པོ). for males, and by that of མ (sometimes of མོ), for females, several nouns may be formed, denoting a male or female person, of any country, place, nation, tribe or caste, religion, profession, sect, or a follower of, &c., as བོད་པ, a Tibetan; བོད་མོ, a Tibetan woman; རྒྱ་གར་པ, an Indian; རྒྱ་གར་མ, a female person of India; རྒྱ་ནག་པ, (or རྒྱ་མི), a Chinese man; རྒྱ་ནག་མ, (or རྒྱ་མོ), a Chinese woman; སོག་པོ, a Mongol; སོག་མོ, a Mongol woman; ཧོར་-པོ, a Turk; ཧོར་མོ, a Turkish woman; བལ་པོ་པ, a man of Nepal or a Nepalese; བལ་མོ, a Nepalese woman; ཕྱི་གླིང་པ, a European; ཕྱི་གླིང་མ, a female person of Europe; རྒྱ་ཕྱི་གླིང་-པ, m. རྒྱ་ཕྱི་གླིང་-མ, f., one of British India, or a European residing in India; ཁ་ཆེ་པ, (or ཁ་ཆེ), a Cashmerian; ཁ་ཆེ་མོ, a Cashmerian woman; བྲམ་ཟེ་པ, one of the Brahman tribe, or a follower of the Hindu religion; བྲམ་ཟེ་མོ, a Brahman's wife, or the follower of ditto; སངས་རྒྱས་-པ, m. མ, f., a follower of Buddha, a Buddhist; ཚོང་པ, a trader; ཚོང་མ, a she trader; ས་སྐྱ་པ, a man of the Sa-skya religious sect in Tibet; ས་སྐྱ་མ, a woman of ditto.

§ 75. Diminutive nouns may be formed, generally, from primitives, by adding to them the particle ཆུང, small or little; as ཁང་ཆུང་, a small or little house. But there are many diminutives that are formed by turning the *a* or *o* vowel of the primitive into *é*, and adding to the end འུ (with or without the above ཆུང་), as from རྟ a horse; རྟེའུ, a colt; from བ, a cow; བེའུ, a calf; from བྱ, a bird; བྱེའུ, a little bird; from སྒོ, a door; སྒེའུ, a little door; from རྡོ, a stone; རྡེའུ, a little stone; from མཚོ, a lake; མཚེའུ, a little lake, &c. Some are formed by adding the *u* vowel, and so making two syllables of the former one; as from ལུག, a sheep; ལུ་གུ, a lamb; from ཐག་པ, a rope;

ཐ་ཟུ, a cord; from ཕྲུག, a child or young, ཕྲུ་གུ, a little child, the young of an animal. And, some are formed by adding to the primitives the particle ཟུ; as from ཁུད, a sack; ཁུད་ཟུ, a little sack: or by adding འུ; as from མི, a man; མིའུ, a dwarf.

Of Declension.

§ 76. There is no irregularity whatever in the declension of nouns, adjectives, numerals, pronouns and participles; they all are declined in the same manner by the addition of certain postpositive particles. As the nouns, &c. may be with or without their respective articles, the postpositive particles, in the genitive, instrumental and dative cases, must be selected in accordance with the final letter of the nominative; in the other cases they follow the nominative indiscriminately.

§ 77. In the nominative the person or thing is named simply without any additional syllable. The other cases are formed by certain postpositive particles, thus:

§ 78. The agentive or instrumentive case is formed by either ཀྱིས, གིས, གྱིས, འིས, or ཡིས (or instead of འིས by -ས, the འི being dropped according to modern orthography) signifying, by, with.

§ 79. The genitive or possessive case is formed by the same particles with the omission of the final ས, thus: ཀྱི, གི, གྱི, འི, or ཡི, signifying, 's, of, pertaining, relating, belonging to.

Note. After a vowel the adjuncts འི or ཡི may be used indiscriminately, (as also -ས and ཡིས;) the first making but one syllable with the preceding, and the last a distinct one; as ངའི, *ňa'i* (pron. *ňé*,) ང་ཡི, *ňa yi*, mine; ངས, *ňas*, or ང་ཡིས, *ňayis*, by me, I.

§ 80. The dative is formed by ལ, applied to the nominative indiscriminately, signifying: to, on, upon, into, unto, with regard or respect to, for, &c. Or by one of these, ཏུ, དུ, རུ or -ར, སུ, put after the nominative, according to its final letter, signifying (in addition to what has been said before of ལ), motion or progression to, into, or change, turn into, promotion, &c. This case is used sometimes for the locative also; that is to say, the above enumerated particles denote frequently, rest in, at, on, a place.

§ 81. The accusative or objective case is the same with the nominative. It seems sometimes to assume the ལ of the dative.

§ 82. The vocative is the same with the nominative, except that the vocative particle ཀྱེ (signifying O !) or some other of similar purport is put before it. But, in general, address or exhortation is made without any such particle; as རིགས་ཀྱི་བུ་དག, gentlemen ! དགེ་སློང་དག, priests !

§ 83. The locative is formed by ན and ལ, signifying, rest in, at, on, a place. This case sometimes is expressed by the particles enumerated above under the dative. But properly they signify motion to, or towards, a place.

§ 84. The ablative is formed by adding to the nominative ནས་ or ལས, signifying, of, out of, from.

Of the Plural Number.

§ 85. The Plural signs in general, are : ཅག, དག, རྣམས. The first, ཅག, or ཅག་རྣམས, is peculiar to the personal pronouns, which have likewise དག, རྣམས, or དག་རྣམས. Besides these, occasionally occur ཚོག, དགུ, བཅས, མཐའ་དག, སྣ, ཐམས་ཅད, ཡོངས, སོགས ཚོ, and ཚོགས, all of which denote a collective or plural number.

(*Note.* The Sanskrit duals have been, generally, rendered by དག, in Tibetan, but in this language there is no dual, and the term དག is used as a plural sign, except when it is added to a personal pronoun, speaking respectfully to one. But here also, it is used mostly in a plural sense.)

Any of the above particles put after the nominative singular, may form the nominative plural, and the other cases of the plural are made up by the same postpositive particles as in the singular ; but here the particles forming the agentive or instrumentive, genitive, or possessive, and dative cases, must be used with respect to the final letter of the nominative plural.

§ 86. The following is the general form of declension, according to which may be declined adjectives, numerals, pronouns, and participles, as well as nouns.

Singular.

1 *Nominative.*	
2 *Instrumentive or agentive,*	གྱིས, ཀིས, གྱིས -ས, or ཡིས ; by, with.
3 *Genitive or possessive,*	གྱི, ཀི, གྱི, འི or ཡི ; of, 's.
4 *Dative,*	ལ། ཏུ, དུ, སུ or -ར རུ ; to, for, &c.

5 *Accusative or objective,*	like the nominative.
6 *Vocative,*	ཀྱེ, O.
7 *Locative,*	ན or ལ ; in, at, on.
8 *Ablative,*	ནས or ལས; from, of, out of, from on.

PLURAL.

1 *Nominative,*	རྣམས། or དག (ཅག)
2 *Instrumentive or agentive,*	རྣམས་ཀྱིས། དག་གིས
3 *Genitive or possessive,*	རྣམས་ཀྱི། དག་གི
4 *Dative,*	རྣམས་ལ། དག་ལ
5 *Accusative or objective,*	རྣམས། དག
6 *Vocative,*	ཀྱེ་ རྣམས། ཀྱེ་དག
7 *Locative,*	རྣམས་ན། དག་ན
	or—ལ། or—ལ
8 *Ablative,*	རྣམས་ནས། དག་ནས
	or—ལས or—ལས

§ 87. Example: *Singular.* *Plural.*

1 *Nom.*	སངས་རྒྱས	Buddha.	སངས་རྒྱས་རྣམས	the Buddhas.
2 *Inst.*	སངས་རྒྱས་ཀྱིས	by Buddha.	སངས་རྒྱས་རྣམས་ཀྱིས	by the Buddhas.
3 *Gen.*	སངས་རྒྱས་ཀྱི	of Buddha.	སངས་རྒྱས་རྣམས་ཀྱི	of the Buddhas.
4 *Dat.*	སངས་རྒྱས་ལ	to Buddha.	སངས་རྒྱས་རྣམས་ལ	to the Buddhas.
5 *Accus.*	སངས་རྒྱས	Buddha.	སངས་རྒྱས་རྣམས	the Buddhas.
6 *Voc.*	ཀྱེ་སངས་རྒྱས	O Buddha.	ཀྱེ་སངས་རྒྱས་རྣམས	O Buddhas.
7 *Locat.*	སངས་རྒྱས་ན	on Buddha.	སངས་རྒྱས་རྣམས་ན	on the Buddhas.
8 *Abl.*	སངས་རྒྱས་ནས	from Buddha.	སངས་རྒྱས་རྣམས་ནས	from the Buddhas.

(*Note.* In the examples given hereafter, the vocative and locative cases may be omitted: since they may easily be formed when required, according to the scheme of general declension.)

§ 88. The particles forming the 2nd, 3rd and 4th cases (see the form of general declension), are used in the following manner.

ཀྱིས and ཀྱི are used after a nominative terminating in ད, བ, or ས ; as from ཁྱོད, thou ; རྒྱབ, the back ; ལུས, the body, are made ཁྱོད་ཀྱིས, by thee ; རྒྱབ་ཀྱིས, with the back ; ལུས་ཀྱིས, with or by the body. And ཁྱོད་ཀྱི, of thee, thine, thy ; རྒྱབ་ཀྱི, the back's ; ལུས་ཀྱི, of the body.

གིས and གི, after a nominative ending in ག, or ་ང ; as from མིག, the eye ; མིང་, a name ; are formed, མིག་གིས, by or with the eye ; མིང་གིས, by or with a name. And མིག་གི, of or belonging to the eye ; མིང་གི, of or belonging to a name. And so on with the rest.

གྱིས and གྱི, after a nominative ending in ན, མ, ར, or ལ ; as, རིན, price ; གཏམ, speech ; གསེར, gold ; དངུལ, silver ; form རིན་གྱིས and རིན་གྱི ; གཏམ་གྱིས and གཏམ་གྱི, གསེར་གྱིས and གསེར་གྱི ; དངུལ་གྱིས, and དངུལ་གྱི.

འིས or -ས, ཡིས and འི, or ཡི, are used after a nominative ending in any vowel ; as མ mother ; མི, man ; ཆུ, water ; མེ, fire ; སོ, a tooth ; form, མས or མ་ཡིས, and མའི or མ་ཡི ; མིས or མི་ཡིས, and མིའི or མི་ཡི ; ཆུས or ཆུ་ཡིས, and ཆུའི or ཆུ་ཡི ; མེས or མེ་ཡིས, and མེའི or མེ་ཡི ; སོས or སོ་ཡིས, and སོའི or སོ་ཡི.

ལ is the general dative sign, applied to any nominative.

ཏུ is used after ག་བ, as ལག་ཏུ, into the hand ; ནུབ་ཏུ, to the west. And after ན་ར་ལ (for ནད, རད, ལད), as ཀུན་ཏུ (for ཀུནད་ཏུ), every where ; ཤར་ཏུ (for ཤརད་ཏུ), to the east ; ཕ་རོལ་ཏུ (for ཕ་རོལད་ཏུ), to the other side.

དུ is used after ང, ད, ན, མ, ར, ལ : as མིང་དུ, for a name ; བོད་དུ, into Tibet ; རིན་དུ, for a price ; ལམ་དུ, to a way, (road journey ;) གསེར་དུ, into gold ; ཡུལ་དུ, into, to a place.

རུ or ར, after འ or any vowel ; as ལྷོ་རུ or ལྷོར, to the south ; མིར, into a man ; མེར into, to, fire ; ཆུར, into water ; ལྷར, into a god.

སུ, after a nominative ending in ས ; as གཡས་སུ, to the right (hand or side).

Examples of Declension.

§ 89. All sorts of declinable words terminating in the letters ད, བ, or ས, as ཁྱོད, thou ; སྣོད, a vessel, (an utensil ;) འོད, shine, lustre ; ཁབ, a needle ; ཡབ, father, (respectfully ;) ཞིབ, fine flour or meal of parched barley, (*satu* ;) རས, cotton cloth ; དུས, time, season ; རིས, part, division ; ཡེ་ཤེས, wisdom ; ཆོས, religion ; may be declined after the following paradigm.

	Singular.		Plural.	
1 *Nom.*	ལུས,	the body,	ལུས་རྣམས,	bodies.
2 *Instr.*	ལུས་ཀྱིས,	by or with the body,	ལུས་རྣམས་ཀྱིས,	with bodies.
3 *Poss.*	ལུས་ཀྱི,	of the body,	ལུས་རྣམས་ཀྱི,	of bodies.
4 *Dat.*	ལུས་ལ,	to the body,	ལུས་རྣམས་ལ,	to bodies.
5 *Acc.*	ལུས,	the body,	ལུས་རྣམས,	bodies.
6 *Abl.*	ལུས་ནས,	from the body,	ལུས་རྣམས་ནས,	from bodies.

§ 90. All sorts of nouns terminating in any of ག་ ང་ may be declined after the following example:

	Singular.		Plural.	
1 *Nom.*	མིག,	the eye,	མིག་རྣམས or མིག་དག,	the eyes.
2 *Instr.*	མིག་གིས,	by or with the eye,	མིག་རྣམས་ཀྱིས,	by the eyes.
3 *Poss.*	མིག་གི,	of the eye,	མིག་རྣམས་ཀྱི,	of the eyes.
4 *Dat.*	མིག་ལ,	to the eye,	མིག་རྣམས་ལ,	to the eyes.
5 *Acc.*	མིག,	the eye,	མིག་རྣམས,	the eyes.
6 *Abl.*	མིག་ནས,	from the eye,	མིག་རྣམས་ནས,	from the eyes.

Examples to be declined: གཡོག, a servant, subject: ཕྲུག, a whole piece of cloth; གཡག, the Tibet yak, (Bos grunniens;) ལག, the hand; ལུག, a sheep; ཤིག, a louse; རེག, touch; ཐོག, thunderbolt; རང་, one's self; ཤིང, wood, tree; ཟུང, a pair, couple; ཡིག་ཕྲེང་, a line of letters; མེ་ལོང་, a looking glass, mirror.

§ 91. All nouns ending in the letters ན་ མ་ ར་ ལ་, (as: ལན, answer; ཡོན, a reward, fee; ལམ, way, road; ཡུམ, a matron, mother; གསེར, gold; ལག་སོར, the hand's finger; ཡུལ, place, country; དཀར་ཡོལ, porcelain,) may be declined after the following example:

	Singular.		Plural.	
1 *Nom.*	རིན,	price,	རིན་རྣམས,	prices.
2 *Instr.*	རིན་གྱིས,	with or by a price,	རིན་རྣམས་ཀྱིས,	by prices.
3 *Poss.*	རིན་གྱི,	of the price,	རིན་རྣམས་ཀྱི,	of prices.
4 *Dat.*	རིན་ལ,	to the price,	རིན་རྣམས་ལ,	to prices.
5 *Acc.*	རིན,	the price,	རིན་རྣམས,	prices.
6 *Abl.*	རིན་ནས,	from the price,	རིན་རྣམས་ནས,	from prices.

§ 92. All nouns that end in འ, *i. e.* in any of the five vowels, as: བཀའ, precept; མ, mother; མི, man; མུ, limit; མེ, fire; and མོ, a female, may be declined after the following example.

		Singular.		*Plural.*	
1	*Nom.*	རྒྱལ་པོ,	a, or the, king,	རྒྱལ་པོ་རྣམས,	kings.
2	*Instr.*	རྒྱལ་པོས,	by the king,	རྒྱལ་པོ་རྣམས་ཀྱིས,	by kings.
3	*Poss.*	རྒྱལ་པོའི,	the king's,	རྒྱལ་པོ་རྣམས་ཀྱི,	kings.
4	*Dat.*	རྒྱལ་པོ་ལ,	to the king,	རྒྱལ་པོ་རྣམས་ལ,	to kings.
5	*Acc.*	རྒྱལ་པོ,	the king,	རྒྱལ་པོ་རྣམས,	kings.
6	*Abl.*	རྒྱལ་པོ་ནས,	from the king,	རྒྱལ་པོ་རྣམས་ནས,	from kings.

§ 93. All words ending in a vowel, or having any of the 21 articles enumerated, may be declined after this form. Such as are,

ཕ, father.
མ, mother.
མི, man.
བུ, child, son.
མེ, fire.
མགོ, the head.
སོ, the tooth.
ལོ, a year, &c.
ལག་པ, the hand.
ཉི་མ, the sun.
ཀ་བ, the pillar.
ལུས་པོ, the body.

མིག་པོ, the eye.
གཟུགས་པོ, the body, object.
རི་པོ, the mountain.
མགོ་པོ, the head.
རི་མོ, the figure, image.
སེང་གེ, the lion.
དཔྱིད་ཀ, the spring season.
དབྱར་ཁ, the summer.
རི་ཀ, the hill, mountain.
དགོན་པ་པ, resident in a monastery.
གླ་པ་མོ, a hired working woman.

ADJECTIVES.

§ 94. Adjectives can hardly be discriminated, in many cases, from substantives, having the same terminations or articles; and being used sometimes adjectively, and sometimes substantively; as, ངན་པ, the bad, bad, a bad man.

Adjectives, when put before a substantive, are invariable in all cases of both numbers; but, when taken absolutely, or when they stand after the substantive, they are declined exactly according to the form of general declension, the substantive being then invariable; as སྐམ་ས, dry land; དཀར་ཕྱོགས, the white or enlightened half of the moon, or of a lunation; ནག་ཕྱོགས, the black or darkened half of ditto; ཆེན་པོ, the great; མཁས་པ, the learned; མི་ངན, a bad man; ཁང་བཟང, a good house; ལུང་པ་ནག་པོ or ལུང་ནག, the black valley.

But it is very seldom that the adjective is used before a substantive; when it does, the adjective stands either without any additional particle, or the article is put in the genitive form 'i, or has an འི annexed; as བཟང་མི or བཟང་བའི་མི or བཟང་པོའི་མི, good man, a good man, the good man.

§ 95. The primitive adjectives appear very frequently without any of their additional terminations, which are in fact a sort of articles; as བཟང་, good; ངན, bad; དཀར, white; ནག, black; དཀའ, difficult; སླ, easy, &c. But they may have also their respective articles, as: བཟང་བ, བཟང་པོ, བཟང་མོ, a, or the, good; ངན་པ, ངན་པོ, ངན་མོ, a, or the, bad; དཀར་བ, དཀར་པོ, དཀར་མོ, a, or the, white; ནག་པ, ནག་པོ ནག་མོ, a, or the, black; དཀའ་བ, དཀའ་བོ, དཀའ་མོ, difficult, hard; སླ་བ, སླ་བོ, སླ་མོ, easy, &c. In all such adjectives the termination པ and བ denotes a thing or person, or they are substantive signs. But, in general, when taken substantively, so as to denote the abstract quality, they should have the particle, ཉིད, after them thus; བཟང་བ་ཉིད, goodness; ནག་པ་ཉིད, blackness; དཀའ་བ་ཉིད, difficulty, hardship; སླ་བ་ཉིད, easiness.

§ 96. Some adjectives have but one termination, namely, the article མ: as སྔ་མ, former, prior; ཕྱི་མ, latter, posterior, outer; ནང་མ, inner, interior, inward; ཕྱི་མ or ཕྱི་རོལ་མ, outer, outward; འོག་མ, lower, inferior; གོང་མ (or བླ་མ,) upper, superior; མདུན་མ, anterior, fore; རྟིང་མ or རྒྱབ་མ, posterior, backward; as in འགྲེལ་བྱེད་སྔ་མ་རྣམས, former or ancient interpreters; འགྲེལ་བྱེད་ཕྱི་མ་རྣམས, latter or modern interpreters.

§ 97. Many adjectives may be formed from substantives, adverbs, &c., by adding either of the genitive signs; as from ལུས, the body; ལུས་ཀྱི, of or belonging to the body, bodily; from དམག, war; དམག་གི, of or belonging to war, warlike; from ཤིང་, wood; ཤིང་གི, of wood, wooden; from གསེར, gold; གསེར་གྱི, of gold, golden; from མི, man; མི་ཡི, of man, human; from དེ་རིང, to-day; དེ་རིང་གི, of this day, this day's; from ད་ལྟར, now; ད་ལྟར་གྱི, of this present, this, &c.

§ 98, Various affirmative adjectives are formed from substantives by adding some one of the following particles: ཅན, ལྡན, ལྡན་ཅན, བཅས་པ, མངའ་བ, ཡོད་པ, signifying:

having, possessing, -ed, -ful, full of, -eous, -ous, -y, &c. ; as in དབུ་ཅན or མགོ་ཅན, having a head, headed, capital (letter); ནོར་ལྡན, possessing wealth, wealthy ; གཤེར་ལྡན་ཅན, full of moisture ; སྡིག་པ་དང་བཅས་པ or སྡིག་བཅས, sinful ; ཡོན་ཏན་མངའ་བ, talented, talentful ; དོན་ཡོད་པ, intelligent, reasonable ; from དབང་, power ; དབང་ཅན, དབང་ལྡན, དབང་ལྡན་ཅན, དབང་བཅས, དབང་མངའ, དབང་ཡོད, powerful, mighty ; from ནོར, wealth, riches : ནོར་ལྡན, ནོར་ཅན, ནོར་ལྡན་ཅན, ནོར་བཅས, ནོར་མངའ, ནོར་ཡོད, wealthy, rich, opulent.

§ 99. Negative adjectives are formed by མེད, མི་ལྡན, མི་མངའ, བྲལ, ཡས, མི, མ, signifying : -less, wanting, not having, without, destitute of ; in (il, im, ir,) un, dis : as དབུ་མེད or མགོ་མེད, headless or without a head, (small, not capital, character ;) ནོར་མི་ལྡན or ནོར་མེད, having no wealth, destitute of wealth ; སྐྱོན་མི་མངའ, without defects ; ལུས་བྲལ, incorporeal ; མཐའ་ཡས, infinite ; དཔག་ཡས, immense ; ཚུལ་མེད, irregular, immethodical ; མི་འོས་པ, unbecoming ; མི་རུང་བ, inconvenient ; མ་ཐོས་པ, unheard ; མ་སྨིན་པ, unripe, immature, not ripe.

§ 100. Adjectives terminating, in English, in -able, and -ible, may be expressed by རུང་བ, fit, convenient, apt for, put after the gerund of a verb ; as, འཐུང་དུ་རུང་བ, potable or drinkable ; ཟར or བཟར་རུང་བ, edible, esculent ; ཀློག་ཏུ་རུང་བ, legible, that may be read or perused. The negatives of these are formed by putting མི between them, thus ; ཀློག་ཏུ་མི་རུང་བ, illegible. The gerund sign is frequently dropt before རུང་བ, together with the བ termination, as འཐུང་རུང, potable.

§ 101. Some adjectives are expressed by the participle future in བྱ, as འཆི་བྱ, for འཆི་བ་ཅན, mortal, obnoxious to death ; འགྱུར་བྱ for འགྱུར་བ་ཅན, mutable, alterable : the negatives of which are formed, thus : འཆི་བ་མེད་པ or འཆི་མེད, immortal ; འགྱུར་བ་མེད་པ, or འགྱུར་མེད, immutable.

§ 102. When an adjective is reduplicated, with any of the particles ཀྱང་ འང་ ཡང་ put between the reduplication, it denotes a kind of superlative degree, and may be expressed by "very ;" as, མཛེས་ཀྱང་མཛེས, very beautiful ; ཆེའང་ཆེ, very great ; ཐུང་ཡང་ཐུང་, very short.

§ 103. When the last or final letter is reduplicated with the è vowel over it, followed by the articles བ or མ ; it denotes it to be taken in a small degree, and may be expressed by 'somewhat :' as མཛེས་སེ་བ, somewhat beautiful ; ཆུང་ངེ་བ, somewhat little ; རྟོག་གེ་བ, petty or sophistical reasoning.

Of Comparison.

§ 104. In adjectives the comparative degree is expressed sometimes by རྗེ, more, and the superlative by རབ, most; as, མཐོ, high; རྗེ་མཐོ, more high or higher; རབ་མཐོ most high, or the highest. But this form seldom occurs.

Degrees of comparison are properly expressed by the terms ལས, པས, or བས, (signifying, than, more than) put after the name of the person or thing to which comparison is made; as, བདག་ལས་ཁྱོད་ཆེ or བདག་པས (or ང་བས), ཁྱོད་ཆེ, thou art (or you are) greater than I; འདི་ལས་དེ་བཟང་ or འདི་བས་དེ་བཟང, that is better than this. The superlative or a comparison with totality is expressed by ཐམས་ཅད་ལས or ཀུན་ལས, than all; as, དེ་ཀུན་ལས or ཐམས་ཅད་ལས་ཆེའོ, that is greater than all, or that is the greatest. The particles, ལྷག་པར, more; and ཆེས, by a great deal; are also in use for expressing any great degree of excellence or of the contrary.

§ 105. The superlative degree, without comparison, is expressed by the following adverbial particles; རབ་ཏུ, eminently; ཤིན་ཏུ, very; ཀུན་ཏུ, altogether, entirely; མཆོག་ཏུ, chiefly; ཡོངས་སུ, wholly; ཡང་དག་པར, thoroughly; ཁྱད་པར, especially; as, རབ་ཏུ་མཁས་པ, eminently wise, or the wisest; ཀུན་ཏུ་བཟང་པོ, entirely good, or the best; ཤིན་ཏུ་གསལ་པོ, very clear, or the clearest.

§ 106. List of Adjectives.

ཀྱག, (པ, པོ, མོ) crooked.

ཀྱག་ཀྱག, very crooked.

ཀུན, all, whole, entire, every.

ཀྱུམ, (པ, པོ, མོ) contracted, cringing.

ཀོང་, (བ, པོ, མོ) concave, not plane.

ཀོང་ ཀོང, ditto.

ཁྱག། ཁྱག་ཁྱག, thick, run into clots.

ཁྱག་ཁྱོག, curve, crooked.

ཁྲང་, (བ, པོ, མོ) straight, right.

ཁྲང་ཁྲང་, straight all along.

ཁྱར། ཁྱར་ཁྱར, flat, not globular.

ཁྱར་ཁྱོར, weak, feeble.

ཁྱལ། ཁྱལ་ཁྱལ, long and flat, not globular.

ཁྱིར། ཁྱིར་ཁྱིར, round, circular.

ཁྱོག། ཁྱོག་ཁྱོག, curved, crooked, bent.

ཁྱོང་། ཁྱོང་ཁྱོང་, oblong.

ཁྱོམ། ཁྱམ་ཁྱོམ, soft, pliant, flexible.

ཁྱོར། ཁྱོར་ཁྱོར, feeble, weak.

ཁྲོང་། ཁྲོང་ཁྲོང་, standing in an erect posture.

ཁ་བ, bitter.

ཁ་དྲག, mighty, powerful, potent.

ཁེ་ཅན, gainful.

ཁེ་མེད, profitless.

ཁེངས་ཅན, haughty, proud.

ཁེངས་ལྡན, ditto.

ཁེངས་མེད, void of pride.

ཁེངས་བྲལ, ditto.

ཁྱད་ཅན། ཁྱད་པར་ཅན, special, particular; eminent, excellent.

ཁྱོག, curved, crooked; cunning.

ཁྲིམས་ལྡན, lawful, legal; of good morals.

ཁྲིམས་མེད, illegal; unusual.

ཁྲེལ་ལྡན, bashful, modest.

ཁྲེལ་ཅན, ditto.

ཁྲེལ་ཡོད, ditto.

ཁྲེལ་མེད, impudent.

ཁྲོ་བ་ཅན, angry, wrathful; cruel.

གང་, (བ, པོ, མོ,) full, replete.

གངས་ཅན, snowy, icy; full of frozen snow.

གན་རྒྱལ, supine, lying with the face upwards.

གལ་ཅན, important, of consequence.

གུང་, middle.

གུས་པ་ཅན, respectful.

གོ་བ་ཅན, intelligent, sagacious.

གོ་ས་ཅན, having a rank or dignity.

གོང་, upper, superior.

གོམས་པ, accustomed, wonted, wont.

ཀ་ཀྱུ་ཅན, crafty, sly, deceitful.

ཀྱོག་པ, curved, crooked.

ཀྱོང་པོ, hard, rough, rude, impolite.

གྲགས་པ་ཅན, illustrious, famous, celebrated, renowned.

གྲགས་ལྡན, ditto.

གྲང་, (བ, པོ, མོ,) cold.

གྲངས་ཅན, numerous, numeral.

གྲངས་མེད, innumerable.

གྲམ་པ་ཅན, swampy, marshy.

གྲིབ་མ་ཅན, shadowy, full of shade.

གྲུ་ཅན, having corners or angles.

གྲུ་མང, having many angles, polygonal.

གྲུམ་པ, broken, maimed.

གྲོས་ཅན, careful, cautious.

གྲོས་མེད, careless, heedless.

གླེན, (པ, པོ, མོ,) foolish, stupid.

གཅང་པོ, clever, dexterous.

གཅིག, (པ, མ,) homogeneous, consisting of one.

གཅིག་པོ, consisting of one; single, alone.

གཅིག་པུ, alone.

གཅེར།-བུ, simple, naked.

གཅེས, (པ, པོ, མ, མོ,) dear, beloved.

གཉིས་ཀ, both.

གཉིས་པ, second.

གཉིས་པོ, consisting of two.

གཉུག་མ, natural, not artificial.

གཉེན་པོ, opposite, adverse, contrary.

གཉེར་མ་ཅན, full of wrinkles.

གཉོད་ཅན, strong, vigorous.

གཉོད་མེད, weak, feeble, languid.

གཏུམ, (པོ, པོ, མོ) fierce, cruel, furious.

གདུག་པ་ཅན, mischievous, hurtful.

གནའ་, (བོ,) ancient, old, of old time.

གནོད་པ་ཅན, hurtful.

གནོད་པ་དང་བཅས་པ, ditto.

གནོད་བཅས, ditto.

གཙང་, (བ, པོ, མ, མོ,) clean, pure, clear; holy.

གཙོ, (བོ, མོ,) chief, principal.

གཞན, (པ, མ,) other.

གཞན་ཞིག, another.

གཞལ་དུ་མེད་པ, immeasurable, immense.

གཞལ་མེད, ditto.

གཞལ་ཡས, ditto.

གཞུ་ཅན, arched ; having a bow.

གཞེང་ཅན, broad, wide.

གཞེང་མེད, void of breadth, narrow.

གཞོན, (པ, མ,) young, not old.

གཞོན་ནུ, (མ,) young, virgin.

གཟི་ཅན, bright, shining.

གཟུ་བོ, straight, right ; upright, honest.

གཟུ་ལུམ་ཅན, inconsiderate, rash.

གཟུགས་ཅན, corporal, bodily, material.

གཟུགས་མེད incorporeal, immaterial, spiritual.

གཟུང་དུ་ཡོད་པ, comprehensible, conceivable.

གཟུང་དུ་མེད་པ, incomprehensible, inconceivable.

གཡང་ཅན, lucky, fortunate.

གཡང་མེད, unlucky, unfortunate.

གཡན་པ་ཅན, itchy.

གཡར, (པོ, མོ,) borrowed, adopted.

གཡས, (པ, མ,) the right (hand or side).

གཡུང, (བ, པོ, མོ,) tame, domestic.

གཡེང་བ་ཅན, inattentive, negligent.

གཡོ་ཅན, crafty, cunning, deceitful.

གཡོ་སྒྱུ་ཅན, ditto.

གཡོགས་པ, covered.

གཡོན་ཅན, crafty.

གཡོན, (མ,) crafty, the left hand or side.

གཤིན་པ, good, excellent, fine.

གཤིན་པོ, the dead.

གཤེར, (བ,) moist, wet, fresh ; recent.

གསང, (བ,) secret, not common.

གསར, (པ, པོ, མོ,) new, fresh, virgin.

གསལ, (བ, པོ, མོ,) clear ; evident.

གསུམ་ཀ, all the three.

གསུམ་པོ, consisting of three.

གསུམ་པ, the third.

གསེར་གྱི, of gold, golden.

གསེར་ཅན, golden ; gilt.

གསོན, (པ, པོ, མ, མོ,) living, alive.

ང་རྒྱལ་ཅན, proud, arrogant.

ངན, (པ, པོ, མོ,) bad, ill, wicked.

ངན་ངོན, mean, pitiful, very bad ; coarse.

ངར་ཅན, strong, vigorous ; hard, sharp.

ངར་མེད, weak, blunt.

ངར་ངར་པོ, hoarse, disagreeable.

ངལ་བ, tired, fatigued, weary.

ངལ་བ་མེད་པ, indefatigable.

ངལ་མེད, ditto.

ངེས་པ, certain, real, true.

ངོ་ཅན, natural.

ངོ་ཚ་ཅན, shamefaced, bashful, modest.

ངོ་ཚ་ཡོད, ditto.

ངོ་ཚ་ཤེས, ditto.

ངོ་ཚ་མེད་པ, shameless, impudent.

ངོ་མཚར་ཅན, wonderful.

ངོམས་པ, satisfied, not wishing more.

ངོམས་མེད, insatiable.

ཅ་ཅོ་ཅན, noisy, clamorous.

ཅི་ཅེར for སྤྱི་ཅེར, bald, having no hair on the head.

ཅོང་ཅོང, not flat or globular ; acuminated.

ཆུང་, (ཆུང་ངུ, ཆུང་བ,) small, little, the younger.

ཆུང་ཆུང, very small, little.

ཆེ, (ཆེ་བ,) great (the great, the elder).

ཆེན, (པོ, མོ,) great, large, big.

ཆོས་མེད, irreligious, impious.

ཆོས་ལྡན, religious, pious, godly.

ཉུང་, ། ཉུང་ངུ, little, few.

ཉེ། ཉེ་མོ, near, not far distant.

ཉེ་རིང་མེད་པ, impartial.

ཉེན་ཅན, dangerous.

ཉེས་པ་ཅན, faulty, wicked, sinful.

ཉོན་མོངས་ཅན, corrupt, wicked, sinful.

ཉོན་མོངས་མེད, sinless.

ཏི་ཕྲག, bad, mean, silly.

ཐ་དད, (པ,) contrary, opposite.

ཐ་མལ་པ, vulgar, common, mean, plebeian.

ཐག་རིང་, far, distant, remote.

ཐང་, open, plain ; clear.

ཐམས་ཅད, whole, entire, all.

ཐར་པ, free, freed.

ཐལ་བ་ཅན, dusty, full of ashes.

ཐིག་ལེ་ཅན, spotted, full of spots.

ཐིབ, (པོ, མོ,) dense, thick, close, compact.

ཐུ, (བོ, མོ,) chief, principal.

ཐུགས་རྗེ་ཅན, generous, liberal.

ཐུགས་རྗེ་དང་ལྡན་པ, ditto.

ཐུགས་རྗེ་མེད, illiberal.

ཐུགས་བརྩེ་བ་ཅན, affectionate, loving.

ཐུགས་རྟོག, heart-trying.

ཐུང་། ཐུང་ངུ, short, brief.

ཐུན་མོང, general, common.

ཐུལ, (བ,) soft, tame, mild.

ཐེ་ཚོམ་ཅན, doubtful, dubious, uncertain.

ཐེང་, (པོ, མོ,) lame, cripple.

དག, (པ, པོ,) clean, pure, sincere.

དང་པོ, first.

དྭངས་པ, pure, clean, clear ; sincere.

དད་པ་ཅན, faithful, believing.

དད་མེད, faithless, unbelieving, infidel.

དམ་པ, excellent, holy, saint ; noble.

དམ་པོ, strict, not loose ; exact.

དལ, (བ, པོ, མོ,) still, quiet, slow ; soft.

དུ་མ, many, much.

དུད་པ, bent, inclined, prone.

དུན་ཅན, diligent.

དུབ་པ, tired, weary, fatigued.

དུབ་ཅན, tiresome.

དུབ་མེད, unwearied, not tired, indefatigable.

དུལ, (བ, པོ, མོ,) soft, gentle, tame.

དོག, (པོ, མོ,) narrow, not wide, needy.

དྲག, (པོ, མོ,) strong, stout ; brave, valiant ; fierce, cruel, furious ; heavy.

དྲག་ཤུལ་ཅན, violent, cruel, tyrannical.

དྲང་, (པོ, མོ,) right, straight, upright.

དྲེགས་པ་ཅན, arrogant, proud.

དྲོ། དྲོན་པོ། དྲོན་མོ, warm.

དཀའ, (བ, བོ,མོ,) hard, difficult.

དཀར, (བ, པོ, མོ,) white.

དཀོན (པ, པོ, མོ,) rare, scarce, dear.

དགའ, (བ, བོ, མོ) glad, merry, rejoicing.

དགའ་བ་ཅན, joyful, cheerful.

དགའ་ལྡན, ditto.

དགུན་གྱི, of winter, wintery, hyemal.

དགུར, (པོ, མོ,) crooked, bent, curved, crooked-backed.

དགེ་བ་ཅན, virtuous.

དགོས་པ, necessary, needful.

དགོས་པ་ཅན, ditto.

དགོས་ཅན, ditto.

དགོས་པ་མེད་པ, unnecessary.

དགོས་མེད, ditto.

དགྱེས་པ, joyful, merry, glad.

དགྲ་བོ་ཅན, hostile, inimical.

དགྲ་ཅན, ditto.

དངུལ་གྱི, of silver, silver.

དངོས་ཅན, material, real.

དངོས་མེད, immaterial, not existing.

དཔག་ཏུ་ཡོད་པ, measurable, that may be measured.

དཔག་ཏུ་མེད་པ། དཔག་མེད, immeasurable.

དཔག་བྲལ, measureless.

དཔག་ཡས, immense.

དཔའ་བ་ཅན, courageous, brave; strong.

དཔའ་ཅན, ditto.

དཔལ, (པོ, མོ,) noble, illustrious; prosperous.

དཔྱིད་ཀ, of spring, vernal.

དབང་ཅན, mighty, powerful, potent.

དབང་ལྡན, ditto.

དབུ་ཅན, headed, with a head, capital.

དབུ་མེད, without a head, headless.

དབུགས་ཅན, aspirated, aspirate.

དབུལ, (བ, པོ, མོ,) poor, indigent.

དབེན, (པོ, མོ) solitary, retired.

དབྱངས་ཅན, harmonious, melodious, vocal.

དབྱར་གྱི, of or relating to the summer, estival.

དབྱིག་ལྡན, wealthy, rich, opulent.

དབྱེར་མེད, indivisible, inseparable.

དམན, (པ,) low, mean, humble.

དམའ, (བ, བོ, མོ,) low, mean, not high.

དམར, (བ, པོ, མོ,) red.

དམུ་ཆུ་ཅན, dropsical.

དམུན་པ་ཅན, dim, stupid.

ནག, (པ, པོ, མོ,) black.

ནང་མ། ནང་གི, inner, inward; domestic.

ནང་པ, intrinsic, esoteric; orthodox.

ནད་ཅན, sick, diseased.

ནད་མེད, not sick, healthy.

ནུབ་ཀྱི, occidental, western.

ནུས་པ་ཅན, efficacious, strong, nutritive.

ནུས་པ་མེད, inefficacious.

ནོག, (པ, པོ,) obscure, gloomy, dim.

ནོག་ནོག, (པོ) very obscure, gloomy.

ནོངས་པ་ཅན, faulty.

ནོར་ཅན, wealthy, opulent.

ནོར་ལྡན, ditto.

ཕ་ཡི, of the father, paternal.

ཕ་མ་ཡི, of the father and mother, parental.

ཕན་པ་ཅན, useful, wholesome.

ཕལ, (པ, པོ, མོ,) common, vulgar; mean, coarse.

ཕོངས་པ, indigent, poor.

ཕོད་པ། ཕོད་པ་ཅན, daring, bold.

ཕྱི། ཕྱི་མ, last, modern, of late.

ཕྱུག, (པ, པོ, མོ,) rich, wealthy, opulent.

ཕྱེད, (པ, པོ, མ, མོ,) half, the half of.

ཕྲ, (བོ, མོ,) small, minute, subtile, thin.

ཕྲ་དོག་ཅན, envious.

ཕྲག་དོག་ཅན, ditto.

བྱང་གི, northern, of the north.

བྱང་, (བ,) purified, perfect, accomplished.

བྱམས་པ་ཅན, clement, merciful.

བྱམས་མེད, merciless, unmerciful.

བྱེ་བྲག་ཅན, singular, distinguished, different.

བྲོ་བ་ཅན, savoury, flavorous, palatable.

བྲོ་བ་མེད། བྲོ་མེད, insipid, tasteless.

བླ, (མ,) upper, superior, higher.

བླུན, (པ, པོ, མོ,) stupid, ignorant, foolish.

བློ་ཅན། བློ་ལྡན། བློ་ལྡན་ཅན, intelligent, sagacious, ingenious.

བློ་མེད, unintelligent, foolish.

བློ་གྲོས་ཅན, prudent, intelligent.

བློ་གྲོས་མེད, imprudent.

བསྐ་བ, bitter, of a disagreeable taste.

བདེ་བ་ཅན, happy, blissful.

བདེན, (པ, པོ,) true, just.

བདེན་བྲལ, unjust.

བདོག་པ་ཅན, wealthy, rich.

བརྟན, (པོ,) secure, firm, strong.

བཙུན, (པ, པོ, མ, མོ,) honourable, respectable, reverend.

བརྩེ་བ་ཅན, affectionate, kind, merciful.

བརྩེ་ལྡན, ditto.

བརྩེ་བ་མེད་པ། བརྩེ་མེད, unkind; merciless.

བརྩེ་བ་མེད་པ་ཅན, ditto.

བརྩོན་པ་ཅན, diligent, industrious.

བརྩོན་འགྲུས་ཅན, diligent, industrious.

བརྩོན་ལྡན, ditto.

བརྩོན་མེད, idle, indolent.

བརྫུན་ཅན or རྫུན་ཅན, lying, false.

བཟང་, (བ, པོ, མོ,) good.

བསིལ, (བ, པོ, མ,) cool, fresh, somewhat cold.

བསུང་ཅན, fragrant, having a scent, scented.

བསོད, (པ,) fine, pleasant, savoury.

མ་ཡི། མའི, of the mother, maternal.

མང་, (པོ,) many, much.

མན, (པ, མ,) lower.

མས། མས་ཀྱི, lower, last, final.

མིག་སེར་ཅན, jealous.

མིང་གི, nominal.

མིང་ཅན, having a name, famous.

མུ་མེད, boundless, infinite.

མུ་ཟི་ཅན, sulphureous.

མུན་པ།-ཅན, dark, obscure, gloomy.

མོད་པོ, cheap, of little value.

མོས་པ་ཅན, respectful, regardful.

མྱ་ངན་ཅན, sorrowful, grievous.

མྱ་ངན་མེད, sorrowless.

མྱོས་པ, intoxicated; drunk.

མཁས, (པ, པོ, མོ,) wise, skilful, learned, prudent.

མཁྱེན, (པ, མ,) knowing, understanding.

མཁྱེན་པ་ཅན, intelligent, skilful.

མཁྱེན་མེད, ignorant, unskilful.

མཁྲང, (བ, པོ, མོ,) hard, solid, compact.

མཁྲེགས་པ, hard, solid.

མཁྲེགས་པར་གྱུར་པ, hardened.

མགོ་ཅན, having a head, headed, capital.

མགྱོགས, (པ,) swift, speedy, nimble, quick.
མངར, (བ, པོ, མོ,) sweet.
མངོན་པ, evident, open, clear; eminent.
མཉམ་པ, even, level; equal, like.
མཉམ་མེད, having no equal, unequalled.
མཉམ་ཟླ, matchless, incomparable.
མཉེན་པ, soft, pliable.
མཐའ་ཡོད, limited.
མཐའ་མེད, unlimited, boundless.
མཐའ་ཡས, ditto, infinite.
མཐུ་མེད, weak, feeble; inefficacious, impotent.
མཐུ་ལྡན, strong, powerful, potent; efficacious.
མཐུན་པ, agreeing, concordant, similar.
མཐོ, (བ,) མཐོན, (པོ, མོ,) high, elevated.
མདོག་ཅན། མདོག་ལྡན, having a colour, coloured.
མདོག་མེད, colourless.
མཚུངས་པ, equal, like.
མཚུངས་མེད, having no equal, matchless.
མཆེར་ཅན, sorrowful.
མཛངས, (པ, མ,) wise, clever, learned; brave.
མཛེས, (པ, མ,) beautiful, handsome, fair, elegant, graceful.
ཚབ་ཚུབ་ཅན, hasty, precipitant, hurry.
ཙེབ་ཙེབ, sharp, pointed.
ཚ, ཚན, hot, biting hot, (as a spice.)
ཚད་པ་ཅན, hot, sultry, torrid.
ཚད་མེད, measureless; immoderate.
ཚད་ལྡན, moderate, temperate.
ཚད་ལས་འདས་པ, beyond measure.
ཚབས་ཅན, dangerous; criminal, faulty.
ཚིག་པ, burnt, hurt by fire.

ཚིམ་པ, content or contented, satisfied.
ཚུ་རོལ་གྱི, of this side.
ཚུབ་ཅན, turbulent, tempestuous, boisterous.
ཚུལ་ཅན, regular, methodical.
ཚུལ་ལྡན, ditto.
ཚུལ་མེད, irregular.
ཚུལ་ཁྲིམས་ཅན, of good moral conduct.
ཚུལ་ཁྲིམས་ལྡན, ditto.
ཚུལ་ཁྲིམས་མེད, of bad morals, dissolute.
ཚེ་རིང, longevous, living long.
ཚེ་ཐུང, (ཅན,) living a short time.
ཚེ་མེད, lifeless.
ཚེ་ཡོད, living.
ཚེ་ལས་འདས་པ, deceased, the late.
ཚེ་འདས་པ, ditto.
ཚེ་གཉིས་པ, amphibious.
ཚེགས, hard, difficult.
ཚེར་མ་ཅན, prickly, full of thorns.
ཚོད་ཅན, moderate, observing due measure.
ཚོད་ལྡན, ditto.
ཚོད་མེད, immoderate.
ཝ་ལེ, clear, not obscure.
ཞ, (པ, བོ, མོ,) lame, cripple, maimed.
ཞག་ཅན greasy, oily, fat.
ཞག་མེད, destitute of fat, &c.
ཞར, (བ, པོ, མོ,) blind.
ཞི་བ, calm, quiet, still, mild, gentle.
ཞིབ, (པོ, མོ,) minute, fine, subtle.
ཞིམ, (པ, པོ,) flavorous, savoury, sweet.
ཞུན, (པོ,) fine, good, pure.
ཞེང་ཅན, wide, broad.

ཞེང་མེད, not wide, narrow.

ཞིལ་པོ, mean, pitiful, coarse.

ཟག་པ་ཅན, defective, wicked, corrupt, calamitous.

ཟངས་ཀྱི, of copper.

ཟངས་མདོག་ཅན, of copper colour, copper coloured.

ཟད་མེད, never-failing, inexhaustible.

ཟབ, (པ, པོ,མོ,) deep, profound.

ཛིན་མེད, inexhaustible.

ཟེ་སྣ་ཅན, nitrous.

ཟོག་ཅན, crafty, cunning, deceitful.

ཟོལ་ཟོག་ཅན, crafty, sly.

ཟླུམ་པོ, round, circular, globular.

འོག་ཅན, entire, not castrated.

འོད་ཅན, shining, bright.

འོན་པ, (པོ, མོ,) deaf.

འོས་པ, becoming, convenient, meet, fit, worthy of.

འཁྱགས་པ, frozen, congealed.

འཁྱམས་པ, gone astray, erred.

འཁྲུགས་པ, stirred up, troubled.

འཁྲུངས་པ, born, produced.

འགགས་པ, prohibited ; stopped.

འགན་ཅན, burdensome.

འགལ་ཚབས་ཅན, faulty, criminal.

འགྱུར་བ་ཅན, mutable, changeable, alterable.

འགྱུར་བ་མེད་པ or འགྱུར་མེད, immutable.

འགྱོད་པ་ཅན, sorrowful, penitent.

འཆི་བ་མེད་པ or འཆི་མེད, immortal.

འཆི་བ, mortal.

འཇམ, (པ, པོ,) soft, smooth, mild.

འཇིག་པ་ཅན, perishable, frail.

འཇིགས་པ་ཅན or འཇིགས་ཅན, fearful, timorous ; dreadful, frightful.

འཇིགས་སུ་རུང་བ, dreadful, horrible, awful.

འཇིགས་མེད, intrepid, fearless, bold.

འཇིགས་བྲལ, ditto.

འཇེབས, (པ, པོ), agreeable, pleasant.

འཇེམ་པོ, clever, dexterous, prudent, wise.

འཐད་པ, fit, meet, proper, becoming.

འཐུག, (པོ, མོ,) dense, thick, heavy, close.

འཐུམས་པ, covered, overcast.

འདུས་བྱས, compounded.

འདུས་མ་བྱས, uncompounded, simple.

འདྲ, (བ,) like, similar, equal.

འདྲེས་པ, mixed, mingled.

འཕགས་པ, eminent, excellent, high ; venerable, respectable, reverend.

འབྲེལ་བ་མེད་པ། འབྲེལ་མེད, inseparable.

འབྲལ་བ་མེད་པ། འབྲལ་མེད, inseparable, incoherent.

འཚོག, plump, fat, thick, gross.

འཚེ་བ་ཅན, hurtful, mischievous, noxious.

འཚེ་བ་མེད་པ, innocuous, harmless.

འཚེད, ditto.

འཛངས, (པ, མ,) wise, clever, learned ; brave.

འཛེམ་པ་ཅན, bashful, modest.

འཛེམ་པ་མེད་པ། འཛེམ་མེད, impudent.

ཡ་མཚན་ཅན, wonderful, strange, curious.

ཡངས, (པ. པོ,) wide, ample, diffuse, copious.

ཡིད་དུ་འོང་བ, pleasing, pleasant, delightful.

ཡིད་དུ་མི་འོང་བ, disagreeable.

ཡོན་པོ, crooked; wrong; deceitful, false.

ཡོམ, (པ, པོ,) inconstant, changing.

ཡོར་པོ, dull, heavy, blunt.

རགས་པ, large, extensive, huge, vast; thick, gross.

རིག་པ་ཅན, learned, intelligent, skilful.

རིགས་པ, reasonable, just, convenient.

རིང, (བ, པོ, མོ,) long; distant.

རིངས་པ, swift, speedy.

རིད, (པ, པོ, མོ,) lean, meagre.

རིན་ཆེན, precious, valuable, costly.

རིས་ཅན, partial, siding with one party.

རིས་མེད, impartial.

རུང་བ, convenient, apt, fit, meet, becoming.

རུལ, (བ, པ,) rotten, putrid.

རེངས་པ, stiff, hard.

རེད་པ, ready.

རེམ་པ, stout, strong.

རོད, (པ, པོ,) stiff.

རྐྱང་, (པ,) simple, not compound.

རྒ། རྒད། རྒན, old, aged.

རྒ་སཔ, grown old.

རྒལ་དུ་ཡོད་པ, fordable.

རྒལ་དུ་མེདཔ, not fordable.

རྒོད, (པ, པོ, མོ,) wild, not domestic.

རྒྱགས་པ, fat, thick.

རྒྱས་པ, extensive, large, copious; ample, wide.

རྔམ་པོ, bright, shining; awful.

རྗེན་པ, raw, not subdued by fire; naked.

རྙིང་པ། རྙིངས་པ, old, ancient; worn out.

རྙིད་པ, withered, pined away.

རྙོག་པ་ཅན, turbid, muddy; thick, not clear.

རྟག་པ, firm, steady, durable, lasting.

རྟས་པ, copious, abundant, fat, thick.

རྟུལ་པོ, blunt, dull.

རྟོགས་པ་ཅན, judicious.

རྟུགས་པོ, blunt, dull.

རྡུང་དུ་རུང་བ, malleable.

རྡུམ་པོ, maimed, mutilated, defective.

རྡུལ་ཅན, dusty.

རྡོས་བཅས, real, substantial.

རྣག་ཅན, purulent, full of corrupt matter.

རྣོ, (པོ,) རྣོན། པོ, sharp, acute, edged.

སྟོད། སྟོད་སྟོད, thick, dense.

རྨུགས་པ་ཅན, foggy, misty.

རྨུན་པོ, dull, heavy, stupid.

རྨུས་པ, dull, heavy; foggy, misty, overcast.

རྨོངས་པ, dull, stupid, ignorant.

རྩལ་མེད, unskilful.

རྩལ་ལྡན, skilful, exercised, expert.

རྩིང་, (པོ,) rough, harsh, full of hard particles.

རྩུབ, (པོ, མོ,) harsh, rough; of unequal surface.

རྩེ་མོ་ཅན། རྩེ་ཅན, pointed, having a top or apex.

རྩེད་མོ་ཅན, playful.

རྩོལ་བ་ཅན, diligent, industrious.

རྫུན་ཅན, false, lying.

རྫོགས་པ, accomplished, perfect, complete; finished, ended.

རྫབ་པོ, vain, false, empty.

རློན་ཅན, moist, wet.

རློན་པ, moist, wet ; fresh, green, new.

ལང་ཚོ་ཅན, adolescent, young.

ལང་རོཤ, stubborn.

ལས་ཅན, laborious, industrious.

ལས་མེད, idle, lazy, doing nothing.

ལུས་ཅན, bodily, corporal, corporeal.

ལུས་མེད, incorporeal.

ལེ་ལོ་ཅན, idle, lazy, indolent, slothful.

ལེགས་པ, good ; elegant, graceful.

ལེགས་ལྡན, virtuous.

ལེབ, (པོ, མོ,) flat, not globular.

ལྐུགས་པ, dumb, mute.

ལྗི-བ ; ལྗིད་པ, heavy.

ལྗིན་ཏེ, ditto.

ལྷུག, (པ,) flexible, pliant.

ལྗང་ཁུ, green.

ལྗིད་ཅན, heavy, grave, weighty.

ལྗིད་ལྡན, ditto.

ལྷེམ་པོ, overflowing, full.

ལྟོགས་པ, hungry, grown hungry.

ལྷན, common ; both.

ལྷུབ་ཅན, wide, ample, diffused.

ཤིས་པ, blessed.

ཤུགས་ཅན, vehement.

ཤེད་ཅན, strong, vigorous.

ཤེད་མེད, impotent, weak.

ཤེས་རབ་ཅན, ingenious, witty.

ཤེས་ལྡན, intelligent, learned.

ཤོ་ར་ཅན, nitrous.

ཤོ་རེ་ཅན, defective, damaged, broken.

སར་པ for གསར་པ, new, fresh, recent, virgin.

སུན་པོ, tedious, irksome.

སུལ་ཅན, furrowed, having long trenches.

སེམས་མེད, inanimate.

སེམས་ལྡན, animate.

སོ་མ, new, fresh, recent.

སོན་པོ for གསོན་པོ, living, alive.

སྲབ, (པོ, མོ,) thin, slender, lean.

སྲབ་སྲིབ, dark, obscure.

སྲིད་ཅན, affectionate, passionate, desirous.

སྲིད་ལྡན, ditto.

སྲེད་མེད, disaffectionate, unbeloved.

སྲོག་ཅན, animate, living.

སྲོག་ལྡན, ditto.

སྲོག་མེད, inanimate, lifeless.

སྲོལ་ཅན, usual, customary.

སྲོལ་མེད, unusual.

སླ། (བ, བོ, མོ,) light, not heavy ; easy, thin.

སླན་ཏེ, ditto, thin.

སླུ་བ་མེད་པ, not to be deceived, infallible.

སླུ་མེད, ditto.

སྐ, (བ, བོ, མོ,) thick, dense.

སྐན-ཏེ, ditto.

སྐད་ཅན, sonorous, vocal.

སྐམ, (པོ,) dry.

སྐལ་བ་ཅན, happy, fortunate.

སྐལ་ལྡན, ditto.

སྐལ་མེད, unfortunate, unlucky.

སྐོམ, (པ,) thirsty.

སྐྱ, (བོ,) white, grey.

སྐྱིད, (པོ,) happy, fortunate, at ease.

སྐྱུར, (པོ, མོ,) sour, acid.

སྐྱེག་ཅན, hurtful, unlucky.

སྐྱོན་ཅན, faulty.

སྐྱོན་མེད, faultless.

སྐྲག་མེད, intrepid.

སྒུར་པོ, crooked, curved, bent.

སྒོམ་དུ་ཡོད་པ, conceivable, imaginable.

སྒོམ་དུ་མེདཔ, inconceivable.

སྒྱུ་ཅན, artful, crafty, cunning.

སྒྲ་ལྡན, sonorous, sounding.

སྒྲ་ཅན, ditto.

སྔ་མ, first, former, prior, antecedent.

སྔོ, (བོ,) སྔོན་-པོ blue ; green.

སྙན, (པ,) agreeable, pleasing.

སྙི་, (བོ,) soft, gentle.

སྙིགས་-པ, degenerate, grown worse.

སྙིང་རྗེ་ཅན, merciful, generous.

སྙིང་རྗེ་མེད་པ, unmerciful, cruel.

སྙིན, (པ, པོ,) soft, gentle.

སྙུན་ཅན, sick, diseased.

སྙེགས་པ, stretched out, straight.

སྙེམ་པ་ཅན, boasting, bragging.

སྟུག, (པ, པོ, མོ,) thick, dense ; heavy.

སྟོང་པ, empty, void.

སྟོབས་ཅན, strong, vigorous.

སྟོབས་ལྡན, ditto.

སྟོབས་མེད, weak, feeble.

སྡང་བ་ཅན, angry, passionate.

སྡར་མ, trembling, frightful.

སྡིག་ཅན, vicious, sinful.

སྡིག་མེད, sinless.

སྡུག, (པ, པོ,) agreeable, pleasing ; fair, handsome, beautiful, delightful.

སྡུག,བསྔལ་ཅན, uneasy, sorrowful.

སྡེར་ཅན, clawed.

སྡེར་མེད, clawless.

ན་ཚོགས་པ, of all sorts, several.

སྤུ་ཅན, hairy.

སྤུ་མེད, hairless, having no hair on.

སྤོགས་ཅན, profitable, advantageous.

སྤོད་ཅན, spicy, seasoned with spice.

སྤོབས་པ་ཅན, courageous, able.

སྤོབས་པ་མེད་པ, cowardly, fearful.

སྤྱང་, (པོ, མོ,) skilful, clever, dexterous, ready, fit.

སྤྱི, general, common ; chief.

སྤྱལ་པ་ཅན, busy, employed, industrious.

སྤྱིག་པ, meagre, lean.

སྦོམ, (པོ,) thick, gross, bulky.

སྦོས་པ, swollen, puffed up.

སྦྲམས་པ, hungry.

སྦྲེས་པ, frozen, stiff, hard.

སྨིན་པ, ripe, mature, perfect.

སྨིན་བྱེད, maturative.

སྨུག་པོ, dark red.

སྨྱོན་པ, mad, lunatick.

སྨྱོས་པ, mad, grown mad, distracted.

ཙར་པོ, dexterous, clever, fine.

རླས་ཅན, moist, wet.

རླས་མེད, void of moisture.

ཞེལ་-ཅན, ample, wide.

ཞེལ་ཞེལ, very ample, wide.

Negative participial adjectives are formed from affirmative ones by the addition of མ, or མི; as in the following list, from སྨིན་པ, ripe; སྨྲས་པ, said; ཐོས་པ, heard, &c. are formed:

མ་སྨིན་པ, unripe.
མ་སྨྲས་པ, unsaid, not spoken.
མ་ཐོས་པ, unheard.
མ་མཐོང་བ, unseen.
མ་གཟིགས་པ, ditto.
མ་གཡོགས་པ, uncovered.
མ་བཀག་པ, unhindered.
མ་བཀང་བ, unfilled, unreplete.
མ་བཟས་པ, uneaten.
མ་བྱས་པ, undone, not made, uncreate.
མ་བགྱིས་པ, ditto.
མ་མཛད་པ, ditto.
འདུས་མ་བྱས་པ, uncompounded, simple.
མ་ཉོས, unbought.
མ་མནན, undaunted, unabashed.
མ་ནུས་པ, unable.
མ་བཤུབས་པ, unabolished.
མ་བླངས་པ, unaccepted.
མ་བཞེས་པ, ditto.
མ་རྫོགས་པ, unaccomplished, unfinished.
མ་ཚང་བ, incomplete.
མ་དག་པ, not clean, inaccurate, incorrect.
མ་གོམས་པ, unaccustomed, unwonted.
མ་བསྒོམས་པ, ditto.
མ་བསྐོས་པ, unelected.
མ་བཤེས་པ, unacquainted, unknown.
མ་འདྲིས་པ, unasked.
མ་འདྲེས་པ, unmixed, pure.
མ་སྦྱར་བ, ditto.
མ་བརྡུངས་པ, unbeaten.

མ་དད་པ, unbelieving.
སྤྱན་མ་དྲངས་པ, uninvited.
ཁ་མ་འབུས་པ, unopened, not yet blown.
མ་བཙགས་པ, unbolted, not sifted.
མ་སྐྱེས་པ, unborn.
མ་བསྐྱིས་པ, unborrowed.
མ་བསླབས་པ, unbred, untaught.
མ་བཏུལ་བ, unbroken, not tamed.
མ་བསྲེགས་པ, unburnt.
མ་བཟུང་བ, uncaught, not taken.
མ་ངེས་པ, uncertain.
བག་མ་ཡིན་པ, unchaste.
འོས་པ་མ་ཡིན་པ, unbecoming.
ཐུན་མོང་མ་ཡིན་པ, uncommon.
སྟུག་པོ་མ་ཡིན་པ, incompact.
མ་བསྡུས་པ, uncollected.
མ་བལྡད་པ, unchewed.
མ་བསམས་པ, unconceived, not imagined.
མ་མཛད་པ, uncreate.
མ་བཞུས་པ, undigested; unmelted.
མ་འཁྱགས་པ, unfrozen, not congealed.
མ་རྨོས་པ, untilled.
མ་སྐྱུག་པ, unpleasing.
མ་ལེགས་པ, unfair; not well, &c.
མ་འཁྲུགས་པ, unerring, not mistaking.
མ་བྱོན་པ, not yet come, future.
མ་འོངས་པ, ditto.
མ་འདས་པ, not escaped.
མ་བླུས་པ, unredeemed, &c. &c.
མི་འོས་པ, unbecoming, indecent, unsuitable.

མི་རྩད་པ, ditto.
མི་གཡོ་བ, immovable.
མི་འགུལ་བ, ditto.
མི་ཤེས་པ, ignorant.
མི་རྟག་པ, unsteady, frail, transient.
མི་རྨོངས་པ, not ignorant.
མི་ཞིམ་པ, unpleasant, disagreeable to the taste.
མི་སྙན་པ, unpleasant (to the ear).
མི་སྲིད་པ, impossible, impracticable.
མི་ཟད་པ, inexhaustible, infinite.
མི་འདྲ, unlike, different.
མི་བརྟན་པ, inconstant, mutable.
མི་ངལ་བ, indefatigable.
མི་ངོམས་པ, not to be satisfied, insatiable.
མི་གཙང་བ, unclean, impure, unholy, defiled.

Some Adjectives with their opposites.

མཐོ་དམན, high (and) low.
འདྲ་མི་འདྲ, like, unlike.
མཉམ་མི་མཉམ, even, uneven ; equal, unequal.
འདུས་བྱས། འདུས་མ་བྱས, compound, simple.
བཟང་ངན, good, bad or ill.
ཆེ་ཆུང་, great, small.
རིང་ཐུང་, long, short.
སྦོམ་ཕྲ, large, small ; coarse, fine.
འཇམ་རྩུབ, soft, harsh ; smooth, rough.
སྲ་སྙི, hard, soft.
ཡང་ལྗི, light, heavy.
ཁྲོང་འབོལ, hard, soft.
སྲབ་འཐུག or སྟུག, thin, thick.
དྲང་པོ། ཀྱོག་པོ, straight, crooked.
དགྱེ་དགུ, bent backwards, forwards.
བརྟན་གཡོ, firm, fixed, movable.
དབང་ཅན། དབང་མེད, powerful, impotent.
དཀའ་སླ, difficult, easy.
སྐྱ་སླ, thick, thin, (as a liquid.)
སྐམ་གཤེར, dry, moist.
དཀར་ནག, white, black.
རྣོན་རྟུལ, sharp, blunt.
གྲང་དྲོ, cold, warm.
མཛེས་མི་མཛེས, fair, unfair.
སྡུག་མི་སྡུག, agreeable, disagreeable ; pleasing, unpleasing (to the eye).
ཞིམ་མི་ཞིམ, agreeable, disagreeable, (to the taste or smell.)
སྙན་མི་སྙན, pleasing, unpleasing, (to the ear.)
བྲོ་བ་ཅན། བྲོ་མེད, savoury, insipid (to the taste.)
དགའ་མི་དགའ, glad, sorrowful ; merry, sad.
ཉེ་རིང, near, far.
རགས་ཕྲ, large, small ; gross, subtle.
དོག་པ། ཡངས་པ, narrow, ample, wide.
གཟུགས་ཅན། གཟུགས་མེད, corporeal, incorporeal.
རིད་པ། རྒྱགས་པ, meagre, fat.
ཟབ་པོ། གཏིང་མེད, deep, shallow.
གཞེང་ཅན། གཞེང་མེད, broad, narrow.

མདོག་ཅན། མདོག་མེད, coloured, colourless.

དབུལ་ཕྱུག, poor, rich.

འཛངས་གླེན, wise, foolish.

དག། མ་དག, pure, impure; clean, unclean.

སྔ་ཕྱི, former, latter; prior, posterior; first, last.

གོང་འོག, upper, lower.

ནང་ཕྱི, inner, outer, &c. &c.

Numerals.

§ 107. **The Cardinal numbers are as follows:**

༡ 1 གཅིག, one.

༢ 2 གཉིས, two.

༣ 3 གསུམ, three.

༤ 4 བཞི, four.

༥ 5 ལྔ, five.

༦ 6 དྲུག, six.

༧ 7 བདུན, seven.

༨ 8 བརྒྱད, eight.

༩ 9 དགུ, nine.

༡༠ 10 བཅུ་ཐམ་པ or བཅུ, ten.

༡༡ 11 བཅུ་གཅིག, eleven.

༡༢ 12 བཅུ་གཉིས, twelve.

༡༣ 13 བཅུ་གསུམ, thirteen.

༡༤ 14 བཅུ་བཞི, fourteen.

༡༥ 15 བཅོ་ལྔ, fifteen.

༡༦ 16 བཅུ་དྲུག, sixteen.

༡༧ 17 བཅུ་བདུན, seventeen.

༡༨ 18 བཅོ་བརྒྱད, eighteen.

༡༩ 19 བཅུ་དགུ, nineteen.

༢༠ 20 ཉི་ཤུ་ཐམ་པ or ཉི་ཤུ, a score, twenty.

༢༡ 21 ཉི་ཤུ་རྩ་གཅིག or ཉེར་གཅིག, twenty-one, &c.

༣༠ 30 སུམ་ཅུ་ཐམ་པ or སུམ་ཅུ, thirty.

༣༡ 31 སུམ་ཅུ་རྩ་གཅིག or སོ་གཅིག, thirty-one, &c.

༤༠ 40 བཞི་བཅུ་ཐམ་པ or བཞི་བཅུ, forty.

༤༡ 41 བཞི་བཅུ་རྩ་གཅིག or ཞེ་གཅིག, forty-one, &c.

༥༠ 50 ལྔ་བཅུ་ཐམ་པ or ལྔ་བཅུ, fifty.

༥༡ 51 ལྔ་བཅུ་རྩ་གཅིག or ང་གཅིག, fifty-one, &c.

༦༠ 60 དྲུག་ཅུ་ཐམ་པ or དྲུག་ཅུ, sixty.

༦༡ 61 དྲུག་ཅུ་རྩ་གཅིག or རེ་གཅིག, sixty-one, &c.

༧༠ 70 བདུན་ཅུ་ཐམ་པ or བདུན་ཅུ, seventy.

༧༡ 71 བདུན་ཅུ་རྩ་གཅིག or དོན་གཅིག, seventy-one, &c.

༨༠ 80 བརྒྱད་ཅུ་ཐམ་པ or བརྒྱད་ཅུ, eighty.

༨༡ 81 བརྒྱད་ཅུ་རྩ་གཅིག or གྱ་གཅིག, eighty-one, &c.

༩༠ 90 དགུ་བཅུ་ཐམ་པ or དགུ་བཅུ, ninety.

༧༡ 91 དགུ་བཅུ་རྩ་གཅིག or གོ་གཅིག, ninety-one, &c.

༡༠༠ 100 བརྒྱ་ཐམ་པ or བརྒྱ, a hundred.

༡༠༠༠ 1000 སྟོང་ or སྟོང་ཕྲག, a thousand.

ཁྲི or ཁྲི་ཚོ, ten thousand, a myriad.

འབུམ or འབུམ་ཚོ, a hundred thousand, one *lakh*.

ས་ཡ, a million.

བྱེ་བ, ten millions.

དུང་ཕྱུར, a hundred millions.

ཐེར་འབུམ, a thousand millions.

ཐེར་འབུམ་ཆེན་པོ, ten thousand millions.

ཁྲག་ཁྲིག, a hundred thousand millions.

ཁྲག་ཁྲིག་ཆེན་པོ, a billion.

Remarks.

1. The units གཅིག, གཉིས, གསུམ, before the tens or any higher number, drop the prefix ག, and are written thus: ཅིག, ཉིས, སུམ; as in ཅིག་བརྒྱ, (100) ཉིས་བརྒྱ, (200) སུམ་བརྒྱ (300); ཅིག་སྟོང, (1,000) ཉིས་སྟོང, (2,000) སུམ་སྟོང, (3,000,) &c. &c. From ཉིས་ཅུ, (twenty) is formed, and now generally used, ཉི་ཤུ.

2. བཅུ and ཅུ are equivalent in signification, བཅུ being used after a vowel, and ཅུ, after a consonant: as in བཞི་བཅུ, ལྔ་བཅུ, and དགུ་བཅུ; and སུམ་ཅུ, དྲུག་ཅུ, བདུན་ཅུ, and བརྒྱད་ཅུ.

3. After the tens are frequently found some of these words; ཐམ་པ, ཕྲག, ཚོ, denoting a collective or integral. ཐམ་པ is used, commonly, after the tens up to one hundred; ཕྲག after བརྒྱ, སྟོང, &c. as well as after any smaller number; as in བདུན་ཕྲག, a week or seven-night. ཚོ, after any great number in general; as ཁྲི་ཚོ, a myriad, འབུམ་ཚོ, a hundred thousand; but sometimes it is used with the smaller numbers also.

4. བཅོ་ལྔ and བཅོ་བརྒྱད are now commonly used, instead of the ancient terms བཅུ་ལྔ or བཅྭ་ལྔ, (fifteen,) and བཅུ་བརྒྱད or བཅྭ་བརྒྱད, eighteen.

5. The units follow the rest of the decades (twenty, thirty, forty, &c.) in the same order as above given from 11 to 19; but, for expressing the decades themselves, there are two modes, as has been shown in the preceding table.

6. When the cardinals are reduplicated, they may be rendered in English thus: གཅིག་གཅིག, single, only one; གསུམ་གསུམ, three by three (as in multiplication), three at once, three to each, &c.; དྲུག་དྲུག, six by six, six at once, six to each, &c.

§ 108. From the above cardinals, numeral adjectives are formed by adding to them the termination པོ (sometimes པ or མ); as གཅིག་པོ, གཉིས་པོ, གསུམ་པོ, &c. consisting of one, two, three, &c.; སུམ་ཅུ་པ, consisting of or containing thirty, (Slocas, &c.); ལེའུ་བཞི་མ, containing four chapters.

§ 109. From the same cardinals, adverbs are formed by putting before them the particle ལན, (turn, time) as, ལན་གཅིག, once; ལན་གཉིས, twice; ལན་གསུམ, thrice; ལན་བཞི, four times; ལན་བཅུ, ten times; ལན་བརྒྱ, a hundred times.

§ 110. The ordinals are formed from the cardinals, by adding to them the article པ in general (and sometimes མ for the female). The first word is however an exception, since instead of གཅིག་པ, the first, དང་པོ is used: but elsewhere the rule is regular;

as བཅུ་གཅིག་པ, the eleventh; ཉེར་གཅིག་པ, the twenty-first, &c.; གཉིས་པ, second, གསུམ་པ, third, &c. all which are formed in conformity therewith.

§ 111. From the ordinals, adverbs are formed by affixing the letter ར, thus: དང་པོར, first, the first time, in the first place; གཉིས་པར, secondly, the second time, in the second place; གསུམ་པར, thirdly, in the third place, and so on with all the rest.

Note. 1. Numerals are often expressed on registers, &c. by the letters of the alphabet, in the following manner:

The thirty simple letters of the alphabet, without vowel signs, (consequently pronounced with the inherent *a*) from ཀ to ཨ, denote the numerals from 1 up to 30. Thence by adding to each letter the *i* (ི) vowel sign in this manner, ཀི—ཨི, the numerals from 31—60 are designed. With the *u* (ུ) vowel sign, thus: ཀུ—ཨུ, the numerals from 61—90 are expressed. With *é* (ེ) thus: ཀེ—ཨེ, those from 91—120. Lastly, with the *o* (ོ) vowel, thus: ཀོ—ཨོ, the numerals from 121—150 are expressed.

Should it be required to continue the register, &c., the letters or syllables of the whole former scheme, being made long, the numbering may be extended as far as 300, thus:

ཀཱ—ཨཱ	denote the numerals	151—180
ཀཱི—ཨཱི	ditto	181—210
ཀཱུ—ཨཱུ	ditto	211—240
ཨཱེ—ཀཱེ	ditto	241—270
ཀཱོ—ཨཱོ	ditto	271—300

Note. 2. In Tibetan books (especially in indexes and quotations from other works) there frequently occurs after these numeral letters some one of the syllables པ, པར, པ་ལ། པ, signifying such and such a volume, or any other thing; and པར or པ་ལ, denoting in such and such a volume, &c.; as, ཀ་པ, the volume, (or any other thing) marked with the letter ཀ; or the first volume, &c.: again, ཀ་པར or ཀ་པ་ལ, in the volume, &c. marked with the letter ཀ *ka*, or in the 1st volume, &c.

These syllables are used in the same manner with all the other numerical letters.

Pronouns.

§ 112. As there is no irregularity in the declension of the pronouns from the nominative singular, the other cases being formed according to the scheme of general declension exhibited above, (§. 86.) it will be unnecessary here to decline every pronoun; the several varieties of them therefore need only be enumerated, with their signification in the nominative singular; and the declension will be confined to a few examples.

§ 113. The Personal Pronouns.

First Person.

ང,	I.
བདག,	
ཁོ་བོ *masc.*	
ཁོ་མོ, *fem.*	
ངེད, *hon.*	
རང,	
ང་རང,	I, myself. I.
ང་བདག,	
ང་ཉིད,	
ང་ཁོ་ན,	
ཉ་ཅི,	
བདག་རང,	
བདག་ཉིད,	
བདག་ཁོ་ན,	
ངེད་རང, *hon.*	
ངེད་ཉིད, *hon.*	
ངེད་ཁོ་ན, *hon.*	
བདག་ཅི,	
ངེད་ཅི, *hon.*	

Second Person.

ཁྱོད,	thou, (you.)
ཁྱེད, *hon.*	
ཁྱོད་རང,	thyself, or thou, you.
ཁྱོད་ཉིད,	
ཁྱོད་ཁོ་ན,	
ཁྱེད་རང, *hon.*	thyself, thou; or yourself, you.
ཁྱེད་ཉིད, *hon.*	
ཁྱེད་ཁོ་ན, *hon.*	

Third Person.

ཁོ *com.*	he, she.
ཁོ་པ, *m.*	
ཁོ་མ, *f.*	
ཁོང, *com. hon.*	
ཁོང་པ, *m. hon.*	
ཁོང་མ, *f. hon.*	
ཁོ་རང,	he himself. she herself.
ཁོ་ཉིད,	
ཁོང་རང, *hon.*	
ཁོང་ཉིད, *hon.*	
ཉིད, *hon.*	

Note. Those that are marked *hon.* are used respectfully. The pronouns ངེད, &c. I; and the second person, ཁྱེད, &c. are used both in the singular and in the plural sense, denoting a degree of civility or politeness, both in the speaker, and in the person or persons addressed.

§ 114. In the strictest sense, the personal pronouns are only these: ང ňá, I; ཁྱོད, *khyod*, thou; ཁོ, *kho*, he, she. But since the others also frequently occur, both in books and common conversation, when speaking with more or less degree of emphasis, and respect, they have been enumerated at length. The Tibetans make frequent use of the compound pronouns, in place of the simple ones.

§ 115. Since the personal pronouns enumerated above frequently occur in the instrumentive case, denoting, before a transitive verb, the agent; which would be rendered among Europeans by the nominative, the instrumentive case of all these pronouns is here inserted at length.

First Person.

ངས or ང་ཡིས,	by me, I.
བདག་གིས,	ditto.
ཁོ་བོས or ཁོ་བོ་ཡིས, *m.*	ditto.
ཁོ་མོས or ཁོ་མོ་ཡིས, *f.*	ditto.
ཇེད་ཀྱིས,	ditto.
རང་གིས,	ditto.
ང་རང་གིས,	ditto.
ང་བདག་གིས,	ditto.
ང་ཉིད་ཀྱིས,	ditto.
ང་ཁོ་ནས,	ditto.
ང་ནི, emphatical and invariable before a transitive verb.	
བདག་རང་གིས,	by myself, I.
བདག་ཉིད་ཀྱིས,	ditto.
བདག་ཁོ་ནས,	ditto.
ཇེད་རང་གིས,	ditto.
ཇེད་ཉིད་ཀྱིས,	ditto.
ཇེད་ཁོ་ནས,	ditto.

Second Person.

ཁྱོད་ཀྱིས,	by thee, thou; you.
ཁྱེད་ཀྱིས,	ditto.
ཁྱོད་རང་གིས,	by thyself; thou, you.
ཁྱོད་ཉིད་ཀྱིས,	ditto.
ཁྱོད་ཁོ་ནས,	ditto.
ཁྱེད་རང་གིས,	by yourself, you, (one.)
ཁྱེད་ཉིད་ཀྱིས,	ditto.
ཁྱེད་ཁོ་ནས,	ditto.

Third Person.

ཁོས or ཁོ་ཡིས, *com.*	by him, her, or he, she.
ཁོ་པས, *m.*	ditto.
ཁོ་མས, *f.*	ditto.
ཁོང་གིས, *com.*	by him, her, he or she.
ཁོང་པས, *m.*	ditto.
ཁོང་མས, *f.*	ditto.
ཁོ་རང་གིས,	by himself.
ཁོ་ཉིད་ཀྱིས,	ditto.
ཁོང་རང་གིས,	ditto.
ཁོང་ཉིད་ཀྱིས,	ditto.
ཉིད་ཀྱིས,	ditto.

§ 116. The nominative plural of the personal pronouns may be formed by adding either of the three following particles or plural signs: ཅག, དག, རྣམས; written also thus, ཅག་རྣམས, དག་རྣམས; as, ང་ཅག, or ང་ཅག་རྣམས, བདག་ཅག or བདག་ཅག་རྣམས, We; ཁྱོད་ཅག or ཁྱོད་ཅག་རྣམས and ཁྱེད་དག or ཁྱེད་དག་རྣམས, Ye or you; ཁོ་ཅག or ཁོ་ཅག་རྣམས, ཁོང་ཅག or ཁོང་ཅག་རྣམས, They.

§ 117. The first person plural is sometimes expressed by ཨུ་སྐོལ or འོ་སྐོལ ཨུ་ཅག, ཨུ་བུ་ཅག or ཡུ་བུ་ཅག, with or without the expletive རྣམས after them.

The instrumentive case, or that of the agent, of the personal pronouns in the plural number, is formed by adding གིས, after ཅག and དག; by ཀྱིས, after རྣམས; and གྱིས after འོ་སྐོལ, as;

ང་ཅག་གིས,	by us, we, (I.)
ཁྱེད་དག་གིས,	by you, ye, (thou.)
ཁོང་རྣམས་ཀྱིས,	by them, they.
འོ་སྐོལ་གྱིས,	by us (me,) we or I.

§ 118. Declension of Personal Pronouns.

First Person.

	Singular.		*Plural.*	
Nom. & Acc.	ང,	I, me.	ང་ཅག or ང་ཅག་རྣམས,	we, us.
Inst.	ངས or ང་ཡིས.	by me.	ང་ཅག་གིས, ང་ཅག་རྣམས་ཀྱིས,	by us.
Gen. or *Pos.*	ངའི or ང་ཡི.	of me.	ང་ཅག་གི, ང་ཅག་རྣམས་ཀྱི,	of us.
Dat.	ང་ལ, (ངར.)	to me.	ང་ཅག་ལ, ང་ཅག་རྣམས་ལ,	to me.
Abl.	ང་ནས or ང་ལས.	from me.	ང་ཅག་ནས, ང་ཅག་རྣམས་ནས,	from us.

	Also, *Singular.*		*Plural.*	
Nom. & Acc.	ངེད,	I, (we.)	ངེད་ཅག, ངེད་རྣམས or ངེད་ཅག་རྣམས,	we, us.
Inst.	ངེད་ཀྱིས,	by me.	ངེད་ཅག་གིས, ངེད་རྣམས་ཀྱིས, &c.	by us.
Gen. or *Pos.*	ངེད་ཀྱི,	of me.	ངེད་ཅག་གི, ངེད་རྣམས་ཀྱི, &c.	of us.
Dat.	ངེད་ལ,	to me.	ངེད་ཅག་ལ, ངེད་རྣམས་ལ, &c.	to us.
Abl.	ངེད་ནས,	from me.	ངེད་ཅག་ནས, ངེད་རྣམས་ནས.	from us.

	Also, *Singular.*		*Plural.*	
Nom. & Acc.	བདག,	I, myself, I, me.	བདག་ཅག or བདག་ཅག་རྣམས,	we, us.
Inst.	བདག་གིས,	by me.	བདག་ཅག་གིས, བདག་ཅག་རྣམས་ཀྱིས,	by us.
Gen. or Poss.	བདག་གི,	of me.	བདག་ཅག་གི, བདག་ཅག་རྣམས་ཀྱི,	of us.
Dat.	བདག་ལ,	to me.	བདག་ཅག་ལ, བདག་ཅག་རྣམས་ལ,	to us.
Abl.	བདག་ནས,	from me.	བདག་ཅག་ནས, བདག་ཅག་རྣམས་ནས,	from us.

§ 119. *Second Person.*

	Singular.		*Plural.*	
Nom. & Acc.	ཁྱོད (also ཁྱེད)	thou, thee.	ཁྱོད་ཅག or ཁྱོད་རྣམས,	you, ye.
Inst.	ཁྱོད་ཀྱིས,	by thee.	ཁྱོད་ཅག་གིས, ཁྱོད་རྣམས་ཀྱིས,	by you.
Gen. or Poss.	ཁྱོད་ཀྱི,	of thee.	ཁྱོད་ཅག་གི, ཁྱོད་རྣམས་ཀྱི,	of you.
Dat.	ཁྱོད་ལ,	to thee.	ཁྱོད་ཅག་ལ, ཁྱོད་རྣམས་ལ,	to you.
Abl.	ཁྱོད་ནས,	from thee.	ཁྱོད་ཅག་ནས, ཁྱོད་རྣམས་ནས,	from you.

§ 120. *Third Person.*

	Singular.		*Plural.*	
Nom. & Acc.	ཁོ,	he, she, him, her.	ཁོ་ཅག or ཁོ་ཅག་རྣམས,	they, them.
Inst.	ཁོས or ཁོ་ཡིས,	by him or her.	ཁོ་ཅག་གིས, &c.	by them.
Gen. or Poss.	ཁོའི or ཁོ་ཡི,	of him or her.	ཁོ་ཅག་གི, &c.	of them.
Dat.	ཁོ་ལ,	to him or her.	ཁོ་ཅག་ལ, &c.	to them.
Abl.	ཁོ་ནས,	from him or her.	ཁོ་ཅག་ནས, &c.	from them.

	Also, *Singular.*		*Plural.*	
Nom. & Acc.	ཁོང,	he, she, him, her (respectfully).	ཁོང་རྣམས or ཁོང་ཅག, &c.	they, them.
Inst.	ཁོང་གིས,	by him or her.	ཁོང་རྣམས་ཀྱིས, &c.	by them.
Gen. or Poss.	ཁོང་གི,	of him or her.	ཁོང་རྣམས་ཀྱི, &c.	of them.
Dat.	ཁོང་ལ,	to him or her.	ཁོང་རྣམས་ལ, &c.	to them.
Abl.	ཁོང་ནས,	from him or her.	ཁོང་རྣམས་ནས, &c.	from them.

§ 121. Possessive Pronouns.

The genitives of the personals are likewise possessive pronouns. They are always put before the substantive, and remain unchanged in all the cases of both numbers.

Possessives formed from the First Person.

Singular.		*Plural.*	
ངའི or ང་ཡི,	my, mine.	ང་ཅག་གི,	our, ours.
བདག་གི,	ditto.	བདག་ཅག་རྣམས་ཀྱི,	ditto.
ཁོ་བོའི,	ditto.	ཁོ་བོ་ཉམས་ཀྱི,	ditto.
ངད་ཀྱི,	ditto.	ངེད་ཅག་གི,	ditto.
ང་རང་གི,	ditto.	ངརང་དག་གི,	ditto.

Second Person.

Singular.		*Plural.*	
ཁྱོད་ཀྱི,	they, thine.	ཁྱོད་ཅག་གི,	your, yours.
ཁྱེད་ཀྱི,	do., (your.)	ཁྱེད་རྣམས་ཀྱི,	ditto.
ཁྱོད་རང་གི,	ditto.	ཁྱོད་ར་ང་དག་གི,	ditto.
ཁྱེད་ཉིད་ཀྱི,	thine, your own.		

Third Person.

Singular.		*Plural.*	
ཁོའི or ཁོ་ཡི,	his, her.	ཁོ་ཅག་གི,	their, theirs.
ཁོང་གི,	ditto.	ཁོང་རྣམས་ཀྱི,	ditto.
ཁོ་རང་གི,	his own, her own.	ཁོ་རང་དག་གི,	ditto.
ཁོང་ཉིད་ཀྱི,	ditto.	ཁོང་ཉིད་དག་གི	ditto.

§ 122. Demonstratives.

The *proximate* demonstrative pronouns are: འདི, this (which is also expressed emphatically, thus: འདི་ནི, འདི་བོ, འདི་ཉིད, འདི་ཁོ་ན, འདི་ཁོ་ན་ཉིད, this very person or thing; འདི་ཀ, འདི་ཀོ, འདི་ག, one, of this place, country, party, sect, profession, &c.) ཚུ་གི, ཨ་གི, this here; ཨུ this; ཨུ་ནི, this here, also sometimes occur.

The *remote* are: དེ, that (emphatically དེ་ནི, དེ་བོ, དེ་ཉིད, དེ་ཁོ་ན, དེ་ཁོ་ན་ཉིད, that very person or thing; དེ་ཀ, དེ་ཀོ, དེ་ག, one of that place or country, party, sect, profession), ཕ་གི, ཕ་གི, that there, ཨོ, that, ཨོ་ནི, that there, also sometimes occurs.

Declension of འདི.

	Singular.		*Plural.*	
Nom. & Acc.	འདི,	this.	འདི་དག, འདི་རྣམས,	these.
Inst.	འདིས or འདི་ཡིས,	by this.	འདི་དག་གིས, འདི་རྣམས་ཀྱིས,	by these.
Gen.	འདིའི or འདི་ཡི,	of this.	འདི་དག་གི, འདི་རྣམས་ཀྱི,	of these.
Dat.	འདི་ལ,	to this.	འདི་དག་ལ, འདི་རྣམས་ལ,	to these.
Abl.	འདི་ནས,	from this.	འདི་དག་ནས, འདི་རྣམས་ནས,	from these.

	Also, Singular.		*Plural.*	
Nom. & Acc.	དེ,	that.	དེ་དག or དེ་རྣམས,	those.
Inst.	དེས or དེ་ཡིས,	by that.	དེ་དག་གིས, དེ་རྣམས་ཀྱིས,	by those.
Gen. & Pos.	དེའི or དེ་ཡི,	of that.	དེ་དག་གི, དེ་རྣམས་ཀྱི,	of those.
Dat.	དེ་ལ,	to that.	དེ་དག་ལ, དེ་རྣམས་ལ,	to those.
Abl.	དེ་ནས,	from that.	དེ་དག་ནས, དེ་རྣམས་ནས,	from those.

§ 123. Interrogative Pronouns.

The Interrogatives are: སུ, who? གང, which? whether? ཅི, what? They are declined thus:

	Singular.		*Plural.*	
Nom. & Acc.	སུ,	who?	སུ་དག or སུ་རྣམས,	who.
Inst.	སུས or སུ་ཡིས,	by whom?	སུ་དག་གིས, སུ་རྣམས་ཀྱིས,	by whom.
Gen. & Pos.	སུའི or སུ་ཡི,	whose? of whom?	སུ་དག་གི, སུ་རྣམས་ཀྱི,	of whom.
Dat.	སུ་ལ,	to whom?	སུ་དག་ལ, སུ་རྣམས་ལ,	to whom.
Abl.	སུ་ནས,	of, from whom?	སུ་དག་ནས, སུ་རྣམས་ནས,	from whom.

	Singular.		*Plural.*
Nom. & Acc.	གང་,	which, whether?	གང་དག or གང་རྣམས,
Inst.	གང་གིས,	by which? by whom?	དང་དག་གིས, གང་རྣམས་ཀྱིས,
Gen.	གང་གི,	whose?	གང་དག་གི, གང་རྣམས་ཀྱི,
Dat.	གང་ལ,	to which? to whom?	གང་དག་ལ, གང་རྣམས་ལ,
Abl.	གང་ནས,	from which?	གང་དག་ནས, གང་རྣམས་ནས.

	Singular.		*Plural.*
Nom. & Acc.	ཅི,	what ?	ཅི་དག,
Inst.	ཅིས or ཅི་ཡིས,	by what ?	ཅི་དག་གིས,
Gen. & Pos.	ཅིའི or ཅི་ཡི,	of what, &c.	ཅི་དག་གི,
Dat.	ཅི་ལ,	to, for what ?	ཅི་དག་ལ,
Abl.	ཅི་ནས,	of, from what ?	ཅི་དག་ནས.

Note. The above interrogatives frequently assume the particle ཞིག, after them. thus སུ་ཞིག, who ? (quisnam ?) གང་ཞིག, which ? ཅི་ཞིག, what ? (quidnam ?) And then the postpositive particles must be added accordingly.

§ 124. Relatives.

The above interrogatives : སུ, who ? གང་, which ? are used in a relative sense likewise. Instead of སུ, sometimes གང་སུ, (he that, that which) is used. Other relatives are གང་ཞིག, whichever, whatever ; ཇི or གང་ཅི, that which, what. They may be declined accordingly to the former examples.

§ 125. Reciprocals.

The reciprocals are, རང, བདག, ཉིད, རང་ཉིད, བདག་ཉིད, signifying : self, one's self.

Examples.

	Singular.		*Plural.*	
Nom. & Acc.	རང,	self, one's self.	རང་དག or རང་རྣམས,	our, your or them-selves.
Inst.	རང་གིས.	by one's self.	རང་དག་གིས,	by selves.
Gen. & Pos.	རང་གི.	of one's self.	རང་དག་གི,	to selves.
Dat.	རང་ལ.	for one's self.	རང་དག་ལ,	for selves.
Abl.	རང་ནས.	of, from one's self.	རང་དག་ནས,	of, from selves.

	Also, Singular.	*Plural.*
Nom. & Acc.	ཉིད, self.	ཉིད་རྣམས or ཉིད་དག, selves.
	&c. &c.	&c. &c.

§ 126. Pronominal Adjectives.

ཐམས་ཅད, every, all, the whole.

ཀུན, all.

འགའ, some.

འགའ་ཞིག, some one, some body.

འགའ་ཡང, (with any negatives,) no one, none.

ཁ་ཅིག, ལ་ལ, ལ་ལ་ཞིག, some, some one.

བདག, རང, one's self.

གཞན, other.

གཞན་ཞིག, another.

སུ་ཞིག, any one.

ཅི་ཞིག, any thing.

འབའ་ཞིག, only, mere.

སུ་ཡང་, every one, each.

སུ་ཡང་རུང།-བ, whoever, whosoever.

གང་ཡང་, either, each, every one.

གང་ཡང་རུང་།-བ, whichever, whichsoever.

ཅི་ཡང་, every thing.

ཅི་ཡང་རུང་།-བ, whatever.

Note. སུ་ཡང, གང་ཡང and ཅི་ཡང, when followed by any of the negative or prohibitive particles མ, མི, མེད, མིན, may be expressed by, none or no one, neither, nothing.

Verbs.

§ 127. Among the verbs there are no terminations in any tense whatever, expressive of persons. It is the preceding noun, pronoun, or the context that must show them. There are many impersonal or indefinite locutions or expressions formed by the participles: present, past, and future. Those of the participle future in བྱ or པར་བྱ and བར་བྱ, may be often expressed in English by 'you must,' or 'you must not;' 'we must,' or 'we must not.

§ 128. The participle present, as a verbal noun, might be taken for the theme of a verb, for fixing the signification of it in a Dictionary, as the Tibetans sometimes do. But, as it is more common, and more consonant with our ideas to take the infinitive, I have most frequently done so. The participle present terminates always in one of the articles པ or བ. It is a participial noun, and may be taken both adjectively and substantively; as བྱེད་པ, doing or a doing; འགྲོ་བ, walking (going), or walking (a going); སྨྲ་བ, speaking, a speaking, speech.

When it denotes the agent, the article may be expressed in several modes; as for a male: བྱེད་པ for བྱེད་པ་པ, a doer; བྱེད་པོ for བྱེད་པ་པོ, the doer or maker; for a female:

བྱེད་མ for བྱེད་པ་མ, a female agent; བྱེད་མོ for བྱེད་པ་མོ, the (female) doer or maker. Such participial nouns are frequently expressed also by adding to the root either བྱེད or མཁན, or sometimes both, thus: བྱེད་མཁན, (with or without the articles པ, for the male and མ for the female,) as: འགྲོ་བྱེད།-པ m. ।-མ, f. འགྲོ་མཁན།-པ m. ।-མ, f. འགྲོ་བྱེད་མཁན, a walker.

§ 129. The infinitive is formed by affixing a ར, to the པ or བ terminations of the participial noun; as, བྱེད་པར, to do, make; འགྲོ་བར, to go, walk. By the infinitive is expressed the supine and the gerund also; but, instead of པར and བར, the latter may assume any of the postpositive particles ཏུ, དུ, རུ, or -ར, སུ; as, བྱེད་དུ, for doing, to do; འགྲོར, for going, to go; ཀློག་ཏུ, for reading, to read; གཟིགས་སུ, for looking on, to look on; ཟ་རུ or ཟར, for eating, to eat.

§ 130. The indicative present is expressed in the several modes following;

1. By the simple root of the verb, dropping the infinitive sign (པར or བར); as བྱེད, he does; འགྲོ, he goes.

2. By the reduplication of the final letter of the root, with the addition of the *o* vowel over it; as, བྱེད་དོ, he does, འགྲོའོ, he walks; also འདུག་གོ, he is or sits, གསུང་ངོ, he commands, ཡོད་དོ, there is, ཡིན་ནོ, it is, འགྲུབ་བོ, he performs, སེམས་སོ, he thinks, སྨྲའ, he speaks, འགྱུར་རོ, he will be, གསོལ་ལོ, he begs, ཤེས་སོ, he knows.

3. By adding to the infinitive, བྱེད or བྱེད་དོ, and dropping the infinitive sign before them; as, འགྲོ་བར་བྱེད or འགྲོ་བྱེད, he does walk; ཟ་བར་བྱེད or ཟ་བྱེད, he does eat.

4. By adding, after the root of the verb, བཞིན་པ; or either of the auxiliaries, འདུག, སྣང, preceded by any of the particles, ཀྱིན་, གིན, གྱིན, འིན or ཡིན, (agreeably to the final letter of the root;) as, བྱེད་བཞིན་པ or བྱེད་ཀྱིན་འདུག, བྱེད་ཀྱིན་སྣང, is doing; འགྲོ་བཞིན་པ or འགྲོའིན་འདུག, འགྲོའིན (or འགྲོ་ཡིན) སྣང་ is going or walking.

§ 131. The root of the perfect participle, preterite or past tense, and of the participle passive, is the same. It is formed regularly in some verbs, by affixing ས to the root of the indicative present; as, from གསུང་, he commands; གསུངས, commanded. Some drop the འ prefix only; others drop the འ prefix, and assume a ས affix; as, from འགྱུར, he becomes, གྱུར, is become, grown; from འབྲི, he writes, བྲིས, wrote, written. In other cases the past tense is formed irregularly. It assumes frequently one of the particles, ཟིན, གྱུར, ཡིན, ཚར, སོང།

§ 132. The imperfect and pluperfect are formed by adding to the root of the present and perfect tense the auxiliary verb, འདུག་པ, was; as, from འོང་བར, to come;

U

འོང་འདུག་པ, was coming ; འོངས་འདུག་པ, had come. But, as an historical imperfect, and pluperfect, they are commonly expressed thus: the imperfect by the participle perfect in པ ; as, སྨྲས་པ, he said ; and the pluperfect, by adding to the former ཡིན་པ ; as, སྨྲས་པ་ཡིན་པ or སྨྲས་ཡིན་པ, he had said.

§ 133. The indicative future is formed regularly, in many verbs, from the infinitive, by adding འགྱུར ; as, བྱེད་པར་འགྱུར, will or shall do: (sometimes the infinitive sign is dropped; as, བྱེད་འགྱུར.) The participle futures in བྱ, པར་བྱ་བ or བར་བྱ་བ, are formed, in many verbs, especially neuters, from the root of the indicative present; as འགྲོ་བྱ, འགྲོ་བར་བྱ་བ, about to go, to be gone. In other cases, they are formed from the roots of the irregular future tenses.

§ 134. The imperative, in some cases, is the same with the root of the present or preterite indicative; as, in འདུག, do sit ; སོང, go away. In some instances the inherent *a* or expressed *é* of the above mentioned tenses or their roots, are changed into *o*; as, from ཟ, to eat, (or he eats,) ཟོ, do eat ; from སེལ, he cures ; སོལ, do cure from སེམས, he thinks; སོམས, do think, consider; sometimes ས, also is affixed ; as, from སྨྲ, he says, speaks ; སྨྲོས-ཤིག, say, do speak.

§ 135. The subjunctive present (or hortative or precative mood,) is formed regularly from the imperative, by adding any of the particles, ཅིག, ཞིག, ཤིག ; as in ཀློག་ཅིག, let him read, he may read ; སོང་ཞིག, let him go, he may go ; སོམས་ཤིག, let him consider, he may consider ; or from the infinitive, by adding གྱུར་ཅིག, ཤོག or ཤོག་ཅིག, signifying let, may ; as, ཤེས་པར་གྱུར་ཅིག, (also ཤེས་གྱུར་ཅིང,) may (he) know or be acquainted with it ; འོང་བར་ཤོག or ཤོག་ཅིག, may it come or happen.

§ 136. The conditional forms of the conjunctive mood are formed by adding ན (*na*) to the roots of the indicative present and preterite : as, བྱེད་ན, if you would do, and བྱས་ན, if you may have done. The conjunctive future may be expressed by the past tense, with the future sign འགྱུར ; as, བྱས་པར་འགྱུར, shall have done ; བཀླགས་པར འགྱུར, shall have read over or perused.

§ 137. When the roots of the indicative present, preterite, and future tenses, and that of the imperative, are known, the rest may be formed regularly by certain adventitious particles or auxiliary verbs.

How the roots alluded to are expressed in many verbs, will be shown, by numerous examples, below.

§ 138. Although there be some verbs in this tongue that commence with a single consonant, and of which the roots never change, the several tenses being distinguished by some additive terminations; yet the greatest part of the verbs, besides such terminations, assume one of the five prefixes (ག་ད་བ་མ་འ,) for the formation of the present, preterite, and future tenses; causing hence many irregularities: these are exhibited in the following scheme, under 10 heads according to the 10 radical letters, ཁ་ག་ཆ་ཇ, ཐ་ད་ཕ་བ་ཚ་ཛ, preceded by འ, in the indicative present.

§ 139. No. 1.

Indicat. pres.	*pret.*	*fut.*	*imperat.*	*signification.*
འཁལ	བཀལ་ཟིན	བཀལ	ཁོལ,	*v. a.* to spin, &c.
འཁུར	བཀུར་ཟིན	བཀུར	ཁུར,	*v. a.* to carry, to respect, &c.
འཁྱིག,	བཀྱིགས,	བཀྱིག	ཁྱིག	*v. a.* to bind, tie.
འཁྲིད	བཀྲིས	བཀྲི	ཁྲིད,	*v. a.* to conduct, lead.
འཁྲུད	བཀྲུས	བཀྲུ	ཁྲུད,	*v. a.* to wash.

In verbs like those here enumerated, the imperative is formed from the indicative present, by dropping the འ prefix, and turning the inherent *a* into the expressed *o* vowel. The future, likewise, is formed from the indicative present, by changing the འ into the བ prefix, and the aspirate ཁ, into the sharp ཀ. The preterite is formed from the future by adding ས; or ཟིན, (the sign of the preterite tense.)

§ 140. No. 2.

Ind. pres.	*pret.*	*fut.*	*imperat.*	*signification.*
འགུགས	བཀུག	དགུག	ཁུག,	*v. a.* to draw down, call, summon.
འགུམ	བཀུམ	དགུམ	ཁུམ,	*v. a.* to destroy, kill, murder, slay.
འགེགས	བཀག	དགག	ཁོག,	*v. a.* to hinder, prohibit.
འགེངས	བཀང་	དགང་	ཁོང་,	*v. a.* to fill, replenish.
འགེབས	བཀབ	དགབ	ཁོབ,	*v. a.* to cover, overspread.
འགེལ	བཀལ	དགལ	ཁོལ,	*v. a.* to load.
འགེས	བཀས	དགས	ཁོས,	*v. a.* to split, cleave.
འགོད	བཀོད	དགོད	ཁོད,	*v. a.* to build, construct.

Ind. pres.	*pret.*	*fut.*	*imperat.*	*signification.*
འགྲེམ	བཀྲམ	དགྲམ	ཁྲོམ,	*v. a.* to scatter, sprinkle.
འགྲེལ	བཀྲོལ	དགྲོལ	ཁྲོལ,	*v. a.* to unfold, explain.

In such verbs as the preceding, the future is formed from the indicative present by turning the འ prefix into that of ད, and the expressed *é* vowel into the inherent *a*, and by dropping the second affix ས. From the future, the preterite is formed by turning the ད into བ, and the hard ག into the sharp ཀ. The imperative is formed from the indicative present, by dropping the འ, and the second affix ས; and by turning the hard ག into the aspirate ཁ, and the *é* vowel into *o*.

In the following eight numbers, the analysis of the several tenses will be left to the learner's sagacity.

§ 141. No. 3.

Ind. pres.	*pret.*	*fut.*	*imperat.*	*signification.*
འཆག	བཅགས	བཅག	ཆོག or ཤོག,	*v. a.* to travel through or over; to go or pass up and down.
འཆང་	བཅངས	བཅང་	ཆོང་,	*v. a.* to keep, hold, wear.
འཆད	བཤད་ཟིན	བཤད	ཤོད,	*v. a.* to explain, tell.
འཆབ	བཅབས	བཅབ	ཆོབ,	*v. a.* to conceal, hide.
འཆའ	བཅས	བཅའ	ཆོས,	*v. a.* to prepare, make ready.
འཆིང་	བཅིངས	བཅིང་	ཆིང་,	*v. a.* to bind, tie, fasten.
འཆིབ	བཅིབས	བཅིབ	ཆིབ,	*v. a.* to mount, ascend.
འཆུ	བཅུས	བཅུ	ཆུས,	*v. a.* to fetch up water, to irrigate, water.
འཆེ	བཅེས	བཅེ	ཆས,	*v. a.* to promise, assure.
འཆེག	བཤགས	བཤག	ཤོག,	*v. a.* to split, cleave; to confess, &c.
འཆོ	བཅོས	བཅོ	ཆོས,	*v. a.* to prepare, make ready.

§ 142. No. 4.

Ind. pres.	*pret.*	*fut.*	*imperat.*	*signification.*
འཇལ	བཅལ	གཞལ	འཇོལ,	*v. a.* to weigh, ponder, &c.
འཇིག	བཤིག	གཞིག	ཤིག,	*v. a.* to destroy, &c.
འཇིབ	བཞིབས	བཞིབ	ཞིབ,	*v. a.* to suck, draw out, &c.

Ind. pres.	*pret.*	*fut.*	*imperat.*	*signification.*
འཇིལ	བཅིལ	གཞིལ	ཆིལ	*v. a.* to depose, divest.
འཇུ	བཞུས	བཞུ	འཇུས,	*v. a.* to digest, concoct.
འཇུག	བཅུག	གཞུག	ཆུག	*v. a.* to put, make, cause.
འཇུན	བཅུན	གཞུན	ཆུན,	*v. a.* to subdue, make tame.
འཇོ	བཞོས	བཞོ	འཇོས,	*v. a.* to express, milk.
འཇོག	བཞག	གཞག	ཞོག,	*v. a.* to put, place, lay down.
འཇོམས	བཅོམ	གཞོམ	ཆོམ,	*v. a.* to subdue, conquer, overcome, &c.

§ 143. No. 5.

Ind. pres.	*pret.*	*fut.*	*imperat.*	*signification.*
འཐགས	བཏགས	བཏག	ཐོག,	*v. a.* to grind ; weave.
འཐིག	བཏིགས	བཏིག	ཐིག,	*v. a.* to let fall in drops.
འཐུང	བཏུངས	བཏུང	འཐུང,	*v. a.* to drink, to drink up.
འཐུབ	བཏུབས	གཏུབ	འཐུབ,	*v. a.* to cut to small pieces.
འཐོར	བཏོར	གཏོར	འཐོར,	*v. a.* to scatter, diffuse.

§ 144. No. 6.

Ind. pres.	*pret.*	*fut.*	*imperat.*	*signification.*
འདིང	བཏིང	གདིང	ཐིང,	*v. a.* to spread on the ground.
འདུལ	བཏུལ	གདུལ	ཐུལ,	*v. a.* to subdue, break.
འདེགས	བཏེག	གདེག	ཐེག,	*v. a.* to lift up.
འདེབས	བཏབ	གདབ	ཐོབ,	*v. a.* to cast, throw, &c.
འདོགས	བཏགས	གདགས	ཐོགས,	*v. a.* to tie, bind.
འདོན	བཏོན	གདོན	ཐོན,	*v. a.* to utter, eject, &c.

§ 145. No. 7.

Ind. pres.	*pret.*	*fut.*	*imperat.*	*signification.*
འཕྲལ	ཕྲལ	དབྲལ	ཕྲོལ,	*v. a.* to separate.
འཕྲི	ཕྲི	འབྲི	ཕྲི,	*v. a.* to make less, subtract.
འཕྲོག	ཕྲོག	དབྲོག	ཕྲོག,	*v. a.* to take by force.

§ 146. No. 8.

Ind. pres.	*pret.*	*fut.*	*imperat.*	*signification.*
འབིགས	ཕིག	དབིག	ཕིག,	*v. a.* to bore, to pierce.
འབུགས	ཕུག	དབུག	ཕུག,	
འབུད	ཕུད	དབུད	ཕུད,	*v. a.* to put off.
འབུབས	ཕུབ	དབུབ	ཕུབ,	*v. a.* to vault, overarch.
འབུལ	ཕུལ	དབུལ	ཕུལ,	*v. a.* to offer, present, give.

འབེབས	ཕབ	དབབ	ཕོབ,	*v. a.* to make descend, to let down.
འབྱིན	ཕྱུང་	དབྱུང	ཕྱུང་,	*v. a.* to draw or pull out.
འབྱེད	ཕྱེ	དབྱེ	ཕྱེ,	*v. a.* to separate, divide, open.

§ 147. No. 9.

འཚག	བཚགས	བཚག	ཚོག	*v. a.* to sift, strain.
འཚབ	བསབས	བསབ	ཚོབ or སོབ,	*v. a.* to repay, give an equivalent for.
འཚིར	བཙིར	གཙིར	ཚིར,	*v. a.* to express, squeeze.
འཚེ	བཙེས	བཙེ or གཙེ,	ཚེས,	*v. a.* to hurt, to do harm to.
འཚེད	བཙོས	བཙོ	ཚོས,	*v. a.* to boil, dress; dye, tinge.
འཚེམ	བཙེམས	བཙེམ	ཚེམ,	*v. a.* to sew, stitch.
འཚོ	བསོས	གསོ	སོས	*v. a.* to feed, keep, nourish; to keep alive.
འཚོག	བཙོགས	བཙོག	ཚོག,	*v. a.* to cut, hew, engrave; to prick, goad.
འཚོང་	བཙོངས	བཙོང་	ཚོང་,	*v. a.* to sell.
འཚོད v. འཚེད,	བཙོས	བཙོ	ཚོས,	*v. a.* to boil, dress; dye, tinge.
འཚོལ	བཙལ་ཞིན	བཙལ	ཚོལ,	*v. a.* to seek, search after.

§ 148. No. 10.

འཛིན	བཟུང་	གཟུང	ཟུང་,	*v. a.* to take, seize.
འཛུག	བཙུག	གཟུག	ཟུག,	*v. a.* to fit, or set, fix, plant.
འཛུད	བཙུད	གཟུད	ཟུད,	*v. a.* to convert, turn, make enter into.
འཛུམ	བཟུམ	གཟུམ	ཟུམ,	*v. a.* to shut, close.
འཛུར	བཟུར	གཟུར	ཟུར,	*v. a.* to shun, avoid.
འཛུལ	བཟུལ	གཟུལ	ཟུལ,	*v. n.* to creep in.
འཛེད	བཟེད	གཟེད	ཟེད,	*v. a.* to hold, keep, receive.
འཛེམ	བཟེམ	གཟེམ	ཟེམ,	*v. n.* to blush, to be ashamed for.

§ 149. *Observations on the five prefixes* (ག་ ད་ བ་ མ་ འ.)

These letters, prefixed to any letter, syllable or word, occur, as has been seen, among other parts of speech as well as the verbs; but it is among the verbs especially that their utility is conspicuous; the formation of the indicative present, preterite, and future tenses depending principally on them.

§ 150. *Use of the prefix* ག :

In some verbs, it is retained in all tenses, as :

Ind. pres.	*pret.*	*fut.*	*imperat.*	*signification.*
གཅི	གཅིས	གཅི་བར་འགྱུར	གཅིས་ཤིག,	to make water.
གཡོག	གཡོགས	གཡོག་པར་འགྱུར	གཡོགས་ཤིག,	to cover.
གསུང	གསུངས	གསུང་བར་འགྱུར	གསུང་ཤིག,	to command, say.
གནས	གནས་ཟིན	གནས་པར་འགྱུར	གནས་པར་ གྱུར་ཅིག,	*v. n.* to dwell, be.

With some verbs it is used only in the present and future (and sometimes in the imperative too) as :

གཅོད	བཅད	གཅད	ཆོད or གཅོད, *v. a.* to cut, to cut off.
གཏོང	བཏང v. བཏངས	གཏང་	ཐོང་, *v. a.* to give.
གཏོད	བཏད	གཏད	ཐོད, *v. a.* to commit to, to entrust.
གསོད	བསད	གསད	སོད or གསོད, to kill, slay, murder.
གསོན	བསན	གསན	གསོན, to hear, hearken to.

With many verbs it is used only in the future, as may be seen in the above scheme Nos. 4, 5, 6, 9, 10.

§ 151. *Use of the prefix* ད :

In some verbs it is retained in all tenses, as :

Ind. pres.	*pret.*	*fut.*	*imperat.*	*signification.*
དཔོག	དཔགས	དཔག	དཔོག,	*v. a.* to measure, weigh, ponder.
དཔོར	དཔར་ཟིན	དཔར	དཔོར,	*v. a.* to dictate, tell what to write.
དཔྱོང་	དཔྱངས	དཔྱང	དཔྱོང་,	*v. a.* to hang, to hang down.
དཔྱོད	དཔྱད་ཟིན	དཔྱད	དཔྱོད,	*v. a.* to try, prove, judge, examine.

In some instances, it is found only with the preterite and future tenses, as :

འཁྲུག	དཀྲུགས	དཀྲུག	ཁྲུག, *v. a.* to trouble, stir up.
འཁྲོལ	དཀྲོལ་ཟིན	དཀྲོལ	ཁྲོལ, *v. a.* to make a noise with a musical instrument to play on.

In many verbs, it is used only in the future, as may be seen above, Nos. 2, 7, 8.

§ 152. *Use of the prefix* བ:

In a few verbs, it is retained in all tenses, as:

བགོད	བགོས	བགོ	བགོས།-ཤིག, *v. a.* to divide, to give in share.
བགྱིད	བགྱིས	བགྱི	གྱིས, *v. a.* to do, make.
བརྡུད	བརྡུས	བརྡུ	རྡུས, *v. a.* to cleanse (rice, &c.) by beating.

In many verbs, the བ is prefixed only to the preterite tense, as to be seen in many instances above, Nos. 2, 4, 6, 10.

In some veıbs it is used both in the preterite and future tenses, as to be seen above, Nos. 1, 3, 5.

§ 153. *Use of the prefix* མ:

The མ prefix is retained in all tenses with some verbs, as:

མཆི	མཆིས	མཆི་བར་འགྱུར, *v. n.* to go, repair to.
མཐོང	མཐོང་ཟིན	མཐོང་བར་འགྱུར, *v. a.* to see, to look on.

In a few instances it is used only in the preterite and future tenses; as in མཉན་པར, *v. a.* to hear fully, to listen to; and in མནན་པར, *v. a.* to depress, ravish, to outdo.

§ 154. *Use of the prefix* འ:

Of the five prefixes, this is the one most extensively employed with the verbs. It is retained in some verbs in all the three tenses, as:

Ind. pres.	*pret.*	*fut.*	*signification.*
འཁྲིག	འཁྲིགས	འཁྲིག་པར་འགྱུར,	*v. n.* to stick to or together.
འཁྲུག	འཁྲུགས	འཁྲུག་པར་འགྱུར,	*v. n.* to be troubled or stirred up.
འགག	འགགས	འགག་པར་འགྱུར,	*v. n.* to stop, stay, still.
འཐུང་	འཐུངས	འཐུང་བར་འགྱུར,	*v. a.* to drink.
འདའ	འདས	འདའ་བར་འགྱུར,	*v. n.* to pass, go away, die.
འཛ	འཛས	འཛ་བརའགྱུར,	*v. n.* to assemble, gather together.

It is dropped very frequently in the preterite, as:

འཁྱེར	ཁྱེར	འཁྱེར་བར་འགྱུར,	*v. a.* to carry.
འཁྲིད	ཁྲིད	འཁྲིད་པར་འགྱུར,	*v. a.* to lead, conduct.
འགས	གས	འགས་པར་འགྱུར,	*v. n.* to be split or cleft.
འགྱུར	གྱུར	འགྱུར་བར་འགྱུར	*v. n.* to become, grow, change, turn.
འཛད	ཟད	འཛད་པར་འགྱུར,	*v. n.* to be spent entirely.

The འ prefix, with most verbs, is used only in the indicative present (with a few exceptions in the imperative), as may be seen in the above scheme, Nos. 1, to 10.

§ 155. From several neuter verbs the active forms are thus derived:

	Ind. pres.	*pret.*	*fut.*	*signification.*
from	འཁུམ	ཁུམས	འཁུམ་པར་འགྱུར,	*v. n.* to shrink, contract himself.
	སྐུམ	བསྐུམས	བསྐུམ,	*v. a* to contract.
from	འཁོད	འཁོད་ཟིན	འཁོད་པར་འགྱུར,	*v. n.* to settle, sit.
	འགོད	བཀོད	དགོད,	*v. a.* to fix, set, build, frame,
from	འཁོར	འཁོར་ཟིན	འཁོར་བར་འགྱུར,	*v. n.* to turn, go, walk round about.
	སྐོར	བསྐོར་ཟིན	བསྐོར,	*v. a.* to turn round; encircle, surround, circumambulate.
from	འགས	གས	འགས་པར་འགྱུར,	*v. n.* to be split or cleft.
	འགེས	བགས	དགས,	*v. a.* to split, cleave.
from	འགག	འགགས	འགག་པར་འགྱུར,	*v. n.* to stop, be hindered.
	འགེགས	བཀག	དགག,	*v. a.* to hinder, prohibit.
from	འགུམ	གུམ*	འགུམ་པར་འགྱུར,	*v. n.* to die, perish, be extinguished.
	འགུམ-པར་བྱེད	བགུམ	དགུམ,	*v. a.* to destroy, kill, extinguish.
from	འགུལ	འགུལ་ཟིན	འགུལ་བར་འགྱུར,	*v. n.* to shake, quake, to agitated.
	སྒུལ	བསྒུལ་ཟིན	བསྒུལ,	*v. a.* to move, agitate, shake.
from	འགྱུར	གྱུར-ཟིན	འགྱུར་བར་འགྱུར,	*v. n.* to become, change, turn.
	སྒྱུར	བསྒྱུར་ཟིན	བསྒྱུར,	*v. a.* to change, turn, translate.
from	འགྱེ	གྱེས	འགྱེ་བར་འགྱུར,	*v. n.* to go asunder, be diffused.
	འགྱེད	བགྱེས	བགྱེ,	*v. a.* to scatter, disperse, diffuse, distribute.
from	འགྱེལ	གྱེལ-ཟིན	འགྱེལ་བར་འགྱུར,	*v. n.* to be turned upside down.
	སྒྱེལ	བསྒྱེལ་ཟིན	བསྒྱེལ,	*v. a.* to turn upside down.
from	འགྲིག	འགྲིག་ཟིན	འགྲིག་པར་འགྱུར,	*v. n.* to congrue, agree, be coherent.
	སྒྲིག	བསྒྲིགས	བསྒྲིག,	*v. a.* to adjust, make agree, compose.
from	འགྲིབ	གྲིབ	འགྲིབ་པར་འགྱུར,	*v. n.* to be offuscated, to grow less.
	སྒྲིབ	བསྒྲིབས	བསྒྲིབ,	*v. a.* to offuscate, darken.

* In the neuter verbs, the future is often formed with the preterite also, thus; གུམ་པར་འགྱུར.

	Ind. pres.	*pret.*	*fut.*	*signification.*
from	འགྲིལ	གྲིལ	འགྲིལ་བར་འགྱུར,	*v. n.* to roll down, to shrink.
	སྒྲིལ	བསྒྲིལ་ཟིན	བསྒྲིལ,	*v. a.* to roll, wrap up.
from	འགྲུབ	གྲུབ	འགྲུབ་པར་འགྱུར,	*v. n.* to be ready, be accomplished.
	སྒྲུབ	བསྒྲུབས	བསྒྲུབ,	*v. a.* to make ready, accomplish.
from	འགྲེང་	འགྲེངས	འགྲེང་བར་འགྱུར,	*v. n.* to arise, stand up.
	སྒྲེང	བསྒྲེངས	བསྒྲེང་,	*v. a.* to raise, erect.
from	འགྲོལ	གྲོལ	འགྲོལ་བར་འགྱུར,	*v. n.* to be loosened, untied.
	འགྲོལ or འགྲེལ	བཀྲོལ	དགྲོལ,	*v. a.* to loosen, untie; explain; deliver, save.
	སྒྲོལ	བསྒྲལ་ཟིན	བསྒྲལ,	
from	འཆག	ཆག	འཆག་པར་འགྱུར,	*v. n.* to break.
	གཅོག	བཅག	གཅོག་པར་འགྱུར,	*v. a.* to break.
from	འཆད	ཆད	འཆད་པར་འགྱུར,	*v. n.* to be rent, dissolved.
	གཅོད	བཅད	གཅད,	*v. a.* to cut off, divide.
from	འཐོན	ཐོན	འཐོན་པར་འགྱུར,	*v. n.* to issue, be uttered.
	འདོན	བཏོན	གདོན,	*v. a.* to utter, eject.
from	འདུ	འདུས	འདུ་བར་འགྱུར,	*v. n.* to assemble, gather together.
	སྡུད	བསྡུས	བསྡུ,	*v. a.* to collect, gather together, amass.
from	འདུམ	དུམ	འདུམ་པར་འགྱུར,	*v. n.* to agree with, be in concord.
	སྡུམ	བསྡུམས	བསྡུམ,	*v. a.* to make agree, reconcile.
from	འཕེལ	ཕེལ-ཟིན	འཕེལ་བར་འགྱུར,	*v. n.* to increase, be augmented.
	སྤེལ	སྤེལ་ཟིན	སྤེལ་བར་འགྱུར,	*v. a.* to augment, &c.
from	འཕོ	འཕོས	འཕོ་བར་འགྱུར,	*v. n.* to shift, change, transmigrate.
	སྤོ	སྤོས	སྤོ་བར་འགྱུར,	*v. a.* to shift, change.
from	འབྲལ	བྲལ	འབྲ་བར་འགྱུར,	*v. n.* to withdraw from, be separated.
	འཕྲལ	ཕྲལ	དབྲལ,	*v. a.* to separate.
from	འབྲི	བྲི	འབྲི་བར་འགྱུར,	*v. n.* to grow less.
	འཕྲི	ཕྲི	དབྲི,	*v. a.* to make less, subtract.
from	འབབ	བབ-ས	འབབ་པར་འགྱུར,	*v. n.* to descend, fall, flow.
	འབེབས	ཕབ	དབབ,	*v. a.* to make descend, let down.

Ind. pres.	*pret.*	*fut.*	*signification.*
from འབྱུང་	བྱུང	འབྱུང་བར་འགྱུར,	*v. n.* to come forth, to be produced; be, become.
འབྱིན	ཕྱུང	དབྱུང,	*v. a.* to draw, pull out, &c.
from འབྱེ	བྱེ	འབྱེ་བར་འགྱུར,	*v. n.* to open, be divided, separated.
འབྱེད	ཕྱེ	དབྱེ,	*v. a.* to open, separate, analyse.
from འཛག	ཟགས	འཛག་པར་འགྱུར,	*v. n.* to drop, fall in drops.
འཚག	བཙགས	བཙག or གཙག,	*v. a.* to strain, let fall in drops.
from སྐྱེ	སྐྱེས	སྐྱེ་བར་འགྱུར,	*v. n.* to be born, or produced.
སྐྱེད	བསྐྱེད་ཟིན	བསྐྱེད,	*v. a.* to generate, produce.
from ནུབ	ནུབ་ཟིན	ནུབ་པར་འགྱུར,	*v. n.* to set, sink.
སྣུབ	བསྣུབས	བསྣུབ,	*v. a.* to abolish, destroy.

From the above examples, the intelligent learner may see, by what contraction, addition or transformation, the actives are usually derived from their respective neuters. In many cases, both the neuter and active are sounded alike, although they differ considerably in orthography.

§ 156. For expressing the substantive verb (am, art, is, are; there is, there are) the Tibetans use several terms, according as they speak to inferiors, equals, or superiors, with more or less respect or politeness. Those terms, or substantive verbs, are: ཡིན, ཡོད, འདུག, བཞུགས, མཆིས, ལགས, མངའ, གདའ, མད, མོད, འཚལ, གནས, སྣང, བཞིན་པ. The negatives of them are thus expressed: མིན or མ་ཡིན, མེད, མི་འདུག, མི་བཞུགས, མ་མཆིས, མ་ལགས, མི་མངའ, མི་གདའ་ཡོད་མིན, མི་འཚལ, མི་གནས, མི་སྣང, མི་བཞིན་པ. They stand in the indicative present, and are invariable after every person of both numbers. Their signification, in general, may be expressed, in English, by am, art, is, are; it is; there is, there are; by the inflection of *do* and *have*. The term འཚལ especially, is used like the auxiliaries *do* and *have* in English, instead of the repetition of the verb of the preceding sentence, as in ཤེས་སམ, འཚལ་ལོ, do you know? I do.

All the above enumerated verbal roots (or substantive verbs) have no variation. When inflected in the several tenses, they are formed by the same particles, as have been before set forth; and especially by the inflexion of the auxiliary verb འགྱུར, and, for the past tense, ཟིན.

§ 157. These substantive verbs frequently occur, when used emphatically, (but with the same signification,) in the form of having the final letter reduplicated with the *o* vowel over them, thus: ཡིན་ནོ *yin-no*, ཡོད་དོ *yod-do*, འདུག་གོ *hdug-go*, བཞུགས་སོ *bzhugs-so*, མཆིས་སོ *mchhis-so*, ལགས་སོ *lags-so*, མངའ་འོ or མངའོ *mṅaho*, གདའོ *gdaho*, མད་དོ *mad-do*, མོད་དོ *mod-do*, འཚལ་ལོ *htshal-lo*, གནས་སོ *gnas-so*, སྣང་ངོ *snang-go*, བཞིན་པའོ *bzhin-paho*.

By such reduplication the substantive verb may be expressed with every sort of noun; as, ངའོ, I am; བདག་གོ, I am, it is I; དེ་དག་གོ, those are, or it is they (or those); ཁྱོད་དོ, thou art; གསུམ་མོ, there are three; ཤིང་ངོ, it is wood or tree; ནག་གོ, it is black; དེ་ལྟར་རོ, it is so.

§ 158. *Examples of the above substantive verbs.*

ཁོ་ཆེན་པོ་ཡིན, he is great; དེ་ལྟར་ཡིན་ནོ, it is so; འདི་ནང་ན་ཅི་ཡོད, what is in this? ང་ཡོད་དོ, I am, I do exist; སུ་འདུག, who is there? མང་པོ་འདུག་གོ, there are many; རྒྱལ་པོ་གང་ན་བཞུགས, where is the king? ཁང་བཟང་ན་བཞུགས་སོ, he is in the palace; འདི་ན་ཇ་མཆིས, how many are here? བརྒྱ་ཙམ་མཆིས་སོ, there are about one hundred; ང་ནི་གདོལ་པའི་རིགས་ལགས་སོ, I am of a low caste; དེ་ལྟར་ལགས, it is so; ཁྱོད་ལ་ནད་མི་མངའ, there is no disease to thee, (or thou art exempt from, desase.) སངས་རྒྱས་ལ་ཡོན་ཏན་མཆོག་མངའ་འོ, Buddha has (there is to him) the chief perfection, དེ་ན་ཅི་གདའ, what is there? མད་དོ, it is true, it is so; དེ་ལྟར་མོད, it is even so; ཞུ་འཚལ་ལོ, I am begging, I do beg, (entreat;) མི་གནས་སོ, there is not; ཁོ་སློག་གིན་སྣང, he is reading; ཁྱོད་སྨྲ་བཞིན་པ, thou speaking, when thou art speaking.

§ 159. *Conjugation of the verb* ཡིན་པར, to be.

INDICATIVE PRESENT.

	Singular.		*Plural.*	
1 *Person.*	ང་ཡིན,	I am.	ང་རྣམས་ཡིན,	we are.
2 *Ditto.*	ཁྱོད་ཡིན,	thou art.	ཁྱོད་རྣམས་ཡིན,	ye are.
3 *Ditto.*	ཁོ་ཡིན,	he, she, is.	ཁོ་རྣམས་ཡིན,	they are.

IMPERFECT.

	Singular.		*Plural.*	
1	ང་འདུག་པ,	I was.	ང་ཚག་འདུག་པ,	we were.
2	ཁྱོད་འདུག་པ,	thou wast.	ཁྱོད་ཚག་འདུག་པ,	ye were.
3	ཁོ་འདུག་པ,	he was.	ཁོ་ཚག་འདུག་པ,	they were.

Perfect Tense.

Singular.		Plural.	
1. ང་ཡོད་པ་ཡིན, vulg. *na yot pin*,	I have been.	ང་ཅག་ཡོད་པ་ཡིན,	we have been.
2. ཁྱོད་ཡོད་པ་ཡིན,	thou hast been.	ཁྱོད་ཅག་ཡོད་པ་ཡིན,	ye have been.
3. ཁོ་ཡོད་པ་ཡིན,	he has been.	ཁོ་ཅག་ཡོད་པ་ཡིན,	they have been.

Pluperfect Tense.

Singular.		Plural.	
1. ང་ཡོད་པ་ཡིན་པ or ང་ཡོད་འཅམ་པ,	I had been.	ང་ཅག་ཡོད་པ་ཡིན་པ,	we had been.
2. ཁྱོད་ཡོད་པ་ཡིན་པ,	thou hadst been.	ཁྱོད་ཅག་ཡོད་པ་ཡིན་པ,	ye had been.
3. ཁོ་ཡོད་པ་ཡིན་པ,	he had been.	ཁོ་ཅག་ཡོད་པ་ཡིན་པ.	they had been.

First Future.

Singular.		Plural.	
1. ང་འགྱུར།-རོ or ང་འགྱུར་བར་འགྱུར།-རོ,	I shall or will be.	ང་ཅག་འགྱུར།-རོ,	we shall or will be.
2. ཁྱོད་འགྱུར།-རོ,	thou shalt or wilt be.	ཁྱོད་ཅག་འགྱུར།-རོ,	ye shall or will be.
3. ཁོ་འགྱུར།-རོ,	he shall or will be.	ཁོ་ཅག་འགྱུར།-རོ,	they shall or will be.

Second Future.

Singular.		Plural.	
1. ང་ཡིན་པར་འགྱུར།-རོ,	I shall have been.	ང་ཅག་ཡིན་པར་འགྱུར།-རོ,	we shall have been.
2. ཁྱོད་ཡིན་པར་འགྱུར།-རོ,	thou shalt have been.	ཁྱོད་ཅགཡིན་པར་འགྱུར།-རོ,	ye shall have been.
3. ཁོ་ཡིན་པར་འགྱུར།-རོ,	he shall have been.	ཁོ་ཅག་ཡིན་རཔར་འགྱུར།-རོ,	they shall have been.

Imperative Mood.

Singular.		Plural.	
1. ང་གྱུར་ཅིག,	let me be.	ང་ཅག་གྱུར་ཅིག,	let us be.
2. ཁྱོད་གྱུར་ཅིག,	be thou.	ཁྱོད་ཅག་གྱུར་ཅིག,	be ye.
3. ཁོ་གྱུར་ཅིག,	let him, her be.	ཁོ་ཅག་གྱུར་ཅིག,	let them be.

Potential Mood.

Present Tense.

Singular.		Plural.	
1. ང་ཡིན་པར་ནུས།-སོ,	I may or can be.	ང་ཅག་ཡིན་པར་ནུས།-སོ,	we may or can be.
2. ཁྱོད་ཡིན་པར་ནུས། སོ,	thou mayst or canst be.	ཁྱོད་ཅག་ཡིན་པར་ནུས།-སོ,	ye may or can be.
3. ཁོ་ཡིན་པར་ནུས།-སོ,	he may or can be.	ཁོ་ཅག་ཡིན་པར་ནུས།-སོ,	they may or can be.
Also, ང་ཡིན་ཆོག,	&c. &c.	Or ང་ཅེ་ཐོག་གོ,	&c. &c.

PRECATIVE MOOD.

	Singular.	Plural.
1.	ང་ཡིན་པར་ཤོག, or ང་འགྱུར་བར་ཤོག, I may be or become.	ང་ཅག་ཡིན་པར་ཤོག or འགྱུར་བར་ཤོག, may we be or become.
2.	ཁྱོད་ཡིན་པར་ཤོག, thou mayst be or become.	ཁྱོད་ཅག་ཡིན་པར་ཤོག, ye may be or become.
3.	ཁོ་ཡིན་པར་ཤོག, he may be or become.	ཁོ་ཅག་ཡིན་པར་ཤོག, they may be or become.

CONDITIONAL.

	Singular.	Plural.
1.	ང་ཡིན་ན, should or would I be, or if I were.	ང་ཅག་ཡིན་ན, should or would we be, or if we were.
2.	ཁྱོད་ཡིན་ན, shouldest or wouldst thou be, or if thou wert.	ཁྱོད་ཅག་ཡིན་ན, should or would ye be, or if ye were.
3.	ཁོ་ཡིན་ན, should or would he be, or if he were.	ཁོ་ཅག་ཡིན་ན, should or would they be, or if they were.

CONDITIONAL PERFECT TENSE.

1. ང་ཡིན་པར་གྱུར་ན, I may or can have been, or if I might have been, &c. And so on with all the persons, in both numbers.

CONDITIONAL PLUPERFECT TENSE

1. ང་ཡིན་པར་གྱུར་པ་ན, I might or should have been, or if I might, &c.

SUBJUNCTIVE MOOD.

Singular.	Plural.
གལ་ཏེ་ང་ཡིན, if I am (or be).	གལ་ཏེ་ང་ཅག་ཡིན, if we are or be.
གལ་ཏེ་ཁྱོད་ཡིན, if thou be.	གལ་ཏེ་ཁྱོད་ཅག་ཡིན, if ye be.
གལ་ཏེ་ཁོ་ཡིན, if he be.	གལ་ཏེ་ཁོ་ཅག་ཡིན, if they be.

IMPERFECT TENSE.

གལ་ཏེ་ང་ཡིན་ན, if I were, and so on.

PERFECT TENSE.

གལ་ཏེ་ང་ཡོད་པ་ཡིན་ན, if I have been, &c. &c.

PLUPERFECT.

གལ་ཏེ་ང་ཡོད་པ་ཡིན་པ་ན, if I had been, &c.

FIRST FUTURE.

གལ་ཏེ་ང་འགྱུར་རོ or འགྱུར་བར་འགྱུར་རོ, if I shall be, or shall become.

Second Future.

གལ་ཏེ་ང་ཡིན་པར་འགྱུར་ན, if I should be or become.

Infinitive.

Present, ཡིན་པར, to be. Perf. ཡོད་པ་ཡིན་པར, to have been.

Participles.

Pres. ཡིན་པ, being ; pref. ཡོད་པ, been. Compound perfect, ཡོད་པ་ཡིན་པ, having been.

---

§ 160. *Conjugation of the substantive verb* ཡོད་པར to be (to one, to be there).

The English verb 'to have' is rendered by ཡོད་པར, to be there, to be to one. It may be conjugated thus :

Indicat. Pres.

Singular.	*Plural.*
1. ང་ལ་ཡོད, (to me is,) I have.	ང་ཅག་ལ་ཡོད, (to us is,) we have, &c.
2. ཁྱོད་ལ་ཡོད, thou hast.	ཁྱོད་ཅག་ལ་ཡོད, ye have.
3. ཁོ་ལ་ཡོད, he has.	ཁོ་ཅག་ལ་ཡོད, they have.

Imperfect. ང་ལ་ཡོད་པ or འདུག་པ, I had, and so on, with all persons, in both numbers.

Perfect tense. ང་ལ་ཡོད་པ་ཡིན, I have had, &c.

Pluperfect tense. ང་ལ་ཡོད་པ་ཡིན་པ or ང་ལ་ཡོད་འདུག་པ, I had had, &c.

Future. ང་ལ་ཡོད་པར་འགྱུར or ཡོད་འགྱུར, I shall have (or there will be to me).

Imperat. ང་ལ་ཡོད་ཅིག or ཡོད་པར་གྱུར་ཅིག, let me have.

Potential. Pres. ང་ལ་ཡོད་ཆོག, or ང་ལ་ཡོད་ཅང, } I may or can have.

Imperf. ང་ལ་ཡོད་འགྱུར་ན, should (or could) I have.

Perfect. ང་ལ་ཡོད་པར་གྱུར, I may or can have had.

Pluperf. ང་ལ་ཡོད་པར་གྱུར་པ་ན, I should (might or could) have had.

Subjunctive Mood.

Present. གལ་ཏེ་ང་ལ་ཡོད, if I have, and so on.

Imperfect. གལ་ཏེ་ང་ལ་ཡོད་ན, if I had, or should I have, &c.

Perfect. གལ་ཏེ་ང་ལ་ཡོད་གྱུར་ན, if I have had, or should I have had.

Pluperfect. གལ་ཏེ་ང་ལ་ཡོད་པར་གྱུར་པ་ན, if I had had.

Future. གལ་ཏེ་ང་ལ་ཡོད་པར་འགྱུར་ན, if I shall have, or should I have hereafter, &c.

Infinitive.

Present. (སུ་ཞིག་ལ) ཡོད་པར, to be (to one), to have.

Perfect. (སུ་ཞིག་ལ) ཡོད་པ་ཡིན་པར, to have been (to one), to have had.

Participles.

Present. (སུ་ཞིག་ལ) ཡོད, being (to one); having.

Perfect. (སུ་ཞིག་ལ) ཡོད་པ, benn (to one) ; had.

Comp. perfect. (སུ་ཞིག་ལ) ཡོད་པ་ཡིན་པ, having been (to one) ; having had.

Note ; This verb, when constructed with the nominative, thus ང་ཡོད or ང་ཡོད་དོ, signifies I am, I exist, or I do exist.

Observations :

By the aid of these two substantive verbs (and their equivalents : འདུག, བཞུགས, མཆིས, ལགས, མངའ, གདའ, མད, མོད, འཚལ, གནས, སྣང, བཞིན་པ ; see § 156.) as also by that of the two auxiliary verbs བྱེད and འགྱུར, which will be described hereafter, (see § 171, 172,) may be formed and conjugated all the tenses of the verbal roots ; as also of every verb in the Tibetan language.

The conjugation of Tibetan verbs is very simple ; it is little else than a participial variation ; and much resembles the following mode of English conjugation :

Indicat. pres. I (thou, he, she, they,) going, ང་འགྲོ་བ, འགྲོའོ or འགྲོ.

Imperfect. I was going, ང་འགྲོ་འདུག་པ.

Perf. p. part. I went, (gone,) ང་སོང*.

Pluperf. I was gone, (or I had went,) ང་སོང་འདུག་པ.

Future. I shall go, ང་འགྲོ་ཟ or འགྲོ་རྒྱུ or ང་འགྲོ་བར་འགྱུར།-རོ.

Conditional. If I (or should I) go, ང་འགྲོ་ན,

Cond. past. If I have gone, ང་སོང་ན.

Cond. fut. If I shall have gone, ང་སོང་བར་འགྱུར་ན.

Infinitive. To go, འགྲོ་བར.

Infinit. future. / *Supine or Ger.* } For going, to g o, འགྲོར or འགྲོ་རུ.

Participles.

Present. Going, འགྲོ་བ.

Pret. Gone, སོང་བ.

* Instead of འགྲོས, which is obsolete, as a perf. tense or participle ; but as a verbal noun, signifying gait, or the manner of going, it is in continual use.

Pluperfect. Having gone, སོང་ཞིང་ or སོང་ནས།སོང་བས also ; སོང་སྟེ, སོང་གིས, སོང་ལ.

Future. About to go, to be gone, འགྲོ་བ, འགྲོ་རྒྱུ, འགྲོ་བར་བྱ་བ.

The reason of the Tibetan verbs being invariable with respect to person and number, is, that properly they are participles ; as, བྱེད, doing or making ; བྱས, done ; བྱ or བྱ་བ, about to do, make, shall do, to be done.

§ 161. Several verbs may be formed from adjectives by the junction of certain auxiliaries. The neuters are formed by ཡིན, འགྱུར, &c. &c. ; as, ནག་པོ་ཡིན་པར, to be black ; སྨིན་འགྱུར་པར to be ripe.

§ 162. The inceptives are formed by འགྱུར and འགྲོ, to become, grow ; as, ནག་པོར་འགྱུར་བར or འགྲོ་བར, to become, grow or turn black.

And the actives are formed by the inflection of བྱེད་པར, to make ; as, ནག་པོར་བྱེད་པར, to make black ; སྨིན་པར་བྱེད་པར, to make ripe.

§ 163. Active and passive verbs ending in བྱེད or བྱེད་དོ, can be discriminated only by the instrumentive and the nominative cases expressed before them ; as, ངས་རྡུང་བར་བྱེད-དོ, (he) is beaten by me, or I do beat (him) ; ང་རྡུང་བར་བྱེད-དོ, I am beaten.

§ 164. All such verbs as end in བྱེད-དོ, and have the instrumentive case before them, may be rendered in English, both in an active and passive sense ; as, ངས་ཁྱོད་རྡུང་བར་བྱེད་དོ, I beat thee, or thou art beaten by me ; but, with the nominative case, only in the passive voice ; as, ཁྱོད་རྡུང་བར་བྱེད, thou art beaten ; འཇིག་རྟེན་འཇིག་པར་བྱེད, the world is destroyed ; འཇིག་རྟེན་འདི་ནི་ཆུ་ཡིས (or ཆུས) མེ་ཡིས (མེས) དང་རླུང་གིས འཇིག (or གཞིག) པར་བྱའོ, this world is to be destroyed by water, fire, and wind.

§ 165. Causal verbs are formed from the actives by adding to the gerund or to the root of the infinitive, the verb འཇུག་པར, (to put, cause, make,) in its several tenses ; as, འཇུག, for the *pres.* ; བཅུག, for the *pret.* ; གཞུག, for the *fut.* ; and ཆུག for the *imperative* ; as, འབྲིར་འཇུག་པར, to cause to write or to be written. Sometimes the gerund sign is dropt ; as, འཁྱེར་འཇུག་པར, (for འཁྱེར་ཏུ་འཇུག་པར,) to cause to carry. Instead of འཇུག་པ, the verb སྩོལ་བ, (*pret.* and *fut.* སྩལ་བ,) is used for forming a causal verb, when speaking respectfully ; as, ཀློག་ཏུ་སྩོལ་བར, to cause to read, or to be instructed in reading.

§ 166. Frequentatives are expressed by repeating the verbal root; as, བྱེད་བྱེད་པར, to do often; འགྲོ་འགྲོ་བར, to go often; འཛུག་འཛུག་པར, to make a practice of sitting, or to sit often; ཀློག་ཀློག་པར, to read often.

§ 167. Potentials are formed by adding to the verbal root, or to the infinitive, either ནུས་པ, ཐུབ་པ, རོ་ཐོག་པ, or ཡོད་པ, to can, be able, to may, to have power, to have courage, to dare; as, བྱེད་ནུས་པར, to can do; འཁྱེར་ཐུབ་པར, to be able to carry away; བསྟོད་པར་རོ་ཐོག་པར, to can or be able to praise one; ང་ནི་དེར་འགྲོ་བར་མི་ཡོད་དོ, I can, or dare, not go thither.

§ 168. Desideratives are expressed by འདོད་པར, བཞེད་པར, to will, wish, desire, intend, &c.; as, འགྲོ་བར་འདོད་པར or འགྲོ་འདོད་པར, to wish or intend to go; མནལ་བར་བཞེད་པར, to wish to sleep.

§ 169. Completive verbs are formed by གྱུར། ཟིན། ཚར། སོང་། grown, become, finished, done, gone. These particles are frequently added to the root of the preterite or past tense, to make a complete perfect of it. They may be expressed in several ways; as, གྱུར། གྱུར་པ། གྱུར་པ་ཡིན། གྱུར་ཏོ། གྱུར་ཟིན། གྱུར་ཟིན་པ། གྱུར་ཟིན་ཏོ།། ཟིན། ཟིན་པ། ཟིན་ཏོ། ཟིན་པ་ཡིན།། ཚར། ཚར་པ། ཚར་ཏོ། ཚར་ཟིན། ཚར་ཟིན་ཏོ།། སོང་། སོང་ཚར། སོང་བ་ཡིན་ནོ།།

Examples, ཁོ་མཁས་པར་གྱུར་ཏོ, he has become learned; ང་ནི་དེ་མ་ཤེས་ཟིན, I have not known that; དཔེ་ཆ་འདི་ད་དུང་མ་ཚར, this book has not yet been finished; ཉི་མ་ཤར་སོང, the sun has arisen; ཟླ་བ་ནུབ་སོང, the moon has set; ཁོ་ཤི་སོང་, he has died, or, he is dead.

§ 170. Active and causal verbs require before them, in general, the instrumentive case (i. e. the nominative with any of these particles; ཀྱིས། གིས། གྱིས། -ས or ཡིས, according to the final letter of the nominative case), and the neuters and passives, in like manner require the nominative or objective case. But, when the active verb is intransitive, the nominative is used; as, ཁོང་ཞབས་འཆག་བྱེད, he walks; ང་མི་འགྲུལ, I do not walk or go. Instead of the instrumentive case, the nominative is also used with the emphatical I; as, ང་ནི་དེ་མ་སྨྲས་སོ for ངས་དེ་མ་སྨྲས་སོ, I have not told (or not said) to (or by me it has not been said). As also, when the objective case takes the ལ particle, the nominative (or accusative) is used, instead of the instrumentive; as, བདག་ཁྱོད་ལ་ཟེར་ཏོ for བདག་གིས, ཁྱོད་ལ་ཟེར་ཏོ I have told thee (or you), it has been said by me to you.

Examples of the use of the instrumentive case; རྒྱལ་པོས་གསུང་ངོ།-གསུངས་སོ།-གསུང་བར་འགྱུར།-རོ།གསུང་བར་གྱུར་ཅིག། གསུང་ན། གསུངས་ན།གསུངས་པར་འགྱུར་ན, &c. &c. The king commands, has commanded, will command, let him (he may) command, should command, may have commanded, shall have commanded, &c. &c.

Examples of the use of the nominative case: རྒྱལ་པོ་སེང་ཁྲི་ལ་བཞུགས, the king sits upon the throne; ཁོང་བཞེངས་སོ, he has stood-up (he has lifted up himself); ང་མི་འགྲོ, I go not; ཁོ་གཉིད་ལོག་འདུག, he sleeps.

རྒྱལ་པོ་ཀུན་གྱིས་བཀུར་བར་བྱེད, the king is respected by all.
— — — — — — བྱས, the king has been respected.
— — — — — འགྱུར, the king will be respected.
— — — — — — བྱ, the king must be respected.
— — — — — བྱོས་ཤིག, the king let him be respected.
— — — — — — ཤོག, the king may he be respected.

§ 171. The two auxiliary verbs that most frequently occur are; བྱེད་པར, to do, make; and འགྱུར་བར, to become, grow, wax, change, turn. By the first are formed many active and passive verbs; and by the second the neuters, actives and passives. When speaking respectfully to or of superiors, instead of བྱེད་པར, the verb མཛད་པར, and (if of one's self or of others before a great personage) བགྱིད་པར are used.

§ 172. Since with respect to persons and numbers there is no variation, the conjugation of these verbs may briefly be thus represented.

THE VERBS བྱེད་པ, to do, make.

Indicat. present,	བྱེད or བྱེད་དོ,	he does, is doing, making.
Imperf.	བྱེད་འདུག་པ,	was doing, did.
Perf.	བྱས། བྱས་པ། བྱས་སོ,	did, has done.
Comp. perf.	བྱས་པ་ཡིན,	has done.
Pluperf.	བྱས་འདུག་པ or བྱས་པ་ཡིན་པ,	had done.
Future,	བྱ or བྱའོ། བྱེད་པར་འགྱུར,	about to do; will or shall do.
Imperative,	བྱོས། བྱོས་ཤིག,	do, let him do.
Hortative,	བྱོས་ཤིག,	let him do, may he do it, may it be done.
Precative,	བྱེད་པར་ཤོག,	
Optative,	བྱེད་པར་གྱུར་ཅིག,	

Conditionals.

Pres. and Fut.	བྱེད་ན,	should he do, or if he would do.
Pret.	བྱས་ན,	should he have done.
Future exact,	བྱས་པར་འགྱུར་ན,	if he shall have done.
Infinitive,	བྱེད་པར,	to do, make.
Infin. fut, / *Supine or gerund*	བྱེད་དུ། བྱར for བྱ་རུ or (བྱེད་པའི་ཕྱིར། བྱེད་པའི་དོན་དུ། བྱ་བའི་ཕྱིར། བྱ་བའི་སླད་དུ)	for doing, to do.

Participles.

Present.	བྱེད། བྱེད་པ,	doing, making.
Nouns of the agent,	བྱེད་མཁན and བྱེད་པ,	*com.* (or *m. et fem.*) a doer, maker.
Masculine,	བྱེད་པ། བྱེད་པ་པ། བྱེད་པ་པོ། བྱེད་པོ,	maker, doer, a maker, a doer.
Femin.	བྱེད་མ། བྱེད་པ་མ། བྱེད་པ་མོ། བྱེད་མོ,	the maker, doer.
Pret. & p. part.	བྱས་པ,	done, made.
Future,	བྱ་བ། or བྱ, བྱེད་རྒྱུ,	to be done; about to do, (faciendum) (facturus).
Sub. Noun,	བྱ་བ,	action, business.

Participial Expressions.

Present,	བྱེད་ཅིང་། བྱེད་དེ,	when doing, at the time of doing.
Pret.	བྱས་ཏེ། བྱས་ནས, བྱས་པས,	having done.
Future,	བྱ་ཞིང་། བྱ་སྟེ,	being about to do, being to be done.
Part. pluperf.	བྱས་ལ,	after having done.

§ 173. The Verb འགྱུར་བ, to become, &c.

Indicat. pres.	འགྱུར or འགྱུར་རོ,	is becoming, changing, turning.
Imperfect.	འགྱུར་འདུག་པ,	was becoming or turning.
Perf.	གྱུར། གྱུར་པ། གྱུར་ཏོ། གྱུར་ཞིན,	(he) became, has become, turned, changed.
Comp. perf.	གྱུར་པ་ཡིན,, &c.	has become.
Pluperf.	གྱུར་འདུག་པ or གྱུར་པ་ཡིན་པ,	had become.
Future,	འགྱུར་བར་འགྱུར་རོ,	shall or will become.
Imperat.	གྱུར། གྱུར་ཅིག,	be, let him be, or become, turned.

Hortative,	གྱུར་ཅིག,	let him be, or become.
Precative,	འགྱུར་བར་ཤོག,	may he become, let him be changed, turned, &c.
Optative.	འགྱུར་བར་གྱུར་ཅིག,	

Conditionals.

Pres. & fut.	འགྱུར་ན,	should he become, or if he would be.
Pret.	གྱུར་ན,	should he have become.
Fut. exact,	གྱུར་པར་འགྱུར་ན,	if he shall have become.
Infinitive,	འགྱུར་བར,	to become, turn, &c.
Infinit. fut. / *Ger. & Supine,*	འགྱུར་རུ (or འགྱུར་བའི་ཕྱིར།) འགྱུར་བའི་དོན་དུ,)	for becoming, to become, turn, grow, &c.

Participles.

Present,	འགྱུར or འགྱུར་བ,	becoming,growing,changing,turning.
Nouns,	འགྱུར་བ། འགྱུར་མཁན,	com. a becomer, &c.
masculine,	འགྱུར་བ། འགྱུར་བ་པ། འགྱུར་བ་པོ།	
fem.	འགྱུར་པོ། འགྱུར་མ། འགྱུར་བ་མ། འགྱུར་བ་མོ། འགྱུར་མོ,	a, or the, becomer, grower, turner, &c.
Abs. Substative,	འགྱུར་བ་ཉིད,	change, turn, vicissitude.
Part. pret.	གྱུར་པ།	grown, become, changed, turned.
Part. fut.	འགྱུར་བྱ། འགྱུར་རྒྱུ,	about to become, &c. subject to change, turn, changeable.

Participial Expressions.

Present & fut.	འགྱུར་དེ or འགྱུར་ཞིང,	when, or at the time of becoming, changing, &c.
Pret. & pluperf.	གྱུར་ཏེ། or གྱུར་ནས། གྱུར་པས། གྱུར་ལ,	having become, being turned, after having become, &c.

§ 174. The verb མཛད་པ (when used respectfully instead of བྱེད་པ) has only one variation, the imperative and hortative being formed by མཛོད ; the rest is supplied by the two auxiliary verbs བྱེད་པ, and འགྱུར་བ.

§ 175. The verb བགྱིད་པ (a respectful verb answering to བྱེད་པ) is used by a person speaking of himself, or of others, before a great personage, and has the following variations:

Indicat. present,	བགྱིད,	he does, &c.
Pret.	བགྱིས,	he did, has done.
Fturen,	བགྱི,	will, shall do.
Imperat.	གྱིས,	do, make.

The other tenses are supplied by the before-named auxiliary verbs (བྱེད and འགྱུར), and by the particles or articles enumerated with them.

Participles.

§ 176. The participles (present, perfect, and future), belong to the class of nouns and adjectives. Among the verbs they form the roots of the indicative present, perfect, and future tenses; as, སྨྲ, སྨྲས, སྨྲ་བྱ. As nouns they may all be used substantively; as, སྨྲ་བ, speaking or a speaking; སྨྲས་པ, spoken, a spoken thing, he that has spoken; སྨྲ་བྱ, about to speak, he that will speak, a thing to be said or spoken of.

§ 177. The present and perfect participles, terminate in པ or བ, according to their final letter, both when taken absolutely or as substantives, and when they stand after the substantive. But before a substantive they stand in the genitive form; thus: པའི, *pahi* pronounced pé or *pai*, བའི, *vahi* pronounced ve or *vai*, (*ai* to be pronounced as in rain, pain.)

Examples: ལས་བྱེད་པ, working, one that works; ལས་བྱེད་པའི་མི, a working man; མང་"སྨྲ་བ, much talking, one that talks much; མང་པོ་སྨྲ་བའི་མི, a man that talks much.

§ 178. When the participle present drops the པ or བ termination, and takes བྱེད or མཁན, or both; thus, བྱེད་མཁན; it denotes a noun, signifying an actor or agent, an instrument or organ; as, སྨྲ་བྱེད། སྨྲ་མཁན། སྨྲ་བྱེད་མཁན, a speaker; རྡུང་བྱེད, that does beat, a hammer; མཐོང་བྱེད, that does, or makes, see, the eye. The first might be expressed by the articles also; thus: སྨྲ་བ་པ or སྨྲ་བ་པོ, a, or the, speaker; སྨྲ་བ་མ or སྨྲ་བ་མོ, a, or the, (female) speaker.

§ 179. The following particles; ཅིང་ ཞིང་ ཤིང་ གྱི་ གི་ ཀྱི་ འི་ ཡི། གྱིན་ གིན་ ཀྱིན་ འིན་ ཡིན། ཏེ་ དེ་ སྟེ། put after the root of the present participle (with respect to its final letter) correspond to the English termination -ing, and are used in the same manner; as, ཞེས་སྨྲ་ཞིང, saying so, or thus saying; དེ་ལྟར་ཡོད་ཀྱི, it being so; ཀློག་གིན་འདུག, he is reading; ཟ་སྟེ་མི་སྨྲ, he does not speak when eating.

§ 180. The participle future terminates in ཅ or ཅ་བ, *chá*, *chá-vá* (taken absolutely, or after a substantive), and ཅའི or ཅ་བའི (taken conjunctively, or before a substantive ;) as, ཟ་ཅ, *adj*. edible, *sub*. any thing to be eaten, meat, food ; ཟ་ཅའི་ཤ, flesh to be eaten ; བཀློག་པར་ཅ་བ, to be read over, that must be read over ; བཀློག་པར་ཅ་བའི་བསྟན་བཅོས, a literary work *(shastra)* to be perused.

§ 181. The pluperfect participle is expressed by any of the following particles, (put after the root of the perfect participle, having regard to its final letter :) པས, ནས། གིས, ཀྱིས, གྱིས, འིས or -ས་ཡིས། ཏེ་སྟེ་དེ། ཅིང་ ཞིང་ ཤིང་ and ལ།. They are used like 'having -ed' or 'being -ed' in English (to join two or more members of a sentence) ; as, སྨྲས་པས། སྨྲས་ནས། སྨྲས་ཏེ། སྨྲས་ཀྱིས། སྨྲས་ཤིང་།, having spoken or said ; སོང་ལ་ཁོ་ལ་ཟེར, having gone tell him, or go and tell him.

ADVERBS.

§ 182. There are many simple and compound primitive and derivative adverbs in this tongue. Here follows a collection of the most common of them, of all sorts.

ADVERBS OF TIME.

ནམ, when?

གང་ཙམ, གང་ཚེ, at what time? when?

འདི་ཙམ, འདི་ཚེ, at this (or such a) time.

དེ་ཙམ, དེ་ཚེ, at that time.

གང་གི་ཙམ—དེའི་ཙམ, or གང་ཙམ—དེ་ཙམ, གང་གི་ཚེ—དེའི་ཚེ, or གང་ཚེ—དེ་ཚེ, correlatively : at which time, at that time.

སྔོན, སྔོན་ཚེ, སྔོན་ཙམ, in old times, of old, formerly, anciently.

རྒྱུན་དུ, ཙམ་རྒྱུན་དུ, རྟག་ཏུ, ཙམ་རྟག་ཏུ, གཏན་དུ, continually, uninterruptedly, always, perpetually.

ནམ་ཡང, ནམ་ཙའང, never.

ཐོག་མར, in the beginning, first.

བར་དུ, in the middle, secondly, afterwards.

ཐ་མར, lastly, ultimately.

གསར་དུ, newly, recently.

གློ་བུར་དུ, suddenly.

དེ་མ་ཐག-ཏུ, immediately, soon, readily.

ནམ་ཞིག-ན, once, at a certain time.

རེས་རེས་སུ, sometimes, now and then.

སྐབས་སྐབས་སུ, occasionally.

རེ་ཞིག, for a while.

རེ་ཞིག—སྟད་ཀྱིས, first—then.

དང་པོར, the first time, first.

གཉིས་པར, the second time, secondly.

དེང་ or དིང་, དེང་ཚེ, དེང་རེས, } now, at this time.

དེང་སང་, དིང་སང་, } now-a-days.

ད་རུང་, as yet, still.

ད་རུང་ཡང, now too.

ད, ད་ལྟ, ད་ལྟ་གིད་རུ, } now, this very instant, or time, this present.

དེ་རིང་, this day, to-day.

མདང་ or མདངས, } yesterday.

ཁ་སང་, ཁ་སྔང་, ཁར་སང་, ཁར་སང་ཞག, } before yesterday, some days ago, lately.

སྔོན་མ་ཞང, three days ago.

ཡང་སྔོན་ཞག, four days ago.

ཡུང་སྔོན་ཞག, five days ago.

སང་, ཐོ་རེ, *vulg.* } to-morrow.

ནངས or གནངས, } after to-morrow.

གཞེས, three days hence.

དགུས, four days hence.

ཆུས, five days hence.

ཞག་དང་ཞག, every day.

ཟླ་དང་ཟླ, every month.

ལོ་དང་ལོ, ལོ་སྦྱར, } every year, year by year.

ལོ་ཆག, every second year.

ད་ལོ, this year.

ན་ནིང་ or ན་ཉིང་, } last year.

ཞེ་ནིང, two years ago, (in the third year ago.)

དགུ་ནིང་, three years ago, &c.

ཆུ་ནིང་, four years ago, &c.

ནང་པར, next year.

སང་པར, two years hence.

ཡང་སང་ or དགུ་པར, } three years hence.

ཡུང་སང་ or ཆུ་པར, } four years hence.

ཉིན་པར, in the day time, by day.

ཉིན་མོ་ལ, by day.

མཚན་མོ་ལ, by night.

ཉིན་མཚན་དུ, day and night.

སྔ་དྲོ་ལ, in the forenoon.

ཕྱི་དྲོ་ལ, in the afternoon.

སྔ་མོ་ལ, ནང་མོ་ལ, } in the morning, early.

ཉིན་དགུང་ལ, at mid-day.

རྒྱ་མོ་ལ, in the evening.

ADVERBS OF NUMBER AND TIME.

ལན་ཚམ, how many times.

ལན་གཅིག, once.

ལན་གཉིས, twice.

ལན་རེ, a single time.

ལན་རེ་རེ, a single time each.

ལན་མང་དུ,
ལན་དུ་མར, } many times.

མཐའ་ཡས་པར, infinitely, immensely.

ལན་འགའ་ཞིག, sometimes.

ལན་འགའ or
རེས་འགའ, } sometimes, now and then, one time or other.

ལན་འགའ — ལན་འགའ, or
རེས་འགའ—རེས་འགའ, } sometime, other time.

ལན་འགའ་ཡང་, not a single time, never.

ADVERBS OF PLACE.

གང་དུ,
ག་རུ,
གར, } whither? where? to what place?

འདི་རུ,
འདིར, } hither, to this place.

དེ་རུ,
དེར, } thither, to that place.

གང་དུ—དེར, *correl.* whither, there, or to which place, to that place.

གང་དུའང་རུང, whithersoever, to whatever place.

གཞན་དུ, to another place; otherwise.

གང་ན,
ག་ན,
གར, } where? at what place?

འདི་ན,
འདིར, } here, at this place.

དེ་ན,
དེར, } there, at that place.

གང་ན—དེ་ན, *correl.* where, there, or at which place, at that place.

གང་ནའང་རུང་, at whatever place, wherever.

གང་ནས,
ག་ནས, } whence? from what place?

འདི་ནས, from this place, hence.

དེ་ནས, from that place, thence.

གང་ནས,
ག་ནས, } དེ་ནས, *correl.* whence, thence, or from which place, from that place.

གང་ནས་ཀྱང་རུང་ or
ག་ནས་ཀྱང་རུང་, } whencesoever, from whencesoever.

ནང་ན, within.

ཕྱི་རོལ་ན, without.

ནང་དུ, into.

ཕྱི་རོལ་ཏུ,
ཕྱིར, } out, onwards.

ནང་ནས, from within.

ཕྱི་རོལ་ནས, from without, from abroad.

མདུན་དུ,
སྔོན་ལ, } forwards, fore, before.

རྒྱབ་ཏུ, backwards, back.

འོག་ཏུ, down, downwards.

འོག་ན, below, beneath.

འོག་ནས, from below.

སྟེང་དུ, } on, upon, over, to, up.
གོང་དུ,
སྒར,

གྱེན་དུ, up, upwards, up hill.

སྟེང་ན, } above, upon, on high.
གོང་ན,
སྒ་ན,

སྟེང་ནས, } from above.
གོང་ནས,
སྒ་ནས,

ཉེ། ཉེ་མོ། ཉེ་མོར, near, at, to a near place.

ཐག་རིང་།-ན, at a far distance.

ཐག་རིང.ཏུ, to a far distance, far.

ཉེ་མོ་ནས, from near, from not far.

ཐག་རིང་ནས, from far, from a great distance.

ཀུན་ཏུ, } everywhere, at whatever place.
གནས་ཀུན་ཏུ,
ཡུལ་ཀུན་ཏུ,
གང་ཏུའང་,

ཡུལ་མང་དུ, on, at, to many places.

ཡུལ་གང་ཏུའང, everywhere, (when followed by a negative) nowhere.

Adverbs of Manner or Quality.

ཅི་ཙུག, } how? on what manner?
ཅི་ལྟར,

འདི་ཙུག, } thus, so, on this manner.
འདི་ལྟར,

དེ་ཙུག, } so, on that manner.
དེ་ལྟར,

ཇི་ཙུག—དེ་ཙུག, } *correl.* as, so, on which manner, on that manner.
ཇི་ལྟར—དེ་ལྟར,

རིམ་པ་བཞིན་དུ, by degrees.

རིམ་གྱིས, gradually.

ཅིག་ཅར or } at once.
གཅིག་ཅར,

རང་བཞིན་གྱིས, by itself, spontaneously.

ངོ་བོ་ཉིད་ཀྱིས, naturally.

སྤྱིར, generally, universally.

ཁྱེ་བྲག་ཏུ, especially, particularly.

ཕལ་མོ་ཆེར, } mostly, for the most part.
ཕལ་ཆེར,

ཐ་མལ་པར, vulgarly.

ཤེས་བཞིན་དུ, knowingly, designedly.

འདུག་སྟེ, sitting.

ཉལ་ཏེ, lying.

འགྲུལ་ཏེ, walking.

མགྱོགས་པར, } swiftly.
ལ་ཧུར,

མྱུར་དུ, } swiftly, speedily.
མྱུར་བར,

མྱུར་བ་མྱུར་བར, } very speedily.
རབ་ཏུ་མྱུར་བར,

རིངས་པར, hastily, speedily.

རིངས་པ་རིངས་པར, very hastily.

ག་ལེ, } slowly.
ག་ལེར,
ལ་འགོར,

དལ་བར, } softly, slowly, gently.
དལ་བུས,

དལ་བུ་དལ་བུས, very softly or slowly.

འདར་འདར་པོར, fearfully, with quaking and trembling.

རབ་ཏུ, eminently.
ཤིན་ཏུ, very.
ཀུན་ཏུ, altogether, entirely.
མཆོག་ཏུ, chiefly.
གཙོ་བོར, principally.
ཡོངས་སུ, wholly, entirely.
ཡང་དག་པར, thoroughly, fully, completely.
ཆེམ་པར, especially.
ངེས་པར, certainly, really.
དངོས་སུ, really.
མངོན་པར, conspicuously.
མངོན་སུམ་དུ, evidently.
གསལ་བོར, }
གསལ་བར, } clearly.
བདེན་པར, truly.
བརྫུན་དུ, or }
རྫུན་དུ, } falsely.
དྲང་པོར, aright; rightly, honestly.
ལོག་པར, wrong, amiss.
བཟང་པོར, well.
ངན་པར, ill, badly.
བདེ་བར, well, happily.
ལེགས་པར, well, elegantly.
མཛེས་པར, beautifully.
ཉེས་པར, viciously, faultily, ill.
ལྷག་པར, more, beyond, in a higher degree.
ལྷུལ་ཏུ, egregiously.
རྗེས་སུ, after, along with.
སོ་སོར, asunder.
སླར, again, back.

ཡང་, again, likewise.
ཡང་ཡང་, }
ཡང་དང་ཡང་, } again and again.
ཡང་དང་ཡང་དུ, }
ཁྱད་པར་དུ, particularly, especially.
མཚུངས་པར, } equally.
འདྲ་བར, } likewise.
མཉམ་པར, } alike.
ལྐོག་ཏུ, }
གསང་བར, } privately, clandestinely, secretly.
ངོས་སུ, openly, before one's face.
གཞན་དུ, otherwise; else.
ཐམས་ཅད་དུ, wholly; in every way.
ཐམས་ཅད་ཀྱི་ཐམས་ཅད་དུ, totally, absolutely.
དབེན་པར, solitarily, retiredly.
རྒྱས་པར, amply, copiously, at large.
བསྡུས་ཏེ, }
མདོར་བསྡུས་ཏེ, } shortly, briefly, concisely, abridgedly.
ནན་ཏན་ཏུ, earnestly; certainly.
བག་ཚོལ་ཏུ, inconsiderately.
གདོན་མི་ཟ་བར, }
ཐེ་ཚོམ་མེད་པར, } undoubtedly.
འཁྲུལ་པ་མེད་པར, }
འཁྲུལ་མེད་དུ, } infallibly.
སླུ་བ་མེད་པར, }
བག་ཡོད་པར, chastely, modestly.
བག་མེད་པར, unchastely, immodestly.
བཏང་སྙོམས་པར, indifferently.
རུང་བར, becomingly, decently.
མི་རུང་བར, unbecomingly, indecently.

རིགས་པར, reasonably, justly.

མི་རིགས་པར, unreasonably, unjustly.

འོས་པར, worthily, becomingly.

མི་འོས་པར, unworthily, unbecomingly.

འགྱུར་བ་མེད་པར, immutably.

ཁ་རོག་གེ, silently, still.

Adverbs of Quantity.

ཙམ or ཙ, how much? how many?

འདི་ཙམ, thus much, or so much (here).

དེ་ཙམ, so much, (there.)

བཅུ་ཙམ, about ten.

བརྒྱ་ཙམ, about one hundred, &c. &c.

མང་། མང་པོ། མང་ཙ, ཙ་མ, } much, many, in a great quantity.

ཉུང་། ཉུང་ཙ, little, few, in a small quantity.

ཕྱེད, half, a half.

ཕྱེད་ཙམ, about the half of, &c.

ཧ་ཅང, too, very.

ཚོད, enough.

ཚོག། ཚོག་ཚོག, it is enough, it is sufficient.

ཚད་མེད།་པར, } immense, immeasurable.
དཔག་མེད། པར, } immensely, immeasurably.

Adverbs of Negation.

མ། མི, not; as in:

ང་ནི་དེ་མ་ཤེས་སོ, I have not known it.

ང་ནི་དེ་མི་ཤེས་སོ, I do not know it.

མེད། མིན, there is not, it is not, as;

དེ་ནང་ན་ཅི་འང་མེད, there is nothing in it.

དེ་མིན་གཞན, that is not, another.

ཁྱོད་ནམ་ཡང་མི་འོང, you never come, &c.

ཁྱོད་ནམ་ཡང་མ་འོངས, you never came, &c.

§ 183. There are several particles used both as postpositions (or prepositions in the occidental languages) and as adverbs. When taken as postpositions, they stand always after the substantive (with or without the genitive sign) as to be seen under the postpositions. When taken adverbially they are put always before the verb, as in the following examples:

ནང་ཏུ་འགྲོ་བར, to go in.

ནང་ན་འདུག་པར, to be, or sit within.

ནང་ནས་འོང་བར, to come from within.

ཕྱིར (ཕྱི་རོལ་དུ) འགྲོ་བར, to go out.

ཕྱི་ན (ཕྱི་རོལ་ན) འདུག་པར, to be or sit out of doors, or on the out side.

ཕྱི་ནས (ཕྱི་རོལ་ནས) འོང་བར, to come from without or from abroad.

འོག་ཏུ་འཇོག་པར, to lay down.

གྱེན་ཏུ་འདེགས་པར, to lift up.

སྟོ་ན་བཞུགས་པར, to be on high, or above.

མདུན་ཏུ་འགྲོ་བར, to go before, (or forwards.)

རྒྱབ་ཏུ་ལྟ་བར, to look back.

གཡས་སུ་འཁོར་བར, to turn (in going) to the right (side or hand).

Postpositions.

§ 184. The prepositions used in the occidental languages, are rendered in this tongue by postpositive particles or postpositions. They are simple and compound. The first are insignificant particles by themselves, and the last have always a significant meaning.

§ 185. The simple postpositions, put after the nominative, form the several cases of a declension, and besides, denote either motion to, towards, into, &c. or rest in, at, on; or motion from, of, out of, a place. Such simple postpositions are:

The genitive signs: ཀྱི། གི། གྱི། འི or ཡི, signifying: of, 's.

The signs of the active or instrumentive case: ཀྱིས། གིས། གྱིས། —ས or ཡིས། signifying: by, with.

The dative sign ལ, to, for.

The ablative signs ནས། ལས, from, of, out of, &c. as have been before set forth in the forms of general declension.

§ 186. The particles ཏུ། དུ། རུ or -ར སུ, (put after the nominative with respect to its final letter) denote motion, progression to, or towards a place; or change, turn, promotion into an other state; as, ནུབ་ཏུ to, towards the west; ཤར་དུ, to the east; རྒྱ་གར་དུ, in India; ལྷོ་རུ or ལྷོར, to or on the south; གཡས་སུ to or on the right, hand. ན and sometimes ལ, denote rest in, at, on a place; as, བོད་ན, in Tibet: ཤིང་ལ, on a tree. ནས and ལས, signify motion from a place; as, བོད་ནས, from Tibet: ཤིང་ལས from on a tree.

§ 187. The compound postpositions require, in general, the genitive case before them. But sometimes the genitive signs being dropt, they are put after the nominative, like the simple postpositions.

Here follow some of them, with a few examples of their application.

Postpositions.	*Examples.*
ཕྱིར་དུ or ཕྱིར, for, sake.	ངའི་ཕྱིར་དུ, for me, for my sake.
ཆེད་དུ or ཆེད, account.	ཅིའི་ཆེད་དུ, for what? why?
དོན་དུ or དོན, cause, reason.	གཞན་གྱི་དོན་དུ, for other's sake.
སླད་དུ or སླད, in behalf of.	སུའི་སླད་དུ or སུ་སླད, for whom? in whose behalf?
ནང་དུ, to, into.	ཁང་པའི་ནང་དུ, into the house.

Postpositions.	*Examples.*
ནང་ན, in, at, among.	ཁང་པའི་ནང་ན, in the house.
ནང་ནས, from, out of, from among.	ཁང་པའི་ནང་ནས, out of, or from the house.
འོག་ཏུ, under (to.)	སའི་འོག་ཏུ, under the earth or ground.
འོག་ན, below, beneath.	སའི་འོག་ན, below the earth, &c.
འོག་ནས, from below.	སའི་འོག་ནས, from below the earth, &c.
གོང་དུ or སྟེང་དུ, to, on, upon, to the top of.	དེའི་སྟེང་དུ, to or above that.
གོང་ན or སྟེང་ན, on, upon, above.	དེའི་སྟེང་ན, on or above that.
གོང་ནས or སྟེང་ནས, from on, from above.	དེའི་སྟེང་ནས, from on that.
མདུན་དུ, before, to.	ཁྱོད་ཀྱི་མདུན་དུ, before (thee) you.
— ན, before, in, at the sight of, &c.	— — — ན, in the sight of you.
— ནས, from before.	— — — ནས, from before you.
སྤྱན་སྔར, before, unto the sight of.	བླ་མའི་སྤྱན་སྔར, before a or the Lama.
— སྔ་ན, before, in, at.	— — — སྔ་ན, before the Lama.
— — ནས, from before.	— — — སྔ་ནས, from before, &c.
རྒྱབ་ཏུ, རྟིང་དུ, རྗེས་སུ } to the back of. after, behind.	རིའི་རྒྱབ་ཏུ, to the back of the mountain. དེའི་རྟིང་དུ, after that. ངའི་རྗེས་སུ, after me.
རྒྱབ་ན, རྟིང་ན, རྗེས་ན } in, at, on the back of, behind.	རིའི་རྒྱབ་ན, behind the hill. དེའི་རྟིང་ན, after or behind it. ངའི་རྗེས་ན, behind me.
རྒྱབ་ནས, རྟིང་ནས, རྗེས་ནས, } from the back of. from behind, &c.	རིའི་རྒྱབ་ནས, from behind the hill. དེའི་རྟིང་ནས, from behind it. ཁང་པའི་རྗེས་ནས, from behind the house.
དྲུང་དུ, གན་དུ, ཐད་དུ, } to, to the side of, by, near to.	ཁོང་གི་དྲུང་དུ, to, near him. — — གན་དུ, ditto. — — ཐད་དུ, ditto.
དྲུང་ན, གན་ན, ཐད་ན, } at the side of, by, near to.	ཁོང་གི་དྲུང་ན, at his side, or near him. — — གན་ན, ditto. — — ཐད་ན, ditto.

Postpositions.	*Examples.*
རྫུང་ནས, } from the side of, from.	ཁོང་གི་རྫུང་ནས, from him, &c.
གན་ནས, } from the side of, from.	— — གན་ནས, ditto.
ཐད་ནས, } from the side of, from.	— — ཐད་ནས, ditto.
བར་དུ, into the middle of, between.	གཉིས་ཀའི་བར་དུ, into, between the two.
བར་ན, in, at, on the middle of, betwixt.	— — བར་ན, betwixt or between the two.
བར་ནས, from the middle of, from between, from among.	— — བར་ནས, from between the two.
ཁོངས་སུ, into, among, under, or into the number of.	མཁས་པ་རྣམས་ཀྱི་ཁོངས་སུ, under (or into the number of) learned men.
ཁོངས་ན, among, amongst.	— — — — ཁོངས་ན, among ditto.
ཁོངས་ནས, from among.	— — — — ཁོངས་ནས, from among the learned.

Postpositions of this kind may be formed from many substantives and adjectives, by adding any of the particles, ཏུ། དུ། རུ or -ར། སུ། ན། ནས། ; as has been shown in the above examples.

Postpositions.	*Examples.*
ལྷན་ཅིག, } along with, in company, together with.	ཁྱོད་དང་ལྷན་ཅིག, together with thee (you).
མཉམ་དུ, } along with, in company, together with.	ཁོང་དང་མཉམ་དུ, in his company, with him.
བཅས་པ, } along with, in company, together with.	རྒྱལ་པོ་བཀའ་བློན་དང་བཅས་པ, the king together with the prime minister.

These generally assume the conjunction དང་ (and) before them, as the examples also manifest.

ཐུག, till, to, as far as.	མཐར་ཐུག for མཐའ་རུ་ཐུག, to, (as far as,) the limit, or boundary.
བར།-དུ, till, (including from to.)	གཞིས་ཀ་རྩེ་བར, till, as far as, &c. &c. S'hikàtsé, (the capital of Tsáng in Tibet.)
ནས — བར, from—till, to (the whole space between.)	ལྷ་ས་ནས་བལ་པོ་བར, from Lhassa to Nepal, (as far as).

The following twenty Sanskrit prepositive particles have been rendered by the Tibetan translators, thus,

	*Sanskrit**.		*English.*	*Tibetan.*	
1	अति	*ati,*	beyond,	དག་པར,	*dag-par.*
2	अधि	*adhi,*	over,	ཤིན་ཏུ,	*shin-tu.*
3	अनु	*anu,*	after,	རྗེས་སུ,	*rjes-su.*
4	अप	*apa,*	un, de,	ལྷག་པར,	*lhag-par.*
5	अपि	*api,*	to,	སླར,	*slar.*
6	अभि	*abhi,*	towards,	མངོན་པར,	*mňon-par.*
7	अव	*ava,*	from,	ཕུལ་དུ,	*phul-du.*
8	आ	*a'* or *ang,*	unto,	ལེགས་པར,	*legs-par.*
9	उत्	*ut,*	up,	མཐོ་བའི,	*mtho-vahi.*
10	उप	*upa,*	near,	ཉེ་བར,	*nye-var.*
11	दुर्	*dur,*	far,	ངན་པ,	*ňan-pa.*
12	नि	*ni,*	into,	ངེས་པར,	*nes-par.*
13	निर्	*nir,*	out,	བྲལ་བ,	*bral-va.*
14	परा	*pará,*	far,	མཆོག་ཏུ,	*mchhog-tu.*
15	परि	*pari,*	round,	ཡོངས་སུ,	*yougs-su.*
16	प्र	*pra,*	forth,	རབ་ཏུ,	*rab-tu.*
17	प्रति	*prati,*	re,	སོ་སོར,	*so-sor.*
18	वि	*vi,*	in,	རྣམ་པར,	*rnam-par.*
19	सं	*sam,*	with,	ཡང་དག་པར,	*yang-dag-par.*
20	सु	*su,*	well,	བདེ་བར,	*bdé-var.*

Conjunctions.

§ 188. Here follow some of the conjunctions that occur frequently in the Tibet books.

དང་, and.

ཀྱང་, འང་, ཡང་, } too, also; though, although; notwithstanding.

དེ་བས་ན, དེས་ན, དེ་ལྟ་བས་ན, དེ་ལྟ་ན, } therefore, then.

* Taken from Mr. Yates' Grammar.

ཡང་ན, or, or else.

ཡང་ན—ཡང་ན, either, or, or else.

གམ, ངམ, དམ, ནམ, བམ, མམ, འམ, རམ, ལམ, སམ, ཏམ, — are interrogative signs, or express a doubt, whether, or? they may be formed of any word, by reduplicating its final letter, and adding a མ; as in བདག་གམ་ཁྱོད; ངའམ་ཁོ, whether I or he, I or he?

ཅེ་འམ, ཞེ་འམ, ཤེ་འམ, — or, or so, or; thus, or.

འོ་ན, འོ་ན་ཀི, འི་ན་ཡང, — then, therefore, nevertheless.

འོན་ཀྱང, འོན་ཏང, འོན་དང, — though, although, albeit, notwithstanding.

མོད་ཀྱང, མད་ཀྱང, — though, although.

མོད་ཀྱང—ད་དུང, although—yet.

ད་དུང, yet, but yet, as yet.

ད་དུང་ཡང, now too, still.

འོན་ཏེ, འོན་ཏེ་ན, གལ་ཏེ, གལ་ཏེ་ན, — if, but if.

གལ་སྲིད—དེ་ལྟ་ན, གལ་ཏེ—དེ་ལྟ་ན, གལ་ཏེ—དེ་ཚེ, — if—then, so.

ཇི་སྟེ, if.

དེ་སྟེ, if, (then).

དེ་སྟེ—དེ་སྟེ, if, if, or but if; as,

དེ་སྟེ་ནུས་ན—དེ་སྟེ་མ་ནུས་ན, if you can, but if you cannot, &c.

ཐ་ན, not even so much as, not even, &c.; as, ཐ་ན་འབྲུ་གཅིག་ཀྱང་མི་འདུག, (there is, not even so much as a single grain (or corn).

དེར་མ་ཟད, nay, nay rather; yea, what is more; besides; yet more.

ཅེ་ན, ཞེ་ན, ཤེ་ན, — pray, I pray; for, because.

§ 189. Interjections.

ཨོཾ, a mystical interjection, denoting the essential body or person of a **Buddha** or any other divinity.

ཨཱཿ, ditto, denoting the word or doctrine of ditto.

ཧཱུྃ, ditto, denoting the mind or mercy of ditto.

ཀྭ། ཀྭ་ཀྭ། ཀྭ་ཀྱེ,
ཝགས། ཀྭ་ཝགས,
སྭ། སྭའི། སྭ་ཡེ,
ཀྱེ། ཀྱེ་ཀྱེ། ཨ་རེ,
ཕྱ། དཔའ། ཕྱ་ཨི། དཔའ་ཡི,
ཨ་ཝེ། ཡ་འོ། ཚོ་རེ། ཚོ་རེ་ཚེ, — are vocative particles, O, holla! &c.

ཀྱེ་མ། ཀྱེ་ཧུད། ཀྱི་ཧུད, } *interj.* expressing grief;
འོ་དོད། ཧུ་ཧུ, } alas ! oh ! woe ! O !

ཨེ་མ། ཨེ་མའོ། ཨེ་མ་ཧོ,
ཨ་ཧོ། ཨ་ཧོ་ཨ་ཧོ, } *interj.* of admiration.

ཨ་ལ་ལ། ཨ་ལ་ལ་ཧོ, ditto of wonder.

ཨ་ལ་ལ་ཨ་ལ་ལ, ditto of great joy, happiness.

ཧ་ཧ, *interj.* of joy, of admiration.

ཨ་ཨཱ ཨེ་ཨོ་ཡ་ཡ, *interj.* of recollection, ho ! yes.

ཨ་ཧོ། ལེགས་སོ། བསྟོད་དོ,
ཡིན་ནོ། ངེས་སོ། བདེན་ནོ,
ལེགས་སོ། ལེགས་སོ་ལེགས་སོ,
མད་དོ། དེ་བཞིན་ནོ། དེ་དེ་བཞིན་ནོ, } denote approbation ; O rare ! well done ! well ! very well ! true ! truth ! yes truly ! &c.

ཨ་ཁ། ཨ་ཁ་ཁ,
འ་ཁ། འ་ཁ་ཁ, } *interj.* of disapprobation, displeasure.

དགའ་འོ། ཨའོ། འབར་རེ,
དགོས་སེ། ཟུ་ཟུ, } *interj.* of endearment or affection.

ཨ་ཏ་ཏ། ཀ་ཀ་པ།,
ཙ་ཙ་པ, } *interj.* expressive of pain.

ཨ་ན། ཨ་ན་ན།,
ཨ་ར། ཨ་ར་ར, } ditto of sorrow or anguish.

ཨ་ཙུ། ཨ་ཙུ་ཙུ, ditto of pain from cold.

ཨ་ཚ། ཨ་ཚ་ཚ, ditto of pain from heat.

ཨ་ཚི། ཨ་ཚི་ཚི, ditto of fright, horror, dread.

SYNTAX.

§ 190. If the structure or construction of the Tibetan language be compared to that of the English, the first seems, in many instances, to be totally the reverse of the last. Thus in the sentence བདག་གིས་མཐོང་བའི་དཔེ་ཞིག་ན, *in a book seen by me*, the actual order of the words will be found on translation to be exactly inverted: *me by seen book a in.*

In the Tibetan, the articles, both definite and indefinite, are put always after the noun ; as, མིག་པོ, the eye ; མི་ཞིག, a man ; རི་བོ, the mountain ; ལག་པ, a or the hand ; བླ་མ, the or a superior ; བུད་མེད་ཅིག, a woman ; བུ་ཞིག, a child ; གོས་ཤིག, a garment, &c.

§ 191. The several cases of a declension are formed by postpositive particles ; and further, all the English prepositions are expressed in this tongue by postpositions. As for instance in a declension :

Singular.

Nom.	the hand,	ལག་པ.
Gen.	of the hand,	ལག་པའི.
Inst.	by or with hand,	ལག་པས.
Dat.	to, into, hand,	ལག་པ་ལ། ལག་པར། ལག་ཏུ.
Accus.	the hand,	ལག་པ.

Locat. in the hand.	ལག་པ་ན། ལག་པར.
Abl. from, out of the hand.	ལག་པ་ནས.

§ 192. **Relation of Prepositions and Postpositions.**

to the ocean or sea,	རྒྱ་མཚོ་ལ or རྒྱ་མཚོར.
in, on ditto.	རྒྱ་མཚོ་ན.
out of, from ditto.	རྒྱ་མཚོ་ནས.
to, up to a hill.	རི་ལ.
on, upon ditto.	རི་ན.
from on ditto.	རི་ལས or རི་ནས.
to mount a horse.	རྟ་ལ་བཞོན་པར.
sitting on a horse.	རྟ་ན་འདུག་པ.
descending from a horse.	རྟ་ལས་འབབ་པ.
to beat with the hand.	ལག་པས་བརྡུང་བར.
to go together with him.	ཁོང་དང་ལྷན་ཅིག་འགྲོ་བར,
come before me.	ངའི་མདུན་དུ་སོང.
stay not in the way.	ལམ་ན་མ་སྡོད.
from whom hast thou that obtained.	ཁྱོད་ཀྱིས་དེ་སུ་ནས་ཐོབ.
for me?	ངའི་ཕྱིར་དུ.
to, near, by thee.	ཁྱོད་ཀྱི་དྲུང་དུ.
from the town.	གྲོང་ཁྱེར་ནས.
to the town.	— — དུ
in, at, the town.	— — ན
to go to, into, heaven.	གནམ་དུ་གཤེགས་པར.
to sit, or be in ditto.	གནམ་ན་བཞུགས་པར.
to descend from ditto.	གནམ་ནས་འབབ་པར.

§ 193. The nouns in general, precede their attributes, and the verbs stand, for the most part, at the end of the sentence; as, མི་བཟང, a good man; མི་ངན, a bad man; མི་གཅིག, one man; མི་གསུམ་པ, the third man; མི་མང་པོ་ཤེས་པ, a much-knowing man; མི་མང་དུ་ཐོས་པ, a man that has heard much (very expert); མི་བསླབ་པར་བྱ་བ, a man that must be taught or instructed.

§ 194. Verbs occur at the end of sentences, thus: ང་ནི་དེ་མི་ཤེས་སོ, I do not know that; ང་ཡང་དང་པོར་དེ་མ་ཤེས་ཤིན, I myself also did not know it at first (or have not known).

ཁྱོད་ལ་དེ་སུས་ཟེར, by whom is it told or said to thee? or, who told it you?

སངས་རྒྱས་ལ་ཕྱག་འཚལ་ལོ, reverence (be) to Buddha.

ཁྱོད་ཡུན་རིང་དུ་འཚོ་བར་གྱུར་ཅིག, may you (thou) live long!

འདུལ་བ་པོས་གདུལ་བར་བྱ་བ་དག་བཏུལ or གདུལ་བྱ་འདུལ་པོས་བཏུལ, the subduer (instructor) has subdued (disciplined) those that were to be subdued (civilized).

§ 195. The auxiliaries follow the principal verb, and it is they only that are conjugated in the several tenses, the root of the principal verb being invariable; as, in བྱེད་དུ་འཇུག་པར, to cause make; བྱེད་ནུས་པར, to can make; བྱེད་འདོད་པར, to wish (or will) to do; (in these the verbs བྱེད་དུ, and བྱེད, remain in all tenses invariable.)

§ 196. The article is expressed sometimes, when speaking definitely, both after the substantive and adjective; as, རྒྱལ་པོ་ཆེན་པོ, the great king. Sometimes it is dropt after both; as, རྒྱལ་ཆེན་བཞི, the four great (fabulous) kings; ལུང་པ་ནག་པོ or ལུང་ནག, the black valley; ལུང་པ་ནག་པོ་པ or ལུང་ནག་པ, a man (or native) of the black valley.

The article is likewise dropt in short and general enumeration; as, ཆེ་ཆུང, great and small; རྒྱལ་བློན, the king and the ministers; མཐོ་དམན, high and low; སྐྱེ། རྒ། ན། འཆི for སྐྱེ་བ་དང་། རྒ་བ་དང་། ན་བ་དང་། འཆི་བའོ།། there is birth, old age, sickness, and death.

But it is dropt especially, when nouns in opposition are enumerated; as, རེ་དོགས (for རེ་བ་དང་དོགས་པ,) hope and fear or anxiety; དགེ་སྡིག, (for དགེ་བ་དང་སྡིག་པ,) virtue and vice; གནམ་ས, (for གནམ་ག་དང་ས་གཞི,) heaven and earth.

§ 197. When two substantives are connected by the genitive sign, the article is generally expressed after the last noun; but when they are contracted into one word, by dropping the genitive sign, the article also is dropt, as in the following examples:

ཤིང་གི་རྩ་བ —	ཤིང་རྩ,	the root or bottom of a tree.
— — སྡོད་པ —	— སྡོད,	the middle part or body of ditto.
— — རྩེ་མོ —	— རྩེ,	the top of ditto.
— — སྡོང་པོ —	— སྡོང་,	the stem of ditto.

ཤིང་གི་ཡལ་ག ཤིང་ཡལ, the branch of a tree.

— — ལོ་མ — ལོ, the leaf of ditto.

— — འབྲས་བུ — འབྲས, the fruit of ditto.

This contracted form is very common; the learner should therefore bear it in mind in difficult sentences.

§ 198. Nouns generally precede their attributes, and then it is only the last of them that is declined in the several cases; as, མི་ཆེན་འདི་དག, these great men:—(here མི་ཆེན་འདི this great man, is in the singular, but by adding to འདི the plural sign དག, the whole is made plural; and now these four syllables remaining invariable, all the other cases are formed according to the rules of general declension.)

§ 199. A noun denoting possession or connexion of any kind with another, or the matter of which any thing is made, is, for the most part, put in the genitive, and always precedes the other noun; as, མིའི་ལུས་པོ, a man's body, or, the body of a man. Such genitives may be expressed adjectively also, in English; as the human body. Other examples: ལག་པའི་སོར་མོ, the finger of the hand; རྐང་པའི་མཐིལ, the sole of the foot; ཁང་པའི་ཐོག, the roof or terrace of a house; ཡུལ་གྱི་འགོ་པ, the head or chief of a village; ལུས་ཀྱི་ཡན་ལག་རྣམས, the limbs or members of the body; གསེར་གྱི་དོང་རྩེ, a gold coin; དངུལ་གྱི་གཞོང་པ, a silver basin; ཤིང་གི་ཕོར་པ, a wooden cup; གསེར་གྱི་ལྕགས་སྒྲོག, golden fetters or chains (for a malefactor); ཆུའི་ཐིགས་པ, a drop of water, &c.

The genitive sign sometimes is dropt, thus: སངས་རྒྱས་བསྟན་པ (for སངས་རྒྱས་ཀྱི་བསྟན་པ) the doctrine, or religion, of Buddha; འཇིག་རྟེན་མགོན་པོ, (for འཇིག་རྟེན་གྱི་མགོན་པོ,) the lord (or patron) of the world (Buddha).

§ 200. When several words are connected in a sentence, they seldom require above one sign of the case they are in; as, ལྷ་ཀླུ་མི་ལ་སོགས་ཀྱིས་སངས་རྒྱས་ལ་ཕྱག་ཚལ་ལོ, the gods, Nagas, men, et cetera, paid homage to (reverenced or saluted) Buddha; རྒྱལ་བློན་འབངས་ཐམས་ཅད་ཀྱི་སྐྱབས་གཅིག་པོ, the only refuge (or protection) of the king, ministers, and of all the subjects (or vassals); རང་གི་ཕ་མ་དང་མི་གཞན་ཐམས་ཅད་ལ, to my own (father and mother) parents, and to every other person.

§ 201. The adjectives, generally, are put after their nouns, and are declined in the several cases of both numbers, according to the form of general declension, the nouns being then invariable before them; as:

	Singular.	Plural.
Nom. & Acc.	མི་བཟང་པོ, a (or the) good man.	མི་བཟང་པོ་རྣམས, good men.
Instr.	མི་བཟང་པོས, by a good man.	མི་བཟང་པོ་རྣམས་ཀྱིས, by good men.
Gen. or *Poss.*	མི་བཟང་པོའི, a good man's.	མི་བཟང་པོ་རྣམས་ཀྱི, good men's.
Dat.	མི་བཟང་པོ་ལ, to a good man.	མི་བཟང་པོ་རྣམས་ལ, to good men.
Abl.	མི་བཟང་པོ་ནས, from a good man.	མི་བཟང་པོ་རྣམས་ནས, from good men.

§ 202. When the adjectives precede their nouns they are invariable in all cases, and stand either without any article, or in the genitive form; as, དམ་ཆོས or དམ་པའི་ཆོས, holy religion; སྐམ་ས, dry land, the continent; སྐམ་སར་སྐྱེབ་པར, to arrive at dry land (to reach the continent, or to land).

§ 203. Numerals, both cardinal and ordinal, like adjectives, are put always after the substantives with which they are connected; as, ལོ་གཅིག, one year; ལེའུ་བཅུ་པ, the tenth chapter.

§ 204. Cardinals, expressive of any great quantity, require, in general, that the preceding noun be in the singular; as, མི་བཅུ, ten men; ལོ་བརྒྱ, a hundred years; དམག་མི་སྟོང་ཕྲག་བརྒྱ, a hundred thousand soldiers, (or warriors;) གྲོང་ཁྲི་ཚོ་གཅིག, a myriad of dwelling places or houses; གྲོང་ཁྱེར་འབུམ་ཕྲག, a hundred thousand towns, (or cities;) སྡོང་མི་ས་ཡ, a million of inhabitants, &c. &c.

§ 205. To facilitate the formation of sentences, and the distinction of the subject and the predicate in them, here follow some questions (together with answers to them) made by the interrogative pronouns, སུ and སུས, who? and by whom? གང, which? whether? གང་གིས, by which? by whom? ཅི, what? ཅིས or ཅི་ཡིས, by or with what? The answer must conform with the question in the repetition of the postpositions, &c.

§ 206. སུ, who? དཀོན་མཆོག, God; སངས་རྒྱས, Buddha; རྒྱལ་པོ, the king; བླ་མ, the chief priest; བློན་པོ་རྣམས, the ministers or officers; འབངས་ཐམས་ཅད, all the people or subjects.

§ 207. འདི་སུས་མཛད (བཟོས or བྱས), by whom is made this? or who has made this?

དེ་དཀོན་མཆོག་གིས་མཛད, it is made by God, or God has made it.

དེ་སངས་རྒྱས་ཀྱིས་མཛད, it is made by Buddha, or Buddha has made it.

དེ་རྒྱལ་པོས་མཛད, it is made by the king, or the king has made it.

དེ་བླ་མས་མཛད, it is made by the cheif priest, or the cheif priest has made it.

དེ་བློན་པོ་རྣམས་ཀྱིས་བཟོས, it is made by the ministers, or the ministers have made it.

དེ་འབངས་ཐམས་ཅད་ཀྱིས་བྱས, it is made by all the people, or all the people have made it.

§ 208. གང་ or གང་ཞིག, which? whether? who? (quis? uter? quisnam?) གང་དག, plural, who?

འདི, this; འདི་ནི, this here; འདི་དག, these; འདི་དག་ནི, these here.

དེ, that; དེ་ནི, that there; དེ་དག, those; དེ་དག་ནི, those there; ཨ་གི, this here; ཕ་གི, that there. ཚུ་གི་དག, these here (on this side); ཕ་གི་དག, those there (on the other side). གང་, གང་ཞིག, whether? or which of two or of more?

ཆེ་བ, the greater one, or the elder; ཆུང་བ, the little one or the younger.

མཐོ་བ, the high or higher; དམའ་བ, the low or lower.

ལྕི་བ, the heavy; ཡང་བ, the light.

དཀར་བ, the white; ནག་པ, the black.

ཕྱུག་པ, the rich; དབུལ་བ, the poor.

འཛངས་པ, the wise; བླུན་པ, the fool.

གཡས་པ, the right, (hand or side;) གཡོན་པ, the left, (hand or side.)

§ 209. འདི་གང་གིས་བྲིས-སོ, by which, or by whom, is this written; or who wrote this?

དེ་བདག་གིས་བྲིས-སོ, } it is written by me.
— ངས, — — } or I wrote it.
— ཁོ་བོས, — — ditto.
— འདིས, — — this wrote it.
— དེས, — — that ditto.
— ཡིག་མཁན.གྱིས, — — it is written by the clerk.
or དེ་ཡི་གེ་པས, — — or, the writer wrote it.

§ 210. དེ་ཅི་འཙམ or ཅི་ཡིན, what is it? དེ་རྣམས་ཅི་དག་ཡིན, what are they or those?

དཔེ་ཆ་ཞིག, a book; ལུག་ཅིག, a sheep; གོས་དཀར་པོ་ཞིག, a white garment; ཡོས་ཤིག or རི་བོང་ཞིག, a hare; ཞྭ་མོ་ཞིག, a cap or hat; འདི་དག་ནི་དམག་མི་དག་ཡིན་ནོ, these are soldiers (or warriors).

དེ་ན་ཅི་ཡོད, what is there? སངས་རྒྱས་ཀྱི་ཞབས་རྗེས, the foot step, (or the impression of the foot step) of Buddha; གསེར་ཡིག་གིས་བྲིས་པའི་གླེགས་བམ་ཞིག, a volume written in golden character; དཔེ་ཆ་པར་མ་ཞིག, a printed book; དམག་གི་ལག་ཆ་དག་མོ or དམག་ཆས་རྣམས་སོ, there are warlike instruments.

§ 211. Examples of the agentive and instrumentive cases being used in the same sentence ; as, ཁོང་གིས, ལག་པས, by him, with the hand, or he with ditto ; ཁོང་གིས་ཁྱོད་ཅིས་ (or ཅི་ཡིས) བརྡུངས, with what has he beaten thee ? (or with what thing has thou been beaten by him ?)

ཁོང་གིས་ང་ལག་པས་བརྡུངས, he beat me with the hand.
— — — — པའི་རྒྱབ་ཀྱིས —, he beat me with the back of the hand.
— — — དབྱུག་པས —, he beat me with a stick.
— — — ལྕུག་མས —, he beat me with a rod.
— — — ཤིང་གི་ཐོ་བས —, he beat me with a wooden hammer.

§ 212. འཇིག་རྟེན་འདི་ཅིས (or ཅི་ཡིས) འཇིག or འཇིག་པར་བྱེད (or འཇིག་པར་འགྱུར), by what is (or will be) this world destroyed ; མེས or མེ་ཡིས, by fire ; ཆུས or ཆུ་ཡིས, by water ; རླུང་གིས, by wind ; རྒྱུ་དང་རྐྱེན་སྣ་ཚོགས་ཀྱིས, by all sorts of efficient causes.

§ 213. འདི་སུའི (or སུ་ཡི) ཡིན, whose is this ? དཀོན་མཆོག་གི, God's ; སངས་རྒྱས་ཀྱི, Buddha's ; རྒྱལ་པོའི, the king's ; བླ་མའི, the chief priest's or high priest's ; བློན་པོ་རྣམས་ཀྱི, the minister's or officer's ; ཡུལ་མི་དག་གི, the villagers' ; པཎ་ཆེན་གྱི, the great Lama's of Teshi-lunpo ; (བཀྲ་ཤིས་ལྷུན་པོ) རྒྱ་ནག་གོང་མ་ཆེན་པོའི, the Chinese Emperor's.

§ 214. སུའི་ཕྱིར, (-ཆེད་དུ-དོན་དུ-སླད་དུ,) on whose account ? in whose behalf ? for whom ? དཀོན་མཆོག་གི་ཕྱིར (or ཕྱིར་དུ, ཆེད or ཆེད་དུ, དོན or དོན་དུ, སླད or སླད་དུ,) for God's sake, on account of God, &c. &c., (add ཆེད་དུ in the same manner to each of the genitive or possessive cases in § 213 so far as ; རྒྱ་ནག་གོང་མ་ཆེན་པོའི ཆེད་དུ, on account of, for, in behalf of the Chinese Emperor.)

§ 215. སུ་ལ, to whom ; དཀོན་མཆོག་ལ, to God ; སངས་རྒྱས་ལ, to Buddha ; རྒྱལ་པོ་ལ, to the king ; བླ་མ་ལ, to the chief priest ; བློན་པོ་རྣམས་ལ, to the ministers or officers ; གྲོང་མི་རྣམས་ལ, to the citizens.

§ 216. དེ་ཅིར (for ཅི་རུ) འགྱུར, into what will that be changed or turned ? or, what will (or shall) that become ? དཀོན་མཆོག་ཏུ, into God ; ཁོང་སངས་རྒྱས་སུ་འགྱུར, he will become (or turn into) a Buddha ; ལྷར—(for ལྷ་རུ) ditto a God ; རྒྱལ་པོར་འགྱུར, he shall become a king ; བླ་མར,—into a Lama or a Lama ; མིར—(for མི་རུ), into a man, or a man.

§ 217. སུ་ནས or སུ་ལས, of whom ? from whom ?

དཀོན་མཆོག་ནས, } of or from God.
or — — ལས, }

སངས་རྒྱས་ནས,
or —— ལས, } of or from BUDDHA.

རྒྱལ་པོ་ནས,
or —— ལས, } of or from the king.

ཕྱོགས་ཐམས་ཅད་ནས, from all quarters.

མི་ཀུན་ལས, from all men.

§ 118. The expressions formed in English, by the auxiliary verb 'to have' and to have not, (or not to have) are rendered here by the substantive verb ཡོད 'to be' (to one) and མེད not to be; as:

སུ་ལ་ཡོད, to whom is? or who has?

དཀོན་མཆོག་ལ་ཡོན་ཏན་ཐམས་ཅད་ཡོད, (to GOD are, &c.) or GOD has all good qualities or perfections.

སངས་རྒྱས་ལ་སྐྱོན་ཅི་ཡང་མེད, (there is no defect, &c.) BUDDHA has no defects, or is without imperfections.

རྒྱལ་པོ་ལ་ནོར་ཡོད, the king has riches.

བླ་མ་ལ་ཆོས་ཀྱི་རྒྱལ་སྲིད་ཡོད, the high priest (or LAMA) has spiritual dominion.

བློན་པོ་རྣམས་ལ་དབང་ཡོད, the ministers (officers or magistrates) have power or authority.

ཡུལ་མི་རྣམས་ལ་བྱ་བ་མང་པོ་འདུག, the country people have much to do.

§ 219. The use of the correlative pronouns གང—དེ (གང་ལ—དེ་ལ, to whom—to him, or who—to him.)

" གང་ལ་ཡོན་ཏན་མཆོག་མངའ་བ།
སངས་རྒྱས་དེ་ལ་ཕྱག་འཚལ་ལོ།།"

" I pay homage to that BUDDHA,
Who has the chief perfection."
(or salutation to the Supreme Intelligence).

§ 220. Since there is no variation in verbs, with respect to person and number; these are determined by the preceding subject, consisting of a pronoun, noun or proper name; as, ང་, I; ཁྱོད, thou; ཁོ, he, she; ང་ཅག, we; ཁྱོད་ཅག, ye; ཁོ་ཅག, they, འགྲོ, going: for, I go, thou goest, he goes, we go, ye go, they go.

དེ་སུས་ཁྱོང་, by whom has it been brought? or who brought it?

མི་འདི་དག་གིས་ཁྱོང, by these men has it been brought, or these men brought it.

དེ་ངེད་ཀྱིས་བཀླགས་སོ, I have perused (read over) it.

དེ་ཁྱེད,ཀྱིས — —, you (thou hast) have ditto.

དེ་ཁོང་གིས — —, he has perused it, (or it has been read over by me, thee, and him.)

དེ་དག་ངེད་རྣམས་ཀྱིས་བཀླགས་སོ, we have perused those (read over).

དེ་དག་ཁྱེད་རྣམས་ཀྱིས — —, you have ditto.

དེ་དག་ཁོང་རྣམས་ཀྱིས — —, they have ditto, (or they have been read over by us, you and them.)

བཅོམ་ལྡན་འདས་ཀྱིས་བཀའ་སྩལ་པ, Bhagavan commanded or said.

སངས་རྒྱས་རྣམས་ཀྱིས་བཀའསྩལ་པ, the Buddhas commanded or said.

ཀུན་དགའ་བོས་གསོལ་པ, Ananda begged, (or asked, requested.)

ཉན་ཐོས་རྣམས་ཀྱིས་གསོལ་པ, the hearers *(shrávakas)* begged (requested or asked).

§ 221. The objective is the same with the nominative in Tibetan, and this case is used before neuter and intransitive verbs, even when it denotes the object of action; as, ང་འགྲོའོ, I go; དེ་ཅི་ཡིན, what is that; རྒྱལ་པོ་ག་ན་བཞུགས, where is the king? ཁོ་གཉིད་མ་ལོག, he has not slept; ཁྱོད་ཅི་བྱེད་འདུག, what art thou doing? ཁྱེད་ནམ་ཕེབས, when are you come, (or arrived)? ཉི་མ་ཤར་སོང་ or ཤར་ཆེར, the sun has arisen; ཟླ་བ་ནུབ་སོང་, the moon has set; ཁོ་རྡུང་བར་བྱེད, he is beaten; འཇིག་རྟེན་འཇིག་པར་བྱེད, the world is destroyed.

§ 222. The case denoting the agent, by whom, or the instrument with which, any action is produced, is called the instrumentive. This case occurs very frequently, since it is used both before active and passive verbs, or before every verb denoting a transitive action on an object or person. In the languages of Europe, it may be rendered properly by the subjective or nominative case, and by the preposition 'with' or 'by' (when any instrument, manner, or way of action is to be expressed); and in the passive form or voice, with the particle 'by'; as, དེ་བདག་གིས་རང་གི་ལག་པས་བྲིས, I wrote it with my own hand, or it is written by me; རྒྱལ་པོ་ཀུན་གྱིསབཀུར or བཀུར་བར་བྱེད, the king is respected by all, or, all do respect the king.

ཆོས་འདི་སངས་རྒྱས་ཀྱིས་གསུངས་སོ, གསུང་ངོ་, གསུང་བར་འགྱུར་རོ།། this doctrine has been, is, and will be taught (commanded) by Buddha; or, Buddha has taught, is teaching, and will teach this doctrine.

PROSODY.

§ 223. In Tibetan, verse differs little from prose; since there is no distinction of vowels into short and long, accented and emphatical; consequently there are no poetical feet measured by short and long syllables. All poetical compositions are in a sort of blank verse (rhyme not being in use, except in some few instances) differing from each other (or from one another) only in the number of syllables.

Although several poetical works, (as, the "*Kavyádarsha,*" by DANDI,) have been translated by the Tibetans, they have not adopted the metrical feet used in Sanskrit versification.

§ 224. The several poetical pieces (or verses) occurring in the KAH-GYUR and STAN-GYUR, and in other works derived from India, have been rendered by the Tibetans, in blank verses, consisting, generally, of four lines each of seven syllables. But in the invocations and benedictions, at the beginning and end of some treatises or works, a few verses or stanzas of four lines, are sometimes introduced, consisting each of 9, 11, 13 or more syllables.

§ 225. By adopting the mythological and religious systems of the Brahmanists and Buddhists of India, the Tibetans have indeed formed a copious poetical language; borrowing many epithets and mythological embellishments from those sources. But since their verses are free from the fetters of rhyme and metre, all the poetical pieces in Tibetan, originals or translations, may be read with as much ease, as if they had been written in prose.

LIST OF VERBS.

§ 226. *Note.* The པ, *pa*, and བ, *va*, terminations are used with this difference, that the པ is put after the following final letters of the verbal root; viz. ག་ད་ན་བ་མ་ས, and the བ after ང་འ ར་ལ (or after any vowel). The verbs in the following list, as they now stand with the པ and བ terminations, are properly participial or verbal nouns. In the infinitive the terminations would be པར, *par*, and བར, *var*, which likewise frequently occur in this language; but, since the participial form is more consistent with the Tibetan practice, they have been so expressed in the following list, in that language; while the English meaning is given in the infinitive.

Alphabetical List of Tibetan Verbs:

ཀླག་པ, *v. a.* to read, peruse ; *v.* བཀླག་པ.

ཀླན་ཀ་བྱེད་པ or ཀླན་ཀ་འཚོལ་བ, *v. a.* to censure, blame.

ཀླན་པ, *v. a.* to mend, patch.

ཀློག་པ, *v. a.* to read ; *v.* ཀླག་པ.

ཀློན་པ, *v. a.* to mend, patch shoes, &c.; *v.* ཀླན་པ.

ཁ་གཅོད་པ, *v. a.* to cover (the mouth of a vessel, &c.)

ཁ་གསག་བྱེད་པ, *v. a.* to flatter.

ཁ་ཙང་བྱེད་པ, *v. a.* to give fair words.

ཁ་ཟེར་བ, *v. a.* to abuse by ill words.

ཁ་ཧོན་བྱེད་པ, *v. a.* to say, utter, repeat with a loud voice.

ཁ་དབྲི་བ, *v. a.* to subtract, diminish.

ཁ་འབབ་པ, *v. n.* to snow, to fall (as snow).

ཁ་འབུ་བ, *v. n.* to open, blow (as a flower).

ཁ་འགྱུར་བ, *v. n.* to change in colour.

ཁ་འབྱེ་བ, *v. n.* to open, to blow (as a flower).

ཁ་འབྱེད་པ, *v. a.* to open his, &c. mouth.

ཁ་རོག་པ, *v. n.* to be still, silent, not to speak.

ཁ་རོག་ཏེ་འདུག་པ, *v. n.* to sit still, to hold his peace.

ཁ་ཕྱད་བྱེད་པ, *v. a.* to boast, brag, glory in.

ཁ་སྒྱུར་བ, *v. a.* to change the colour of, &c.

ཁྱབ་པ, *v. a.* to encompass, pervade, comprehend, include ; to conceive.

གང་བ or གང་ཡིན་པ, *v. n.* to be full or replete.

གང་བར་བྱེད་པ, *v. a.* to make full, to fill.

གང་བར་འགྱུར་བ, *v. n.* to become full.

གབ་པ, *v. n.* to abscond.

གར་བྱེད་པ, *v. a.* to dance.

གོ་བ, *v. a.* to perceive, understand.

གོན་པ, *v. a.* to put on, wear.

གྱོན་པ, *v. a.* ditto.

གྱལ་བ, *v. n.* to yawn, to gape.

གླེང་བ, *v. n.* to discourse, talk.

གླེབ་པ, *v. a.* to make flat, level.

གློད་པ, *v. a.* to loose, relax, slacken.

གཅག་པ, *v. a.* to conceive, mind, fix in the mind.

གཅད་པ, *v. n.* to cut off.

གཅལ་བ, *v. a.* to scatter, spread, put asunder.

གཅི་བ, *v.* to make water.

གཅུ་བ, *v. a.* to twist, wreath, wind.

གཅུན་པ, *v. a.* to make soft, pliant, tame.

གཅུར་བ, *v. a.* to compress, include, bring one to an extremity.

གཅེར་ཉལ་བ, *v. n.* to lie naked.

གཅོག་པ, *v. a.* to break, to break asunder, off.

གཅོད་པ, *v. a.* to cut ; v. གཅད་པ.

གཅོར་བ, *v. a.* to spread, scatter, disperse.

གཉུལ་བ, *v. a.* to examine, explore, spy.

གཉེར་བ, *v. a.* to get, acquire, procure, provide.

གཉོག་པ, *v.* to desire, wish earnestly, strive, endeavour.

གཏང་བ, *v. a.* to give over, to bestow on ; v. གཏོང་བ.

གཏང་རག་བྱེད་པ, *v. a.* to give thanks ; to remunerate.

གཏང་རག་འབུལ་བ, *v. a.* ditto.

གཏད་པ, *v. a.* to give to, intrust, commit to; v. གཏོད་པ.

གཏར་བ, *v. a.* to bleed, to let blood.

གཏིག་པ, *v. n.* to drop, drip, fall in drops.

གཏིབ་པ, *v. n.* to be overcast with.

གཏུག་པ, *v. a.* to touch, reach to, join, meet.

གཏུབ་པ, *v. a.* to cut into small pieces.

གཏུལ་བ, *v. a.* to reduce into powder, to grind.

གཏོག་པ, *v. a.* to make a noise with the fingers.

གཏོགས་པ, *v. n.* to belong, appertain to, to be taken to.

གཏོང་བ, *v. a.* to give, yield, bestow, grant; v. གཏང་བ.

གཏོང་ཏུ་འཇུག་པ, *v. c.* to cause to give.

གཏོང་བར་ནུས་པ, to be able to give.

གཏོང་བར་མི་ནུས་པ, not to be able to give.

གཏོང་བར་བྱེད་པ, the act of giving, or the state of being given.

གཏོད་པ, *v. a.* to give, commit, entrust to; v. གཏད་པ.

གཏོར་བ, *v. a.* scatter, spread, disseminate; v. འཐོར་བ.

གདགས་པ, *v. a.* to tie, bind, fasten, compose; v. འདོགས་པ.

གདང་བ, *v. a.* to open wide, to menace.

གདབ་པ *v. a.* to cast, spread, scatter; make; v. འདེབས་པ.

གདམས་པ, *v. a.* to advise, counsel.

གདའ་བ, *v. n.* to be, to be found.

གདིང་བ, *v.a.* to spread on the ground; v. འདིང་བ.

གདུ་བ, *v. a.* to gather together; v. སྡུ་བ། འདུ་བ.

གདུལ་བ, *v. a.* to make tame, break, subdue, to discipline, educate; v. འདུལ་བ.

གདེག་པ, *v. a.* to lift, hold, take up, to weigh; v. འདེགས་པ.

གདོན་པ, *v. a.* to utter, say, tell with a loud voice; v. འདོན་པ.

གནང་བ, *v. a.* to allow, grant; yield, permit.

གནས་པ, *v. n.* to dwell, abide; be, continue.

གནོང་བ, *v. n.* to be ashamed.

གནོད་པ, *v. a.* to hurt, to do harm to.

གནོན་པ, *v. a.* to depress, humble, deject; surpass; v. ནོན་པ.

གཙག་པ, *v. a.* to strain, filter; let out blood; v. འཚག་པ། འཛག་པ.

གཙུབ་པ, *v. a.* ro rub together.

གཙེ་བ, *v. a.* to hurt, to do harm to; v. འཚེ་བ.

གཙེར་བ, *v. a.* to injure, hurt, do wrong to.

གཞག་པ, *v. a.* to lay, place, put; v. འཇོག་པ.

གཞལ་བ, *v. a.* to weigh, measure; pay, repay; v. འཇལ་བ.

གཞིག་པ, *v. a.* to try, prove, examine; to be ruined; v. འཇིག་པ.

གཞིབ་པ, *v. a.* to suck out; v. འཇིབ་པ.

གཞིབས་པ, *v. a.* to put, place in order, to arrange.

གཞིལ་བ, *v. a.* to overpower, subdue, conquer; v. འཇིལ་བ.

གཞུ་བ, *v. a.* to smite, beat.

གཞུག་པ, *v. a.* to lay, put; shut; v. འཇུག་པ.

གཞུང་བ, *v. n.* to attend, be heedful.

གཅུར་བ, *v. a.* to cut away the branches and leaves, to prune, lop trees.

གཞེས་པ, *v. n.* to sit, be, exist.

གཞོག་པ, *v. a.* to cut, hew, chop ; v. འཇོག་པ.

གཞོམ་པ, *v. a.* to subdue, vanquish, conquer, (entirely ;) v. འཇོམས་པ.

གཞོལ་བ, *v. a.* to apply himself earnestly to a thing.

གཟག་པ, *v. a.* to strain, percolate ; v. གཙོག་པ.

གཟན་པ, *v. n.* to eat up, to eat ; feed on.

གཟར་བ, *v. a.* to lay, put on.

གཟས་པ, *v. a.* to begin, to have intention to do.

གཟིགས་པ, *v. a.* to look on, see, view, regard, behold.

གཟིམ་པ, *v. n.* to go to bed, to sleep.

གཟིར་བ, *v. a.* to press, squeeze, to crush, &c. ; v. འཛིར་བ.

གཟུག་པ, *v. n.* to ache, to be in pain.

གཟུགས་པ, *v. a.* to set, place, fix, plant, fix thoroughly ; v. འཛུག་པ, also བཙུག་པ.

གཟུང་བ, *v. a.* to seize, take, hold fast, conceive, comprehend ; v. འཛིན་པ། བཟུང་བ.

གཟུད་པ, *v. a.* to turn, convert to, make to enter into ; v. འཛུད་པ.

གཟུམ་པ, *v. a.* to shut, close entirely ; v. འཛུམ་པ.

གཟུར་བ, *v. a.* to turn out of one's way, to go aside (not to meet, &c.) ; v. འཛུར་བ.

གཟུལ་བ, *v. n.* to creep or enter in an inclined posture ; v. འཛུལ་བ.

གཟེད་པ, *v. a.* to keep, hold ; put, lay on ; v. འཛེད་པ.

གཟེམ་པ, *v. n.* to be ashamed, to be in confusion ; v. འཛེམ་པ.

གཟེར་བ, *v. n.* to ache, to be in continued pain.

གཟོ་བ, *v. a.* to own, to acknowledge.

གཟོན་པ, *v. n.* to be spent in vain.

གཡར་བ, *v. a.* to borrow any thing ; to adopt.

གཡལ་བ, *v. n.* to yawn, gape.

གཡིག་པ, *v. n.* to be hindered, stopped.

གཡུར་བ, *v. n.* to bend, to bow down.

གཡེང་བ, *v. n.* to fluctuate, be unsteady, be agitated ; to be inattentive.

གཡེམ་པ, *v.* to practise fornication.

གཡེལ་བ, *v. n.* to be negligent, idle ; *v. a.* to forget.

གཡོ་བ, *v. n.* to be agitated, moved, shaken ; *v. a.* to dress.

གཡོག་པ, *v.* to cover ; shelter.

གཡོབ་པ, *v. a.* to wave, shake, brandish, turn, fan.

གཡོར་བ, *v. a.* to cover, offuscate, darken.

གཡོས་པ, *v. a.* to bake ; dress victuals.

གཤག་པ, *v. a.* to split, cleave ; confess.

གཤད་པ for བཤད་པ, *v. a.* to unfold, explain ; tell.

གཤིབས་པ, *v. n.* to sit in order, series.

གཤུང་བ, *v. a.* to chide, rebuke, reprehend.

གཤེ་བ, *v. n.* to abuse, revile, speak ill.

གཤེག་པ, (v. གཤག་པ) *v. a.* to split, cleave ; confess.

གཤེགས་པ, *v. n.* to go, walk stately ; to die.

གཤེར་བ, *v. a.* to ask, beg.

གཤོ་བ, *v. a.* to pour out, shed, diffuse.

གཤོག་པ, *v. a.* to split, cleave, divide; v. གཤག་པ.

གཤོད་པ, *v. a.* to unfold, dress, comb; v. གཤད་པ.

གཤན་པ, *v. a.* to put on or upon.

གཤོམ་པ, *v. a.* to prepare, make ready.

གཤོར་བ, *v. a.* to measure; to let go one after another; to chase, hunt.

གསང་བ, to conceal, hide, keep secret.

གསད་པ, *v. a.* to kill, slay, murder.

གསན་པ, *v. a.* to hear fully, to hearken to.

གསབ་པ, *v. a.* to return a kindness; to repay.

གསིག་པ, *v. a.* to cast or fling back, up.

གསིལ་བ, *v. a.* to toll, sound, ring; split, divide.

གསུང་བ, *v. a.* to command, order, bid.

གསེ་བ or **གསེད་པ**, *v. a.* to pick, cleanse, put asunder.

གསོ་བ, *v. a.* to repair, mend; cure, heal; feed, bring up.

གསོག་པ, *v. a.* to collect, gather together, heap up, make ready.

གསོང་བ, *v, a.* to conceal, hide, keep secret; v. གསང་བ.

གསོད་པ, *v. a.* to kill, slay, murder, destroy; v. གསད་པ.

གསོབ་པ, *v. a.* to repay a kindness, repay; v. གསབ་པ.

གསོར་བ, *v. a.* to turn, brandish, (in one's hand.)

གསོལ་བ, *v. a.* to pray, entreat, beg, petition; to take of meat and drink; to put on a garment, &c.

ངལ་བ, *v. n.* to be weary, fatigued.

ངུ་བ, *v. n.* to weep, lament.

ངུ་འབོད་པ, *v. n.* to weep and sob, to weep with convulsive sighs.

ངུར་བ, *v. n.* to grunt, to make a grumbling noise.

ངོ་ཤེས་པ, *v. a.* to know, to be acquainted with.

ཅང་ཤེས་པ, *v. a.* to know every thing.

ཆགས་པ, *v. n.* to be conceived, to be originated.

ཆས་པ, *v. n.* to begin, intend, go.

ཉན་པ, *v. a.* to hear, hearken to.

ཉལ་བ, *v. n.* to lie down, to sleep.

ཉིལ་བ, *v. n.* to fall or break down.

ཉུག་པ, *v.* to feel, touch, handle, search after.

ཉུལ་བ, *v. n.* to creep, move slowly; *v. a.* spy, observe.

ཉེ་བར་འགྲོ་བ, *v. n.* to approach, go near to.

ཉེད་པ, *v. a.* to soften, mollify, make soft; v. མཉེ་བ། མཉེད་པ.

ཉོ་བ, *v. a.* to buy, purchase.

ཏོན་བྱེད་པ, *v. a.* to endeavour, be diligent.

ཐུག་པ, *v.* to reach, go, come, to.

ཐོབ་པ, *v. a.* to find, get; discover; v. འཐོབ་པ.

ཐོས་པ, *v. a.* to hear, to be informed or have notice of.

དྲང་བ, *v. a.* to draw, cite, quote; invite; v. འདྲེན་པ.

དྲན་པ, *v. n.* to remember, have in memory; *v. a.* to recollect.

དྲན་པར་བྱེད་པ, *v. a.* to bring or put into one's memory, or notice.

དཀྱུ་བ, *v. a.* to run a race; to run a horse.

དཀྲི་བ, *v. a.* to wrap round about, wind.

དཀྲུག་པ, *v. a.* to trouble, stir, shake, move up and down; coagulate, curdle; to churn.

དཀྲོག་པ, *v. a.* coagulate, curdle; to churn.

དཀྲོལ་བ, *v. a.* to play on a musical instrument.

དགག་པ, *v. a.* to stop, hinder, preclude, prohibit; v. འགེགས་པ.

དགང་བ, *v. a.* to fill entirely, replenish, make full; v. འགེངས་པ.

དགབ་པ, *v. a.* to cover; overspread; v. འགེབས་པ.

དགར་བ, *v. a.* to separate, seclude, fold up.

དགལ་བ, *v. a.* to load, put a load on; v. འགེལ་བ.

དགས་པ, *v. a.* to tear, rend, cleave, divide; v. འགེས་པ.

དགུམ་པ, *v. a.* to kill, destroy, murder, extinguish; v. འགེམ or འགེམས་པ.

དགོངས་པ, *v. a.* to think on, remember, be merciful to.

དགོད་པ, *v. n.* to laugh, smile; *v. a.* to build, frame, prepare; v. འགོད་པ.

དགོས་པ, *v. n.* to want, to be necessary.

དགྱེ་བ, *v. n.* to sit in a reclined posture.

དགྱེས་པ, *v. n.* to be merry or glad.

དགྲམ་པ, *v. a.* to scatter, spread; v. འགྲེམ་པ.

དགྲོང་བ, *v. a.* to kill, murder, destroy; v. འགྲོངས་པ.

དགྲོལ་བ, *v. a.* to unfold, untie, explain; v. འགྲོལ་བ། འགྲེལ་བ.

དངག་པ or དངགས་པ, *v. a.* to commend, praise.

དངང་བ, *v. n.* to be terrified, afraid.

དཔག་པ, *v. a.* to weigh, ponder (mentally), measure, mete; v. དཔོག་པ.

དཔར་བ, *v. a.* to dictate, say or tell what to write.

དཔོག་པ, *v. a.* to weigh, measure, &c.; v. དཔག་པ

དཔོར་བ, *v. a.* to dictate, &c.; v. དཔར་བ.

དཔྱང་བ, *v. a.* to hang, suspend; v. དཔྱོང་བ.

དཔྱད་པ, *v. a.* to examine, prove, try, essay; v. དཔྱོད་པ.

དཔྱོང་བ, *v. a.* v. དཔྱང་བ.

དཔྱོད་པ, *v. a.* v. དཔྱད་པ.

དབག་པ, *v. a.* to maculate, stain, spot.

དབབ་པ, *v. a.* to let down, to put in order, arrange; v. འབེབས་པ.

དབུག་པ, *v. a.* to bore or pierce through; v. འབུགས་པ.

དབུབ་པ, *v. a.* to extend, dilate, expand, cover, fix; v. འབུབས་པ.

འབུར་བ, *v. a.* to make smooth or even.

དབུལ་བ, *v. a.* to offer, present, give; v. འབུལ་བ.

དབོ་བ, *v. a.* to pour out, empty; v. འབོ་བ.

དབོག་པ, *v. a.* to give, bestow, transfer, impart, communicate; to maculate, stain; v. དབག་པ.

དབོལ་བ (for བཙོལ་བ,) *v. a.* to squeeze, force out.

དབྲི་བ, *v. a.* to blot out, efface; v. འབྲི་བ.

དབྱུག་པ, *v. a.* to brandish, wave, wag, move.

དབྱེ་བ, *v. a.* to divide, separate, open; v. འབྱེད་པ.

དབྲལ་བ, *v. a.* to separate, force, or put asunder; v. འབྲལ་བ.

དབྲི་བ, *v. a.* to diminish, subtract, lessen; v. འབྲི་བ.

དབྲོག་པ, *v. a.* to take or carry away by force; v. འབྲོག་པ.

དཟུལ་བ, *v. n.* to smile.

དམེ་བ, *v. a.* to defile, pollute.

དམོད་པ, *v. a.* to abuse, curse, censure.

དཛུལ་བ or དཛུལ་བར་བྱེད་པ, *v. a.* to grind, reduce to fine powder.

དཛུག་པ, *v. a.* to show, or point at.

ན་བ, *v. a.* to be sick.

ནུ་བ, *v. a.* to suck, draw milk from the breast.

ནུད་པ, *v. a.* to suckle, nurse.

ནུབ་པ, *v. n.* to set, sink, decline, decay.

ནུར་བ, *v. n.* to approach, draw near to.

ནུས་པ, *v. a.* to can, to be able to do.

ནེར་བ, *v. n.* to sink down.

ནོང་བ, *v. n.* to commit a fault, be faulty.

ནོད་པ, *v. a.* to perceive, take, receive.

ནོན་པ, *v. a.* to depress, humble, surpass, outdo; v. གནོན་པ and མནན་པ.

ནོམ་པ, *v. n.* to be satisfied or content with.

ནོར་བ, *v. n.* to err, mistake, or to be mistaken.

ནོལ་བ, *v. n.* to agree, meet.

ཕམ་པ, *v. n.* to be defeated, to lose the field, not to win, to fail.

ཕེབ་པ, *v. n.* to come to, arrive at, a place.

ཕེར་བ, *v. n.* to be proper, fit, decent, becoming.

ཕོད་པ, *v. n.* to dare, be bold, have courage, be audacious.

ཕྱིན་པ, *v. n.* to go, walk, travel, arrive at.

ཕྱོགས་པ, *v. n.* to turn to or towards.

ཕྲག་པ, *v.* to envy, to impart unwillingly.

ཕྲད་པ, *v.* to meet, join, encounter, find.

བྱུག་པ, *v. n.* to flow.

བྱེད་པ, *v. a.* to do, make, act, perform.

བླང་བ, *v. a.* to take, receive, accept; v. ལེན་པ.

བླད་པ, *v. a.* to chew, grind with the teeth.

བླུ་བ, *v. a.* to ransom, redeem.

བླུག་པ, *v. a.* to pour into.

བླུད་པ, *v. a.* to make or cause to drink.

བཀག་པ, *part. pret.* of འགེགས་པ, to hinder, prohibit, &c.

བཀང་བ, *part. pret.* of འགེངས་པ, to fill, make full.

བཀན་པ, *v. a.* to hold fast, to extend.

བཀབ་པ, *part. pret.* of འགེབས་པ, to cover, spread over.

བཀར་བ, to be separated, selected; banished

བཀལ་བ, to be laden, to spin.

བཀས་པ, to be split, rent, cleft.

བཀུག་པ, to be drawn down; to be called, summoned, gathered together.

བཀུམ་པ, *pret. pass.* of འགུམས་པ, to destroy, kill, cut off.

བཀུར་བ, *v. a.* to carry, convey, to respect, reverence, honour.

བཀོག་པ, *part. pass.* of འགོག་པ, to pull, pluck, draw violently.

བཀོང་བ, *part. pass.* of འཁོང་བ, to frighten.

བཀོད་པ, *part. pass.* or *pret.* to build, make, frame, fabricate; bring to.

བཀོན་པ, *v. n.* to be angry with.

བཀོལ་བ, *v. a.* to spare, not to use much.

བཀྱལ་བ, *v. n.* to talk nonsense.

བཀྱིག་བ, *v. a.* to bind, tie; to bind hand and foot; v. འཁྱིག་པ.

བཀྱེ་བ, *v. a.* to spread, diffuse, scatter.

བཀྱེད་པ, *v. a.* to extend, widen.

བཀྱོན་པ, *v. a.* to reprove, rebuke.

བཀྲབ་པ, *v. a.* to select, choose.

བཀྲམ་པ, *part. pret.* of འཁྲེམ་པ, to scatter, diffuse, show, display.

བཀྲལ་བ, *part. pret.* of འཁྲེལ་བ, to unfold, explain, explicate.

བཀྲི་བ, *v. a.* to conduct, guide; v. འཁྲིད་པ.

བཀྲུ་བ, *v. a.* to wash clean, to cleanse; v. འཁྲུད་པ.

བཀྲེན་པ, *v. n.* to be indigent, poor, hungry.

བཀྲོལ་བ, *part. pret.* of འཁྲེལ་བ or འཁྲོལ་བ, to untie, unfold, explain.

བཀླག་པ, *v. a.* to read over, peruse; v. ཀླག་པ། ཀློག་པ.

བརྐམ་པ, *v. a.* to desire earnestly, to long for.

བརྐུ་བ, *v. a.* to steal away; v. རྐུ་བ.

བརྐོ་བ, *v. a.* to dig up or out; v. རྐོ་བ.

བརྐྱང་བ, *v. a.* to stretch out, extend.

བསྐང་བ, *v. a.* to fulfil, accomplish, make up, satiate, satisfy, content, perform.

བསྐམ་པ, to be made dry.

བསྐར་བ, *v. a.* to separate, fold up.

བསྐུ་བ, *v. a.* to besmear, bedaub, anoint.

བསྐུང་བ, *v. a.* to hide, conceal.

བསྐུམ་པ, *v. a.* to contract, shrink up.

བསྐུར་བ, *v. a.* to send, dispatch, bestow, give.

བསྐུལ་བ, *v. a.* to exhort, incite, bid.

བསྐོ་བ, *v. a.* to choose, elect.

བསྐོན་པ, *v. a.* to put on (as a garment).

བསྐོར་བ, *v. a.* to encircle, surround; to make turn round; v. སྐོར་བ.

བསྐོལ་བ, *v. a.* to make boil, to boil; v. སྐོལ་བ.

བསྐྱ་བ, *v. a.* to carry, convey, take away.

བསྐྱག་པ, *v. a.* to spend all.

བསྐྱང་བ, *v. a.* to protect, defend, keep safe; v. སྐྱོང་བ.

བསྐྱད་པ, *v. a.* to measure out.

བསྐྱབ་པ, *v. a.* to protect, defend; v. སྐྱོབ་པ.

བསྐྱམ་པ, *v. a.* to stir, move, shake up; v. སྐྱོམ་པ

བསྐྱར་བ, *v. a.* to repeat, add to; keep or hold up; v. སྐྱོར་བ.

བསྐྱལ་བ, *v. a.* to conduct, convey, carry, send: v. སྐྱེལ་བ.

བསྐྱི་བ, *v. a.* to borrow, take on loan; v. སྐྱི་བ.

བསྐྱིལ་བ, to be gathered together, to assemble in the middle.

བསྐྱུང་བ, *v. a.* to leave off, put aside, renounce, forsake, relinquish; v. སྐྱུང་བ.

བསྐྱུད་པ, *v. a.* to forget; v. སྐྱུད་པ.

བསྐྱུར་བ, *v. a.* to leave off, cast away, relinquish; v. སྐྱུར་བ.

བསྐྱེད་པ, *v. a.* to produce, generate, form, make, cause, breed, rear up, beget, procreate ; v. སྐྱེད་པ, *v. a.* སྐྱེ་བ, *v. n.*

བསྐྱོད་པ, *v. a.* to move, agitate, shake ; to move one's self, to go, walk ; v. སྐྱོད་པ.

བསྐྱོན་པ, *v. a.* to put, lay, hang on ; v. སྐྱོན་པ.

བསྐྲད་པ, *v. n.* to expel, eject, banish ; v. སྐྲོད་པ.

བསྒུ་བ, *v. a.* to expect, wait for.

བསྐྲུན་པ, *v. a.* to beget, procreate, form, make, cause, breed, rear.

བསྒྲོག་པ, to rattle, make a noise.

བགག་པ, *v. a.* to hinder, obstruct ; *v. n.* to be stopped, hindered.

བགད་པ, *v.* to laugh, deride.

བགམ་པ, *v. a.* to try, prove, tempt.

བགོ་བ, *v. a.* to put on a garment, to divide.

བགོད་པ, *v. a.* to divide.

བགོར་བ, *v. n.* to linger, tarry, remain long, to be long on one's way.

བསྒྱང་བ, *v. a.* to prolong, procrastinate.

བགྱི་བ, *v. a.* to do (hereafter).

བགྱིད་པ, *v. a.* to do, make, act, perform, &c.

བགྲང་བ, *v. a.* to number, count up, to compute ; *v. n.* to grow cold.

བགྲད་པ, *v. a.* to open wide, to menace.

བགྲིལ་བ, *v. a.* to roll, to roll up.

བགྲུ་བ, *v. a.* to cleanse, make clear (from the husks, &c.)

བགྲུང་བ, *v. a.* to defecate, strain, let sit down.

བགྲུད་པ, *v. a.* v. བགྲུ་བ.

བགྲེ་བ, *v. n.* to grow old.

བསྒྲེང་བ, *v. a.* to raise, erect, build ; v. སྒྲེང་བ.

བགྲོ་བ, *v.* to argue, reason, consider.

བགྲོད་པ, *v. n.* to go on or over.

བརྒལ་བ, *v. a.* to ford ; argue, dispute ; v. རྒལ་བ། or རྒོལ་བ.

བརྒྱང་བ, *v. a.* to extend, dilate, widen.

བརྒྱན་པ, *v. a.* to adorn, embellish.

བརྒྱབ་པ, *v. a.* to hurl, fling, dart, throw with violence ; v. རྒྱབ་པ། རྒྱོབ་པ.

བརྒྱལ་བ, *v. n.* to fall down senseless, to faint.

བརྒྱུ་བ, *v. a.* to put into a cord, order, series.

བརྒྱུག་པ, *v. n.* to run, to run away.

བསྒག་པ, *v. a.* to put on oath.

བསྒང་བ, *v. n.* to be or become full or replete with ; v. སྒང་བ.

བསྒར་བ, *v. a.* to make dense or thick.

བསྒུག་པ, *v. a.* to expect one, to wait on, to tarry till one arrives.

བསྒུལ་བ, *v. a.* to move, agitate, shake ; v. སྒུལ་བ.

བསྒོ་བ, *v. a.* to proclaim, publish, make known ; v. སྒོ་བ.

བསྒོང་བ, *v. a.* to conglomerate, make into an oval figure, to make round.

བསྒོམ་པ, *v. a.* to imagine, represent in one's mind ; v. སྒོམ་པ.

བསྒོར་བ, *v. a.* to detain, withhold ; thicken, &c.

བསྒྱིང་བ, *v. n.* to stretch with yawning ; v. སྒྱིང་བ.

བསྒྱུར་བ, *v. a.* to turn, change ; translate ; to multiply (as in arithmetic) ; v. སྒྱུར་བ.

བསྒྱེལ་བ, *v. a.* to turn upside down, to overthrow ; v. སྒྱེལ་བ.

བསྒྲག་པ, *v. a.* to proclaim, tell openly, publish, preach.

བསྒྲང་བ, *v. a.* to enumerate, count up ; upbraid ; to cool, make cool ; v. བགྲང་བ, v. སྒྲང་བ.

བསྒྲལ་བ, *v. a.* to save, deliver, rescue ; v. སྒྲོལ་བ.

བསྒྲིག་པ, *v. a.* to adjust, compose, put together; v. སྒྲིག་པ.

བསྒྲིབ་པ, *v. a.* to offuscate, overshadow ; v. སྒྲིབ་པ.

བསྒྲིམ་པ, to endeavour, make great efforts ; v. སྒྲིམ་པ.

བསྒྲིལ་བ, *v. a.* to wrap, roll, wind up, twist ; v. སྒྲིལ་བ.

བསྒྲུག་པ, *v. a.* to pick up, gather, collect.

བསྒྲུང་བ, *v. a.* to mix, mingle, put together ; to contrive, feign, relate falsely ; v. སྒྲུང་བ.

བསྒྲུན་པ, *v. a.* to liken, compare, estimate ; v. སྒྲུན་པ.

བསྒྲུབ་པ, *v. a.* to prepare, make ready, render propitious ; to acquire, learn, obtain, get ; v. སྒྲུབ་པ.

བསྒྲེ་བ, *v. a.* to repeat, (what belongs to the same class.)

བསྒྲོད་པ, *v. a.* to go on ; perambulate ; v. སྒྲོད་པ.

བསྒྲོན་པ, *v. a.* to embellish, decorate with ; v. སྒྲོན་པ.

བརྔ་བ, *v. a.* to reap, cut down ; v. རྔ་བ.

བརྔན་པ, *v. a.* to reward, give a reward ; v. རྔན་པ.

བརྔུབ་པ, *v. a.* to draw in and let out breath, to inhale and exhale, to breathe ; v. རྔུབ་པ

བརྔོད་པ, *v. a.* to parch or broil, to deceive ; v. རྔོད་པ.

བརྔོན་པ, *v. a.* to chase, hunt ; deceive ; v. རྔོན་པ.

བསྔག་པ, *v. a.* to praise, commend.

བསྔབ་བ, *v. n.* to be faint, weary, tired ; to decay.

བསྔོ་བ, *v. n.* to become green, mouldy, rotten ; to prosper ; *v. a.* to bless, give benediction ; v. སྔོ་བ.

བསྔོ་བར་མཛད་པ, *v. a.* to make green ; bless, prosper.

བསྔོག་པ, *v. a.* to fret, vex.

བཅག་པ, *part. pret.* of གཅོག་པ, *v. a.* to break, the *fut.* of འཆག་པ, to walk over, perambulate ; *v. a.*

བཅང་བ, *v. a.* to wear, carry, use; v. འཆང་བ.

བཅད་པ, *part. pret.* of གཅོད་པ, *v. a.* to cut off.

བཅབ་པ, *v. a.* to conceal, hide, keep secret, cover ; v. འཆབ་པ.

བཅམ་པ, *v. a.* to bargain, make an agreement ; to dance, jump ; v. འཆམ་པ.

བཅའ་བ, *v. a.* to make, prepare, make ready ; v. འཆའ་བ.

བཅར་བ, *v. a.* to wreathe ; to pull by force.

བཅལ་བ, *part. pret.* of འཇལ་བ, to weigh, ponder, measure ; pay, pay back.

བཅིང་བ, *v. a.* to bind, tie, fasten ; v. འཆིང་བ.

བཅིབ་པ, *v. a.* to ascend, mount a vehicle, horse, &c. ; v. འཆིབ་པ.

བཅིར་བ for བཅིར་བ, *v. a.* to squeeze, press out entirely ; v. འཆིར་བ.

བཅིལ་བ, *part. pret.* of འཇིལ་བ, *v. a.* to depose, divest, expel, cast out, eject, drive out, banish.

བཅུ་བ, *v. a.* to fetch or draw up water, &c. ; v. འཆུ་བ.

བཅུག་པ, *part. pret.* of འཇུག་པ, *v. a.* to put, lay, place ; close, shut ; make, cause.

བཅུམ་པ, *v. n.* to contract, shrink up ; v. འཆུམ་པ.

བཅེ་བ, *v. a.* to promise, assure, affirm ; v. འཆེ་བ.

བཅེམ་པ, *v. a.* to chew or grind with the teeth ; v. འཆེམས་པ.

བཅེར་བ, *v. a.* to heap or pile up.

བཅོ་བ, *v. a.* to make, prepare, form ; v. འཆོ་བ.

བཅོམ་པ, *part. pret.* of འཇོམས་པ, *v. a.* to overcome, subdue, conquer.

བཅོལ་བ, *part. pret.* of འཆོལ་བ, to commend, commit to, entrust ; v. འཆོལ་བ.

བརྗིད་པ, *v. n.* to shine, glisten, glitter, &c.

བརྗེ་བ, *v. a.* to barter, change, turn ; v. རྗེ་བ.

བརྗེད་པ, *v. a.* to honour, reverence ; to forget ; v. རྗེད་པ.

བརྗོད་པ, *v. a.* to say, utter, pronounce ; v. རྗོད་པ.

བརྙན་པ, *v. a.* to borrow, take from others.

བརྙས་པ, *v. a.* to scorn, disdain, contemn.

བརྙིང་བ, *v. n.* to grow old ; be worn out ; v. རྙིང་བ.

བརྙིད་པ, *v. n.* to fade or wither away ; v. རྙིད་པ.

བརྙེད་པ, *v. a.* to find, get ; v. རྙེད་པ.

བརྙོག་པ, *v. n.* to be troubled or stirred up, dirty ; v. རྙོག་པ.

བསྙད་པ, *v. a.* to tell, say, report, give notice of ; v. སྙད་པ.

བསྙབ་པ, *v. a.* to extend, stretch out ; v. སྙོབ་པ.

བསྙམ་པ, *v. a.* to make even or level, equal ; to balance ; v. སྙམ་པ.

བསྙལ་བ, *v. a.* to lay flat on the ground, to lay to sleep ; v. སྙོལ་བ, *v. u.* ཉལ་བ, *v. n.*

བསྙིགས་པ, *v. a.* to give over to another, to return.

བསྙིལ་བ, *v. n.* to break or fall down (as a rock) ; v. སྙིལ་བ.

བསྙུག་པ, *v. a.* to dip, immerge, moisten ; v. སྙུག་པ.

བསྙུང་བ, *v. a.* to make less, to reduce ; v. སྙུང་བ.

བསྙུན་པ, *v. n.* to grow or become sick ; v. སྙུན་པ.

བསྙུལ་བ, *v. a.* to wash, cleanse (the hands, &c.)

བསྙེག་པ or བསྙག་པ, to endeavour, make haste ; v. སྙེག་པ.

བསྙེང་བ, *v. n.* to be afraid, to fear ; v. སྙེངས་པ.

བསྙེན་པ, *v.* to approach to ; propitiate, gain, to induce to favour ; v. སྙེན་པ.

བསྒྲེར་བ, *v. a.* to make grimaces to.

བསྙེལ་བ, *v. a.* to forget, neglect.

བསྙོག་པ, *v. a.* to have a desire or lust, to desire earnestly, to long for.

བསྙོད་པ, *v. a.* to give over, to deliver, to give into one's hand.

བསྙོན་པ, *v. a.* to accuse, charge with a crime.

བཏག་པ, *v. a.* to weave ; to grind.

བཏང་བ, *part. pret.* of གཏོང་བ, to give.

བཏབ་པ, *part. pret.* of འདེབས་པ, to throw, cast, hurl, fling.

བཏིག་པ, *v. a.* to drop, to let fall in drops.

བཏིང་བ, *part. pret.* of འདིང་བ, to spread on the ground.

བཏུ་བ, *v. a.* to pick up, gather, collect ; v. འཐུ་བ.

བཏུག་པ, *v. a.* to cast down one's self at the feet of another.

བཏུང་བ, *v. a.* to drink up the whole ; v. འཐུང་བ.

བཏུད་པ, *v. a.* to bow down ; v. འདུད་པ.

བཏུམ་པ, *v. a.* to cover, put a cover on ; v. འཐུམ་པ.

བཏུལ་བ, *part. pret.* of འདུལ་བ, to subdue, overcome.

བཏེག་པ, *part. pret.* of འདེགས་པ, to lift up.

བཏོག་པ, *v. a.* to pull, pluck, up, out.

བཏོན་པ, *part. pret.* of འདོན་པ, to eject; cast out, draw out.

བརྟ་བ, *v. n.* to grow thick or fat.

བརྟག་པ, *v. a.* to examine, investigate, try, &c.; v. རྟོག་པ.

བརྟབ་པ, *v. n.* to be in confusion or hurry ; v. རྟབ་པ.

བརྟིབ་པ, *v. a.* to pull down ; v. རྟིབ་པ.

བརྟེན་པ, *v. a.* to hold, support, depend on ; v. རྟེན་པ.

བརྟོད་པ, *v. a.* to fasten with a peg and rope.

བརྟོལ་བ, *v. a.* to squeeze or force out ; v. རྟོལ་བ.

བལྟ་བ, *v. a.* to look on, behold ; v. ལྟ་བ.

བལྟབ་པ, *v. a.* to fold up, (as a garment;) v. ལྟབ་པ.

བལྟམ་པ, *v. n.* to be full or replete, to be born.

བསྟད་པ, *v. a.* to put on a saddle, to saddle.

བསྟན་པ, *v. a.* to show ; instruct, teach ; v. སྟོན་པ.

བསྟབ་པ, *v. a.* to give, offer, present, bestow ; v. སྟབ་པ, afford.

བསྟར་བ, *v. a.* to decorate, embellish, put into order or series ; v. སྟར་བ.

བསྟི་བ, *v. a.* to receive kindly, refresh, put to rest or respite ; v. སྟི་བ.

བསྟིང་བ, *v. a.* to chide, reproach, abuse ; v. སྟིང་བ.

བསྟིམ་པ, *v. a.* to infuse, instil, inspire, pour into ; v. སྟིམ་པ.

བསྡུང་བ, *v. a.* to shorten, abbreviate ; v. སྡུང་བ.

བསྡུད་པ, *v. a.* to repeat, to do many times ; v. སྡུད་པ.

བསྡུན་པ, *v. a.* to make agree, concord, to confer ; v. སྡུན་པ.

བསྟེན་པ, *v. a.* to keep, hold, support, maintain; v. སྟེན་པ.

བསྟེར་བ, *v. a.* to give, bestow, grant; v. སྟེར་བ.

བསྟོད་པ, *v. a.* to exalt, praise, commend.

བདའ་བ, *v. a.* to carry, convey, take with, off.

བདར་བ, *v. a.* to file, polish, cleanse; to fret; whet, sharpen.

བདུག་པ, *v. a.* to fumigate, perfume, smoke.

བདུང་བ, *v. a.* to strike, beat.

བརྡབ་པ, *v. a.* to clap, beat, strike, knock: v. རྡབ་པ or རྡོབ་པ.

བརྡར་བ, *v. a.* to whet, sharpen; v. རྡར་བ or རྡོར་བ.

བརྡལ་བ, *v. a.* to spread, scatter, extend; v. རྡལ་བ or རྡོལ་བ.

བརྡུང་བ, *v. a.* to beat, strike on, to thresh; v. རྡུང་བ.

བརྡེག་པ, *v. a.* to beat, strike, smite; v. རྡེག་པ.

བལྡག་པ, *v. a.* to lick all over, to lick; v. ལྡག་པ.

བལྡད་པ, *v. a.* to chew the cud (entirely), to chew, to ruminate, to muse; v. ལྡད་པ.

བཟླབ་པ, *v. a.* to repeat, say again; v. ཟླབ་པ.

བསྡད་པ, *v. n.* to sit down; to wait for; v. སྡོད་པ.

བསྡམ་པ, *v. a.* to bind, tie, fasten; oblige one's self, &c.; v. སྡོམ་པ.

བསྡི་བ or བསྡིགས་པ, *v. a.* to menace, threaten; v. སྡིགས་པ.

བསྡུ་བ, *v. a.* to collect, gather together; to abridge; v. སྡུད་པ.

བསྡུམ་པ, *v. a.* to make agree, to reconcile; v. སྡུམ་པ.

བསྡུར་བ, *v. a.* to confer, compare.

བསྡེབ་པ, *v. a.* to exchange, barter; to mix; v. སྡེབ་པ.

བསྡོ་བ, *v. a.* to hazard, to expose to accident or danger.

བསྡོག་པ, *v. a.* to compose, prepare, make ready.

བསྡོང་བ, *v. a.* to associate, unite with.

བསྡོམ་པ, *v. a.* to add together.

བརྣག་པ, *v. n.* to mind to suffer; to grow full of corrupt matter (as a sore).

བརྣང་བ, *v. n.* to be suffocated or choked by any thing in the throat.

བརྣན་པ, *v. a.* to attend or look on.

བརྣུ་བ or རྣུར་བ, *v. a.* to draw to, to attract.

བསྣད་པ, *v. a.* to hurt, to make a wound on.

བསྣན་པ, *v. a.* to increase, augment, add to.

བསྣམ་པ, *v. a.* to take into one's hand, to put on, receive, to smell the scent of; v. སྣོམ་པ.

བསྣར་བ, *v. a.* to prolong, to lengthen out, to delay, to extend far.

བསྣལ་བ, *v. a.* to draw long, to spin out, to prolong.

བསྣུན་པ, *v. a.* to suckle; to pierce, to stab.

བསྣུབ་པ, *v. a.* to abolish, destroy; v. སྣུབ་པ.

བསྣུམ་པ, *v. a.* to smell, try the smell; v. སྣུམ་པ.

བསྣུར་བ, *v. a.* to make less, smaller, to bring nearer; v. སྣུར་བ.

བསྣེམ་པ, *v. a.* to move, shake, agitate.

བསྣོ་བ, *v. a.* to mix, mingle, make a mixture of; v. སྣོ་བ.

བསྣོམ་པ, *v. a.* to smell, try the smell of; v. སྣོམ་པ.

བསྣོར་བ, *v. a.* to confound, disturb, set in disorder; v. སྣོར་བ.

བཙག་པ, *v. a.* to strain, defecate, purify; v. འཚག་པ.

བཙང་བ, *v. a.* to press forward, to open a way to one's self by pressing among the multitude.

བཙབ་པ, *v. a.* to cut short.

བཙའ་བ, *v.* to watch over, to observe; to bring forth, to be born.

བཙལ་བ, *v. a.* to seek, to look for; v. འཚོལ་བ.

བཙིར་བ, *v. a.* to squeeze, press out.

བཙུག་པ, *v. a.* to set, plant, fix, establish; v. འཛུགས་པ.

བཙུད་པ, *v. a.* to put in, to inject; v. འཛུད་པ.

བཙུམ་པ, *v. a.* to shut or close entirely, (the eye;) v. འཛུམ་པ.

བཙེ་བ, *v. a.* to hurt, injure, do harm to; v. འཚེ་བ.

བཙེམ་པ, *v. a.* to sew (entirely); v. འཚེམ་པ.

བཙོ་བ, *v. n.* to become ripe or mature; *v. a.* to boil, dress, dye, tinge, to refine; v. འཚོ་བ, འཚོད་པ.

བཙོག་པ, *v. a.* to cut, hew, engrave, inoculate, beat, smite; v. འཚོག་པ.

བཙོང་བ, *v. a.* to sell away; v. འཚོང་བ.

བརྩད་པ, *v. a.* to dispute, argue, debate; v. རྩོད་པ.

བརྩམ་པ, *v. a.* to begin, compose, write, make; v. རྩོམ་པ.

བརྩི་བ, *v. a.* to count or number up, to admit, acknowledge; v. རྩི་བ.

བརྩིག་པ, *v. a.* to build or raise up a wall; v. རྩིག་པ.

བརྩེ་བ *v. a.* to love, be kind or merciful to.

བརྩེག་པ, *v. a.* to raise one thing above another, to raise stories; to grind; bind, tie, truss up; v. རྩེག་པ.

བརྩེད་བ, *v. a.* to shorten, gird or tuck up; v. རྩེད་བ.

བརྩོན་པ, *v. n.* to endeavour, strive, labour.

བརྩལ་བ, *v. a.* to give, bestow, afford; v. རྩོལ་བ.

བརྫོང་བ, *v. a.* to send, despatch, commission, put into; v. རྫོང་བ.

བརྫི་བ, *v. a.* to depress, oppress, to tread under one's feet; to make sink; v. རྫི་བ.

བརྫུ་བ, *v. a.* to transform, transfigure miraculously; v. རྫུ་བ.

བརྫེ་བ, *v. a.* to menace, threaten, to make grimaces, to tuck, gird up; v. རྫེ་བ.

བཞག་པ, *part. pret.* of འཇོག་པ, to put, place, lay.

བཞད་པ, *v. n.* to smile, laugh; *v. a.* deride.

བཞབ་པ, *v. n.* to go or creep in unawares; v. འཇབ་པ.

བཞར་བ, *v. a.* to shave, cut with a razor.

བཞུ་བ, *v. a.* to melt, to digest; v. འཇུ་བ.

བཞུགས་པ, *v. n.* to sit (stately), be, exist.

བཞུད་པ, *v. n.* to go, depart.

བཞུར་བ, *v. a.* to cut, chop, shave.

བཞེང་བ, *v. a.* to rise, build, erect; to stand up.

བཞེད་པ, *v. a.* to will, wish, desire.

བཞེས་པ, *v. a.* to take, receive, accept of; to put on.

བཞོ་བ, *v. a.* to milk, draw milk, &c.; v. འཇོ་བ.

བཞོག་པ, *v. a.* to hew, cut, chop with an axe.

བཟའ་བ, *v. a.* to eat up, to eat the whole; to eat; v. ཟ་བ.

བཟི་བ, *v. n.* to be intoxicated.

བཟུང་བ, *part. pret.* of འཛིན་པ, to take into one's hand, to seize, to catch; v. གཟུང་བ.

བཟུར་པ, *pret.* of འཛུར་བ, to turn out, or aside from one's way.

བཟེད་པ, *v. a.* to keep, hold; v. འཛེད་པ.

བཟོ་བ, *v. a.* to make, form, fabricate, work, frame.

བཟོད་པ, *v. a.* to suffer, forbear, have patience.

བཟླ་བ, *v. a.* to repeat, turn round; pass over (a mountain), double (a cape); v. ཟློ་བ or ཟླ་བ.

བཟུམ་པ, *v. a.* to gather or bring together.

བཟློག་པ, *a.* to turn back, to force to go back, to reform; v. ཟློག་པ.

བརླག་པ, *v. a.* to waste, destroy, rase, erase, to turn upside down.

བརླན་པ, *v. a.* to moisten, make wet; *v. n.* to grow wet.

བཤག་པ, *v. a.* to confess, declare.

བཤད་པ, *v. a.* to explain, tell fully; v. འཆད་པ.

བཤམ་པ, *v. a.* to prepare, make ready.

བཤའ་བ, *v. a.* to kill animals for food, to butcher.

བཤར་བ, *v. a.* to put into series; to measure, to hunt.

བཤལ་བ, *v. a.* to cleanse, wash clean, purge.

བཤིག་པ, *part. pret.* of འཇིག་པ, to pull down, destroy; break, violate.

བཤྲིག་པ, *v. a.* to flay, strip, take off the skin; to copy.

བཤུ་བ, *v. a.* to sell, give to another.

བཤུད་པ, *v. a.* to rub.

བཤུམ་པ, *v. a.* to weep over or for, to lament.

བཤུར་བ, *v. a.* to burn slightly.

བཤེར་བ, *v. a.* to confront, compare, to face.

བཤེས་པ, *v. a.* to know, to know a person or thing unknown before.

བཤོ་བ, *v. a.* to spill, shed, pour out.

བཤོར་བ, *v. a.* to chase, course, hunt, pursue.

བཤོལ་བ, *v. a.* to put away, to defer, to delay.

བསག་པ, *v. a.* to collect, assemble; to hoard up; v. སོག་པ.

བསང་བ, *v. a.* to purify, cleanse, clear up.

བསད་པ, *part. pret.* of གསོད་པ, to kill, murder.

བསབ་པ, *v. a.* to return, to do like, to render, repay, supply; v. འཚབ་པ.

བསམ་པ, *v. a.* to think, meditate, muse on, to consider; v. སེམ or སེམས་པ.

བསལ་བ, *v. a.* to put away, cleanse, clear, heal, cure; v. སེལ་བ.

བསིག་པ, *v. a.* to agitate, shake, retake; cast up.

བསིར་བ, *v. a.* to whirl about.

བསིལ་བ, *v. a.* to refresh, cool; wash.

བསུ་བ, *v. a.* to receive one; solemnly to go to meet one, &c.

བསུབ་པ, *v. a.* to efface, blot out, destroy.

བསུམ་པ, *v. a.* to shut or close the mouth, &c.

བསེ་བ, *v. a.* to pull asunder, to anatomise.

བསེད་པ, *v. a.* to pull asunder, to pick, cleanse.

བསྲང་བ, *v. a.* to make right, straight, equal, to keep, hold in equilibrium, to balance.

བསྲན་པ, *v. n.* to harden one's self, to suffer anything.

བསྲབ་པ, *v. a.* to refrain, hold back, to curb, to disperse.

བསྲི་བ, *v. a.* to keep, hold; not to give much.

བསྲིང་བ, *v. a.* to make longer, to protract, to prolong, extend farther; to bring up, breed; to send, despatch.

བསྲུང་བ, *v. a.* to defend, take care of; to observe, keep.

བསྲུབ་པ, *v. a.* to churn, agitate, curdle.

བསྲེ་བ, *v. a.* to add together, collect, aggregate.

བསྲེག་པ, *v. a.* to burn, to consume.

བསྲེལ་བ, *v. a.* to feed, rear, keep.

བསྲོ་བ, *v. a.* to warm, heat moderately.

བསློང་བ, *v. a.* to erect, set up, raise, to lift, hold up, rouse or excite; v. སློང་བ.

བསླད་པ, *v. a.* to mix, mingle, alloy.

བསླན་པ, *v. a.* to patch, mend; v. སླན་པ.

བསླབ་པ, *v. a.* to teach; learn fully; v. སློབ་པ.

བསླུ་བ, *v. a.* to deceive, impose on; v. སླུ་བ.

བསླེ་བ, *v. a.* to twist, wind.

བསླེབ་པ, *v. n.* to arrive at a place.

བསློག་པ, *v. a.* to turn, reverse, to turn inside out.

མིད་པ, *v. a.* to swallow down.

མིན་པ, *v. n.* not to be.

མུར་བ, *v. a.* to grind or cut with the teeth; to chew.

མུལ་བ, *v. n.* to smile.

མེད་པ, *v. n.* not to be, to be wanted.

མོལ་བ, *v. a.* to command, order, say.

མོས་པ, *v. a.* to esteem, have regard for.

མྱང་ང, *v. a.* to taste, enjoy.

མྱུལ་བ, *v. a.* to spy, investigate, explore.

མྱོ་བ, *v. n.* to be intoxicated.

མྱོང་བ, *v. a.* to taste, enjoy.

མཁྱུད་པ, *v. a.* to keep, hold, embrace.

མཁྱེན་པ, *v. a.* to know, understand.

མགུ་བ, *v. n.* to rejoice, be glad.

མངག་པ, *v. a.* to send, commission, ablegate.

མངན་པ, *v. a.* to curse, to wish evil to.

མངའ་བ, *v. n.* to be; *v. a.* to have, to possess.

མཆི་བ, *v. n.* to go or repair to.

མཆིས་པ, *v. n.* to be, to be there.

མཆེད་པ, *v. n.* to spread, to be diffused.

མཆོང་བ, *v. a.* to leap, jump.

མཆོད་པ, *v. a.* to offer, to sacrifice; to worship.

མཆོར་བ, *v. n.* to slip or fall out of the hand.

མཇལ་བ, *v. a.* to meet, visit, have an interview.

མཉན་པར, *v. a.* to hear fully, to hear, hearken to.

མཉམ་པ, *v. n.* to be even, level, equal.

མཉེ་བ, *v. a.* to mollify, soften, rub gently.

མཉེད་པ, *v. a.* ditto.

མཉེལ་བ, *v. n.* to be weary, fatigued.

མཉེས་པ, *v. n.* to be merry, glad.

མཐར་བ, *v. n.* to be freed or delivered.

མཐོང་བ, *v. a.* to see, view, look on.

མཐོལ་བ, *v. a.* to confess, declare.

མནན་པ, *v. a.* to depress, humble, conquer, out-do; v. ནོན་པ, v. གནོན་པ.

མནབ་པ, *v. a.* to put on his clothes, dress.

མནམ་པ for སྣམ་པ, *v. a.* to smell, perceive by the nose; to touch, feel.

མནར་བ, *v. n.* to suffer, be afflicted with.

མནལ་བ, *v. n.* to sleep.

མནོ་བ, *v. a.* to think, or fancy.

མནོག་པ, *v. n.* to be content, or satisfied with.

མནོང་བ, *v. n.* to be conscious of one's fault.

མཚོན་པ, *v. a.* to show, represent, figurate.

མཛད་པ, *v. a.* to do, make, act, create, form.

ཚད་པ or ཚད་ཟ་ཐེད་པ, *v. a.* to measure, prove.

ཚིར་བ, *v. n.* to be done, to be finished.

ཚིམ་པ, *v. n.* to be content or satisfied with.

ཚོར་བ, *v. a.* to feel, perceive, to hear.

ཚོལ་བ for འཚོལ་བ, to seek, look for.

ཞུ་བ, *v. a.* to beg, request, entreat; ask.

ཞུད་པ, *v. a.* to twist, spin.

ཞེན་པ, *v. a.* to desire, wish, will.

ཞོག་པ, for འཇོག་པ, *v. a.* to lay, place, put down.

ཞོན་པ, *v. a.* to mount, ascend (carriage, &c.)

ཟ་བ, *v. a.* to eat, take food; v. བཟའ་བ.

ཟུག་པ, *v. a.* to yelp, bark.

ཟེར་བ, *v. a.* to say, tell, speak.

ཟླ་བ or ཟློ་བ, *v. a.* to pass over, to double, to repeat.

ཟློག་པ, *v. a.* to return, make to go back.

འོང་བ, *v. n.* to come.

འོན་པ, *v. a.* to bring.

འོར་བ, *v. a.* to put, lay down.

འཆད་བ, *v. a.* to censure, accuse.

འཁམ་པ, *v. n.* to be out of one's senses, to fall down.

འཁད་པ, *v. n.* to stop or be stopped.

འཁལ་བ, *v. a.* to spin.

འཁྲུ་བ, *v. a.* to vie with, to hate.

འཁུན་པ, *v. n.* to groan.

འཁུམ་པ, *v. n.* to shrink, contract.

འཁུར་བ, *v. a.* to carry, convey.

འཁུལ་བ, *v. a.* to subdue, subject.

འཁགས་པ, *v. n.* to be stopped or hindered.

འཁེངས་པ, *v. n.* to be full, replete.

འཁོད་པ, *v. n.* to sit down, settle.

འཁོན་པ, *v. n.* to be angry with one.

འཁོབ་པ, *v. a.* to encircle, compass.

འཁོར་བ, *v. n.* to go round about, to wander.

འཁོལ་བ, *v. n.* to boil, to be hot.

འཁྱག་པ, *v. n.* to freeze, be congealed.

འཁྱམ་པ, *v. n.* to err, wander, go astray.

འཁྱར་བ, *v. n.* to go astray, to err.

འཁྱིག་པ, *v. a.* to bind, tie, fasten.

འཁྱིར་བ, *v. n.* to turn, go round about.

འཁྱིལ་བ, *v. n.* to be gathered together.

འཁྱུ་བ, *v. n.* to run, to run away.

འཁྱུག་པ, *v. n.* to run, flee.

འཁྱུད་པ, *v. a.* to embrace, comprise.

འཁྱུར་བ, *v. n.* to be separated, divorced.

འཁྱེད་པ, *v. n.* to be spread, or distributed.

འཁྱེར་བ, *v. a.* to carry, convey, take away.

འཁྱོང་བ, *v. a.* to bring.

འཁྲོམ་པ, *v. n.* to be stirred, moved, troubled.

འཁྱོར་བ, *v. n.* to miss, fail, to be giddy.

འཁྱོལ་བ, *v. n.* to arrive, reach.

འཁྲ་བ, *v. n.* to lean to, to depend on.

འཁྲབ་པ, *v. a.* to strike, beat.

འཁྲི་བ, *v. n.* to be involved in, to wind.

འཁྲིག་པ, *v. n.* to cohere, stick together.

འཁྲིད་པ, *v. a.* to lead, conduct.

འཁྲིལ་བ, *v. n.* to be twisted together or round.

འཁྲུ་བ, *v. n.* to wash one's self, to bathe.

འཁྲུག་པ, *v. n.* to be stirred, troubled.

འཁྲུང་བ, *v. n.* to be born, produced.

འཁྲུད་པ, *v. a.* to wash, cleanse.

འཁྲུལ་བ, *v. n.* to err, be mistaken.

འཁྲེམ་པ, *v. n.* to be scattered.

འཁྲེན་པ, *v. n.* to long for, desire.

འཁྲོལ་བ, *v. a.* to play on a musical instrument.

འགག་པ, *v. n.* to stop, to cease.

འགམ་པ, *v. a.* to taste, to try the taste of, to put into the mouth.

འགལ་བ, *v. n.* to secede, withdraw from.

འགར་བ, *v. a.* to transgress, violate.

འགས་པ, *v. n.* to open, be split or cleft.

འགུགས་པ, *v. a.* to draw down, to call, summon.

འགུད་པ, *v. n.* to decay, decline, be spent.

འགུམ་པ, *v. n.* to die, perish.

འགུལ་བ, *v. n.* to be agitated, to move, shake.

འགེགས་པ, *v. a.* to hinder, prohibit, stop.

འགེངས་པ, *v. a.* to fill, replenish, make full.

འགེད་པ, *v. a.* to diffuse, spread, extend.

འགེབས་པ, *v. a.* to cover, overspread.

འགེམ་པ, *v. a.* to kill, destroy.

འགེལ་བ, *v. a.* to load, put on a burden or load.

འགེས་པ, *v. a.* to split, cleave, divide.

འགོ་བ, *v. n.* to be stained, sullied, inflicted with.

འགོག་པ, *v. a.* to hinder, stop.

འགོང་བ, *v. a.* to bewitch, enchant.

འགོད་པ, *v. a.* to build, frame, construe.

འགོམ་པ, *v. n.* to be accustomed to.

འགོར་བ, *v. n.* to tarry, loiter, linger.

འགོལ་བ, *v. n.* to go astray.

འགྱག་པ, *v. n.* to be sold, spent, expended.

འགྱང་བ, *v. n.* to be a long time, or late, to be delayed.

འགྱིང་བ, *v. n.* to stretch with yawning.

འགྱུ་བ, *v. n.* to run, flee, vanish, disappear.

འགྱུར་བ, *v. n.* to become, be ; change, turn.

འགྱེ་བ, *v. n.* to go asunder, to disperse.

འགྱེད་པ, *v. a.* to disperse, diffuse, scatter.

འགྱེལ་བ, *v. n.* to be turned upside down.

འགྱོད་པ, *v. n.* to repent, be grieved for.

འགྲག་པ, *v. n.* to sound, be rumoured.

འགྲང་བ, *v. a.* to number, count ; be filled, satisfied.

འགྲད་པ, *v. a.* to extend wide.

འགྲན་པ, *v. a.* to vie, contend, strive with.

འགྲམ་པ, *v. n.* to be scattered, diffused, spread.

འགྲིག་པ, *v. n.* to congrue, agree, suit, be coherent.

འགྲིབ་པ, *v. n.* to grow less, decrease ; be offuscated.

འགྲིམ་པ, *v. n.* to go, walk.

འགྲིལ་བ, *v. n.* to roll, fall down.

འགྲུ་བ, *v. n.* to endeavour, strive.

འགྲུབ་པ, *v. n.* to be ready, to be produced.

འགྲུམ་པ, *v. n.* to be broken, maimed.

འགྲུལ་བ, *v. n.* to go, walk, march, pace.

འགྲེ་བ, *v. n.* to be repeated ; to roll about, or on the ground.

འགྲེང་བ, *v. n.* to stand, stay erect.

འགྲེམ་པ, *v. a.* to sprinkle, scatter ; expose to sale.

འགྲེལ་བ, *v. a.* to unfold, explain.

འགྲོ་བ, *v. n.* to go, walk, march.

འགྲོགས་པ, *v. n.* to converse, associate with.

འགྲོངས་པ, *v. n.* to die, cease to live.

འགྲོད་པ, *v. a.* to go on, over, to travel.

འགྲོལ་བ, *v. n.* to be unfolded, untied.

འཆག་པ, *v. n.* to break, to walk ; *v. a.* to full cloth.

འཆང་བ, *v. a.* to wear, put on ; keep, hold, carry.

འཆད་པ, *v. a.* to explain, tell, instruct ; *v. n.* to be rent, torn, dissolved.

འཆབ་པ, *v. a.* to conceal, hide.

འཆམ་པ, *v. n.* to dance, jump.

འཆའ་བ, *v. a.* to prepare, make.

འཆར་བ, *v. n.* to rise, go up.

འཆལ་བ, *v. n.* to fluctuate, be unsteady.

འཆི་བ, *v. n.* to die, cease to live.

འཆིང་བ, *v. a.* to bind, tie, fasten.

འཆིབ་པ, *v. a.* to mount, ascend.

འཆུ་བ, *v. a.* to fetch or draw up water ; to water, irrigate.

འཆུན་པ, *v.* to yield, confess.

འཆུམ་པ, *v. n.* to shrink.

འཆེ་བ, *v. a.* to promise, assure.

འཆེག་པ, *v. a.* to cleave, split, confess.

འཆེམས་པ, *v. a.* to grind, to cut with the teeth.

འཆེལ་བ, *v. a.* to believe, give credit to.

འཆོ་བ, *v. a.* to prepare, make ready.

འཆོར་བ, *v. n.* to run away, escape.

འཆོལ་བ, *v. a.* to command, commit to, intrust.

འཆོས་བ, *v. a.* to prepare, make ready.

འཇག་པ, *v. a.* to establish, settle, fix.

འཇབ་པ, *v. n.* to creep in secretly.

འཇལ་བ, *v. a.* to weigh, ponder, pay.

འཇིག་པ, *v. n.* to be destroyed, ruined, to perish; *v. a.* to destroy.

འཇུག་པ, *v. a.* to put, place, lay, make, cause.

འཇུན་པ, *v. a.* to subdue, make tame.

འཇུམ་པ, *v. n.* to shrink, be afraid of.

འཇོ་བ, *v. a.* to express, squeeze, milk.

འཇོག་པ, *v. a.* to put, place, lay down; cut, hew.

འཇོམས་པ, *v. a.* to overcome, subdue, conquer.

འཇོལ་བ, *v.* to turn aside from the way.

འཐད་པ, *v. n.* to be fit, meet, convenient.

འཐབ་པ, *v.* to fight, quarrel, dispute.

འཐམ་པ, *v. a.* to embrace, include.

འཐལ་བ, *v. n.* to pass away, go beyond.

འཐིག་པ, *v. n.* to drop, fall in drops.

འཐིམ་པ, *v. a.* to pervade, diffuse over.

འཐུ་བ, *v. a.* to gather, collect, pick up.

འཐུང་བ, *v.* to drink.

འཐུབ་པ, *v. a.* to cut into small pieces.

འཐུམ་པ, *v. n.* to cover, cast, spread over.

འཐུལ་བ, *v. n.* to spread wide; to smoke.

འཐེག་པ, *v. n.* to depart, commence a journey.

འཐེན་པ, *v. a.* to draw, make fast.

འཐེབས་པ, *v. a.* to take, seize, hold fast on.

འཐེམས་པ, *v. a.* to shut, comprise, cover, include.

འཐོ་འཚོམས་པ, *v. a* to fret, vex.

འཐོག་པ, *v. a.* to pick, pluck up.

འཐོགས་པ, *v. a.* to take into one's hand; to hold.

འཐོན་པ, *v. n.* to go out, issue, be uttered.

འཐོམ་པ, *v. n.* to doubt, hesitate, mistake, err.

འཐོར་བ, *v. a.* to scatter, diffuse, disperse; v. གཏོར་བ.

འཐོལ་བ, *v. a.* to declare, confess, not to hide.

འདག་པ, *v. n.* to become pure, clean; *v. a.* to lick.

འདམ་པ, *v. a.* to choose, select.

འདའ་བ, *v. n.* to go, pass away, to escape.

འདར་བ, *v. n.* to tremble, quake, shudder.

འདིང་བ, *v. a.* to spread on the ground.

འདུ་བ, *v. n.* to assemble, gather together.

འདུ་ཤེས་པ, *v.* to represent in the mind, be conscious of.

འདུག་པ, *v. n.* to be, exist, sit, be present.

འདུད་པ, *v. n.* to bow, incline, bow down.

འདུན་པ, *v. a.* to desire, wish; will.

འདུབ་པ, *v. n.* to be fatigued, weary, tired.

འདུམ་པ, *v. n.* to agree with, be in concord.

འདུར་བ, *v. n.* to trot, to ride in a trot.

འདུལ་བ, *v. a.* to tame, break, subdue, educate.

འདེགས་པ, *v. a.* to lift, raise, hold up, weigh.

འདེང་བ, *v. n.* to go, resort, to proceed.

འདེད་པ, *v. a.* to follow, carry, convey, lead.

འདེབས་པ, *v. a.* to cast, throw, utter; found, establish.

འདོ་བ, *v. a.* to say, repeat, answer to.

འདོགས་པ, *v. a.* to bind, tie, fasten; v. གདགས་པ.

འདོང་བ, *v. n.* (v. འདེང་བ) to go, march, proceed.

འདོད་པ, *v. a.* to wish, desire, long for ; will.
འདོན་པ, *v. a.* to utter, eject, expel ; *v. n.* to eat, drink.
འདོམ་པ, *v. n.* to meet, come together, unite.
འདོམས་པ, *v. a.* to advise, counsel.
འདོར་བ, *v. a.* to cast off, reject, not to take.
འདྲལ་བ, *v. n.* to be rent, unfolded.
འདྲི་བ, *v. a.* to ask, make a question.
འདྲིད་པ, *v. a.* to deceive, impose on.
འདྲིམ་པ for འབྲིམ་པ, *v. a.* to distribute, to give to each.
འདྲིལ་བ, *v. a.* to roll down, turn about, fall down.
འདྲུ་བ for འབྲུ་བ, *v. a.* to dig, make a hole ; fret, vex.
འདྲུད་པ, *v. a.* to rub, file.
འདྲུབ་པ, *v. a.* to sew, stitch, join together.
འདྲུལ་བ, *v. n.* to become putrid, rancid.
འདྲེ་བ, *v. n.* to mix, mingle, unite with.
འདྲེག་པ, *v. a.* to shave with a razor.
འདྲེན་པ, *v. a.* to draw ; bring, govern, invite.
འདྲེད་པ, *v. n.* to slide, glide, slip.
འཕག་པ, *v. n.* to arise ; lift up one's self ; *v. a.* to rear, to throw his rider (as a horse).
འཕང་བ, *v. a.* to shoot out, ejaculate, throw.
འཕ་མཔ, *v. n.* to lose, be defeated.
འཕར་བ, *v. n.* to spring, rise, be promoted.
འཕུང་བ, *v. n.* to be indigent, poor.
འཕུད་པ, *v. a.* to put off, (as a garment, &c.)
འཕུར་བ, *v. n.* to fly ; *v. a.* to cover, cast over.
འཕུལ་བ, *v. a.* to repel, drive back.

འཕེན་པ, *v. a.* to shoot, throw, cast, ejaculate.
འཕེལ་བ, *v. n.* to increase, multiply, augment.
འཕོ་བ, *v. n.* to shift, change, turn ; migrate.
འཕོག་པ, *v. a.* to strike, hurt, touch.
འཕོངས་པ, *v. n.* to be indigent, poor.
འཕྱ་བ, *v.* to rebuke, chide.
འཕྱག་པ, *v. a.* to sweep, make clean.
འཕྱང་བ, *v. n.* to hang down.
འཕྱན་པ, *v. n.* to go astray, be lost.
འཕྱར་བ, *v. a.* to display, exhibit, show.
འཕྱི་བ, *v. n.* to be blotted out ; *v. a.* to wipe off, blot out.
འཕྱིད་པ, *v. a.* to wipe, to blot out.
འཕྱུག་པ, *v. n.* to blunder, mistake, err.
འཕྱུར་བ, *v. n.* to rise up, be diffused.
འཕྱེ་བ, *v. n.* to crawl, creep, go slowly.
འཕྱོ་བ, *v. n.* to float, to swim on the surface of, &c.
འཕྲ་བ, *v. n.* to kick, strike with the foot.
འཕྲག་པ, *v. a.* to envy.
འཕྲབ་པ, *v. a.* to kick, strike with the foot.
འཕྲལ་བ, *v. a.* to separate, put asunder, divide
འཕྲི་བ, *v. a.* to subtract, diminish, lessen.
འཕྲིག་པ, *v. n.* to palpitate, flutter.
འཕྲིན་པ, *v. a.* to let know, to send intelligence.
འཕྲུག་པ, *v. a.* to scratch, rub.
འཕྲུལ་བ, *v. n.* to change, turn, (miraculously.)
འཕྲེ་བ, *v.* to lean, incline to.
འཕྲོ་བ, *v.* to scatter, diffuse, be scattered.
འཕྲོག་པ, *v. a.* to take by force, to rape.
འཕྲོད་པ, *v. n.* to be delivered, given, paid.

འབང་བ, *v. n.* to be steeped, macerated.

འབད་པ, *v. a.* to endeavour, make an effort.

འབབ་པ, *v. n.* to descend, fall, flow.

འབར་བ, *v. n.* to burn, be inflamed.

འབལ་བ, *v. a.* to pick, make rough, hairy.

འབིགས་པ, *v. a.* to pierce, bore.

འབུ་བ, *v. n.* to open, bud, blow.

འབུགས་པ, *v. a.* to pierce, bore.

འབུངས་པ, *v. a.* to exercise, endeavour.

འབུད་པ, *v. a.* to blow (the fire); to put off (as a garment).

འབུན་པ, *v. n.* to itch.

འབུབ་པ, *v. n.* to fall flat down.

འབུབས་པ, *v. a.* to cover, vault, overarch.

འབུལ་བ, *v. a.* to offer, present, give.

འབེབས་པ, *v. a.* to let down, shower, rain.

འབོ་བ, *v. n.* to be poured or shed out.

འབོགས་པ, *v. a.* to transfer to, confer on.

འབོད་པ, *v. a.* to call, name, invite, summon.

འབོར་བ, *v. a.* to put, place, lay down.

འབྱང་བ, *v. n.* to be purified or clean.

འབྱམ་པ, *v. n.* to overflow, be of wide extent.

འབྱར་བ, *v. n.* to stick to, adhere; to infect.

འབྱི་བ, *v. n.* to be wiped or blotted out.

འབྱིང་བ, *v. n.* to sink, drown, be immerged.

འབྱིད་པ, *v. n.* to pass away, be spent, to slide.

འབྱིན་པ, *v. a.* to draw, pull out; receive into, &c.

འབྱུག་པ, *v. a.* to besmear, bedaub.

འབྱུང་བ, *v. n.* to come forth, be born, rise.

འབྱེ་བ, *v. n.* to open, be divided, separated.

འབྱེད་པ, *v. a.* to open, divide, separate.

འབྱེར་བ, *v. n.* to disappear, vanish.

འབྱོ་བ, *v. a.* to pour out, transfuse.

འབྱོག་པ, *v. a.* to lick, touch with the tongue.

འབྱོང་བ, *v. n.* to be, or made ready.

འབྱོན་པ, *v. n.* to come, arrive.

འབྱོར་བ, *v. n.* to come in, arrive; *v. a.* to find, get, be united with.

འབྱོལ་བ, *v. n.* to deflect, turn aside, deviate.

འབྲང་བ, *v.* to bring, or be brought forth.

འབྲད་པ, *v. a.* to rub, fret, scratch.

འབྲབ་པ, *v. a.* to snatch away.

འབྲལ་བ, *v. n.* to go asunder, separated from.

འབྲི་བ, *v. a.* to write, express in characters, or figures; *v. n.* to grow less, decrease.

འབྲིད་པ, *v. a.* to make less, lessen, deceive.

འབྲིམ་པ, *v. a.* to distribute, give, share.

འབྲུ་བ, *v.* to pick, dig, fret, vex.

འབྲུད་པ, *v. a.* to rub, fret, dig.

འབྲུབ་པ, *v. a.* to distribute, give, lend; *v. n.* to flow.

འབྲེ་བ, *v. a.* to draw, stretch, spread out.

འབྲེག་པ, *v. a.* to shave with a razor; v. **འདྲེག་པ**.

འབྲེང་བ, *v.* to follow, go behind, imitate.

འབྲེལ་བ, *v. n.* to be joined, or united with.

འབྲོས་པ, *v. n.* to run away, desert.

འཚོག་པ, *v. a.* to sift, strain, squeeze.

འཚོང་བ, *v. n.* to be pure, whole, perfect.

འཚོབ་པ, *v. a.* to return, repay; supply.

འཚོབས་པ, *v. n.* to fear, be afraid.

འཚར་བ, *v. n.* to be finished, to grow, be grown up.

འཚལ་བ, *v.* to do, know, require, desire, &c.

འཚིག་པ, *v. n.* to be burnt, or burnt by fire.

འཚིར་བ, *v. a.* to press, squeeze, force out.

འཚུགས་པ, *v. n.* to be established, rooted.

འཚུད་པ, *v. n.* to enter into, be contained in.

འཚུབ་པ, *v.* to turn, whirl, (rapidly.)

འཚེ་བ, *v. a.* to hurt, injure, do harm to.

འཚེག་པ, *v. a.* to return, repay, give back.

འཚེང་བ, *v. n.* to advance, get up, improve.

འཚེད་པ, *v. a.* to boil, dress, dye, tinge, ripen.

འཚེམ་པ, *v. a.* to sew, stitch.

འཚེར་བ, *v. n.* to shine; to grieve for.

འཚོ་བ, *v. n.* to live, to be alive; *v. a.* to feed, cherish, nourish; boil, dress, dye, tinge.

འཚོག་པ, *v. a.* to cut, hew, engrave; to prick, pierce.

འཚོགས་པ, *v. n.* to assemble, associate, flock, come together.

འཚོང་བ, *v. a.* to sell.

འཚོད་པ, *v. a.* to boil, dress victuals; dye, tinge.

འཚོབ་པ, *v.* to act as a deputy, to depute.

འཚོལ་བ, *v. a.* to seek, look for, search after.

འཛག་པ, *v. n.* to drop, fall in drops.

འཛད་པ, *v. n.* to be spent, lack, want.

འཛར་བ, *v. n.* to hang down.

འཛིང་བ, *v.* to quarrel, fight.

འཛིན་པ *v. a.* to take, seize, hold fast, keep.

འཛིར་བ, *v. n.* to drop, fall in drops.

འཛུགས་པ, *v. a.* to fix, put, sit, plant, found, establish, build.

འཛུད་པ, *v. a.* to put, place, lay; turn, convert to.

འཛུམ་པ, *v.* to wink, (close and open again the eyes,) to smile, to look gay.

འཛུར་བ, *v. n.* to turn or go aside from one's way, (not to meet.)

འཛུལ་བ, *v. n.* to creep in, to enter in an inclined posture.

འཛེག་པ, *v.* to climb or ascend.

འཛེད་པ, *v. a.* to hold, contain, receive.

འཛེམ་པ, *v.* to blush, be ashamed for.

འཛེར་བ, *v. n.* to be hoarse; *v. a.* to speak, utter.

འཛོག་པ, *v. a.* to gather, heap together, (confusedly).

འཛོམ་པ, *v. n.* to come together, associate, assemble, meet.

འཛོམ་དུ་འཇུག་པ, *v. c.* to make or cause to meet.

འཛོལ་བ, *v. n.* to err, mistake.

ཡལ་བ, *v. n.* to be insipid or flat.

ཡིབ་པ, *v. n.* to abscond, hide one's self.

ཡུར་བ, *v. n.* to slumber.

རི་བ, *v. n.* to be worthy of so much, to cost, &c.

རིག་པ, *v. a.* to know, understand.

རིགས་པ, *v. n.* to be convenient, just.

རུང་བ, *v. n.* to be apt, fit, meet, convenient, &c.

རུབ་པ, *v. a.* to assault, fall on, attack.

རུལ་བ, *v. n.* to be rotten, putrid, rancid.

རེ་བ, *v.* to hope.

རེག་པ, *v. a.* to touch, feel.

རེང་བ or རེངས་པ, *v. n.* to be stiff, hard.

རོལ་བ, *v. n.* to delight, or to take pleasure in, to amuse one's self with.

རྐམ་པ, *v. a.* to long for, desire earnestly.

རྐུ་བ, *v. a.* to steal, thieve.

རྐོ་བ, *v. a.* to dig, carve, grave, cut.

རྐྱང་བ for བརྐྱང་བ, *v. a.* to stretch out.

རྐྱལ་བ, *v.* to swim.

རྐྱོང་བ, *v. a.* to stretch out, distend, extend.

རྙི་བ, *v. n.* to become, grow old; རྙིས་པ, grown old.

རྒལ་བ, *v. a.* to ford, to pass over without swimming.

རྒོད་པ, *v. n.* to laugh, to be wild.

རྒོལ་བ, *v.* to dispute, oppose.

རྒྱག་པ, *v. a.* to cast, throw, beat.

རྒྱབ་པ, *v. a.* to throw, cast, beat.

རྒྱལ་བ, *v. n.* to triumph, to be victorious, to be emancipated, to arrive at final beatitude.

རྒྱུ་བ, *v. n.* to rise, move, flow, proceed, go, walk.

རྒྱུག་པ, *v. n.* to run, flee.

རྒྱུད་པ, *v. a.* to put into a string, series; to collect, to gather together.

རྒྱོ་བ, *v. a.* to abuse a woman with violence.

རྒྱོང་བ, *v. a.* to extend, widen, dilate.

རྒྱོབ་པ, *v. a.* to cast, throw, hurl.

རྔ་བ, *v. a.* to reap, to cut with a sickle.

རྔན་པ, *v. a.* to reward, give a reward.

རྔབ་པ, *v.* to pant, long for, wish, desire.

རྔམ་པ, *v.* to long for.

རྔམས་པ for ཧམས་པ, idem.

རྔུབ་པ, *v.* to draw in, to breathe.

རྔུལ་བ, *v. n.* to sweat.

རྔོ་བ for རྔོ་ཐོག་པ, to be able, to may, to dare.

རྔོད་པ, *v. a.* to parch, burn slightly; to deceive.

རྔོན་པ, *v. a.* to chase, hunt, pursue; to deceive.

རྙུད་པ or སྙུད་པ, *v. n.* to grow less, abate, decrease.

རྗེ་བ, *v. a.* to barter, exchange; to change.

རྗེད་པ, *v. a.* to honour, reverence.

རྗོད་པ, *v. a.* to say, utter, speak, tell.

རྙང་བ, *v. a.* to cleanse, purge.

རྙིང་བ, *v. n.* to grow old, to be worn out.

རྙིད་པ, *v. n.* to fade, wither, pine away.

རྙིལ་བ, *v. n.* to break or fall down (as a rock).

རྙེད་པ, *v. a.* to find, get, obtain.

རྙོག་པ, *v. n.* to be stirred up, agitated, troubled.

རྙོང་བ, *v. a.* to snare, ensnare, entrap.

རྟག་པ, *v. n.* to be firm, steady, permanent, lasting, never ceasing, durable.

རྟབ་པ, *v. n.* to be in a hurry.

རྟབ་རྟབ་པ, idem.

རྟས.པ,*v. n.* to be copious, abundant; fat, thick.

རྟིབ་པ, *v. a.* to pull, break down.

རྟེན་པ, *v. a.* to keep, hold, support; *v. n.* to lean on, to depend on.

རྡོག་པ, *v. a.* to judge, examine, try, prove.

རྡོལ་བ, *v. a.* to make to spring or gush forth, to squeeze out, to arrive at.

རྡབ *v. a.* to clap, to strike together, to beat on.

རྡར་བ, *v. a.* to whet, to make sharp.

རྡལ་བ, *v. a.* to spread, to extend wide.

རྡིབ་པ, *v. n.* to drop or fall down suddenly, to break in.

རྡུང་བ, *v. a.* to beat, strike, hammer.

རྡེག་པ, *v. a.* to strike, beat, smite.

རྡོབ་པ, *v. a.* to clap, strike together.

རྡོར་བ, *v. a.* to whet, sharpen.

རྡོལ་བ, *v. a.* to spring out, gush forth, to issue; spring a leak, to have a hole.

རྣད་པ, *v. a.* to excite, incite, spur, stir up.

རྣབ་པ, *v. n.* to roll, or fall down.

རྨ་བ, *v. a.* to wound; to ask.

རྨི་བ, *v.* to dream.

རྨུག་པ, *v. a.* to bite, to wound with the teeth.

རྨུར་བ, *v.* to snarl, wrangle, quarrel.

རྨེ་བ, *v. n.* to be defiled, stained with.

རྨེད་པ, *v. a.* to say, speak, ask; to plough and sow.

རྨེལ་བ, *v. a.* to pick, cleanse (as wool).

རྨོ་བ, *v. a.* to plough.

རྨོད་པ, *v. a.* idem.

རྨྱང་བ, *v. n.* to yawn, gape, stretch with yawning.

རྩི་བ, *v. a.* to count, reckon, number; to accept, admit, yield to.

རྩིག་པ, *v. a.* to build, make a wall, construe.

རྩེ་བ, *v. n.* to play, sport, amuse one's self, game, frolick, trifle.

རྩེག་པ, *v. a.* to raise one thing above another, to tuck, truss up.

རྩེང་བ, *v. a.* to tuck, truss up.

རྩེན་པ, *v. n.* to play, sport, game; v. རྩེ་བ.

རྩོད་པ, *v.* to dispute, debate, contest, fight, quarrel.

རྩོམ་པ, *v. a.* to begin, make, compose, write.

རྩོལ་བ, *v.* to endeavour, make an effort.

རྫི་བ *v. a.* to press, force, squeeze, urge, oppress; v. བརྫི་བ.

རྫུ་བ, *v. a.* to change or turn one's self into, to transform.

རྫེ་བ *v. a.* to tuck, truss up.

རྫོང་བ or རྫང་བ, *v. a.* to make ready, to send, despatch.

རླུག་པ, *v. a.* to purge, carry off, produce. an abortion.

རློག་པ, *v. a.* to overthrow, lay waste, destroy.

རློན་པ, *v. n.* to be wet, fresh, green.

(བྱིན་རླབས) རློབ་པ, *v. a.* to bless, to give his benediction to.

རློམ་པ, *v. n.* to boast, be proud with.

ལགས་པ, *v. n.* to be, to exist, to be found.

ལུ་བ, *v. n.* to cough, to get up phlegm.

ལུད་པ, *v. n.* to burst, to overflow suddenly.

ལུས་པ, *v. n.* to remain, to be left.

ལེན་པ, *v. a.* to take, receive, seize, fetch.

ལོག་པ, *pret.* of ལྡོག་པ, *v. n.* to turn back.

ལོང་བ, for ལེན་པ, to take, receive, seize.

ལོང་བ from ལྡོང་བ, to be blind.

ལོབ་པ, *v. a.* to learn ; v. སློབ་པ.

ལྐུག་པ or ལྐུགས་པ, to be dumb or mute.

ལྕུ་བ for གཅུ་བ, *v. a.* to turn round, twist, wreathe ; to turn as a screw.

ལྕུད་པ, *v. a.* idem ; v. གཅུ་བ.

ལྕེབ་པ, *v.* to perish, destroy one's self.

ལྕོག་པ, *v. a.* to shake, quake, to be agitated ; to can, be able to do, may.

ལྡེན་པ, *v.* to enter into, penetrate, affect.

ལྟ་བ, *v. a.* to look, behold, view, see.

ལྟབ་པ, *v. a.* to fold up, to plait.

ལྟམ་པ for བལྟམ་པ, to be full, to be born.

ལྟུང་བ, *v. n.* to fall, to sin.

ལྡག་པ, *v. a.* to lick, touch with the tongue.

ལྡང་བ, *v.* to get of, to be given of ; to rise up, stand up, arise, to be diffused.

ལྡད་པ, *v. a.* to chew, cut with the teeth.

ལྡན་པ, *v. a.* to have, possess ; to be (to one).

ལྡབ་པ, *v. a.* to repeat, reiterate.

ལྡར་བ, *v. n.* to be faint, weary, languid.

ལྡིང་བ, *v. n.* to soar, fly aloft, float.

ལྡིར་བ, *v.* to be puffed up, to make a noise.

ལྡུག་པ, *v. a.* to pour into ; v. བླུག་པ.

ལྡུད་པ, *v. a.* to make or cause to drink (cattle).

ལྡེ་བ, *v. n.* to bask ; sit near the fire.

ལྡེག་པ, *v. n.* to quake, tremble.

ལྡེམ་པ, *v. n.* to shake, quake.

ལྡོག་པ, *v. n.* to return, go back, to be turned upside down, to be overset.

ལྡོང་བ, *v. n.* to be or become blind.

ལྡོན་པ, *v. a.* to return, give or pay back.

ལྡོབ་པ, *v.* to perceive easily, to be witty.

ལྷགས་པ, *v. n.* to arrive at, resort, go, come to.

ལྷུང་བ, *pret.* of ལྟུང་བ, *v. n.* to fall down from.

ལྷེ་བ, *v. a.* to twist, wreathe, wind.

ཤི་བ (*pret.* of འཆི་བ, *v. n.* to die), to be dead.

ཤུ་བ, *v. a.* to flay, strip, take off the skin ; to copy a book, &c.

ཤུང་བ, *v. n.* to breathe with a noise by the nostrils, to snore.

ཤུད་པ, *v. a.* to rub together, to fret.

ཤུབ་པ, *v. n.* to whisper.

ཤུམ་པ, *v. n.* to weep, lament.

ཤུར་བ, *v. a.* to hurt, burn slightly, cut.

ཤེས་པ, *v. a.* to know, understand.

ཤོང་བ, *v. n.* to have room, to be received into (a vessel) ; &c. to shite, to go to stool.

ཤོམ་པ, *v. a.* to prepare, make ready.

ཤོར་བ, *v. a.* to chase, hunt.

སད་པ, *v. a.* to prove, try, tempt, to awake.

སིག་པ, *v. a.* to retake, move or lift up a little.

སིབ་པ, *v. a.* to soak, imbibe.

སིམ་པ, *v. n.* to be refreshed, recreated, satisfied with.

སུད་པ, *v. n.* to cough or breathe with difficulty.

སེད་པ, *v. a.* to pick, cleanse.

སེམ་པ or སེམས་པ, *v.* to think, mind, meditate.

སེལ་བ, *v. a.* to cleanse, make clean, mend, repair, correct, improve, relieve, cure, heal, remedy; disclose, discover; v. བསལ་བ.

སོག་པ, *v. a.* to gather together, collect, hoard up.

སོང་བ, *v. n.* to go, depart, pass away; *pret.* and *imperat.* of འགྲོ་བ.

སོད་པ, *v. a.* to try, prove, tempt; v. སད་པ.

སོན་པ for སོང་བ, to go, come, arrive at a place.

སོན་པ for གསོན་པ, to be alive.

སྲིད་པ for སྤྲིང་བ, *v. a.* to send, despatch, order, commission.

སྲིང་བ, *v. a.* to lengthen, make longer.

སྲུང་བ, *v. a.* to keep, observe, defend, preserve, watch, spy.

སྲུབ་པ, *v. a.* to stir up, agitate, move.

སྲུལ་བ, *v. a.* to make rotten.

སྲེ་བ, *v. a.* to add (as in arithmetic); v. བསྲེ་བ.

སྲེག་པ, *v. a.* to burn.

སྲོ་བ, *v. a.* to warm, heat moderately.

སྲོང་བ, *v. a* to make right, straight, equal, keep in equilibrio, equiponderate, balance.

སླུ་བ, *v. a.* to deceive, impose on.

སླེ་བ, *v. a.* to twist, wind, writhe.

སླེབ་པ, *v. n.* to arrive.

སློག་པ, *v. a.* to change, turn, convert; to turn the outside inward.

སློང་བ, *v. a.* to raise up, erect, gather, amass, ask alms.

སློན་པ, *v. a.* to protrude, force out.

སློབ་པ, *v. a.* to teach, instruct; learn.

སླར་བ, *v. a.* to separate, fold up.

སྐུང་བ, *v. a.* to put under the ground, to hide, bury, to put into a hole.

སྐུད་པ, *v. a.* to smear, bedaub.

སྐུམ་པ, *v. a.* to contract, shrink up.

སྐུར་བ, *v. a.* to send, despatch; bestow, give.

སྐུལ་བ, *v. a.* to exhort, incite, bid.

སྐེམ་པ, *v. a.* to make dry, lean, meagre.

སྐོ་བ, *v. a.* to elect, choose.

སྐོང་བ, *v. a.* to fulfil, accomplish.

སྐོན་པ, *v. a.* to put on (as clothes).

སྐོམ་པ, *v. n.* to thirst, be thirsty.

སྐོར་བ, *v. a.* to turn round, encircle, surround, enclose.

སྐོལ་བ, *v. a.* to boil, make boil; seeth.

སྐུག་པ, *v. a.* to spend, lay out, expend.

སྐྱི་བ, *v. a.* to borrow, ask a loan, take on credit.

སྐྱིག་པ, *v. n.* to vex.

སྐྱིལ་བ, *v. a.* to bend, cross, or put in the form of a cross.

སྐྱུག་པ, *v. a.* to vomit, to cast up from the stomach.

སྐྱུང་བ, *v. a.* to leave off, put aside, renounce, forsake, relinquish, to leave behind.

སྐྱུད་པ, *v. a.* to forget.

སྐྱུར་བ, *v. a.* to leave off, cast away, relinquish.

སྐྱེ་བ, *v. n.* to be born, to be produced, to come forth.

སྐྱེང་བ, *v.* to be ashamed of.

སྐྱེད་པ, *v. a.* to produce, generate, form, make, cause, breed, rear up, beget, procreate.

སྐྱེན་པ, *v.* to make haste, to strive, to endeavour.

སྐོམ་པ, *v. n.* to be thirsty.

སྐྱེལ་བ, *v. a.* to carry, convey; conduct, accompany, lead; bring; send.

སྐྱོ་བ, *v. n.* to grieve, be sorrowful, mournful.

སྐྱོང་བ, *v. a.* to defend, guard, protect, keep safe.

སྐྱོད་པ, *v. n.* to move, go, walk; *v. a.* to move, agitate, shake.

སྐྱོན་པ, *v. a.* to put, place, lay on.

སྐྱོབ་པ, *v. a.* to protect, defend, keep safe.

སྐྱོམ་པ, *v. a.* to stir up, move, shake, agitate.

སྐྱོར་བ, *v. a.* to repeat, add to; keep or hold up.

སྐྲག་པ, *v. n.* to fear, dread, be afraid of.

སྐྲང་བ, *v. n.* to swell, to be swollen; to puff up.

སྐྲབ་པ, *v. a.* to beat the ground with one's feet.

སྐྲི་བ, *v. a.* to lead, conduct; v. འཁྲིད་པ། བཀྲི་བ.

སྐྲོད་པ, *v. a.* to eject, expel, drive out.

སྒང་བ, *v. n.* to be filled or replete; to be fulfilled.

སྒབ་པ, *v. a.* to spread over, to cover with.

སྒུག་པ, *v.* to wait for.

སྒུལ་བ, *v. a.* to move, agitate, shake.

སྒེག་པ, *v. n.* to puff, boast, brag.

སྒོ་བ, *v. a.* to bid, order, proclaim, publish.

སྒོག་པ, *v. a.* to make swear, to put on oath.

སྒོང་བ, *v. a.* to make round or globular, to conglomerate.

སྒོམ་པ, *v.* to be accustomed to, to be exercised in; to represent in the mind, to think on; to fancy, imagine.

སྒོར་བ, *v. a.* to thicken, coagulate, form clots.

སྒྱིང་བ, *v. n.* to stretch with gaping and yawning.

སྒྱེལ་བ, *v. a.* to overset, overthrow, subvert, overturn.

སྒྱོང་བ, *v. n.* to be hidden or secret.

སྒྲང་བ, *v. a.* to enumerate, reckon; v. བསྒྲང་བ.

སྒྲིག་པ, *v. a.* to adjust, compose, make agree, put together.

སྒྲིབ་པ, *v. a.* to offuscate, shadow, darken.

སྒྲིམ་པ, *v. a.* to hold fast, twist together; to endeavour, make an effort.

སྒྲིལ་བ, *v. a.* to roll, wrap, wind up, twist.

སྒྲུང་བ, *v. a.* to mix, feign, relate falsely.

སྒྲུན་པ, *v. a.* to liken, compare, estimate; to emulate, vie, contend with.

སྒྲུབ་པ, *v. a.* to prepare, make ready; render propitious; to acquire, learn, obtain, get.

སྒྲེག་པ, *v.* to belch, to eject wind from the stomach.

སྒྲེང་བ, *v. a.* to raise, erect, lift up.

སྒྲོ་བ, *v.* to argue, reason, consider; to debate, discuss, take measures for; v. བསྒྲོ་བ.

སྒྲོག་པ, *v. a.* to proclaim, publish, preach.

སྒྲོད་པ, *v.* to go on or over.

སྒྲོན་པ, *v. a.* to embellish, decorate.

སྒྲོལ་བ, *v. a.* to untie, loosen, deliver, save.

སྔུར་བ, *v. n.* to snort, make a noise, &c.

སྔོ་བ, *v.* to grow green; *v. a.* to bless.

སྒྲད་པ, *v. a.* to tell, report, relate, say; accuse, charge with.

སྙམ་པ, *v.* to think, suppose.

སྙིགས་པ, *v. n.* to be degenerated, grown worse.

སྙིལ་བ, *v. a.* to break down, destroy.

སྙུག་པ, *v. a.* to dip, immerge, moisten.

སྙུང་བ, *v. a.* to make fewer, or less, to reduce.

སྙུན་པ, *v. n.* to be debilitated, sick ; *v. a.* to disease, afflict.

སྙེ་བ, *v. n.* to lean on, to rest against.

སྙེག་པ, *v.* to make haste, to strive, endeavour.

སྙེངས་པ, *v. n.* to fear, dread, be afraid of.

སྙེན་པ, *v. n.* to approach ; *v. a.* to gain, procure.

སྙེམ་པ, *v. n.* to boast, brag, be proud of.

སྙོད་པ, *v. a.* to feed, to give to eat and drink ; to tell.

སྙོབ་པ, *v. a.* to lift up, stretch out ; *v. n.* to reach to.

སྙོམ་པ, *v. a.* to make equal, level.

སྙོལ་བ, *v. a.* to lay, place, put flat down.

སྟབ་པ, *v. n.* to hurry, to be in confusion.

སྟར་བ, *v. a.* to put in order or series.

སྟི་བ, *v. n.* to rest, refresh one's self.

སྟིང་བ, *v. a.* to rebuke, chide, upbraid.

སྟིམ་པ, *v. a.* to infect, pervade, penetrate.

སྟུང་བ, *v. a.* to shorten, abbreviate, make short.

སྟུད་པ, *v. a.* to iterate, repeat ; to put together.

སྟུན་པ, *v. a.* to make agree, reconcile ; confer.

སྟེན་པ, *v. a* to keep, hold ; to keep in pay.

སྟེར་བ, *v. a.* to give, bestow, grant, allow, permit.

སྟོང་པ་ཡིན་པ, *v. n.* to be empty.

སྟོད་པ, *v. a.* to magnify, extol, exalt, praise.

སྟོན་པ, *v. a.* to show, instruct, teach.

སྟོབ་པ, *v. a.* to give into one's hand, to give, deliver.

སྟོར་བ, *v. n.* to go astray, to be mingled among.

སྡང་བ, *v. n.* to abhor, dislike, be angry.

སྡིགས་པ, *v. a.* to menace, threaten with.

སྡུད་པ, *v. a.* to collect, gather, amass.

སྡུམ་པ, *v. a.* to make agree, pacify, reconcile.

སྡེབ་པ, *v. a.* to mingle, mix ; exchange, barter.

སྡོ་བ, *v.* to hazard, expose to chance or danger.

སྡོད་པ, *v.* to sit, tarry, wait for, attend.

སྡོམ་པ, *v. a.* to bind, restrain ; oblige one's self ; to vow, promise.

སྣང་བ, *v. n.* to be light, to be evident, manifest ; to seem, appear.

སྣད་པ, *v. a.* to hurt, wound, injure, to do harm to.

སྣམ་པ, *v. a.* to take, receive ; put on.

སྣུན་པ, *v. a.* to prick, goad, pierce ; to suckle.

སྣུབ་པ, *v. a.* to abolish, destroy.

སྣུམ་པ, *v. a.* to smell, perceive by the nose.

སྣུར་བ, *v. a.* to make less ; bring nearer, anticipate.

སྣོ་བ, *v. a.* to make small pieces of, to diminish.

སྣོན་པ, *v. a.* to augment, increase, add more to.

སྣོམ་པ, *v. a.* to smell, perceive by the nose ; to take, receive, put on.

སྣོར་བ, *v. a.* to confound, mix, mingle, disturb, to mistake.

སྤོལ་བ, *v. a.* to comprise, include, embrace.

སྤག་པ, *v. a.* to carry, or bring by turns.

སྤང་བ, *v. a.* to leave off, renounce, quit, abandon, cast away.

སྤར་བ, *v. a.* to exalt, promote, raise.

སྤུང་བ, *v. a.* to heap up together.

སྤུད་པ, *v. a.* to adorn, embellish ; put on.

སྤུབ་པ, *v. a.* to turn upside down ; to place with the face or mouth downwards.

སྤུར་བ, *v. a.* to make fly ; to excite, to egg on.

སྤེལ་བ, *v. a.* to augment, increase.

སྤོ་བ, *v. a.* to change, shift, alter.

སྤོག་པ, *v. a.* to carry or bring forwards by turns.

སྤོང་བ, *v. a.* to leave off, cast away.

སྤོར་བ, *v. a.* to raise, promote, advance.

སྤྱང་བ, *v. a.* to let down, to hang down.

སྤྱད་པ, *v. a.* to use, enjoy ; practise, do.

སྤྱིང་བ, *v. a.* to make sink, to submerge.

སྤྱུག་པ, *v. a.* to expel, banish.

སྤྱོ་བ, *v. a.* to mock, ridicule, chide ; rail on ; blame, censure.

སྤྱོད་པ, *v. a.* to use, enjoy; practise, do, perform.

སྤྱོན་པ, *v. n.* to come, arrive.

སྤྱོམ་པ, *v. a.* to show, to expose to view ; to boast, brag.

སྤྲ་བ, *v. a.* to adorn, decorate, embellish.

སྤྲང་བ, *v.* to mendicate, beg, ask alms.

སྤྲད་པ, *v. a.* to give into one's hand, to deliver ; compose ; meet.

སྤྲིང་བ, *v. a.* to give intelligence, make acquainted with ; inform ; send orders.

སྤྲུག་པ, *v. a.* to shake off, cleanse ; rub, scrub.

སྤྲུལ་བ, *v. a.* to change or turn (miraculously).

སྤྲོ་བ, *v. a.* to like, wish, will, be pleased with; to scatter, diffuse.

སྤྲོད་པ, *v. a.* to compose, put together.

སྦ་བ, *v. a.* to hide, conceal, keep secret.

སྦག་པ, *v. a.* to dirty, foul, soil, stain.

སྦང་བ, *v. a.* to macerate, steep in water.

སྦམ་པ, *v. a.* to gather, collect, put together.

སྦར་བ, *v. a.* to kindle, inflame, light.

སྦེད་པ, *v. a.* to hide, conceal, cover, keep secret.

སྦོ་བ, *v.* to puff, swell up.

སྦོག་པ, *v. a.* to make dirty, foul.

སྦོང་བ, *v. a.* to steep, macerate.

སྦོར་བ, *v. a.* to kindle, light, inflame.

སྦྱང.བ, *v. a.* to take away a part, subtract ; cleanse, purify, exercise.

སྦྱར་བ *v. a.* to compose, join, put together, write ; mix, mingle ; dress, prepare.

སྦྱིན་པ, *v. a.* to give alms, to give, bestow, confer on.

སྦྱོང་བ, *v. a.* to diminish, subtract ; cleanse ; exercise.

སྦྱོར་བ, *v. a.* to join, put together.

སྦྲན་པ, *v. a.* to bespot, besprinkle ; summon, call for aid.

སྦྲིད་པ, *v. n.* to sneeze ; to be numb, or benumbed.

སྦྲུ་བ or སྦྲུད་པ, *v. a.* to knead, work dough with the fist.

སྦྲེང་བ, *v.* to play on, or sound a musical instrument.

སྦྲེལ་བ, *v. a.* to join or put together.

སྦྲོན་པ, *v. a.* to call on for aid, to summon ; to bespot, besprinkle.

སྨད་པ, *v. a.* to blame, chide, abuse, curse ; contemn, disdain, scorn ; to bend down, depress.

སྨིན་པ་ཡིན་པ, *v. n.* to be ripe or mature.

སྨོ་བ, *v. a.* to mention, tell, say.

སྨོད་པ, *v. a.* to blame, &c. ; v. སྨད་པ.

སྨོན་པ, *v. a.* to desire, wish, will, long for.

སྨྱུང་བ, *v. n.* to fast, to take no food.

སྨྱུར་བ, *v. a.* to hasten, make haste.

སྨྱོ་བ, *v. n.* to be mad, distracted.

སྨྲ་བ, *v. a.* to speak, say.

སྩལ་བ also སྩོལ་བ, *v. a.* to give, grant ; order.

ཧ་གོ་བ, (v. གོ་བ,) *v. a.* to understand, perceive.

ཧྲིག་པ, *v.* to look to, to twinkle.

ཧྲིག་ཧྲིག་བྱེད་པ, to look hither and thither.

End of the Grammar.

བཀྲ་ཤིས །

APPENDIX.

I. TIBETAN MODES OF RECKONING TIME.

§. 227. The Tibetans, having derived their astronomical and astrological knowledge both from Indian and from Chinese sources, as also from other parts of the eastern world, have thence become possessed of several distinct modes of reckoning and measuring time. The system of astronomy and chronology formed on the Indian principle is called "*Kar-ţis*" (དཀར་རྩིས or སྐར་རྩིས, d,*kar-rtsis* or s*kar-rtsis*) ; astrological calculations (especially the black-art), and the mode of reckoning years, in the Chinese manner, are denominated by the Tibetans "*Nak-çis*" (ནག་རྩིས, *nag-rtsis*). Of both these are an abundance of works in Tibet, expounding the particulars of the various systems.

§ 228. The most common mode of reckoning time among the people at large, especially in calculating the years of the present generation, or in estimating the age of individuals, is that by the cycle of 12 years, in which each year is denominated from a certain animal, in the following order.

Cycle of 12 Years.

	Tibetan.		*English.*		*Tibetan.*		*English.*
1	བྱི་ལོ,	*byi-lo,*	the mouse-year.	7	རྟ་ལོ,	rta-*lo,*	the horse-year.
2	གླང་ལོ,	gl*ang-lo,*	the ox-year.	8	ལུག་ལོ,	*lug-lo,*	the sheep-year.
3	སྟག་ལོ,	s*tag lo,*	the tiger-year.	9	སྤྲེ་ལོ,	s*pré-lo,*	the ape-year.
4	ཡོས་ལོ,	*yos-lo,*	the hare-year.	10	བྱ་ལོ,	*bya-lo,*	the bird-year.
5	འབྲུག་ལོ,	h*brug-lo,*	the dragon-year.	11	ཁྱི་ལོ,	k*hyi-lo,*	the dog-year.
6	སྦྲུལ་ལོ,	s*brul-lo,*	the serpent-year.	12	ཕག་ལོ,	p*hog-lo,*	the hog-year.

But in books, epistolary correspondence, and in every transaction of importance, the Tibetans make use, generally, of the cycle of 60 years. This is of two kinds. The one in the Indian, and the other in the Chinese, manner. We will give them both here below.

§ 229. The years of the Indian Cycle of 60 years, as they are reckoned south of the *Nermada* river in India, (See Col. Warren's Chron. Tab. XXI.,) exactly coincide with the Tibetan era, with the exception only that the Tibetans have translated literally the Sanscrit names into their own language, and that they count the beginning of the first cycle from a more recent epoch than that stated by Col. Warren to be in use among the Hindus. The present year, 1834, (called *Jaya*, in Sanscrit; in Tibetan r*Gyel-va*, རྒྱལ་བ, meaning Victory or Victorious,) is, both in South India and Tibet the 28th year of the cycle. In Tibet, it is the 28th year of the XIV. cycle, reckoning the beginning of the first cycle from the year 1026 of the Christian Era; but the Indians date the commencement of the first cycle from an anterior epoch, sometimes from the *Kaliyuga*, and sometimes from the reign of *Saliváhana*.

§ 230. In order to preserve a correspondence between the years of the Chinese cycle and that of India, the Tibetans give the designation of first to the fourth year of the Chinese cycle; probably that cycle was in general use when they adopted the calendar and computations of India.

The Tibetans, like the Chinese, divide the year into lunar months, calling them thus: the first, second, third month, &c. &c. And during the period of one Lunar Cycle (of 19 solar years), they insert seven intercalary months, generally one every third year, to make them agree with the solar years:—in fact, their calculations exactly correspond with the luni-solar system of the Hindus, which is fully explained in Col. Warren's work above alluded to.

§ 231. The Chinese cycle of sixty years, differs from the Indian, in the mode of naming the years: the latter has a distinct name for each year of the series: the former is made up by combining the names of the five elements, (made ten by affixing the male and female termination), in a regular series, with the names of the zodiacal animals of the cycle of 12 years; the series of 10 is repeated six times, while that of 12 is repeated only five times in the 60 years, which causes a different combination for every year of the cycle.

The names of the five elements, repeated with the masculine and feminine affix, in Chinese, as written in Tibetan, with their translation in Tibetan also and English, are as follows:

The 10 *Elements.*

	Chinese.			*Tibetan.*			*English.*
1	*Kya*	or	ཀྱ	ཤིང (ཕོ)	or	*shing pho,*	Wood, *m.*
2	*Yi*	or	ཡི	ཤིང (མོ)	or	*shing mo,*	Wood, *f.*
3	*Ping*	or	པིང	མེ (ཕོ)	or	*mé pho,*	Fire, *m.*
4	*Ting*	or	ཏིང	མེ (མོ)	or	*mé mo,*	Fire, *f.*
5	*Vou*	or	ཝུ	ས (ཕོ)	or	*sa pho,*	Earth, *m.*
6	*Kyi*	or	ཀྱི	ས (མོ)	or	*sa mo,*	Earth, *f.*
7	*King*	or	ཀིང	ལྕགས (ཕོ)	or	*lchags pho,*	Iron, *m.*
8	*Zin*	or	ཟིན	ལྕགས (མོ)	or	*lchags mo,*	Iron, *f.*
9	*Zhin*	or	ཞིན	ཆུ (ཕོ)	or	*chhu pho,*	Water, *m.*
10	*Kuhi*	or	ཀུའི	ཆུ (མོ)	or	*chhu mo,*	Water, *f.*

The names of the 12 animals or signs of the zodiac, as written in the Tibetan character, are—

	Chinese.			*Tibetan.*			*English.*
1	*Tsi*	or	ཙི,	བྱི,	or	*byi*	Mouse.
2	*Tshihu*	or	ཚིའུ,	གླང་,	or	*glang*	Ox.
3	*Yin*	or	ཡིན,	སྟག,	or	*stag*	Tiger.
4	*Mahu*	or	མའུ,	ཡོས	or	*yos*	Hare.
5	*Shin (tchin?)*	or	ཤིན,	འབྲུག,	or	*hbrug*	Dragon.
6	*Zi*	or	ཟི,	སྦྲུལ,	or	*sbrul*	Serpent.
7	*Hu (u)*	or	ཨུ,	རྟ,	or	*rta*	Horse.
8	*Wuhi*	or	ཝུའི,	ལུག,	or	*lug*	Sheep.
9	*Shing*	or	ཤིང་,	སྤྲེ	or	*spré*	Ape.
10	*Yéhu*	or	ཡེའུ,	བྱ,	or	*bya*	Bird.
11	*Zuhi*	or	ཟུའི,	ཁྱི,	or	*khyi*	Dog.
12	*Huhi*	or	ཧའི,	ཕག,	or	*phag*	Hog.

It should be remarked, that the animals of the cycle of 12 years are to be taken alternately, male and female, thus: ཕོ་བྱི, མོ་གླང, ཕོ་སྟག, མོ་ཡོས, &c. &c. to accord with the genders of the elements. After the five (or ten) elements are frequently introduced, also, the particles ཕོ (male), and མོ (female), thus: ཤིང་ཕོ་བྱི, ཤིང་མོ་གླང., མེ་ཕོ་སྟག, མེ་མོ་ཡོས, &c. but they may be omitted at pleasure, without any danger of obscurity arising therefrom; since the names of the 12 animals are always coupled with different elements throughout the series.

§. 232. Sanscrit and Tibetan names of the years in the Cycle of Sixty years, as they are reckoned south of the river Nermada, in India, and in Tibet, expressed in Roman character. They accord with the Tibetan version of the two first columns in the succeeding table.

	Sanscrit.	*Tibetan.*
1	Prabhava,	Rab-byung.
2	Vibhava,	*r*Nam-*h*byung.
3	Shukla,	*d*Kar-po.
4	Pramodi,	Rab-myos.
5	Prajapati,	*s*Kyes-*b*dag.
6	Angira,	Angira.
7	Srimukha,	*d*Pal-*g*dong.
8	Bhava,	*d*Nos-po.
9	Yuvika,	Na-tshod-*l*dan.
10	Dhritu, or (Dhátá,)	*h*Dsin-byed.
11	Iswara,	*d*Vang-phyug.
12	Bahudanya,	*h*Bru-mang-po.
13	Pramáthi,	Myos-*l*dan.
14	Vikrama,	*r*Nam-*g*non.
15	Vris'habha,	Khyu-*m*chhog.
16	Chitra,	*s*Na-tshogs.
17	Bhánu,	Nyi-ma.
18	Bhánutára,	Nyi-*s*grol-byed.
19	Pirthapa,	Sa-*s*kyong.
20	Aks'haya,	Mi-zad.
21	Sarvajit,	Thams-chad-*h*dul.
22	Sarvadhári,	Kun-*h*dsin.
23	Virodhi,	*h*Gal-va.
24	Vikrita,	*r*Nam-*h*gyur.
25	Khara,	Bong-bu.
26	Nanda,	*d*Gah-va.
27	Vijaya,	*r*Nam-*r*gyal.
28	Jaya,	*r*Gyal-va.
29	Mada (or Manmatha)	Myos-byed.
30	Durmukha,	*g*Dong-ńan.
31	Hémalambhi,	*g*Ser-*h*phyang.
32	Vilambhi,	*r*Nam-*h*phyang.
33	Vicári,	*s*Gyur-byed.
34	Sarvapati,	Kun-*l*dan.
35	Plava, (or Sáva),	*h*Phar-va.
36	Shubhakrit,	*d*Gé-byed,
37	Shobhana,	*m*Dses-byed.
38	Khrodhi,	Khromo.
39	Vishwabandhu, (or Viswávasu,)	*s*Na-tshogs-*d*vyig.
40	Parábhava,	Zil-*g*non.
41	Pravanga, or Plavanga,	*s*Préhu.
42	Kilaka,	Phur-bu.
43	Saumya,	Zhi-va.
44	Sádhárána,	Thun-mong.
45	Virodhakrit,	*h*Gal-byed.
46	Paridharí,	Yongs-*h*dsin.
47	Pramádi,	Bag-med.
48	A'nanda,	Kun-*d*Gah.
49	Rákskasa,	Srin-bu.
50	Anala,	Mé.
51	Pingala,	*d*Mar-*s*er-chan.
52	Káladútí, (or Kálayukta,)	Dus-kyi pho-nya.
53	Siddhárthi,	Don-grub.
54	Rudra,	Drag-po.
55	Durmati,	*b*Lo-ńan.
56	Dundubhi,	*r*Ňa-chhen.
57	Rudhirura, (or Rudirodgari,)	Khrag-*s*kyug.
58	Raktákshi,	Mig-*d*mar.
59	Kródhana,	Khro-vo.
60	Ks'haya, or Ks'hayaka,	Zad-pa.

§. 233. Vrihaspati chakra, or cycle of sixty years.

As written in the Tibetan character.

In Sanscrit and Tibetan. *In Chinese and Tibetan.*

ལོ་རྣམ་ཙུ་སྐོར་གྱི་མིང་གི་རྣམ་གྲངས།

	རྒྱ་གར་གྱི་སྐད།	བོད་ཀྱི་སྐད	རྒྱ་ནག་གི་སྐད	བོད་ཀྱི་སྐད	
1	པྲབྷཝ	རབ་བྱུང་	ཏིང་མཙུ	མེ་ཡོས	༡
2	ཝིབྷཝ	རྣམ་འབྱུང་	ཝུ་ཤིན	ས་འབྲུག	༢
3	ཤུཀླ	དཀར་པོ	ཇི་སྲི	ས་སྦྲུལ	༣
4	པྲམོད	རབ་མྱོས	ཀིང་ཝུ	ལྕགས་རྟ	༤
5	པྲཛཱཔཏི	སྐྱེས་བདག	སྲིན་ཝུའི	ལྕགས་ལུག	༥
6	ཨང་གི་ར	ཨང་གི་ར	ཞིན་ཤིང་	ཆུ་སྤྲེ	༦
7	ཤྲཱིམུཁ	དཔལ་གདོང་	གུའི་ཡེཙུ	ཆུ་བྱ	༧
8	བྷཱཝ	དངོས་པོ	ཅ་ཤུའི	ཤིང་ཁྱི	༨
9	ཡུཝཱན	ན་ཚོད་ལྡན	ཡི་ཧའི	ཤིང་ཕག	༩
10	དྷཱཏྲ	འཛིན་བྱེད	པིང་ཙི	མེ་བྱི	༡༠
11	ཨཱིཤྭར	དབང་ཕྱུག	ཏིང་ཆིཙུ	མེ་གླང་	༡༡
12	བཧུདྷཱནྱ	འབྲུ་མང་པོ	ཝུ་ཡིན	ས་སྟག	༡༢
13	པྲམཱཐི or པྲམཱདི	མྱོས་ལྡན	ཇི་མཙུ	ས་ཡོས	༡༣
14	ཝིཀྲམ	རྣམ་གནོན	ཀིང་ཤིན	ལྕགས་འབྲུག	༡༤
15	ཝྲིཥ	ཁྱུ་མཆོག	སྲིན་སྲི	ལྕགས་སྦྲུལ	༡༥
16	ཙིཏྲ	སྣ་ཚོགས	ཞིན་ཝུ	ཆུ་རྟ	༡༦
17	སྭབྷཱནུ	ཉི་མ	གུའི་ཝུའི	ཆུ་ལུག	༡༧
18	ཏཱཎཱར	ཉི་སྒྲོལ་བྱེད	ཅ་ཤིང་	ཤིང་སྤྲེ	༡༨
19	པཱརྠིཝ	ས་སྐྱོང་	ཡི་ཡེཙུ	ཤིང་བྱ	༡༩
20	ཨཀྵཡ	མི་ཟད	པིང་ཤུའི	མེ་ཁྱི	༢༠
21	སརྦཛིཏ	ཐམས་ཅད་འདུལ	ཏིང་ཧའི	མེ་ཕག	༢༡
22	སརྦདྷཱརི	ཀུན་འཛིན	ཝུ་ཙི	ས་བྱི	༢༢
23	ཝིརོདྷི	འགལ་བ	ཇི་ཆིཙུ	ས་གླང་	༢༣
24	ཝིཀྲིཏ	རྣམ་འགྱུར	ཀིང་ཡིན	ལྕགས་སྟག	༢༤
25	ཁར	བོང་བུ	སྲིན་མཙུ	ལྕགས་ཡོས	༢༥
26	ནནྡ	དགའ་བ	ཞིན་ཤིན	ཆུ་འབྲུག	༢༦
27	ཝིཛཡ	རྣམ་རྒྱལ	གུའི་སྲི	ཆུ་སྦྲུལ	༢༧
28	ཛཡ	རྒྱལ་བ	ཅཝུ	ཤིང་རྟ	༢༨
29	མད	མྱོས་བྱེད	ཡི་ཝུའི	ཤིང་ལུག	༢༩
30	དུརྨུཁ	གདོང་ངན	པིང་ཤིང་	མེ་སྤྲེ	༣༠

CYCLE OF SIXTY YEARS, *Continued.*

	In Sanscrit and Tibetan.		*In Chinese and Tibetan.*		
31	ཧེ་མ་ལམྦི	གསེར་འཕྱང་	ཏིང་ཡེའུ	མེ་བྱ	༣༡
32	བིལམྦི	རྣམ་འབྱུང་	ཝུ་ཤྲུའི	ས་ཁྱི	༣༢
33	བིཀཱརི	སྒྱུར་བྱེད	ཅི་ཧའི	ས་ཕག	༣༣
34	སརྦཱརི	ཀུན་ལྡན	ཀིང་ཙི	ལྕགས་བྱི	༣༤
35	པླབ	འཕར་བ	ཤིན་ཚེའུ	ལྕགས་གླང་	༣༥
36	ཤུབྷཀྲིཏ྄	དགེ་བྱེད	ཞིན་ཡིན	ཆུ་སྟག	༣༦
37	ཤོབྷན	མཛེས་བྱེད	ཀུའི་མའུ	ཆུ་ཡོས	༣༧
38	ཀྲོདྷི	ཁྲོ་མོ	ཅ་ཤིན	ཤིང་འབྲུག	༣༨
39	བིཤྭཱབ་སུ	སྣ་ཚོགས་དབྱིག	ཡི་སྲི	ཤིང་སྦྲུལ	༣༩
40	པརཱབྷབ	ཟིལ་གནོན	པིང་ཝུ	མེ་རྟ	༤༠
41	པླབཾག	སྤྲེའུ	ཏིང་ཝུའི	མེ་ལུག	༤༡
42	ཀཱིལཀ	ཕུར་བུ	ཝུ་ཤིང་	ས་སྤྲེ	༤༢
43	སཽམྱ	ཞི་བ	ཅི་ཡེའུ	ས་བྱ	༤༣
44	སཱདྷཱརཎ	ཐུན་མོང	ཀིང་ཤྲུའི	ལྕགས་ཁྱི	༤༤
45	བིརོདྷཀྲིཏ྄	འགལ་བྱེད	ཤིན་ཧའི	ལྕགས་ཕག	༤༥
46	པརིདྷཱབི	ཡོངས་འཛིན	ཞིན་ཙི	ཆུ་བྱི	༤༦
47	པྲམཱདི	བག་མེད	ཀུའི་ཚེའུ	ཆུ་གླང་	༤༧
48	ཨཱ་ནན་ད	ཀུན་དགའ	ཅ་ཡིན	ཤིང་སྟག	༤༨
59	རཱཀྵས	སྲིན་བུ	ཡི་མའུ	ཤིང་ཡོས	༤༩
50	ཨནལ	མེ	པིང་ཤིན	མེ་འབྲུག	༥༠
51	པིང་ག་ལ	དམར་སེར་ཅན	ཏིང་སྲི	མེ་སྦྲུལ	༥༡
52	ཀཱལཡུཀྟི	དུས་ཀྱི་ཕོ་ཉ	ཝུ་ཝུ	ས་རྟ	༥༢
53	སིད་དྷཱརྠ	དོན་གྲུབ	ཅི་ཝུའི	ས་ལུག	༥༣
54	རཽ་དྲ	དྲག་པོ	ཀིང་ཤིང་	ལྕགས་སྤྲེ	༥༤
55	དུརྨ་ཏི	བློ་ངན	ཤིན་ཡེའུ	ལྕགས་བྱ	༥༥
56	དུན་དུབྷི	རྔ་ཆེན	ཞིན་ཤྲུའི	ཆུ་ཁྱི	༥༦
57	རུདྷིརུར	ཁྲག་སྐྱུག	ཀུའི་ཧའི	ཆུ་ཕག	༥༧
58	རཀ་ཏཱཀྵི	མིག་དམར།	ཅ་ཙི	ཤིང་བྱི	༥༨
59	ཀྲོདྷན	ཁྲོ་བོ།	ཡི་ཚེའུ	ཤིང་གླང་	༥༩
60	ཀྵཡཀ	ཟད་པ།	པིང་ཡིན	མེ་སྟག	༦༠

§ 234. Names of the years of the CYCLE OF SIXTY YEARS, according to the Chinese reckoning, in Roman characters, and bearing reference to the two last columns of the preceding catalogue.

	Chinese.	*Tibetan.*	*English.*
1	Kya tsi,	Shing byi,	Wood-mouse.
2	Yi tshihu,	Shing *g*lang,	Wood-ox.
3	Ping yin,	Mé *s*tag,	Fire-tiger.
4	Ting mahu,	Mé yos,	Fire-hare.
5	Vou shin, (or tchin ?)	Sa *h*brug,	Earth-dragon.
6	Kyi zi,	Sa *s*brul,	Earth-serpent.
7	King hu,	*l*chags *r*ta,	Iron-horse.
8	Zin wuhi,	*l*chags lug,	Iron-sheep.
9	Zhin shing,	Chhu *s*pré,	Water-ape.
10	Kuhi yéhu,	Chhu bya,	Water-bird.
11	Kya zuhi,	Shing khyi,	Wood-dog.
12	Yi hahi,	Shing phag,	Wood-hog.
13	Ping tsi,	Mé byi,	Fire-mouse.
14	Ting tshihu,	Mé *g*lang,	Fire-ox.
15	You yin,	Sa *s*tag,	Earth-tiger.
16	Kyi mahu,	Sa yos,	Earth-hare.
17	King shin,	*l*chags *h*brug,	Iron-dragon.
18	Zin zi,	*l*chags *s*brul,	Iron-serpent.
19	Zhin hu,	Chhu *r*ta,	Water-horse.
20	Kuhi wuhi,	Chhu lug,	Water-sheep.
21	Kya shing,	Shing *s*pré,	Wood-ape.
22	Yi yéhu,	Shing bya,	Wood-bird.
23	Ping zuhi,	Mé khyi,	Fire-dog.
24	Ting hahi,	Mé phag,	Fire-hog.
25	Vou tsi,	Sa byi,	Earth-mouse.
26	Kyi tshihu,	Sa *g*lang,	Earth-ox.
27	King yin,	*l*chags *s*tag,	Iron-tiger.
28	Zin mahu,	*l*chags yos,	Iron-hare.
29	Zhin shin,	Chhu *h*brug,	Water-dragon.
30	Kuhi zi,	Chhu *s*brul,	Water-serpent.

	Chinese.	*Tibetan.*	*English.*
31	Kya hu,	Shing *r*ta,	Wood-horse.
32	Yi wuhi,	Shing lug,	Wood-sheep.
33	Ping shing,	Mé *s*pré,	Fire-ape.
34	Ting yéhu,	Mé bya,	Fire-bird.
35	Vou zuhi,	Sa khyi,	Earth-dog.
36	Kyi hahi,	Sa phag,	Earth-hog.
37	King-tsi,	*l*chags byi,	Iron-mouse.
38	Zin tshihu,	*l*chags *g*lang,	Iron-ox.
39	Zhin yin,	Chhu *s*tag,	Water-tiger.
40	Kuhi mahu,	Chhu yos,	Water-hare.
41	Kya shin,	Shing *h*brug,	Wood-dragon.
42	Yi zi,	Shing *s*brul,	Wood-serpent.
43	Ping hu,	Mé *r*ta,	Fire-horse.
44	Ting wuhi,	Mé lug,	Fire-sheep.
45	Vou shing,	Sa *s*pré,	Earth-ape.
46	Kyi yéhu,	Sa bya,	Earth-bird.
47	King zuhi,	*l*chags khyi,	Iron-dog.
48	Zin hahi,	*l*chags phag,	Iron-hog.
49	Zhin tsi,	Chhu byi,	Water-mouse.
50	Kuhi tshihu,	Chhu *g*lang,	Water-ox.
51	Kya yin,	Shing *s*tag,	Wood-tiger.
52	Yi mahu,	Shing yos,	Wood-hare.
53	Ping shin,	Mé *h*brug,	Fire-dragon.
54	Ting zi,	Mé *s*brul,	Fire-serpent.
55	Vou hu,	Sa *r*ta,	Earth-horse.
56	Kyi wuhi,	Sa lug,	Earth-sheep.
57	King shing,	*l*chags *s*pré,	Iron-ape.
58	Zin yéhu,	*l*chags bya,	Iron-bird.
59	Zhin zuhi,	Chhu khyi,	Water-dog.
60	Kuhi hahi,	Chhu phag,	Water-hog.

§ 235. Tibetan Symbolical Words used as Numerals.

There are great many works on astronomy and astrology in Tibet, exclusive of the treatises on these subjects introduced into the *Kah-gyur* or *Stan-gyar* collections. Of these the most celebrated is the *Bei'dúrya Kárpo,* written by s,*Dé-srid Sangs*-r,*gyas* r,*Gya*-m,*ts'ho* (སྡེ་སྲིད་སངས་རྒྱས་རྒྱ་མཚོ,) a regent or viceroy at *Lhassa,* in the last half of the seventeenth century of our æra. In this and indeed in all works of science, symbolical names (གྲངས་བརྡ *grangs* br*da,* numerical signs), are used instead of numerals, for arithmetical and astronomical calculations. As for instance : + ལག, for + 2 ; མེ, for 3 ; × ཆུ, for × 4 ; ÷ སོ, for ÷ 32.

This mode of expressing numbers in evidently an exact imitation of the Indian system. For some of the numerals there are several synonymous terms, as is also the case in Sanskrit, but it is sufficient to allude in this place to those which are of constant and general occurrence. Although the nine units, together with the zero (0), would have been sufficient to express any sum whatever, yet for a few of the higher numbers corresponding symbols have also been supplied ; they are : 10, 11, 12, 13, 14, 15, 16, 18, 24, 25, 27, and 32.

When dictating to an assistant in symbolical names what to write in figures, the computer commences the operation from right to left : thus if he says ཉི་མ (12), མཁའ (0), མཚོ (4), the other writes 4012, &c. This method is the same with that followed in the Shástras of India, therefore it is unnecessary to add any thing further on the subject.

The rationale of the adaptation of these numerical symbols will be obvious in most cases ; thus the body, the moon, and their synonymes express unity from their singleness : the hand, the eye, wings, twins, &c. denote a double object, or 2 ; &c. many others, as an arrow, for 5 ; Rishi, for 7 &c. are derived from the mythology of the Hindus.

The following is a list of these expressions, with their signification in English, to which the corresponding Sanskrit terms have been added (with a few exceptions).

༡ or 1. གཟུགས*, *gzugs,* body ; S. *sharíram.*

ཟླ, *zla,* the moon ; S. *chandra.*

འོད་དཀར, *hod-dkar,* white brightness, the moon ; S. *shwéta-rochis.*

བསེ་རུ, *bse-ru,* rhinoceros ; S. *gandaka.*

* Note. The articles, (པ, པོ, བ, བོ, མ, མོ, *Pa, po, va, vo, ma, mo,* &c.) have been omitted after the roots, since the words occur mostly in this form.

༢ or 2. ལག, *lag*, the hand ; S. *bhuja, hasta*, or *pani.*

མིག, *mig*, the eye ; S. *nétra, chakshus.*

ཟུང་ཕྱོགས, *zung-phyogs*, or simply ཟུང, *zung*, the two sides, wings, halves, a pair, couple ; S. *chhada, pakshó*, &c.

འཁྲིག *hkhrig*, or བགྲོད, *bgrod*, the twins ; copulation.

༣ or 3. འཇིག་རྟེན, *hjig-rtan*, the world ; S. *loka.*

ཡོན་ཏན, *yon-tan*, quality ; S. *guna.*

མེ, *mé*, fire ; S. *agni* or *anala.*

རྩེ, *rtsé*, top, summit ; S. *agram.*

༤ or 4. མཚོ, (also ཆུ་མཚོ) *mtsho*, a sea or lake ; S. *samudra.*

ཆུ, *chhu*, water ; S. *jala* or *wari.*

རྐང, *rkang*, a foot ; S. *páda.*

རིག་བྱེད, *Rig-byed*, a Véda ; S. *Véda.*

༥ or 5. འབྱུང, h*byung*, an element ; S. *bhutam.*

དབང, *dvang*, an organ of sense ; S. *indrayam.*

མདའ, *mdah*, an arrow : S. *bána* or *vána.*

ཕུང, *phung*, aggregate of the elements constituting the body and soul ; S. *skándha.*

༦ or 6. མཚམས, *mtshams*, the six cardinal points : the north, east, south, west, zenith, and nadir.

རོ་བྲོ་བ, *ro,bro-va*, taste, savour ; S. *rasa.*

དུས, *dus*, time, season ; S. *samaya.*

༧ or 7. ཐུབ་པ, *Thub-pa*, a sage ; S. *Muni.*

དྲང་སྲོང, *Drang-srong*, an hermit ; S. *Rishi.*

རི, *ri*, a hill or mountain ; S. *parvata.*

རེས་གཟའ, *Res-gzah*, a special or chief planet ; S. *Graha.*

༨ or 8. ཀླུ, *klu*, an hydra or snake ; S. *nága.*

སྦྲུལ, *sbrul*, serpent ; S. *sarpa.*

གདེངས་ཅན, *gdengs-chan*, a hooded-snake ; S. ?

ལྟོ་འགྲོ, *lto-hgro*, creeping on its belly ; S. *uraga.*

ནོར *nor* or ནོར་ལྷ, *nor-lha*, wealth, or the eight gods of wealth : S. *Vasu* or *vasudéva.*

སྲེད་པ, *sred-pa*, affection, passion ; S. *Trisńá.*

༩ or 9. རྩ, *rtsa*, root (or vein); S. *mula.*

གཏེར, *gter*, treasure; S. *kosham.*

གཟའ, *gzah*, a planet; S. *graha.*

བུ་ག, *bu-ga*, a hole; S. *chiddra.*

སྲིན་པོ, *Srín-po*, an imp or goblin; S. *Rákshasa.*

༡༠ or 10. ཕྱོགས, *phyogs*, corner, quarter, point; S. *Dik* or *Dish.* The ten points, (4 cardinal, 4 intermediate, the zenith and the nadir.)

༡༡ or 11 འཕྲོག་བྱེད, *h,phrog-byed*, that takes by force; S. *Hari* for *Siva.*

དྲག་པོ, *Drag-po*, the brave or fierce; S. *Rudra*, for *Siva.*

བདེ་འབྱུང, *Bde-hbyung*, the source of happiness; S. *Shambu*, a name of *Siva.*

དབང་ཕྱུག, *Dvang-phyug*, the powerful; S. *Ishwara*, for *Siva.*

༡༢ or 12. ཉི་མ, *Nyi-ma*, the sun; S. *Surya, Arka, Bhánu.*

ཁྱིམ, *khyim*, the sun's place in the zodiac; S. *Griha*, the 12 zodiacal signs.

༡༣ or 13. འདོད་པ, *hdod-pa*, lust, desire, wish, Cupid; S. *Káma.*

སྨྱོས་བྱེད or སྨྱོས་བྱེད, *myos-byed*, that infuriates or makes mad, lust, desire, wish, Cupido; S. *Madana, Káma Déva.*

༡༤ or 14. ཡིད, *yid*, the mind; S. *manas.*

མནུ, *Manu*, ditto; S. *manu.*

སྲིད་པ, *Srid-pa*, existence, birth, the world; S. *Bhuvanam.*

༡༥ or 15. ཚེས། ཉིན་ཞག, *tshes, nyin-zhag*, the 15th day of a lunar month; any day of the semi-lunation; S. *Aha* or *Ahan.*

༡༦ or 16. མི་བདག, *Mi-bdag*, lord of men, a sovereign; S. *Narapati.*

རྒྱལ་པོ, *Rgyal-po*, a king, prince; S. *Rája.*

༡༨ or 18, ཉེས་པ, or སྐྱོན, *nyes-pa*, or *skyon*, vice, fault, blemish; S. *Dosha.*

༢༤ or 24, རྒྱལ་བ, *Rgyal-va*, he that has been victorious, a Jina or Buddha; S. *Jina.*

༢༥ or 25, དེ་ཉིད, *de-nyid*, the same, self; S. *tatwam.*

༢༧ or 27, སྐར་མ, *Skur-ma*, a star, one of the 27 constellations in the path of the moon; S. *Nakshatra.*

༣༢ or 32, སོ, *So*, a tooth; S. *danta.*

༠ or 0. མཁའ, *mkhah*, void, space; S. *kha, ákásha, gaganam.*

ཐིག, *thig*, a spot, stain; S. ? *nabhas.*

སྟོང་པ, *Stong-pa*, the vacuum; empty space, zero; S. *shúnyam.*

II.—SPECIMENS OF THE TIBETAN LANGUAGE.

From the Kah-gyur and other classical Works.

1. ATTRIBUTES OF A VIRTUOUS WOMAN.

[Extracted from the *Bkah-hgyur, mdo, kha,* leaf 106-7 ; corresponding with the 12th chapter of the *Lalita vistara,* the original Sanskrit text.]

§. 236. The required qualities in a maiden who may aspire to be united in marriage with SHA'KYA are thus defined by himself :

See བཀའ་འགྱུར, མདོ, volume ཁ. leaf 106-7

༄༅།། གང་ལ་སྤྱོད་ལམ་ཡོན་ཏན་ བདེན་པའི་ཚིག་མེད་པ །
བུད་མེད་ཐལ་པ་གང་ཡང་ བདག་གི་ཚུལ་ མཐུན་མིན །
གང་ཞིག་ བདག་གི་སེམས་ནི་ མངོན་པར་དགའ་བྱེད་ཅིང་ །
བག་ཡོད་ གཟུགས་དང་ ན་ཚོད་ རྒྱུས་རིགས་དག་པ་ འོས །
དེས་ ནི་ཡོན་ཏན་ཚོགས་སུ་བཅད་དེ་ཡི་གེར་ བྲིས །
འདི་འདྲའི་ བུ་མོ་ མཆིས་ན་ གདག་ལ་ བཀའ་ སྩོལ་ཅིག །
སྐྱེ་བོ་ཐལ་པ་ མ་བརྙམས་ བདག་ ལ་མཁོ་མ་ལགས །
ཡོན་ཏན་ བརྗོད་པ་འདི་ལྡན་ མཆིས་ན་ བདག་སྩོལ་ཅིག །
དར་ཅིང་ གཟུགས་ བཟང་ལྡན་ཡང་ གཟུགས་ཀྱི་རིགས་དང་བྲལ
ཕུ་ནུ་མ་ལ་ ཁྲམས་ ལྟར་ ཁྲམས་པའི་ སེམས་ལྡན་ཞིང་ །
གཏོང་ལ་ དགའ་སྟེ་ དགེ་སློང་ བྲམ་ཟེ་ སྦྱིན་ཚུལ་ཅན །
དེ་འདྲའི་ བུ་མོ་ མཆིས་ན་ ཡབ་ཀྱིས་ བདག་སྩོལ་ཅིག །
གང་ལ་ང་ རྒྱལ་ ཁེངས་དང་ ཞེ་སྡང་མ་ མཆིས་ཤིང་ །
གཡོ་དང་ ཕྲག་དོག་སྒྱུ་ སྤངས་ དྲང་བའི་ ངང་ཚུལ་ཅན །
མི་ལམ་ན་ཡང་ སྐྱེས་པ་གཞན་ལ་ཆགས་དང་བྲལ །
བདག་གི་ ཆོས་ནི་ ཆོག་ འཚོལ་ཏེག་སྨོམ་བག་མཆིས་ལ །
རྒྱགས་པ་མ་མཆིས་ མི་ གཡེང་ ཁྲང་ ཁྲབ་ ཚུལ་ འཆང་ཞིང་ །
ང་རྒྱལ་ མ་མཆིས་ འཕྲིད་དང་ ཁྲལ་བས་ ཁྲན་མོ་བཞིན །
སྦྲ་རི་ར་ལ་ མ་ཆགས་ ཆང་ལ་ མ་ཆགས་ཏེ །
འདོད་ ཁྲལ་ བཙན་ སེམས་ མ་མཆིས་རང་གི་ནོར་ཁྱིས་ འཚོལ །

བདེན་ལ་ གནས་ཤིང་ མི་འཕྱར་ གཡེང་བ་ མ་ལགས་པ།
ངོ་ཚའི་གོས་འཆལ་ སོད་དང་ ཁེངས་པ་ མ་མཆིས་ གནས།
སྒྲ་དང་ བཟླ་ཤིས་ མ་ཆགས་ རྟག་ཏུ་ཆོས་ལ་ བརྩོན།
གཟུགས་དང་ ངག་དང་ ཡིད་ཀྱི་ དངོས་པོ་ རབ་དག་པ།
གཉིད་དང་ རྨུགས་པ་ མི་ མངའ་ ང་རྒྱལ་ ཞེན་བྲལ་ཞིང་།
ཐོགས་ དང་ ལྡན་ལ་ ལེགས་ པའི་ལས་ ནམས་ རྟག་སྤྱོད་དེ།
ཆོས་ སྒྲུབ་ གཉིས་འཐང་ སྟོན་པ་བཞིན་གྱི་རིམ་ གྲོར་ལྡན།
ཟན་དང་ ཟན་མོ་ ཀུན་འཐང་ བདག་བཞིན་ བྱམས་ སེམས་པ།
སྐད་འཆོང་ བཞིན་དུ་ བསྟན་བཅོས་ ཚོ་ག་ འཆོལ་ཞིང་ མཁས།
སྨད་ཀྱིས་ ཉལ་ཞིང་ སྟོན་དུ་ མལ་ནས་ལྡང་ བཅིད་པ།
ཐམས་པས་ རྗེས་སློགས་ མ་བཞིན་ རྒྱལ་ འཆོས་ མ་ མཆིས་པ།
དེ་འདྲའི་ བུད་ མེད་ མཆིས་ན་ཡབ་ཀྱིས་ བདག་སྤོལ་ ཅིག།

དེ་ནས་རྒྱལ་པོ་ཟས་གཙང་ མས་ ཚིགས་སུ་ བཅད་པ་ འདི་ དག་ཐོས་ནས། མདུན་ན་ འདོན་ལ་ སྨྲས་པ། བྲམ་ཟེ་ཆེན་པོ་ ཁྱོད་ སེར་སྐྱའི་ གནས་ཀྱི་ གྲོང་ཁྱེར་ ཆེན་པོར་ སོང་ལ། ཁྱིམ་ཐམས་ཅད་དུ་འདང་ སོང་སྟེ། བུ་མོ་དག་ ལྟོས་ལ་ གང་འདང་ རྒྱང་སྟེ་ ཡོང་ཏན་ དེ་ལྟ་བུ་དག་ཡོད་ན། ——— བུ་མོ་དེ་དག་ འདིར་འོང་ཅིག ——— དེའི་ཚེ་ ཚིགས་སུ་ བཅད་པ་ འདི་དག་ཀྱང་སྨྲས་སོ :

རྒྱལ་རིགས་བྲམ་ཟེའི་བུ་ མོ་དང་ ༎ རྗེའུ་རིགས་དམངས་རིགས་དེ་བཞིན་ཏེ།
སུ་ལ་ཡོན་ཏན་འདི་ཡོད་པའི ༎ བུ་མོ་དེ་ནི་འདིར་འོང་ཅིག།
ང་ཡི་བུ་འདི་རིགས་དག་དང་ ༎ རུས་ལ་ང་མཚར་འཛིན་མ་ཡིན།
ཡོན་ཏན་བདེན་པ་ཆོས་ཀྱི་ནམས ༎ དེ་ལ་འདི་ཡི་ཡིད་དགའོ ༎

Translation.

"No ordinary woman is suitable to my taste and habits; none who is incorrect in her behaviour; who has bad qualities, or who does not speak the truth. But she alone will be pleasing and fit for me, who, exhilarating my mind, is chaste, young, of good complexion, and of a pure family and descent." He indited a catalogue of these qualifications in verse, and said to his father, "If there shall be found any girl with the virtues I have described, since I like not an unrestrained woman, let her be given to me in marriage." "She, who is young, well portioned, and elegant, yet not boastful of her beauty, (lit. with her body;)—who is affectionate towards her brother, sister, and mother;—who, always rejoicing in giving alms, knoweth the proper manner how to bestow them on the priests and brahmans:—if there be found any such damsel, father, let her be brought to me. One, who being without arrogance, pride, and passion, hath left off artifice, envy, deceit, and is of an upright nature;—who even in her dreams hath not lusted after any other man;—who resteth content with her husband, and is always submissive and chaste: —who is firm and not wavering;—who is not proud or haughty, but full of humility like a female slave;—who hath no excessive fondness for the vanities of sound, smell, taste, (music, perfumes, and exquisite meats,) nor for wine;—who is void of cupidity;—who hath not a covetous heart, but is content with her own possessions;—who, being upright, goeth not astray; is not fluctuating; is modest in her dress, and doth not indulge in laughing and boasting;—who is diligent in her moral duties, without being too much addicted to the gods and festivals (or righteous overmuch). Who is very clean and pure in her body, her speech and her mind;—who is not drowsy nor dull, proud nor stupid;—but being of good judgment, doth every thing with due reflection;—who hath for her father and mother-in-law equal reverence as for a spiritual teacher;—who treateth her servants, both male and female, with constant mildness;—who is as well versed as any courtesan in the rites and ceremonies described in the Shastras;—who goeth last to sleep and riseth earliest from her couch:—who maketh every endeavour with mildness, like a mother without affection;—if there be any such maiden to be found, father, give her unto me as a wife."

Afterwards, the king (Sans. *Shaddhodana*, Tib. *Zas-Qtsang-ma*), directs his brahman minister (Sans. *Purohita*, Tib. *Mdhun-na-hdon*), to go into the great city of *Capila-vastu*, (Tib. *Ser-skya-qzhi*,) and to inquire there in every house after a girl possessed with these good qualities, shewing at the same time Shakya's letter, and uttering two *Slokas*, or verses, of the following meaning:

"Bring hither that maiden who has the required qualities, whether she be of the royal tribe, or of the brahman caste; of the gentry, or of the plebeian class. My son regardeth not tribe nor family extraction: his delight is in good qualities, truth, and virtue alone."

2. Verses against wearing the veil.

The objections of the Buddhists to the seclusion of woman may be gathered from the following imaginary conversation of Shakya's wife, extracted from the Kah-gyur, Do. vol. Kh. leaf 120-121, (corresponding with the Sanskrit *Lalita vistara*,) at the end of the 12th chapter.

§. 237. ༄༅། དེ་ནས་ཤཱཀྱའི་བྲ་མོ་ས་འཚོ་མ་ ཚོ་བླུག་གམ་ནང་མི་གང་ མཐོང་ཡང་རྡུང་སྟེ། གདོང་མི་སྟེང་དོ།
དེ་དག་ཀྱང་དེ་ལ་བག་སར་མོ་ནི་ཞུམ་ཞུམ་པོར་འདུག་ པའི་རིགས་ན། འདི་ནི་རིག་རྩ་མ་གཡོགས་སོ་ཞེས་འཕྱ་སྨོད་ཅིང་
མི་སྙན་པར་ཟེར་རོ།། དེའི་ཚེ་ ཤཱཀྱའི་བུ་མོ་ས་འཚོ་མས་ གདམ་ དེ་ཐོས་ནས་ ནང་མི་རྣམས་ཀྱི་ མཙན་ཙ་ འཙག་སྟེ།
ཚིགས་སུ་བཅད་པ་འདི་དག་སྨྲས་སོ།།

1. "འཙག་དང་ འཕྱིང་དང་འཆག་པ་ལ། །འཕགས་པ་དག་ནི་མ་ གཡོགས་ མཛེས།
ནོར་བུ་རིན་ཆེན་ འོད་གསལ་བ། །རྒྱལ་མཚན་རྩེ་མོར་ གསལ་ན་མཛེས།།

2. འཕགས་པ་ འགྲོ་ནའང་ མཛེས་པ་སྟེ། །འོང་ནའང་ དེ་བཞིན་ མཛེས་པ་ཡིན།
འཕྱེང་བའམ་དེ་ བཞིན་ འཙག་པ་དང་ ། །ཐམས་ཅད་ཙ་འང་ འཕགས་པ་མཛེས།།

3. འསགས་པ་སྨྲ་ནའང་ མཛེས་པ་སྟེ། །མི་སྨྲར་ འཙག་ཀྱང་ དེ་བཞིན་ མཛེས།
དཔེར་ན་ ཀ་ལ་བིང་ཀ་ནི། །མཐོང་ དང་སྒྲ་ཐོས་དེ་བཞིན་ནོ།།

4. ལྷ་ཤའི་གོས་ནི་ གྱོན་པ་དང་ ། །གོས་དན་ གྱོན་དང་ལུས་ རིད་པ།
དེ་ནི་རང་གི་ གཟི་ཡིས་ མཛེས། ཡོན་ཏན་ལྡན་པ་ཡོན་ཏན་ བརྒྱན།།

5. གང་ལ་སྡིག་པ་མེད་གྱུར་པ། །འཕགས་པ་ཀུན་ཏུ་དགེ་བ་ཡིན།
ཆོལ་པ་སྡིག་པ་བྱེད་པ་ནི། །རྗེ་སྟེད་བརྒྱན་ཀྱང་ མཛེས་མ་ཡིན།།

6. གང་དག་ སྙིང་ལ་ སྡིག་པ་ཡོད་ཅིང་ ཚིག་ འཇམ་པ།
དེ་དག་ ཙག་གི་ བུམ་པར་ བདུད་རྩི་ བླུགས་པ་ བཞིན།
བྲག་གི་ སེར་ག་ རྡུབ་པ་ལྟ་བུར་ ནང་ ཡང་ རྡུབ།
དེ་འདྲ་ དེ་དག་ སྦྲུལ་གྱི་ཁ་ལ་ ཀུག་པ་ བཞིན།།

7. དེས་པ་དེ་དག་ གན་ཏུ་ ཀུན་འོང་ ཀུན་སྤྱག་ འཚོལ།
འབབ་ ཕྱོགས་ ཐམས་ཅད་ ལྟ་བུར་ འགྲོ་བ་ཀུན་ཕྱིས་གསོ།
འཕགས་པ་དག་ནི་ རྟག་ཏུ་ འོ་ཞེས་ བཀང་ བུམ་འདྲ།
བདག་ ཉིད་ དག་པ་དེ་ འདྲ་ མཐོང་ན་ བཀྲ་ཤིས་ དགེ།།

8. གང་དག་ སྡིག་པའི་ ཕྱགས་པོ་ཡུན་རིང་ ཡོངས་ སྤོང་ ཞིང་།
དགེ་བའི་ བཤེས་ གཉེན་ རིན་པོ་ཆེས་ནི་ ཡོངས་ བཟུང་ལ།
སྡིག་པ་ ནམ་སྤྲོང་ སངས་རྒྱས་ ཆོས་ལ་ མངོན་ ཆགས་པ།
དེ་ལྟ་བུ་དག་ མཐོང་བ་ བཀྲ་ཤིས་ འབྲས་བུ་ ཡོད།།

9. གང་དག་ལུས་ བསྡམས་ ལུས་ཀྱི་སྐྱོན་ རྣམས་ རབ་ བསྡམས་དང་ །
གང་དག་ ཚིག་ བསྡམས་ རྟག་ཏུ་ ཚིག་ འཆལ་མེད་ གྱུར་ལ།
དབང་པོ་ ཐུལ་ ཤིང་ ཤིང་ཏུ་ བསྡམས་ལ་ཡིད་དང་བ།
དེ་ལྟ་བུ་ དག་ གདོང་ གཡོགས་ཏེ་ནི་ ཅི་ཞིག་བྱ།།

10. གལ་ཏེ་ ལུས་ལ་ གོས་ནི་ སྟོང་གིས་ གཡོགས་ གྱུར་ ཀྱང་ །
གང་དག་ སེམས་ བསྒྲུས་ངོ་ ཚ་མེད་ ཅིང་ཁྲེལ་ མེད་དང་ །

གང་དག་ འདི་ འདྲའི་ ཡོན་ཏན་མེད་ཅིང་ བདེན་ ཚིག་མེད །
དེ་དག་ སྒེན་མོ་བས་ཀྱང་ སྒྲེན་མོར་ འཇིག་ རྟེན་རྒྱུ །

11. གང་ཞིག་ སེམས་ སྦས་ རྟག་ཏུ་དབང་པོ་ བསྡམས་གྱུར་ཅིང་ །
བདག་གི་ ཡོན་ ཚོག་ སེམས་ཅན་ གཞན་ལ་མི་ སེམས་པ །
དེ་འདྲ་བ་དག་གི་རྒྱ་ བཞིན་ཏུ་མ་ གཡོགས་ སྣང་ །
དེ་འདྲ་བ་དག་ གདོང་ གཡོགས་ཏེ་ནི་ཅི་ཞིག་བྱ ། །

12. གཞན་ཡང་ །
རྡལ་སྤོང་ བདག་ཉིད་ ཚེ་དང་ གཞན་ སེམས་ སྤྱོ་མཆས་དང་ །
དེ་བཞིན་ ལྷ་ཚོགས་ དག་གིས་ ཁོ་མོའི་ བསམ་པ་དང་ །
ཁོ་མོའི་ ཚུལ་ ཁྲིམས་ ཡོན་ཏན་ རྣམ་དང་ བག་ཡོད་ མཁྱེན །
དེ་ལྟ་བས་ན་ ཁོ་མོས་ གདོང་ བཀབ་ ཅི་ཞིག་ དགོས ། །"

དགེ་སློང་དག། རྒྱལ་པོ་ཟས་གཙང་མས་ ཤཱཀྱའི་བུ་མོ་ ས་འཚོ་མའི་ སྤོབས་པ་དང་ བསྟན་པའི་ ཚིགས་སུ་བཅད་པ་ རྣམ་པ་ འདི་ལྟ་བུ་ འདི་ཐོས་སོ ། །ཐོས་ནས་ཀྱང་ ཚིམ་ཞིང་ མགུ་ལ་ཡི་ རངས་ཏེ་ རབ་ཏུ་དགའ་ཞིང་ དགའ་བ་དང་ཡིད་ བདེ་བ་སྐྱེས་ནས་ ། རས་ བཅོས་བུ་བཟང་པོ་ རིན་པོ་ཆེ་ ཙ་མས་སྤྲས་པ་བྱུང་གཅིག་དང་ ། མུ་ཏིག་གི་ དོ་ཤལ་སྦྱང་ཐེ་བ་ བརྒྱ་སྟོང་ རི་བ་དང་ ། མུ་ཏིག་དམར་པོ་ བཟང་ པོས་སྤྲས་པའི་ གསེར་གྱི་ ཕྲེང་བས་ ཤཱཀྱའི་བུ་ མོས་ འཚོ་མ་ལ་ བཀབ་ནས་ ཆེད་དུ་བརྗོད་པ་འདི་ ཆེད་དུ་ བརྗོད་དོ* ། །

13. " ཁོ་བོའི་བུ་ནི་ ཡོན་ཏན་ ཇི་འདྲས་ བརྩུན་པ་དང་ །
མཚའ་མ་ རང་གི་ཡོན་ཏན་ ཇི་ལྟར་ རབ་སྣ་བ །
སེམས་ཅན་དག་པ་དེ་ གཉིས་ ཕྲད་པར་ གྱུར་པ་ནི །
མར་དང་ མར་གྱི་ ཉིང་ཁུ་ ཇི་ལྟར་ འདྲ་བ་ བཞིན ། །"

སྒྲུ་རྩལ་བསྟན་པའི་ལེའུ་ སྟེ་བཅུ་ གཉིས་པའོ ། །

[This is the twelfth chapter; On the displaying of dexterity in the arts.]

Literal Translation.

Thereafter SAHTS'HOMA† (S. GOPA) the daughter of SHAKYA (*Lagna béchonchan :* ལག་ན་བེ་ཅོན་ཅན, the gladiator) when in the sight of her father-in-law, and mother-in-law, or of any of the domestics, neglects to conceal her face (with a veil). They say of her : "It would be proper that this new bride remain with some restraint, for she never veileth herself."

* These few lines of the text are translated only in general terms.

† Shis is called also GRAGS *HDSIN-MA*, the celebrated woman, (གྲགས་འཛིན་མ, in Sans. YASHODHARÁ.)

Then, SHATS'HOMA, the daughter of SHAKYA (the gladiator), having heard this disagreeable upbraiding and talk of herself, sitting before the domestics uttered the following verses:

1. "Sitting, standing, and walking, those that are venerable, are pleasing when not concealed. A bright gem will give more lustre if put on the top of the standard. 2. The venerable are pleasing when they go; they are agreeable also when they come. They are so whether they stand, or whether they are sitting. In every manner the venerable are pleasing. 3. The man excellent in virtue is pleasing when he speaks; he is so also when he sits still. As an example, doth not the *Kalapinka* bird appear more beautiful when she chaunteth her lovely song in your presence? 4. The venerable man who putteth on a garment made of the *kusha* grass, or whose squalid clothing concealeth not his emaciated body, still shineth with his own lustre. He that hath good qualities is adorned by those qualifications. 5. They who have put off all vices are venerable. Fools, committing vices, how much soever they be adorned, are never pleasing. 6. Those that have malice in their heart, yet speak a sweet language, are like a poisoned bowl into which nectar is poured; or a cleft on a rock that is rough both inside and outside. Communion with such men is like contact with the mouth of a snake. 7. With respect to the venerable, all resort to them, all reverence them. They are supported and cherished by all men, as the stairs descending to the water's edge are kept in repair by the multitude. The venerable are always like a bowl full of milk and curd. It is a great happiness to see human nature capable of such purity. 8. Fraught with blissful consequences is the gift of such men as have renounced the company of the wicked, and being directed by a venerable religious guide, are become enamoured of the doctrine of the most perfect (Buddha). 9. For such as have restrained their body, have suppressed the several defects of it, have refrained their speech, and never used a deceitful language; and having subdued the flesh, are held in restraint by a pure conscience: for such, to what purpose is the veiling of the face? 10. They that have a cunning heart are impudent and shameless; and having not the required qualities, do not speak the truth:—though they should cover their body even with a thousand clothes, they would go about in the world more naked than the unclothed. 11. They that have concealed their passions, and have kept them under subjection, and are content with their own husbands, and think not on any other;—such women, when not concealed by a veil, shine forth like the sun and moon: for such, to what purpose is the veiling of the face? 12. Moreover, DRANG-SRONG, (S. *Ris'hi,*) the great Lord (God), who is wise in knowing the hearts of others

yea, also the whole company of the gods, know my thoughts, my good morals, my virtues, my vows, and my chastity. Therefore, why should I conceal my face ?"

Zas-Qtsang-ma, (S. *Shuddhodana*, the father of Shakya,) her father-in-law, was much pleased with these expressions, and presented her with several precious things. He uttered at the same time a *slóka*, the meaning of which is this: 13 "My son being adorned with such qualities as he has, and my daughter-in-law having such virtuous qualifications as she describes; to see two such pure persons united together, is like when butter and ghee (clarified butter) are mixed together."

3. Ratnavali's Letter to Shakya.

§. 238. *Mutig-chen*, (S. *Ratnavali*,) a young princess of Ceylon, the daughter of the king of Singala, having been informed by some merchants of Central India (*Madhyam*) of Buddha and of his doctrine, she was much pleased with it; and, when those merchants returned home, she sent some presents to Chom-dan-das (Shakya), with a letter of the following contents :

༄༅། ལྷ་དང་ལྷ་མིན་མི་ཡིས་ཕྱག་བགྱིས་པ། །སྐྱེ་དང་བསྒུད་དང་བསྐྲེངས་ལས་ངེས་གྲོལ་ཞིང་།
གཙོ་བོ་གྲགས་པ་ཆེ་ཆེར་རབ་གྲགས་པ། །དྲང་སྲོང་བདུད་རྩི་ཆ་ལས་ཐུགས་རྗེས་གནང་།།

"Reverenced by the *Suras*, *Asuras*, and men ; really delivered from birth, sickness, and fear ; Lord ! who art greatly celebrated by thy far extending renown, from the sage's ambrosial portion, kindly grant me ! (meaning religious instruction or wisdom.")

Shakya received this letter, and sent to the princess a picture of *Buddha* on cotton cloth, with some verses written above and below the image, containing the terms upon which refuge is obtained with *Buddha ; Dharma*, and *Sangha*, and a few fundamental articles of the faith ; together with two stanzas recommendatory of Buddhism. In a letter to the king of Singala, Shakya prescribes with what solemnity this image should be received, the letter perused, and made known in Ceylon.

The stanzas are these. See *Dulvá*, vol. 5, leaf 30.

1. ༄༅། བརྩམ་པར་བྱ་ཞིང་འབྱུང་བར་བྱ། །སངས་རྒྱས་བསྟན་ལ་འཇུག་པར་བྱ།
འདམ་བུའི་ཁྱིམ་ན་གླང་ཆེན་བཞིན། །འཆི་བདག་སྡེ་ནི་གཞོམ་པར་བྱ།
2. གང་ཞིག་རབ་ཏུ་བག་ཡོད་པར། །ཆོས་འདུལ་འདི་ལ་སྤྱོད་གྱུར་པ།
སྐྱེ་བའི་འཁོར་བ་རབ་སྤངས་ནས། །སྡུག་བསྔལ་ཐ་མར་བྱེད་པར་འགྱུར།།

1. "Arise, commence a new course of life. Turn to the religion of *Buddha*. Conquer the host of the lord of death, (the passions,) that are like an elephant in this muddy

house, (the body,) (or conquer your passions, like as an elephant subdues every thing under his feet in a muddy lake.) 2. Whoever has lived a pure or chaste life, according to the precepts of this *Dulvá*, shall be free from transmigration, and shall put an end to all his miseries."

4. Compendium of the doctrine of Buddha in one sloka.

§. 239. ༄༅།། སྡིག་པ་ཅི་ཡང་མི་བྱ་སྟེ། "No vice is to be committed,
དགེ་བ་ཕུན་སུམ་ཚོགས་པར་བྱ། Virtue must perfectly be practised,—
རང་གི་སེམས་ནི་ཡོངས་སུ་གདུལ། Subdue entirely your thoughts.
འདི་ནི་སངས་རྒྱས་བསྟན་པ་ཡིན། This is the doctrine of *Buddha.*"

5. A Moral Maxim.

§. 240. ༄༅།། ཐམས་ཅད་ཆོས་ནི་མཉན་པར་བྱ། ། ཐོས་ནས་རབ་ཏུ་གཟུང་བྱ་སྟེ།
" གང་ཞིག་བདག་ཉིད་མི་འདོད་པ། ། དེ་དག་གཞན་ལ་མི་བྱའོ།།"

See བསྟན་འགྱུར, མདོ, vol. གོ, leaf 174.

The same in English.

Hear ye all this moral maxim, and having heard it keep it well: "Whatever is unpleasing to yourself never do it to another*." (Do unto others as you would be done by.)

6. Another Maxim.

§. 241. ༄༅།། འཇིག་རྟེན་བདེ་བ་ཇི་སྙེད་པ། ། དེ་ཀུན་གཞན་བདེ་འདོད་ལས་བྱུང་།
འཇིག་རྟེན་སྡུག་བསྔལ་ཇི་སྙེད་པ། ། དེ་ཀུན་བདག་བདེ་འདོད་ལས་བྱུང་།

See བསྟན་འགྱུར, མདོ, vol. ལ, leaf 27.

English.

Whatever happiness is in the world, it has all arisen from a wish for the welfare of others. Whatever misery (distress) is in the world, it has all arisen from a wish for our own welfare.

7. Why God is called Konchok, in Tibetan, "The Chief of Rarity."

§. 242. ༄༅།། (དཀོན་མཆོག, *d*kon *m*chhog, rare or precious chief)
འབྱུང་བ་དཀོན་ཕྱིར་དྲི་མེད་ཕྱིར། ། མཐུ་ལྡན་ཕྱིར་དང་འཇིག་རྟེན་གྱི།
རྒྱན་གྱུར་ཕྱིར་དང་མཆོག་ཉིད་ཕྱིར། ། འགྱུར་བ་མེད་ཕྱིར་དཀོན་མཆོག་ཉིད།།

See the དཀར་ཆག (Index) to the Kah-gyur; also, elsewhere.

English.

On account of his rare appearance (manifestation), *and on account of* his spotlessness, *and on account of* his power, *and on account of* his having become the ornament of the world,

* The phrase that expresses this moral maxim, both in Latin and French, agrees very closely with the Tibetan text; thus, in Latin: "Quod tu tibi non vis, alteri non feceris." In French: "Ne faites pas à autrui ce que vous ne voudriez pas qu'on vous fit." See also St. Matth. vii. 12.

and on account of his being chief and immutable, he is called the chief of rarity (or the rarest Being).

8. Who is the Supreme of all ?

སྟོན་པ་གཽ་ཏ་མས་བྲམ་ཟེ་པད་མའི་སྙིང་པོ་ལ་།

By the teacher Goutama, (Shakya) to a brahman (called) Padma Garbbha.

See འདུལ་བ, vol. ཁ, leaf 190, in the བཀའ་འགྱུར.

§. 243. ༄༅ །། སྦྱིན་སྲེག་མཆོད་སྦྱིན་རྣམས་ཀྱི་མཆོག ། །སྡེབ་སྦྱོར་མཆོག་ནི་ཉི་མའི་ལྷ།
མི་ཡི་མཆོག་ནི་རྒྱལ་པོ་སྟེ། །རྒྱ་མཚོ་ཆུ་བོ་རྣམས་ཀྱི་མཆོག །
ཟླ་བ་རྒྱུ་སྐར་རྣམས་ཀྱི་གཙོ། །ཉི་མ་སྣང་བྱེད་རྣམས་ཀྱི་གཙོ།
སྟེང་དང་འོག་དང་ཐད་ཀར་ཡང་། །འགྲོ་བའི་འགྲོ་བ་ཇི་སྙེད་པ།
ལྷ་དང་བཅས་པའི་འཇིག་རྟེན་ན། །སྨྲ་བའི་མཆོག་ནི་རྫོགས་སངས་རྒྱས།།

Translation.

Burnt-offering (of fragrant substances) is, the chief of all sacrifices. The prince of poetry (or versification) is, the god (or regent) of the sun. (Apollo). The chief of men is, the king. The ocean is the chief of all waters. The moon is the principal of the planets (moving stars). The sun is the principal of all the luminous bodies. Whatever walking (rational) beings are in this world, above, below, and round about (us), including all the gods (angels) also, the speaking (or rational) chief (of them all) is, THE ALL-PERFECT BUDDHA.

9. Who is the true Protector ?

§. 244. ༄༅ །། ཚངས་པ་དང་ནི་ཁྱབ་འཇུག་དང་། །མཆུ་དེ་ལྷ་ལ་སོགས་དང་།
ཀླུ་དང་གནོད་སྦྱིན་གྲུལ་བུམ་དང་། །ཉི་མ་ཟླ་བ་གཟའ་རྣམས་དང་།
རི་འམ་མཚོ་འམ་ལྗོན་ཤིང་དང་། །རྡོ་དང་རི་ཡི་ལྷ་རྣམས་ནི།
དེ་དག་ཐམས་ཅད་སྐྱབས་མ་ཡིན།
དམ་པའི་དོན་དུ་འགྲོ་བ་ཡི། །སྐྱབས་ནི་སངས་རྒྱས་ཉག་གཅིག་ཡིན།
ཆོས་རྣམ་གཉིས་དང་འཕགས་པའི་ཚོགས། །གཏན་གྱི་སྐྱབས་མཆོག་མ་ཡིན་ནོ།།

See བཀའ་འགྱུར, རྒྱུད, vol. ཁ, རྒྱུད་བླ་མ, (Sans. *Uttara Tantra.*)

Translation.

BRAHMA, VISHNU, and the great God (ISHWARA) et cet. ;—the *Nágás*, *Yakshás*, and *Kumbhandás* (demi-gods) ;—the sun, the moon, and the planets ; any mountain (or hill), lake, and green tree ; any rock (or large mass of stone,) and the hill gods,—all these are no protections. The only refuge for him, who aspires to true perfection, is BUDDHA alone. The two kinds of moral instruction (dogmatic and argumentative), and the collective body of priests, are no permanent refuge.

10. With whom refuge may be taken.

See བསྟན་འགྱུར། བསྟོད་ཚོགས, vol. ཀ, leaf 89.

§. 245. ༄༅། །གང་ལ་སྐྱོན་ནི་མི་མངའ་ཞིང་། །ཡོན་ཏན་དཔག་མེད་མངའ་བ་དང་།
ཐམས་ཅད་མཁྱེན་དང་ཐུགས་རྗེ་ཅན། །དེ་ལ་བདག་ནི་སྐྱབས་སུ་མཆི།།

Translation.

Who is void of all defects, and who abounds with immense good qualities (perfections); who is all-knowing and merciful, to Him will I fly for protection.

10. On the same subject.

Ibid. leaf 47-48.

§. 346. ༄༅། །གང་ལ་སྐྱོན་ཀུན་ཡོད་མིན་ལ། །ཡོན་ཏན་ཐམས་ཅད་ཡོད་གྱུར་ན།
ཚངས་དང་ཁྱབ་འཇུག་དབང་ཕྱུག་ཆེ། །དེ་ཡང་གདག་གི་སྟོན་པ་ཡིན།།

Translation.

In whom there are no defects, and who has all the perfections (required in a Buddha); be he called Brahma, Vishnu, or the great Ishwara. He also is my teacher (or Buddha).

---

11. Here follow two specimens of Tibetan translation from the great Sanscrit Epic, the *Mahá Bhárata*, by Vyása, the Rishi, called in Tibetan དྲང་སྲོང་རྒྱས་པ (Drang srong rgyas-pa, meaning: the copious hermit or sage); first, the speech of Arjuna, and secondly, a short description of the quality of the soul.

11. The address of Arjuna to Vishnu.

Extracted from the Stan-gyur བསྟོད་ཚོགས, vol. ཀ leaf 25, also leaf 51, 52.

§. 247. ༄༅། །ཀུན་ཏིའི་བུ་ལ་ནི་དེ་བལྟས་ན། །ཐམས་ཅད་གཉེན་ཙ་ནམ་པར་གནས།
མཆོག་ཏུ་བརྩེ་བས་ནོན་པ་ཡིས། །ཞུམ་པ་ཡིས་ནི་འདི་སྐད་སྨྲས།།
ཁྱབ་འཇུག་གཉེན་ནམས་མཐོང་བས་ན། །འཐབ་པར་འདོད་དེ་གནས་པ་ལ།
བདག་གི་ལུས་ནི་ཞུམ་གྱུར་ཅིང་། །ཁ་ཡང་ཡོངས་སུ་སྐམ་པར་བྱེད།
ང་ཡི་ལུས་ནི་འདར་གྱུར་ཅིང་། །སྤུ་ཡང་ནམ་པར་ལྡང་བར་འགྱུར།
གཞུ་ནི་ལག་ནས་ལྷུང་གྱུར་ཅིང་། །པགས་པའང་ཡོངས་སུ་ཚིག་པར་འགྱུར།།
ང་ཡི་ཡིད་ནི་ནམ་འཁོར་བས། །གནས་པར་ཐ་བར་ནུས་མ་གྱུར།
གང་གི་དོན་ཏུ་རྒྱལ་སྲིད་དང་། །ལོངས་སྤྱོད་བདེ་བ་འདོད་གྱུར་པ།
དེ་ཉིད་སྲོག་དང་ནོར་ནམས་ནི། །སྤངས་ནས་ང་དང་འཐབ་པར་གནས།།

Translation.

The son of Kunti (Arjuna), perceiving that they were all his relations, being greatly affected through compassion for them, and seized with horror, thus said:

"Having beheld, O Vishnu, my kindred waiting ready for the fight, my body is seized with horror, my mouth also is entirely dry; my frame trembleth with anguish, the hair standeth on end upon my body; my bow escaped (escapeth) from my hand, my skin also is all over parched. My mind being in confusion, I am unable to fix it. Those for whom I wished dominion, wealth, and the enjoyments of life, they, abandoning life and fortune, are ready to fight against me."

12. The Nature of the soul.

Ibid. leaf 35.

§. 248. ༄༅། །འདི་ནི་མཚོན་གྱིས་མི་གཅོད་ཅིང་། །འདི་ནི་མེ་ཡིས་མི་འཚིག་ལ། །
ཆུ་ཡིས་འདྲུལ་བར་མི་འགྱུར་དེ། །འདི་ནི་རླུང་གིས་སྐེམས་མི་འགྱུར། །

Translation.

The weapon cutteth it (this) not; the fire burneth it not; the water corrupteth it not; the wind drieth it not away*.

13. How the doctrine of Shakya should be received by the learned, and the priests.

See བཀའ་འགྱུར, མདོ, vol. ཁ leaf 230, also བསྟན་འགྱུར, མདོ, vol. ཆོ leaf 26, and elsewhere.

§. 249. ༄༅། །བསྲེགས་བཅད་བརྡར་བའི་གསེར་བཞིན་དུ། །མཁས་པ་རྣམས་ཀྱིས་ཡོངས་བརྟགས་ནས། །
བདག་གསུང་བླང་བྱ་དགེ་སློང་དག །གུས་པའི་ཕྱིར་ནི་མ་ཡིན་ནོ། །

Translation.

Priests! like as gold is tried by burning, cutting and filing, the learned must examine my commandments (doctrine) and receive them accordingly, and not out of respect (for me).

14. Shakya of the Scythian race.

བཀའ་འགྱུར, མདོ, vol. ཅ, leaf 288, 291, in the Lankavatara Sutra.

§. 250. ༄༅། །ང་ནི་ཤཱ་ཀྱ་ཡ་ནའི་རིགས། །གཙང་མའི་གནས་ནས་བྱུང་བ་སྟེ། །
མྱ་ངན་འདས་པའི་གྲོང་འགྲོ་བའི། །ཆོས་ནི་སེམས་ཅན་རྣམས་ལ་སྟོན། །

Translation.

I (Shakya) am of the Scythian nation, born of an undefiled place. I teach a religion (doctrine) to animal beings (men) for entering into the city exempt from pain, (i. e. I teach how to be emancipated, or delivered from bodily existence.)

* When the author was prosecuting his Tibetan studies at the monastery of Kanum, he was struck with two passages in the *Stan-gyur* collection, which he immediately recognised as having met with in a duodecimo volume of Robertson's Disquisition on India, presented to him by Mr. Moorcroft in Cashmír. The two extracts in the text above are those alluded to; he mentioned to Dr. Gerard having found these Tibetan translations from the Mahábhárata, and was some months afterwards surprized to see in the Calcutta newspapers, an announcement that he had discovered the *lost volumes* of that great Indian epic! The object of the present note is merely to correct the misapprehension which thus got abroad, as it was only from Dr. Wilkin's English translation of the passages in question that he was enabled to recognise the Tibetan translations to be taken from the same work.

15. Moral Sentence.

The following moral sentiment taken from Chan'aka's Nití Shástra: "*Svadéshé pújyaté Rájá ; Vidván sarvatra pújyaté,*" (the literal version of which, in Latin, is: "*Suo regno colitur rex ; doctus ubique colitur,*") has been thus rendered by the Tibetans:

§. 251. ༄༅། །རྒྱལ་པོ་རང་གི་ཡུལ་ན་བཀུར། །ཡོན་ཏན་ལྡན་པ་ཀུན་ཏུ་བཀུར།།

A king is honoured in his own dominion ; a talented man is everywhere respected.

---

16. Remarkable Sayings,

(taken from a work entitled, in Tibetan: ༄༅། །ལེགས་པར་བཤད་པ་རིན་པོ་ཆེའི་གཏེར་ཞེས་བྱ་བའི་བསྟན་བཅོས། in Sanscrit: *Subhás'hita Ratna Nidhi Náma Shástra*, that is, "A Work of Elegant Sayings, entitled: *A Treasury of Jewels,*" written by *Kungá Gyel-tsan* (ཀུན་དགའ་རྒྱལ་མཚན), in Sanscrit *A'nanda Dwaja*, the celebrated *Sa-skya Pánd'ita*, in the 13th century after Christ.)

---

§. 252. ༄༅། །སངས་རྒྱས་མགོན་པོ་ཡོངས་སྤངས་ཏེ། །ལྷ་གཞན་ཆེ་ལ་ཕྱག་བྱེད་པ།
བློ་ངན་གང་ཀླུའི་འགྲམ་རུ་ནི། །སྐོམ་ནས་ཁྲོན་པ་བྱེད་དང་མཚུངས།།

He who entirely rejects Buddha, the Patron, and pays reverence to other Gods, acts like that foolish man, who, being thirsty, sinks a well on the bank of the Ganges.

༄༅། །ཤེས་རབ་དང་མཉམ་མིག་མེད་དེ། །མོངས་པ་དང་མཉམ་མུན་པ་མེད།
ནད་དང་འདྲ་བའི་དགྲ་མེད་དེ། །འཆི་བ་དང་མཉམ་འཇིགས་པ་མེད།།

There is no eye like the understanding: there is no blindness like ignorance: there is no enemy like sickness: nothing dreaded like death.

༄༅། །ནོར་རམ་རིག་པ་ལྡན་གྱུར་ན། །དམན་པ་ཉམས་ནི་རྡིགས་པར་འགྱུར།
གོ་འཕང་གཉིས་པོ་དེ་དག་གིས། །མཁས་པ་ཤིན་ཏུ་ཙལ་བར་འགྱུར།།

Low-minded men, should they become wealthy or learned, grow arrogant: a wise man, by these excellencies, becomes the more humble.

༄༅། །གཞན་ལས་འཚོལ་ཞིང་ཟས་ཞིམ་འདོད། །སློང་མོས་འཚོ་ཞིང་ཁེངས་པ་ཆེ།
བསྟན་བཅོས་ཤེས་མེད་རྩོད་པར་འདོད། །ཚོད་ཀྱི་དེ་གསུམ་བཞད་གད་རྒྱུ།།

To seek to get from others, and yet to desire to fare on delicacies: to live by begging, and yet to have great pride: to be ignorant of literary works, and yet to wish to dispute; these three actions make you ridiculous to others.

III. COLLOQUIAL PHRASES.

§ 253. ༄༅། བདེ་ལེགས་སུ་གྱུར་ཅིག, may you be happy (may you prosper), may it please (your honour).

རྒྱལ་བར་གྱུར་ཅིག, may you be victorious.

བཀྲ་ཤིས་པར་གྱུར་ཅིག, may you be glorified and blessed.

ཕྱག་འཚལ་ལོ, I salute you (I thank you).

བྱོན་པ་ལེགས་སོ, you are welcome.

ནང་ཏུ་ཞུགས་ཤིག, } please to enter.

or ནང་ཏུ་སྦྱོད་ཅིག, } please to walk in.

གདན་འདི་ལ་བཞུགས་སུ་གསོལ, I beg (you) to sit on this couch (stuffed seat).

ཡང་ན་བཞུགས་ཁྲི་འདི་ལ, or on this chair.

བདེ་བར་ཕེབས་སམ, are you happily arrived?

ང་བདེ་མོ་ཕྱེབས་ཟིན, I have happily arrived.

སྐུ་གཟུགས་བདེ་མོ་འཛག་གམ, are you in good health ?

ནད་མི་མངའ་འམ, have you no sickness ?

དཀོན་མཆོག་གི་ཐུགས་རྗེ་ཡིས། ང་ལ་ད་ལྟ་ལུས་དང་སེམས་ཀྱི་བདེ་བ་གཉིས་ཀ་ཡོད, by the grace of God, I am well now, both in body and mind.

ཇོད (or སྐུ་གཞོགས, Sir, or your honour,) ནམ་ཕེབས, when are you come ? (when did you arrive ?)

མདང་ཉི་མ་ནུབ་ཁ་ན, yesterday at sunset.

ལམ་ན་སྐུ་ངལ་བར (མཉེལ་བར) མ་གྱུར་ཏམ, have you not been fatigued on the road ?

ང་ཅིའང་ངལ་མ་སོང་, I was not fatigued at all.

ཅི་ལ་བཞོན་དེ་ཕེབས, on what sort of carriage came you ?

ང་འཇོགས་དཔྱང་ལ་འོངས, I came in a palanquin.

གྲུ་ཧྲི་འམ་ཤིང་རྟ་ཐོབ་མ་ནུས་སོ, I could not find a boat (ship), neither a horse or carriage.

ད་རེ་ཞིག་འདི་ན་སྐུ་ངལ་གསོ་བ་མཛོད་ཅིག, now please to rest here for a while.

ཐུགས་རྗེ་ཆེ, (great mercy!) I thank you: (or I thank for your offered kindness).

གཟིམ་ཁང་འདི་ན་བཞུགས་འཛང་མཛོད་ཅིག, please to take your lodgings in this apartment.

ཇི་དང་ཇི་དགོས་པ་འབྱུང་ན་ང་ལ་མོལ་ཅིག (or བཀའ་སྩོལ་ཅིག) ང་བདག་གིས་དེ་ཐམས་ཅད་དབུལ་བར་བྱའོ, whatever you may want, please to command me, and I will furnish it.

ནང་མོ་བདེ་ལེགས, good morning.

ཉིན་མོ་བདེ་ལེགས, good day.

ནུབ་མོ་བདེ་ལེགས, good evening.

མཚན་མོ་བདེ་ལེགས, good night.

བདེ་བར་གཟིམས་ཤིག, may you sleep well.

བདེ་བར་གཟིམས་སམ, have you slept well ?

ང་ཅག་དང་མཉམ་པོ་གསོལ་ཇ་ཞིག་མི་འདྲེན་ནམ, will you not drink some tea with us ?

གཟུགས་ཚོད་དང་དགོངས་འཛམ་མི་གསོལ་ལམ, will you not dine and sup (with us) ?

ཁྱེད་ཅག་ལ་ནས་ཆང་ (h. སྐྱེམས་འཐུང་) དང་ཨ་རག (h. འདྲེན་རག) ཡོད་དམ, have you some acid liquor (distilled from barley), and brandy ?

གཉིས་ཀ་འཛུག, ང་ཅག་ལ་རྒུན་ཆང་ཡང་ (h. རྒུན་སྐྱེམས) ཡོད, ང་ལ་སྔོན་ལ་ཅུང་ཟད་ཅིག་ཨ་རག་བྱུ, I beg to give me first a little brandy.

ཞིམ་པོ་འཛུག་གམ, is it (savoury) pleasing to the taste ?

ཞིམ་པོ་འཛུག, it is pleasing.

ཞིམ་པོ་འཛུག་ན་ཇེ་ཙམ་འཐད་འདྲེན་ཅིག་ང་ཅག་གིས་གཞན་ཡང་དབུལ་ཐུའོ, if you find it to your taste, please to drink, we will present you another (bottle) also.

ཐུགས་རྗེ་ཆེ, I thank you.

འདི་ཙམ་ཆོད, this is enough.

ནས་ཆང་འདི་ཅུང་ཟད་སྐྱུར་མོ་འཛུག, this liquor of barley is a little sour.

རྒུན་ཆང་འདི་གང་ཡུལ་ནས་ཡིན, from what country is this wine ?

དེ་ང་ཅག་ག་རྒུན་ཚལ་ནས་ཡིན, it is from our vineyard.

ད་ལོ་རྒུན་འབྲུམ་ཡགས་པོ (འཇམ་པོ) བྱུང, this year we had fine grapes.

ཁྱེད་ཅག་གི་ཁང་པ་ན་ད་དུང་རྒུན་འབྲུམ་ཡོད་ན་ང་ལ་ཅུང་ཟད་སྤྲུལ་ཙ་གསོལ, should you still have any grapes, in your house, I beg you to favour me with some.

འདི་ནི་རྒུན་དཀར་པོ, འདི་ནི རྒུན་ནག་གོ, these are white grapes, these are black grapes.

གཉིས་ཀ་བདེ་མོ་དང་མངར་མོ་འཛུག, they both (each of them is) are beautiful and sweet.

རྒུན་འབྲུམ་འདི་ཙམ་ཆེན་པོ་བདག་གིས་ནམ་ཡང་མ་མཐོང, I have never seen such large grapes as these are.

ད་དུང་འདྲེན་ཅིག, be pleased to take yet more, (to help yourself again.)

ད་ཆོད, (ཚོག་ཚོག,) མང་པོ་ཟོས, enough, I have eaten much.

ཐུགས་རྗེ་ཆེ, I thank you.

ཁྱེད་ཅག་ཐམས་ཅད་བདེ་མོ་བཞུགས་ཤིག, may you all remain in peace.

ཁྱོད་ལམ་ན་བདེ་བར་སྐྱོད་ཅིག, may you well proceed on your way.

དེ་ན་བགོད་པ་ཆེན་པོ་དེ་ཅི་ཡིན, what is that large building yonder ?

དེ་དགོན་པ་ཞིག་ཡིན, it is a monastery.

དེ་ནང་ན་སུ་དག་གནས་སོ, who dwell there ? who inhabit it ?

ཆོས་པ་རྣམས་སོ, or ཆོས་མཛད་པ་རྣམས་སོ, religious men.

དེ་དག་གི་དགོན་པར་ནང་དུ་འཛུལ་རུང་ངམ, is it allowable to enter their monastery ?

རུང་ངོ, it is allowable (one may enter).

གནང་བ་ཐོབ་ན་དེ་ནང་ན་ཡོད་པ་ཐམས་ཅད་བདག་གིས་ཡོངས་སུ་བལྟ་བར་འདོད་དོ, should I be permitted, I wish to see (examine thoroughly) every thing, that is to be found there.

སུ་ཞིག་གིས་དྲིས་ལན་འདེབས་ནུས་པའི་ཆོས་པ་མཁྱེན་པ་ཅན་ཞིག་ངའི་རྩར་དུ་འདིར་ཤོག་ཞུས་ཤིག, let any one (go and) request (or beg of) an intelligent *gélong* (religious man) who is able to answer my inquiries, to come hither to me.

དེ་ཡིས་ཁྲིད་དེ་ང་ནང་དུ་འགྲོའོ, conducted by him, I will enter.

ཁྱོད་ཀྱི་འདོད་པ་བཞིན་དུ་དགེ་སློང་ཞིག་འདིར་ཕེབས་སོ, here is a *gélong* (priest) come according to your wish.

བྱོན་པ་ལེགས་སོ, you are welcome.

ཁྱེད་ཀྱི་མཚན, (what is) your name ?

ངའི་ཆོས་མིང་ཚུལ་ཁྲིམས་རྒྱ་མཚོ་ཡིན, my religious name is *Tshul-khrims rGya-mtsho*, " Ocean of good Morals."

དགོན་པ་འདིའི་ནང་ན་ཇི་དང་ཇི་ཡོད་ཁྱེད་ཀྱིས་ང་ལ་ཞིབ་ཏུ་བཤད་དུ་གསོལ, I beg you to tell me, in detail, every thing that is to be found in this monastery.

ཁྱེད་ཀྱི་བཞེད་པ་བཞིན་དུ་བདག་གིས་དེ་ཐམས་ཅད་བཤད་པར་བྱའོ, I will explain every thing according to your (honour's) wishes.

འདི་ནི་བླ་མའི་བཞུགས་ས་ཡིན, this (chamber) is the residence of the Lama (superior, or high priest).

དེ་ཕྱོགས་ན་དེ་ནི་མཁན་པོའི་གཟིམ་ཁང་ཡིན, there on that side is the principal's chamber.

ཕྱོགས་འདི་ན་ནི་སློབ་དཔོན་གྱི་བཞུགས་གནས་སོ, on this side is the professor's (teacher's) apartment (or dwelling place).

ཁང་པ་ཆེན་པོ་དེ་ནང་ན། སྟེང་ན་ཕྱག་མཛོད་བཞུགས་སོ, in that large room, in the upper story, resides the treasurer.

དེའི་འོག་ན་ཡོད་པའི་ཁང་པ་དག་ན་གཉེར་པ་གནས་སོ, in the rooms below it, dwells the steward (butler, caterer, provider of victuals, &c.)

སྟེང་། བར། འོག་གི་བརྩེགས་པའི.ཁང་མིག་འདི་དག་ནི་དགེ་འདུན་གྱི་གནས་ཁང་དག་གོ, these small staired rooms (cells) above, in the middle and below, are the dwelling places of the priests (or monks).

འདི་ནི་དགེ་འདུན་གྱི་འདུ་ཁང་ཡིན, this is the place of congregation for the priests.

དེའི་གོང་ན་དེ་ནི་མཆོད་ཁང་ཡིན་, that above it is the place of sacrifice (or offering).

འདོ་དག་ནི་མཆོད་པའི་ལག་ཆ་དག་གོ, these are the implements of sacrifice.

དེའི་གོང་ན་དེ་ནི་དྲི་གཙང་ཁང་ཡིན, that above the latter is the holy chapel (or shrine).

འདི་ནི་ལྷ་ཁང་ཆེན་པོ་ཞིག་ཡིན, this is the large temple of the gods.

སྒོ་ཁང་ན་སྐུ་འདྲ་འདི་དག་ནི་རྒྱལ་ཆེན་བཞི་དང་ । ཆོས་སྐྱོང་རྣམས་ཀྱི་རི་མོ་ དག་ཡིན་ལགས་སོ, these pictures here in the vestibule are the (painted) images of the four great (fabulous) kings, and of the guardians or defenders of religion.

ནང་ན་རྩིག་པའི་ལོགས་ན་ཡོད་པའི་རི་མོ་དག་ནི་སངས་རྒྱས་དང་ །བྱང་ཆུབ་སེམས་དཔའ་རྣམས་ཀྱི་སྐུ་འདྲ་དག་གོ, the images, within, found on the side of the wall, are representations of Buddhas and of Bodhisatwas.

འདི་ནི.ཟིས་སྐུའོ, this is a picture (painted image).

འདི་ནི་ལུགས་སྐུའོ, this is a cast (molten) image.

འདི་ནི་འབུར་སྐུའོ, this is a carved image (bass-relief).

དེ་ནི་ཐགས་སྐུའོ, that is a woven image.

འདི་ནི་སྐུ་རྟེན་དང་,	these here	a Buddha's person, i. e. a Buddha image.
འདི་ནི་གསུང་རྟེན་དང,	are the repre-	his doctrine, i. e. a sacred volume.
འདི་ནི་ཐུགས་རྟེན་དག་ཡིན་ནོ	sentations of	his grace or mercy, i. e. a holy shrine, or small pyramidial building.

གླེགས་བམ་འདི་དག་ན་སངས་རྒྱས་བཅོམ་ལྡན་འདས་དང་བྱང་ཆུབ་སེམས་དཔའ་དག་དང་། སྔོན་གྱི་མཁས་པ་རྣམས་ཀྱིས་གསུངས་པའི་ཆོས་རྣམས་བཞུགས་སོ, in these volumes are contained the moral instructions, delivered (commanded) by Buddha, that has been victorious; by Bodhisatwas, and by ancient learned men.

གླེགས་བམ་ཞིག་བསྒྲོལ་ཏེ་བདག་ལ་བསྟན་ཏ་གསོལ, I beg you to open a volume, and to show it me.

གླེགས་བམ་འདི་ནི་མཚལ་པར་ཡིན, this volume is printed with vermilion (red ink).

འདི་ནང་ན་གླེགས་བུ (or ཤོག་བུ) ལྔ་བརྒྱ་ཙམ་མཆིས་སོ, in this (volume) there are about 500 leaves.

འདི་ནི་མགོ, འདི་ནི་ མཇུག་གོ, this is the beginning, and this the end.

ཤོག་བུའི་མདུན་ལོགས་དང་རྒྱབ་ལོགས་རེ་རེ་ལ་ཡིག་ཕྲེང་བདུན་བདུན་ཡོད, there are on the front and back of each leaf seven lines.

པར་གསལ་པོ་འདུག, དག་ཡིག་དང་ཞུས་དག་དང་དེ་དང་འདྲ་བ་ཡོད་ན་འདི་ལ་རིན་ཆེན་པོ་མཆིས་སོ, the print of it is clean ; if orthography and the correction of the errata be in accordance therewith, this volume is of great value.

འདི་ནི་གསེར་ཕྲ་དང་དངུལ་ཕྲས་བྲིས་པའི་གླེགས་བམ་མ་ཚང་བ་ཞིག་ཡིན, this is an incomplete volume, written with gold and silver pigment.

འདི་དག་ནི་པར་མ, དེ་དག་ནི་རྡོ་པར་གྱི་དཔེ་ཆ་དག་ཡིན་ནོ, these are printed, those lithographed books.

འདི་ན་ཡི་གེ་དབུ་ཅན་དབུ་མེད་ཀྱི་བྲིས་ མ་རྣམས་ཀྱང་མང་པོ་བཞུགས་སོ, there are here many MSS. (manuscripts) also, both in the capital and small character.

འདི་ན་པར་ཁང་ག་ན་ཡོད, where is (here) the printing house?

དེ་དེ་ཕྱོགས་ན་འདུག, it is on that side.

མི་དེ་ནི་པར་དཔོན་ཡིན, དེའི་དྲུང་ན་གཞན་དེ་དག་ནི་པར་གཡོག་རྣམས་སོ, that man yonder is the principal printer, the others near to him are his working men.

མི་འདི་གང་པ་ཡིན or གང་ལུང་པ་ཡིན, from what place is this man? or what countryman is this man?

ཁོ་འདི་པ་ཡིན or ལུང་འདི་པ་ཡིན, he is from this place, or he is from this country.

དེ་པ་ཡིན or ལུང་དེ་པ་ཡིན, he is from thence, or from that place, he is from that country.

ཁོ་ང་ཚག་པ་ཡིན། ཁོ་ང་ཚག་གི་ལུང་པ་ཡིན, he is from us, he is our countryman.

འདི་འཛམ་བུ་གླིང་པ་ཡིན, དི་ཕྱི་གླིང་པ་ཡིན, this is an Asiatic, that is an European.

འདི་རྒྱ་གར་པ, དེ་རྒྱ་ནག་པ་ཡིན, this is an Indian, that is a Chinese man.

ང་ཏ་ཟིག་པ་ཡིན, I am a Tájik, (a Persian.)

འདི་བོད་པ, དེ་བལ་པོ་པ་ཡིན, this is a Tibetan, that is a Nepalese.

འདི་ཧོར་པ, དེ་སོག་པོ་ཡིན, this is a Turk, that is a Mongol.

འདི་ནི་ཧོར་མོ་ཞིག་ཡིན, this is a Turkish woman.

འདི་ན་ཧོར་ཕྲུག་ཅིག་འདུག, there is a Turkish boy.

འདི་ཁམས་པ, དེ་དབུས་གཙང་པ་ཡིན, this is of Khams-land (or a Khámbá), that is of Utsang (or middle Tibet).

འདི་དབུས་པ, དེ་གཙང་པ་ཡིན, this is of (the province) U, that is of (the province) Tsang.

འདི་ལྷོ་པ or ལྷོ་འབྲུག་པའི་ཡུལ་པ་ཡིན, དེ་མོན་ཡུལ་པ་ཡིན, this is of Bhután, that is a Mon.

འདི་མངའ་རིས་པ, དེ་ནི་ཁ་ཆེ་པ་ཡིན, this is of Ńári, that is a Cashmerian.

འདི་ནི་ཆེ་མོ་ཞིག་ཡིན, this is a Cashmerian woman.

འདི་ལ་དྭགས་པ, དེ་ནི་སྦལ་ཏི་ཡུལ་པ་ཡིན, this is of Ladák, that is of Beltistan or Little Tibet.

འདི་ལྷ་ས་པ, དེ་ནི་གཞིས་ཀ་རྩེ་པ་ཡིན, this is of Lassa, that is of Zhikatsé.

འདི་སངས་རྒྱས་པ, དེ་བོན་པོ་པ་ཡིན, this is a Buddhist, that is of the Bon religious sect.

འདི་བྲམ་ཟེ་པ, དེ་མུ་སྟེགས་པ་ཡིན, this is a Brahmanist, that is a Tirthíka, or Tirthakara (a Jaina ?)

འདི་ཡེ་ཤུས་པ, དེ་མོ་ཤེས་པ་ཡིན, this is a follower of Jesus, that is the same of Moses.

འདི་མུ་ཧམ་མེད་པ, དེ་ཀླ་ཀློ་པ་ཡིན*, this is a Muhammedan, that is an infidel, a pagan.

འདི་ནི་ཆོས་འདི་པ་ཡིན་, དེ་ནི ཆོས་གཞན་པ་ཡིན, this is of this religion, that is of another religion.

འདི་ང་ཅག་གི་ཆོས་ལུགས་པ་ཡིན, this is of our religious sect.

འདི་ནི་ནང་པ་ཡིན, དེ་ནི་ཕྱི་པ (or ཕྱི་རོལ་པ) ཡིན, (properly intrinsic and exotic,) this is of the orthodox, that of the heterodox, church, (or doctrine.)

བོད་ན་ནང་པ་སངས་རྒྱས་པའི་ནང་ན་ཆོས་ལུགས་སོ་སོ་ཙམ་འདུག, how many different religious sects are there in Tibet among the orthodox Buddhists ?

མང་པོ་འདུག་གོ, there are many.

ཆོས་ལུགས་ཆེ་བ་དག་འདི་དག་ཡིན་ནོ, the principal sects are as follows : རྙིང་མ་པ, 1, Nyigmápá ; ཨུ་རྒྱན་པ, 2, Urgyenpá ; བཀའ་གདམས་པ, 3, Kahdámpá ; དགེ་ལུགས་པ, 4, Gélukpá, or དགའ་ལྡན་པ, Gáldánpá, (or དགེ་ལྡན་པ, .Ghéldámpá,) ས་སྐྱ་པ' 5, Sakyapá ; བཀའ་བརྒྱུད་པ, 6, Kargyutpá ; ཀརྨ་པ, 7, Karmapá ; འབྲི་ཁུང་པ, 8, Brikungpá ; དང་འབྲུག་པ, and 9, Brukpá.

འདི་ནི་ང་དང་ཆོས་གཅིག་པ་ཡིན, this person is of the same religion with me.

དེ་ནི་ཁྱོད་དང་ཆོས.གཅིག་པ་ཡིན, that is of the same religion with thee.

འདི་ནི་ང་དང་ཡུལ་གཅིག་པ་ཡིན, this is of the same place (or country) with me, or this is my countryman.

* The Tibetans call the Muhammedans in general by this name. This word ཀླ་ཀློ (pronounced *Lálo*) answers to the Sanscrit *Mlechchha*.

མི་འདི་དག་ནི་ཡུལ་དང་ཆོས་མི་གཅིག་པ་དག་ཡིན་ནོ, these men are all of different countries and of different religions.

ཁྱོད་སུ་ཡིན, who art thou? who are you?

གང་ནས་འོངས (h. ག་ནས་ཕེབས), whence are you come?

ཁྱོད་ལ་ལམ་ཡིག་ཡོད་དམ, have you a passport?

ཡ་དོ (or གྲོགས་པོ) ཚམ་འདུག, how many companions have you? (or how many men, &c.)

ཁྱོད་དང་མཉམ་པོ་མི་གྲ་ཚམ་ཡོད, how many men (or persons) are with you?

ང་ཕི་གླིང་པ་ཡིན, I am a European.

འབྲི་ཧིན་ཆེན་མོ་པ, of Great Britain.

ད་ལྟ་འདི་རུ་རྒྱ་གར་ནས (or རྒྱ་ཕི་གླིང་ནས) འོངས་པ་ཡིན, I am come now hither from India, (from European or British India.)

ང་ལ་ལམ་ཡིག་མི་འདུག, I have no passport.

དེ་མེད་ན་ང་ཅག་གིས་ཁྱོད་ལ་ལམ་མི་གཏོང་ (or གཏང་ཐུ་མིན), without it (without a passport) we will give you no way, or we will not allow you to proceed on your journey.

ཁྱོད་འདིར་ཅི་ལ་འོངས, why are you come hither?

ཁྱོད་ཚོང་པ་ཡིན་ནམ། ཡང་ན་རྒྱལ་པོ་ཞིག་གི་པོ་ཉ་ཡིན, are you a merchant, or are you the envoy of any king?

ང་ཚོང་པ་ཡང་མིན། པོ་ཉ་ཡང་མིན། ང་ཡུལ་འཁོར་པ་ཞིག་ཡིན, I am neither merchant, nor envoy; I am a traveller.

བོད་བྱེ་བྲག་ཏུ་འཕགས་པའི་ཡུལ་ཡིན་པའི་ཕྱིར་ང་ལ་འདི་མཐོང་བའི་འདོད་པ་ཡོད་པ་ཡིན, on account of Tibet being particularly a high country, I had a desire to see it.

ཡུལ་འདིའི་མཐོ་བ་ཉིད་རྒྱ་མཚོ་ལ་ལྟོས་ཏེ་དཔག་ཚད་ཚམ་འདུག་ད་བདག་གིས་ཤེས་སོ, I know now, what is the elevation of this country above the sea, (or how many miles be, &c.)

དེ་བཞིན་ཙ་གྲང་གི་ལྗི་ཡང་དང་། རྡོ་ཤད་དང་། སྣམ་གཞིར་ཕྱི་ཚད་བདག་གིས་ཐོབ་ཟིན, as also (I have found) the measure of the heaviness and lightness of the heat and cold, and of the dryness and humidity of the air.

འདི་ན་འབྲུའི་རིགས་ཅི་སྐྱེ, what sort of corn is produced here?

ང་ཅག་གི་ཡུལ་ལ་རྒྱ་གར་མཚོགས་འབྲུ་རིགས་མང་པོ་མི་འབྱུང, in our country there do not grow so many kinds of corn, as in India.

ཁྱེད་བོད་པ་དག་སྟོན་པ་སུའི་བསྟན.པ་ལ་དགའ (འམ་ཆོས་ལུགས་གང་ཡིན), you, who are Tibetans, in what teacher's doctrine do you delight? (who is the teacher or founder of your religion?) or what religious sect are you?

ང་ཅག་ནི་བཅོམ་ལྡན་འདས་ཤཱཀྱ་ཐུབ་པས་གསུངས་པའི་དམ་པའི་ཆོས་ལ་དད་པ་བྱེད་དོ, we believe in the holy religion taught by Bhagavan Shákya Muni, (the triumpher, the mighty Shákya.)

རྒྱ་གར་ན་ཤཱཀྱའི་རིགས་ལ་དབྱེ་བ་གསུམ་པོ་འདི་ལྟར་ཡོད་པ་ཡིན, this triple division was of the Shákya race, in India.

ཤཱཀྱ་ཆེན་པོ་དང་། ཤཱཀྱ་ལི་ཙ་བྱི་དང་། ཤཱཀྱ་རི་བྲག་པའོ།། Shákya the Great, Shákya Litsabyi, and Shákya the mountaineer or highlander.

བོད་ན་རྒྱལ་པོ་རྣམས་ཀྱི་ཐོག་མ་གཉའ་ཁྲི་བཙན་པོ་ཡིན, in Tibet, the kings begin with Nyákhritsánpo (about 250 years before Christ.)

དེ་རྒྱ་གར་ན་ཤཱཀྱ་ལི་ཙ.བྱི་རིགས་ནས་འཁྲུངས, he was born of the Litsabyi race, in India.

དེ་རྒྱ་གར་ནས་སྐྲགས་ཏེ་འམ་དམག་གི་ཙལ་སུ་གཡུལ་ན་ཕམ་པར་བྱུར་ནས་བོད་ཙ་ཕེབས་དང་བོད་བོན་པོ་དག་གིས་རང་གི་རྒྱལ་པོར་བཀུར, he being expelled from India, (or after being defeated in battle,) went to Tibet, and by the Bons of Tibet was honored (acknowledged) as their king.

རྒྱལ་པོ་འདིའི་རབས་ན་རིམ་པ་བཞིན་རྒྱལ་པོ་མང་པོ་བྱོན, in the family (generation or dynasty) of this king, there came (succeeded) many princes in a regular series.

ཉི་ཤུ་རྩ་བདུན་པ་ལྷ་ཐོ་ཐོ་རི་ཡིན, the 27th is Lha Thothori, (500 years after the first king, in the 3rd century after Christ.)

འདིས་ཡོ་བྲང་ཡམ་བུ་བརྐབ, this (prince) founded (built) the residence at Yambu.

འདིའི་སྐུ་རིང་ལ་ནམ་མཁའ་ནས་རིན་པོ་ཆེའི་སྒྲོམ་བུ་བབས, in the time of this (king) there fell from heaven a precious chest.

དེའི་ནང་ན་ཟ་མ་ཏོག་བཀོད་པའི་མདོ་དང་། གསེར་གྱི་མཆོད་རྟེན་ལ་སོགས་པ་བཞུགས་སོ།། there was found in it a Sutra (treatise) called the "Constructed Vessel" (a work on moral subjects), and a *chaitya* of gold, &c. (a small pyramidal shrine).

ཡི་གེ་དེ་སུས་ཀྱང་དེ་ཙས་སུ་མ་ཤེས་སོ, at that time, no one knew those letters.

སུམ་ཅུ་རྩ་གཉིས་པ་སྲོང་བཙན་སྒམ་པོ་ཡིན, the 32nd (king) is "Srongtsan Gambo."

འདི་ལོ་བརྒྱད་ཅུ་ཙམ་བཞུགས, he lived about 80 years.

འདིས་བལ་པོ་དང་རྒྱ་ནག་ནས་བཙུན་མོ་བླངས, this (king) married (took his wives) from Nepal and China.

ལྷ་མོ་འདི་དག་གིས་སངས་རྒྱས་ཀྱི་སྐུ་གཟུགས་དང་དམ་པའི་ཆོས་ཀྱི་གླེགས་བམ་རྣམས་བོད་དུ་ཁྱོངས, by these ladies, images of Buddha, and some volumes containing orthodox (or holy) religion, were brought to Tibet.

དེ་ནས་རྒྱལ་མོ་འདི་ དག་གིས་གཙུག་ལག་ཁང ་དག་བཞེངས་ཏེ་བོད་ན ་འང་སངས་ རྒྱས་ཀྱི་བསྟན ་པ་དར, afterwards, these queens (or princesses) having erected colleges, the religion of Buddha was propagated also in Tibet.

བོད་ན་མཁས་པ་རྣམས་ཀྱི་ཐོག་མ་ཐུ་མི་སམ་བྷོ་ཊ་ཡིན, in Tibet, "Thumi Sembhota" was the first learned man.

འདིས་རྒྱ་གར་ན་ལེགས་སྦྱར་གྱི་སྐད་ལེགས་པར་བསླབས་དང་ཁ་ཆེའི་ཡི་གེ་ནས་དཔེ་བླངས་ཏེ་བོད་ཀྱི་ཡིག་གཟུགས་དབུ་ཅན་དབུ་མེད་ཀྱི་རྩོལ་བསྟན་དང་ །ཐུ་མ་ར་རྟའི་བསྟན་བཅོས་རྣམས་མཛད་དང་ ། ཆོས་རི་བསྒྱུར་ད་པ་ཡིན, he became well acquainted with the Sanskrit language in India. And, in conformity with the Cashmerian characters, he taught the manner of forming the figures of the Tibetan letters, both capital and small.

རྒྱལ་པོ་སུམ་ཅུ་རྩ་བརྒྱད་པ། ཁྲི་སྲོང་ལྡེའུ་བཙན་གྱི་དུས་སུ་དང ། དེའི་སྲས་དང་ཚ་བོ་ (or དབོན་པོ) རྣམས་ཀྱི་རིང་ལ་དམ་པའི་ཆོས་དར་ཏེ་བོན་པོའི་ཆོས་ནུབ་པར་གྱུར་ཏོ ॥ in the time of "Khri srong dehu tsan" (in the 8th and 9th century after Christ) the 38th king, and under his sons and grandsons, the orthodox (Buddhistic) religion being propagated, that of the "Bonpo" declined.

རལ་པ་ཅན་ནམ་ཁྲི་ལྡེ་སྲོང་བཙན་གྱི་དུས་སུ་རྒྱ་གར་གྱི་པཎྜི་ཏ་དང་བོད་ཀྱི་ལོ་ཙཱ་བ་མང་པོ་དག་གིས་རྒྱ་གར་སྐད་ནས་བོད་སྐད་དུ་གླེགས་བམ་མང་པོ་བསྒྱུར་ད་ཟིན, in the time of "Ralpachen" or "Khri de srong tsán" (in the 9th century) there were translated many volumes from Sanskrit into Tibetan, by several Indian Pandits and Tibetan Lotsavas, (interpreters, translators.)

དེ་རྗེས་ནས་གླང་དར་མས་སངས་རྒྱས་བསྟན་པ་བསྣུབས, afterwards (in the 10th century) Langtarma abolished the Buddhistic religion.

ཡང་དེ་ཕྱིན་ནས་རྒྱ་གར་གྱི་པཎྜི་ཏ་ཇོ་བོ་ཨ་ཏི་ཤ་དང ། བོད་ཀྱི་དགེ་བ ཤེས་འབྲོམ་སྟོན་ལ་སོགས་པ་མཁས་པ་མང་པོ་དག་གིས་སླར་བསོས་ཏེ་དམ་པའི་ཆོས་ཁ་བ་ཅན་ཐམས་ཅད་དུ་དར་བར་གྱུར་ཏོ ॥ again (in the 11th century) the holy religion being revived by "Chovo Atisha" (the lord Atisha) by the Tibetan learned priest "Bromston" and by many other learned men, it was diffused (or propagated) in the whole snowy country, (Tibet.)

དམ་པའི་ཆོས་ཡུན་རིང་དུ་གནས་པར་གྱུར་ཅིག, may the holy religion remain (or continue) long.

ཡུལ་ཀུན་ཏུ་ཆོས་འདོད་པ་དག་ལ་སྒྲོགས་པར་གྱུར་ཅིག, may it be proclaimed (preached) in every country, to such as wish for religious instruction.

བོད་སྐད་ལ་བཞུགས་པའི་གསུང་རྟེན་རྣམས་སའི་སྟེང་ན་ཉི་ཟླ་ལྟར་གྱུར་ཅིག, may the sacred volumes (the representatives of the doctrine of Buddha) be on the face of the (whole) earth, like the sun and moon.

སྐྱེ་འགྲོ་ཐམས་ཅད་བདེ་བར་གྱུར་ཅིག, may all, that is born and walks, be saved (or arrive at happiness. Sans. *Shubham astu sarva jagatam)*.

བཀྲ་ཤིས, (Sans. *Mañgalam)* glory (and) praise.

ང་ལ་བོད་ཙ་ཡོད་པའི་བསྟན་བཅོས་རྣམས་ཀྱི་དཀར་ཆག་གམ་ཐོ་ཡིག་ཅིག་ཕུལ་ཙ་གསོལ, I beg (you) to favour me with a register or list of the literary works that are to be found in Tibet.

དེ་རྣམས་ཀྱི་མིང་ཆེན་གྲངས་མེད་དེ། དེ་དག་ཐམས་ཅད་བདག་གིས་བཤད་པར་མི་ནུས་སོ ༎ ཆེ་བ་དག་འདི་ལྟར་ལགས་སོ, their titles being numberless, I cannot tell all of them; the larger ones are as follows:

1. བཀའ་འགྱུར (སྡེ་བདུན་ལ) གླེགས་བམ་བརྒྱ, Translation of Commandments (in 7 classes) 100 vols. སྡེ་དག་ནི, the classes are: 1, འདུལ་བ, S. *Vinaya*, discipline or education, 13 vols. 2, ཤེས་རབ་ཀྱི་ཕ་རོལ་ཏུ་ཕྱིན་པ, (or *contractedly* ཤེར་ཕྱིན,) S. *Prajnyá Páramitá*, Transcendental Wisdom, 21 vols.. 3, སངས་རྒྱས་ཕལ་པོ་ཆེ, (or *contractedly* ཕལ་ཆེན,) S. *Buddhavata Sangha*, Association of Buddhas, 6 vols. 4, དཀོན་མཆོག་བརྩེགས་པ, (or *contractedly* དཀོན་བརྩེགས,) S. *Ratnakuta*, Accumulated Jewels, 6 vols. 5, མདོ་སྡེ (or མདོ), S. *Sutra*, Tract or Treatise, 30 vols. 6, མྱ་ངན་ལས་འདས་པ (or *contractedly* མྱང་འདས), S. *Nirvanam*, Deliverance from Pain, 2 vols. 7, རྒྱུད, S. *Tantra*, Mysticism, 22 vols.

2. བསྟན་འགྱུར, (collection of) literary works translated (from Sanscrit) in 225 vols. *Note:* Instead of བཀའ་འགྱུར་དང་བསྟན་འགྱུར་, frequently occurs this contracted form, བཀའ་བསྟན, as also, གསུང་རབ, S. *Pravachanam*, and བསྟན་བཅོས, S. *Shástram*.

The b*Stan*-hgyur consists of two classes: the r*Gyud* (རྒྱུད, in 88 vols.) and the m*Do* (མདོ, in 137 vols.) In the r*Gyud* there are 24 different tantrika systems (contained in 2,640 tracts or different large and small treatises), among which the first is that of དུས་ཀྱི་འཁོར་ལོ, S. *Kála Chakra*, the circle of time, (on the doctrine of *Adibuddha*) in 5 vols. In the m*Do* class under several heads, there are many learned theological, philosophical, logical, medical, philological or grammatical, &c. works*.

* For further information upon the several parts of the two Tibetan compilations above-described, see the "GLEANINGS IN SCIENCE," No. 32, Aug. 1831, p. 243. Also, the "JOURNAL OF THE ASIATIC SOCIETY OF BENGAL," No. 1. Jan., p. 1, and No. 9, Sept. 1832, p. 375.

Besides the works contained in the b*Kah*-hgyur and b*Stan*-hgyur there are a great number of books, in Tibet, under various names. To give some idea of them, we will enumerate a few, in Tibetan and English. 1, ལོ་རྒྱུས, annals, chronicle, history. 2, གཏམ་རྒྱུད, oral account, tradition, traditional history, S. *Akhyánam*. 3, ཆོས་འབྱུང་, elements (or origin and progress) of (the Buddhistic) religion. 4, རྟོགས་བརྗོད, judicious sayings, (or memoirs, reflections, critiques, biographical notices.) 5, རྣམ་ཐར (properly emancipation or liberation), biography (of a remarkable person), legendary account. 6, སྒྲུངས, a fable, tale, fiction; fabulous history. The གེ་སར་སྒྲུངས, *Qésar sgrungs*, is the fabulous history (in Tibetan) of a celebrated warlike king (called *Qésar*) in the high, central, or northern part of Asia; but the time, in which he lived, the Tibetans cannot determine. 7, དེབ་ཐེར or དེབ་གཏེར, (a *defter)* register, records, annals. 8, དེབ་ཐེར་སྔོན་པོ, ancient records. 9, ཡིག་ཚང་, or ཡིག་གཟུང་, records, annals, chronicle. 10, ཡིག་རྙིང་, ancient writ, chronicle. 11, བོད་ཀྱི་ཡིག་ཚང་, Tibetan records. 12, ས་སྐྱ་ཡིག་ཚང, records of the *Sa-skya* sect. 13, རྒྱའི་ཡིག་ཚང་ Chinese records. 14, ཤེས་བྱ་རབ་གསལ, very clear science, history. 15, རྒྱལ་རབས, royal pedigree, history of dynasties. 16, རྒྱལ་རབས་གསལ་བའི་མེ་ལོང་, a clear mirror of royal pedigree, or history of dynasties (in Tibet). 17, རྒྱལ་རབས་དཔག་བསམ་ལྗོན་ཤིང་, a work on royal pedigree or dynasty, called the all-bestowing tree (the *Kalpavrixa* or *Kalpa-druma* of the Indians). 18, ཞལ་ཡིག or བཀའ་ཞལ་, written advice or instruction. 19, བཀའ་འབུམ, a hundred thousand precepts, i. e. a collection of precepts and instructions. 20, བཀའ་ཆེམས, testament or last will; བཀའ་ཚོམས, fragments of commandments or precepts. 21, ཕྲིན་ཡིག, epistles, letters, epistolary correspondence on business. 22, བསྟོད་ཚོགས, a collection of praises or hymns. 23, སྨོན་ལམ, prayer. 24, གླུ, a song; བསྟོད་གླུ, a song of praise, a hymn; ཁྲད་གླུ, a satirical song, a satire; གླུ་འབུམ, a hundred thousand songs, i. e. a collection of songs. 25, བསྟན་རྩིས, chronology or calculation of some events or epochs occurring in the sacred volumes.

IV. CHRONOLOGICAL TABLE.

§ 254. The following short account of some remarkable events, in the history of Buddhism, and in Tibet, is extracted from a work entitled *Bai'dúrya* d*kar-po* (བཻཌཱུརྱ་དཀར་པོ) written by s*Dé-srid Sangs*-r*gyas* r*gya-mtsho* (སྡེ་སྲིད་སངས་རྒྱས་རྒྱ་མཚོ) a regent at Lhassa. (1)

He wrote at the beginning of the 12th cycle of sixty years (the Tibetans counting the beginning of the first cycle from 1026 of the Christian æra, and the present year, 1834, being the 28th year of the 14th cycle) consequently at the beginning of 1686 A. D. His table expresses the years elapsed from each event up to the time when he wrote. In the following translation, besides this mode of computation, the corresponding year of the vulgar era, in which each event occurred, before or after Christ, has been added.

Some explanatory notes have been appended, to which reference is made from the text by the figures in brackets.

			Years elapsed up to 1686 A. D.	Year of the Christian æra B. C.
༄༅། །བཅོམ་ལྡན་འདས་བལྟམས་ནས, ...	༢༦༤༧	From the incarnation or birth of b*Chom*-l*dan* h*das* (Sha'kya),...	2647	962
རབ་ཏུ་བྱུང་ནས, ...	༢༦༡༩	Since he took the religious character, ...	2619	934
སངས་རྒྱས་ཏེ་ཆོས་འཁོར་དང་པོ་བསྐོར་ནས, ...	༢༦༡༣	Since he became Buddha, and commanded to teach his doctrine (first turned the wheel of the law),	2613	928
ཆོ་འཕྲུལ་ཆེན་པོ་བསྟན་པས་མུ་སྟེགས་ཀྱི་སྟོན་པ་དྲུག་བཅུལ་ནས, ...	༢༥༩༡	Since he displayed great prodigies and overcame the six *Tirthika* teachers, (2) ...	2591	906
དུས་ཀྱི་འཁོར་ལོ་གསུངས་ནས, ...	༢༥༦༧	Since he taught the Kála Chakra (religious system), (3) ...	2567	882
མྱ་ངན་ལས་འདས་ནས, ...	do.	Since he was delivered from pain (or from his death), ...	do.	do.
ཞམ་ལྷ་ལའི་ཚལ་པོ་ཀླ་བ་བཟང་གིས་རྩ་རྒྱུད་བསྡུས་ནས, ..	༢༥༦༦	From the time that the r*tsa*-r*gyud* (S. *Múla Tantra)* was col-		

		B. C.
	lected (or compiled) by *Zla*-b*zang*, the king of Shambhala, (4) ... 2566	881
ཟླ་བཟང་གཤེགས་ནས, .. ༢༥༦༤	From the death of *Zla*-b*zang*, 2564	879
པད་མ་འབྱུང་གནས་འཁྲུངས་ནས,... ༢༥༦༣	From the birth of *Padma* h*byung* g,*nas* (pron. Padma jungné, S. Padma Sambhava), (5) ... 2563	878
རྒྱ་ནག་ཙ་ཧེ་བཙུན་འཇམ་དབྱངས་ཏྲི་ཀྵའི་ ཤིང་ལས་འཁྲུངས་ནས, ... ༢༥༢༣	From the birth of the revered master h*jam* d*vyangs* (6) (S. *Manju ghos'ha*) in China, out of the Trik-s'ha tree, ... 2523	838
ཀླུ་སྒྲུབ་འཁྲུངས་ནས, ... ༢༡༦༧	From the birth of k*Lu*-s*grub* (S. Nágarjuna), (7) ... 2167	482
ཤམ་བྷ་ལར་རིགས་ལྡན་གྲགས་པ་རྒྱལ་ སར་ཕེབས་ནས, ... ༡༩༦༣	Since *Rigs*-l*dangrags-pa* (8) succeeded to the throne, in Shambhala, 1963	278
		Aft. Chr.
བོད་ཀྱི་རྒྱལ་པོ་ཐོ་ཐོ་རི་གཉན་བཙན་ འཁྲུངས་ནས, ... ༡༤༣༣	From the birth of *Tho-tho-ri* g*Nyan*-b*tsan*, the king of Tibet,... 1433	252
མདོ་སྡེ་ཟ་མ་ཏོག་སོགས་ཐོ་ཐོ་རིའི་ མཁར་དུ་བབས་ནས, ... ༡༣༥༤	Since a chest with the treatise *Zamatog* (a religious book), &c. fell from heaven into the court of *Tho-tho-ri*, (9) ... 1354	331
གཉན་བཙན་གཤེགས་ནས, ... ༡༣༡༤	From the death of g*Nyan* b*tsan* (or *Tho-tho-ri*), ... 1314	371
འབྲས་བུའི་བསྟན་པ་རྫོགས་ཏེ། སྒྲུབ་ པའི་བསྟན་པ་ཚུགས་ནས, ... ༡༠༦༧	Since the doctrine of endeavouring perfection succeeded to that of fruits (immediate consequences of good morals), (10) ... 1067	618
ཤམ་བྷ་ལར་རྒྱ་མཚོ་རྣམ་རྒྱལ་ཕེབས། མེ་མཁའ་རྒྱ་མཚོའི་མགོ་ཚུགས། མ་ཁར་ ཟླ་སྒོ་ཕྱུགས་ནས, ... ༡༠༦༣	Since r*gya*-m*tsho* r*Nam*-r*gyal* (11) (a king) arrived at Shambhala. Since the period of 403 years, called *Mekha gya-tso*, commenced, (12)	

			A. D.
	And since the infidels (or Muhammadans) entered Makha (Mecca), ...	1063	622
སྲོང་བཙན་(སྒམ་པོ)འཁྲུངས་ནས, ... ༡༠༥༨	From the birth of *Srong* b*tsan* (*sgam-bo*), (13) ...	1058	627
ཀོང་ཇོ་བོད་དུ་ཕེབས་ནས, ... ༡༠༤༦	Since the arrival of *Kong-cho* (a Chinese Princess) in Tibet, (14)	1046	639
ལྷ་ལའི་འཕྲུལ་སྣང་གི་གཙུག,ལག་ཁང་བཞེངས་ནས, ... ༡༠༣༤	Since the *'phrul snang* college (or *vihar*, was built at Lhassa, (15) ...	1034	651
བོད་རྗེ་ཁྲི་སྲོང་ལྡེ་བཙན་བལྟམས་ནས, ༩༥༧	From the birth of *Khri srong* l*dé* b*tsan*, the *master* of Tibet or king, (16) ...	957	728
པད་འབྱུང་བོད་དུ་ཕེབས་ནས, ... ༩༣༨	From the arrival of *Padjung* (S. Padma Sambhava) in Tibet, ...	938	747
བསམ་ཡས་བཞེངས་ནས, ... ༩༣༦	Since b*Sam-yas* was built, ...	936	749
ཁྲི་སྲོང་ (ལྡེའུ་བཙན) གཤེགས་ནས, ... ༨༩༩	From the decease of Khrisrong (*l*déhu *b*tsan), ...	899	786
པད་འབྱུང་རྒྱ་གར་གཤེགས་ནས, ... ༨༨༣	Since *Padjung* returned to India,	883	802
རྩིས་འགོ་ཐོག་མ་བཟུག་ནས, ... ༨༨༡	From the beginning of (a new period or) astronomical calculation, ...	881	804
གླང་དར་བཙས་ནས, ... ༨༢༤	From the birth of g*Lang-dar* or Langtarma, ...	824	861
ཁྲི་རལ་འཁྲུངས་ནས, ... ༨༢༡	From the birth of *Khri-ral* (or Ralpachen), ...	821	864
གླང་དར་གྱིས་ཆོས་བསྣུབས་ནས, ... ༧༨༦	Since g*Lang-dar* abolished the (Buddhistic) religion, ...	786	899
གླང་དར་བསྒྲོངས་ནས, ... ༧༨༥	Since g*Lang-dar* was murdered,	785	900
ཤམ་བྷ་ལ་ནས་དུས་འཁོར་རྒྱ་གར་དུ་ཕེབས་ནས, ... ༧༢༠	Since the *Kála-chakra* (religious system) was introduced into India, (17) ...	720	965

				A. D.
བོད་དུ་བསྟན་པ་ཕྱི་དར་ཐོག་མ་བྱུང་ནས, ...	༧༡༤	Since the beginning of the last propagation of the Buddhistic religion in Tibet, (18) ...	714	971
ཨ་ཏི་ཤ་འཁྲུངས་ནས, ...	༧༠༥	From the birth of *Atisha*, ...	705	980
འབྲོམ་སྟོན་འཁྲུངས་ནས, ...	༦༨༣	From the birth of h*Brom-ston* (or Brom, the teacher), ...	683	1,002
གསོལ་ནག་ཐང་ཆེན་གྱི་དགོན་པ་བཏབ་ནས, ...	༦༧༠	Since the monastery of *Great* g,*Sol-nag thang* was founded, ...	670	1,015
མེ་མཁའ་རྒྱ་མཚོའི་འདས་ལོ་རྫོགས་ནས, ...	༦༦༡	From the end of the *Me mkhá rgya mtsho* (or period of 403 years),	661	1,024
དུས་འཁོར་བོད་དུ་ཕེབས། རབ་བྱུང་ཐོག་མ་ཟིལ་ནས, ...	༦༦༠	Since the Kála Chakra was introduced into Tibet, and since the 1st year of the cycle of 60 years began, ...	660	1,025
མི་ལ་རས་པ་འཁྲུངས་ནས, ...	༦༤༧	From the birth of *Mi-la-ras-pa*,	647	1,038
ཨ་ཏི་ཤ་གཤེགས། གླང་རི་ཐང་པ་འཁྲུངས་ནས, ...	༦༣༣	From the decease of *Atisha* and the birth of g,*Lang rithang-pa*,...	633	1,052
ར་སྒྲེང་གི་གཙུག་ལག་ཁང་བཏབ་ནས, ...	༦༣༠	Since the college (or *vihar)* of *Ra sgreng* was founded, ...	630	1,055
ལོ་ཙྪ་བ་བློ་ལྡན་ཤེས་རབ་འཁྲུངས་ནས,	༦༢༨	From the birth of b*Lo-ldan shes-rab*, the interpreter or translator, ...	628	1,057
གསང་ཕུའི་ཆོས་སྡེ་དང་། ས་སྐྱ་བཏབ་ནས, ...	༦༡༤	Since the monastery of g,*Sang phu* and that of *Sa-skya* was founded, (19) ...	614	1,071
དྭགས་པོ་ལྷ་རྗེ་འཁྲུངས་ནས, ...	༦༠༨	From the birth of *Tagpo lha rje*, ...	608	1,077
གྲྭ་ཐང་དགོན་པ་བཏབ་ནས, ...	༦༠༦	Since the *Gra thang* monastery was founded, ...	606	1,079
རས་ཆུང་པ་འཁྲུངས་ནས, ...	༦༠༣	From the birth of *Ras-chhung-pa*, ...	603	1,082

				A. D.
ས་ཆེན་ཀུན་དགའ་སྙིང་པོ་ འཁྲུངས་ནས,	༥༩༥	From the birth of *Kun-dgah Snying-po,* the Great Sa-skya (Lama), ...	595	1090
བློ་ལྡན་ཤེས་རབ་ གཤེགས་ནས, ...	༥༧༨	From the decease of b*Lo-ldan shes-rab,* ...	578	1107
ཕག་མོ་གྲུབ་པ་འཁྲུངས་ནས, ...	༥༧༧	From the birth of *Phag-mo grub-pa,* ...	577	1108
ལྷག་མཐོང་རྫོགས། ཏིང་འཛིན་སྒོམ་མགོ་རྩོམས་ནས, ...	༥༦༧	Since the period of 'more-seeing' being finished, that of 'deep meditation' commenced, (20) ...	567	1118
གཡུ་བྲག་པ་འཁྲུངས་ནས, ...	༥༦༤	From the birth of g*Yu-brag-pa,*	564	1121
ཤཱཀྱ་ཤྲཱི་འཁྲུངས་ནས, ...	༥༦༠	From the birth of *Shákya Sri,* (21) ...	560	1125
མངའ་བདག་ཉང་འཁྲུངས་ནས, ...	༥༥༡	From the birth of *Nyang,* the prince or lord, ..	551	1134
ས་ཆེན་གཤེགས། གདན་ས་ཐེལ་གྱི་ཆོས་སྡེ་བཏབ་ནས, ...	༥༢༩	From the decease of *Su-chhen,* (the great Sa-skya Lama,) and since the *Thel* or g*Dan-sa thel* monastery was founded, ...	529	1156
ཚལ་གྱི་ཆོས་སྡེ་བཏབ་ནས, ...	༥༡༢	Since the monastery of *Tshal* was founded, ...	512	1173
འབྲི་གུང་བཏབ་ནས, ...	༥༠༨	Since the h*Bri-gung* monastery was founded, ...	508	1177
སྟག་ལུང་ཆོས་སྡེ་བཏབ་ནས, ...	༥༠༧	Since the *Stag-lung* monastery was founded, ...	507	1178
ས་སྐྱ་པཎ་ཆེན་བལྟམས་ནས, ...	༥༠༥	From the birth of the Great *Sa-skya Pan'ditá,* (22) ...	505	1180
གུང་ཐང་བཏབ་ནས, ...	༥༠༠	Since *Gung-thang* (a monastery) was founded, ...	500	1185

			A. D.
ཁ་ཆེ་པཎ་ཆེན་བོད་དུ་ཐེབས། ཀརྨ་པཀྴི་འཁྲུངས་ནས, ... ༤༨༣	Since the great Cashmirian Pan'ditá (*Shakya Sri*) arrived in Tibet. And since *Kar-ma Paks'hi* was born, ...	483	1202
གཏེར་སྟོན་གུ་རུ་ཆོས་དབང་འཁྲུངས་ནས, .. ༤༧༥	From the birth of g,*Ter-ston Guru chhos-dvang* (the prince of religion, the LAMA teaching hidden treasures), ...	475	1210
གླང་ཐང་ཆོས་སྡེ་བཏབ། རྒྱལ་བ་ཡང་དགོན་པ་འཁྲུངས་ནས, ... ༤༧༤	Since the g*Lang-thang* monastery was founded, and since r*Gyel-va yang* d*gonpa* was born, ..	474	1211
བྱང་རྡོར་གཉིས་ཀྱི་ཆོས་སྡེ་ཆགས་ནས, .. ༤༦༢	Since the two monasteries at *Byang* (Chang) and at r*Dor* were founded, ..	462	1223
འགྲོ་མགོན་འཕགས་པ་འཁྲུངས་ནས, ༤༥༢	From the birth of h*Gro mgon* h*phags-pa*, ..	452	1233
འགྲོ་མགོན་འཕགས་པ་བོད་ཁམས་ཡོངས་ཀྱི་རྗེ་བོར་གྱུར་ནས, ... ༤༣༤	Since (as before) he became the Master of the whole Tibet,	434	1251
ཆོས་ལུང་ཚོགས་པའི་ཆོས་སྡེ་བཏབ་ནས, ... ༤༣༢	Since the *Chhos-lung ts'hogs-pa* monastery was founded, ..	432	1253
བུ་སྟོན་འཁྲུངས་ནས, .. ༣༩༧	From the birth of *Bu-ston*, ..	397	1288
ཏ་སི་བྱང་ཆུབ་རྒྱལ་མཚན་འཁྲུངས་ནས, ... ༣༨༥	From the birth of *Ta-si byang chhub* r*gyal mtshan*, ...	385	1300
ཐེག་ཆེན་ཆོས་རྒྱལ་འཁྲུངས། ཏ་སི་བོད་ཁམས་ཀྱི་རྗེ་བོར་གྱུར་ནས, ... ༣༣༨	From the birth of *Theg chhen chhos* r*gyal;* and since *Tasi* became the Master of Tibet, ...	338	1347
རྩེས་ཐང་གི་ཆོས་སྡེ་བཏབ་ནས, ༣༣༦	Since the r*Tses-thang* monastery was founded, ...	336	1349
ཙོང་ཁ་པ་བལྟམས་ནས, ... ༣༣༠	From the incarnation (or birth) of *Tsong khapa*, (23) ..	330	1355

			A. D.
ཐང་སྟོང་རྒྱལ་པོ་འཁྲུངས་ནས, .. ༣༠༢	From the birth of *Thang stong rgyal-po*, ..	302	1383
དགེ་འདུན་གྲུབ་པ་འཁྲུངས་ནས,... ༢༩༦	From the birth of d*Ge*-h*dun grub-pa*, (24) ...	296	1389
ལོ་ཆེན་ཤེས་རབ་རིན་ཆེན་འཁྲུངས་ནས, ༢༨༢	From the birth of *Shes-rab rin-chhen*, the great Lotsáva, (translator or interpreter,) ...	282	1403
ཙོང་ཁ་པ་ཆེན་པོས་སྨོན་ལམ་ཆེན་མོ་གཙུགས། དགའ་ལྡན་བཏབ་ནས, ... ༢༧༨	Since the great *Tsong-kha-pa* established the feast of the great supplication or prayer (to be yearly celebrated at Lassa); and since he founded the d*Ga*-l*dan* monastery, ..	278	1407
འཇམ་དབྱངས་ཆོས་རྗེས་འབྲས་སྤུངས་ཀྱི་དགོན་པ་བཏབ། ཀརྨ་པ་མཐོང་བ་དོན་ལྡན་འཁྲུངས་ནས, ... ༢༧༡	From the foundation of the h*Bras-spungs* monastery (or convent by h*jam*-d*Vyangs chhos rjé;* and from the birth of *Karmapa* m*Thong va don* l*dan*, ..	271	1414
བྱམས་ཆེན་ཆོས་རྗེས་སེ་རའི་ཆོས་སྡེ་བཏབ། རྗེ་ཙོང་ཁ་པ་གཤེགས། དར་མ་རིན་ཆེན་དགའ་ལྡན་ཁྲིར་ཕེབས་ནས, ... ༢༦༨	Since the foundation of the *Séra* monastery, by *Byams chhen chhos rjé.* The death of the Rev. Tsong-kha-pa; and since *Dar-ma rin chhen* succeeded to the chair at d*Gah*-l*dan*, ..	268	1417
གསང་སྔགས་མཁར་གྱི་ཆོས་སྡེ་བཏབ་ནས, ... ༢༦༦	Since the g*Sang sñags* m*khar* monastery was founded, ...	266	1419
དུས་ཞབས་ནོར་བཟང་རྒྱ་མཚོ་འཁྲུངས་ནས, ... ༢༦༤	From the birth of *Dus zhabs nor* b*zang* r*gya* m*ts'ho*, ...	264	1421
ས་སྐྱ་ངོར་གྱི་ཆོས་སྡེ་བཏབ་ནས, ... ༢༥༨	Since the *Nor* monastery was founded by those of the Sa-skya sect, ...	258	142

			A. D.
དགེ་ལེགས་དཔལ་ལྡན་དགའ་ལྡན་ཁྲིར་ ཕེབས་ནས, ... ༢༥༦	Since d*Gé-legs* d*pal*-l*dan*, succeeded to the chair at d*Gah*-l*dan*, ..	256	1429
ན་ལེན་དའི་ཆོས་སྡེ་བཏབ་ནས, ... ༢༥༢	Since the *Nálenda* monastery was founded, ...	252	1433
ཆབ་མདོ་བྱམས་གླིང་བཏབ་ནས, ... ༢༥༠	Since the *Chhab mdo byams gling* monastery was founded,	250	1435
ཞ་ལུ་ལེགས་པ་རྒྱལ་མཚན་དགའ་ལྡན་ ཁྲིར་ཕེབས་ནས, ... ༢༤༩	Since *Zha-lu legs-pa* r*gyal*-m*tshan* succeeded to the chair at d*Gah*-l*dan*, ...	249	1436
དཔལ་འཁོར་ཆོས་སྡེ་མཆོད་རྟེན་བརྩིགས་ ནས, ... ༢༤༨	Since the d*Pal*-h*khor* monastery's *mchhod*-r*ten* (S. Chaitya, a shrine or fane), was built, ..	248	1437
ལོ་ཙཱ་བ་ཆོས་སྐྱོང་བཟང་པོ་འཁྲུངས་ ནས, ... ༢༤༦	Since the birth of *Lo-tsáva chhos skyong bzang-po*, ..	246	1439
ཕུག་སྤྱིས་པད་དཀར་ཞལ་ལུང་བརྩམས་ ནས། ཆོས་སྐྱོང་གཟའ་ལྔའི་ངེས་པ་མཛད། ལོ་ཆེན་ཆོས་རྒྱལ་འཁྲུངས་དགེ་འདུན་ གྲུབ་གིས་བཀྲ་ཤིས་ལྷུན་པོ་བཏབ་ ནས, ... ༢༤༠	Since the astronomical work titled *Pad*-d*kar zhal lung* was written by *Phug pa pa*, &c. to ascertain the lunations and the five planets. Since *chhos* r*Gyal*, the great *Lo-tsáva* was born; and since d*Gé*-h*dun grub* founded the monastery, called b*kra-shis lhun-po*, ...	240	1445
འབྲས་ཡུལ་སྐྱེད་ཚལ་ཆོས་སྡེ་བཏབ་ ནས, ... ༢༣༨	Since the h*Bras-yul skyed tshal* monastery was founded, ...	238	1447
བློ་གྲོས་ཆོས་སྐྱོང་དགའ་ལྡན་ཁྲིར་ ཕེབས་ནས, ... ༢༣༧	Since b*Lo-gros chhos skyong* succeeded to the chair at d*Gah*-l*dan*, ...	237	1448
བ་སོ་ཆོས་རྒྱན་དགའ་ལྡན་ཁྲིར་ ཕེབས་ནས, ... ༢༢༤	Since *Ba-so chhos* r*Gyan* succeeded to the chair at d*Gah* l*dan*, ...	224	1461

			A. D.
གོང་དཀར་ཆོས་སྡེ་བཏབ་ནས, ...	༢༢༣	Since the *Gong* d*kar* monastery was founded, ... 223	1462
གསེར་མདོག་ཅན་གྱི་ཆོས་སྡེ་བཏབ་ནས, ..	༢༡༨	Since the g*Ser*-m*dog-chan* monastery was founded, .. 218	1467
བྱམས་གླིང་ཆོས་སྡེ་བཏབ་ནས, ...	༢༡༥	Since the *Byams-g,ling* monastery was founded, ... 215	1470
བློ་གྲོས་བརྟན་པ་དགའ་ལྡན་ཁྲིར་ཕེབས་ནས, ...	༢༡༤	Since b*Lo-gros* br*tan-pa* succeeded to the chair at d*Gah*-l*dan*, 214	1471
དགེ་འདུན་གྲུབ་གཤེགས་ནས, ...	༢༡༢	From the decease of d*Gé*-h*dun grub*, ... 212	1473
དགེ་འདུན་རྒྱ་མཚོ་བལྟམས་ནས, ...	༢༡༡	From the birth (incarnation) of d*Gé*-h*dun* r*gya*-m*tsho*, (25) ... 211	1474
རྟ་ནག་ཐུབ་བསྟན་རྣམ་རྒྱལ་བཏབ་ནས, ...	༢༠༩	Since the r*Ta-nag thub* b*stan*-r*nam* r*gyal* monastery was founded, 209	1476
སྨོན་ལམ་དཔལ་དགའ་ལྡན་ཁྲིར་ཕེབས་ནས, ...	༢༠༧	Since s*Mon-lam* d*pal* succeeded to the chair at d*Gah*-l*dan*, 207	1478
ཚར་ཆེན་འཁྲུངས་ནས, ...	༡༨༥	From the birth of *Tshar-chhen*, ... 185	1500
ཆོས་འཁོར་རྒྱལ་བཏབ་ནས, ...	༡༧༨	Since the *Chhos*-h*khor* r*Gyal* monastery was founded, ... 178	1507
མཁས་གྲུབ་དཔལ་གྱི་སེང་གེ་འཁྲུངས་ནས, ...	༡༥༠	From the birth of m*Khas grub* d*pal-gyi Seňgé*, ... 150	1535
དགེ་འདུན་རྒྱ་མཚོ་གཤེགས་ནས, ...	༡༤༥	From the decease of d*Gé*-h*dun* r*gya*-m*tsho*, ... 145	1540
བསོད་ནམས་རྒྱ་མཚོ་འཁྲུངས་ནས,	༡༤༤	From the birth of b*Sod-nams* r*gya*-m*tsho*, (25) ... 144	1541
ཨལ་ཐན་རྒྱལ་པོས་གདན་དྲངས་ནས,	༡༡༠	Since he was invited by *Althun khan* (a Mongol prince), ... 110	1575
ཆོས་འཁོར་གླིང་བཞེངས་ནས, ...	༡༠༩	Since he erected (or built) the *Chhos* h*khor* g,*ling* monastery,... 109	1576

				A. D.
བསོད་ནམས་རྒྱ་མཚོ་གཤེགས་ནས,...	༩༩	From the decease of b*Sod-nams* r*gya*-m*tsho*, ...	99	1586
ཡོན་ཏན་རྒྱ་མཚོ་བལྟམས་ནས, ...	༩༨	From the birth (incarnation) of *Yon-tan* r*gya*-m*tsho*, (25) ...	98	1587
ཡོན་ཏན་རྒྱ་མཚོ་གཤེགས་ནས, ...	༧༡	From the demise of *Yon-tan* r*gya*-m*tsho*, ...	71	1614
ངག་དབང་བློ.བཟང་རྒྱ་མཚོ་བལྟམས་ནས, ...	༧༠	From the incarnation of *Ňag* d*vang* b*lo* b*zang* r*gya*-m*tsho*, (25)	70	1615
ཉིད་འཛིན་སྒོམ་པ་རྫོགས་ནས། ཚུལ་ཁྲིམས་སྒོམ་མགོ་ཚུགས, ...	༦༧	Since the period of deep meditation being finished, that of morality (or good moral conduct)was begun, see note, (10)...	67	1618
རབ་བྱུང.བཅུ་གཅིག་པའི་ཐོག་མར་རིགས་ལྡན་སེང་གེ་ཁྲིར་ཕེབས་ནས, ...	༦༠	Since, in the beginning of the eleventh cycle, *Rigs*-l*dan Seňgé* succeeded to the chair (at d*Gah*-l*dan*), ...	60	1625
བསྟན་འཛིན་ཆོས་རྒྱལ་བོད་ཀྱི་རྒྱལ་པོར་སྒྱུར་ནས, ...	༤༦	Since b*Stan*-h*dsin chhos* r*gyel* became the king of Tibet, ...	46	1639
ངག་དབང་བློ་བཟང་རྒྱ་མཚོ་བོད་ཁམས་ཡོངས་ཀྱི་རྗེ་པོར་གྱུར་ནས, ...	༤༥	Since *Ňag* d*vang* b*Lo* b*zang* r*gya*-m*tsho* became the master of the whole of Tibet, ...	45	1640
ཕོ་བྲང་པོ་ཏ་ལ་བཏབ་ནས, ...	༤༢	Since he founded the *Potala* (residence), (25) ...	42	1643
ངག་དབང་བློ་བཟང་རྒྱ་མཚོ་རྒྱ་ནག་ཏུ་ཕེབས་ནས, ...	༣༥	Since *Nag*-d*vang* b*Lo* b*zang* r*gya*-m*tsho* went to (arrived in) China, (26) ...	35	1650
སླར་བོད་དུ་ལོག་ཕེབས་ནས, ...	༣༤	Since he again returned to (arrived in) Tibet, ...	34	1651

			A. D.
དེ་ནས་ལོ་སོ་བཞི་ འདས་པ་རབ་བྱུང་བཅུ་གཉིས་པའི་ཐོག་མ་པྲ་བྷ་བ་ཞེས་མེ་མོ་ཡོས་ལ་བཻ་ཌཱུརྱ་དཀར་པོའི་རྩིས་གཞི་མཛད་དོ།། །།	Thence thirty-four years being elapsed, in the beginning of the twelfth cycle, in the year, (called in Sans. *Prabhava*, (in Tibetan) *Mé-mo Yos*, (this) *Bai-'durya* d*karpohi* r*tsis* d*zhi* (ground work on computation) was written, ...	0	1686

Notes to the Chronological Table.

(1.) For the character of this regent (སྡེ་སྲིད, vulg. *Tisri)* see the *Alphabetum Tibetanum*, by the P. Georgi. He was both a fine scholar and a great politician. He wrote several excellent works, as the *Baidúrya sňon-po* (བཻ་ཌཱུརྱ་སྔོན་པོ) on medicine; which is the best commentary on the r*Gyud sdé* b*zhi* (རྒྱུད་སྡེ་བཞི) a large volume, translated from the Sanscrit. This work has not been introduced either into the *Kah-gyur* or the *Stan-gyur* compilation; the contents of both which, in an English translation, I have had the honour to present to the Asiatic Society, through Mr. H. H. Wilson. This author compiled the *Baidúrya Karpo*, a work on Astronomy, Astrology, &c. (from which the present Chronological Table has been taken; from the *Padkar Zhal-lung* (པད་དཀར་ཞལ་ལུང་) a work written by *Phug-pa-pa* m*khas* d*vang* l*hun-grug* r*gya-mtsho*, and *Nor* b*zang* r*gya-mtsho* (ཕུག་པ་པ་མཁས་དབང་ལྷུན་གྲུབ་རྒྱ་མཚོ་དང་། ནོར་བཟང་རྒྱ་མཚོ). One of Tisri's other works is entitled: g*Yah-sel* (གཡའ་སེལ) "the Effacer of Stains," in which he answers the objections of several learned men,' who criticised his works. He wrote also the h*Bél* g*tam* (འབེལ་གཏམ) political discourses, and some other works. But he distinguished himself especially, as a good politician, in the administration of Tibet, by visiting, *sub-incognito*, several provinces, and afterwards remunerating or punishing the officers according to their merits. He concealed also the death of the *Dalai Lama* for 12, or as some say, for 18 years. He is generally believed, in Tibet, to have been the natural son of that Lama *Ňag*-d*vang* b*lo* b*zang* r*gya-msth*o (ངག་དབང་བློ་བཟང་རྒྱ་མཚོ་) the 5th of the great Lamas, that are now styled, r*Gyelva Rin-po chhé* (རྒྱལ་བ་རིན་པོ་ཆེ), "his precious (or holy) Majesty," or as some call them "*Dalai Lama*." The Dalai Lama, upon an invitation to Pekin, from the first Emperor of those Manchus who had conquered China in 1644, paid a visit to that country, in 1650. His ambition had been gratified with the kingdom of Tibet, as a donation to him from that Mogol prince, who had conquered it in 1640; afterwards the Manchus endeavoured to acquire influence in the country through him, which brought so many calamities over Tibet, that the regent had good reason for concealing his death, and thus delivering the kingdom from a continuance of the pernicious domination of the Hierarchy.

(2.) At the first rise of Buddhism in Central India, the great antagonists of that doctrine are styled in the Buddhistic works, *Tir-thi-kas* or *Tir-tha-ka-ras*, in Sans.; *Mu-stegs-chen* or *Mu-stegs-pa*, in Tib. (མུ་སྟེགས་ཅན or མུ་སྟེགས་པ, a Determinist.) SHA'KYA and his followers are frequently stated in the *Dulva*, and elsewhere, to have had many disputes with them. They are represented to have been indecent in their dress, and grossly atheistic in their principles. See the beginning of the first volume of the *Dulva*, in the *Káh-gyur*.

(3.) The *Kála Chakra*, religious system, to which so many volumes of the *Stan-gyur* and other works are devoted, is not mentioned in the really ancient Buddhistic works of India, with the exception of one. This system in fact was first introduced into India towards the end of the tenth century (in 965), and afterwards, viâ *Kashmir* into Tibet. See Journal As. Soc. of Bengal, vol. ii. p. 57.

(4.) The *Kála Chakra* doctrine of *Adibuddha* was delivered by SHA'KYA, in his 80th year, at *Shrí Dhanya kataka, (Cattak in Orissa,)* called in Tib. d*Pal-ldan* h*Bras-spungs* (དཔལ་ལྡན་འབྲས་སྤུངས, " *the noble city, called accumulated rice,*") upon the request of zla *bzang* (ཟླ་བཟང་,) pron. vulg. *Dázáng* or *Dává Zángpo*, S. Chandra Bhadra (or Soma Bhadra ?) a king of *Shambha la*, a fabulous country or city in the north beyond the *Jaxartes*, who in his 99th year visited SHA'KYA there, in a miraculous manner. Upon his return home, he compiled in the course of the next year, the r*Tsa-rgyud* (རྩ་རྒྱུད, S. *Múla Tantra)*, in accordance with what he had heard from SHA'KYA, and two years afterwards he died. This work is the source of all the subsequent voluminous compilations, increased modifications and interpolations. In the *Múla Tántra*, SHA'KYA foretels to Dázang 25 kings, who will successively reign at *Shambhala*, each for a hundred years. The six first of them are called *Chhos-kyi rgyel-po* (ཆོས་ཀྱི་རྒྱལ་པོ, S. *Dharma Rájá*, a religious king or patron of religion) and the others are styled *Rigs-lden*, S. *Kulika*, " *the Noble* or *Illustrious*." He foretells also that after 600 years from that date, (or of that of his death) *Rigs-ldan Grags-pa* (རིགས་ལྡན་གྲགས་པ,) S. *Kulika Kirti*, " the celebrated noble one;" (the Epiphanes of the Greeks ?) will succeed to the throne at Shambhala, and that 800 years afterwards, the k*la* k*lo* ཀླ་ཀློ vulg. *Lálo*, S. Mlechha, or *Muhammadan* religion, will rise at *Makha* (Mecca). There are in the subsequent interpolated and greatly increased compilation many stories on the rise, destructive progress, and final decline of Muhammadanism, and the glorious re-establishment of Buddhism in the north. It would be interesting to ascertain how the doctrine taught at *Cuttack* in *Orissa*, was brought beyond the *Jaxartes* to *Shambhala*, or what reason the Buddhists had for inventing this story.

Since in the Múla Tantra (ཙ་རྒྱུད) SHA'KYA explicitly declares, in the prophetical form, that the above-mentioned *Rigs-ldan Grags-pa*, &c., will be of his own *Shákya* race, and of the nation of *Dázáng*, the natural interpretation is that they both were of the Scythian nation, or of the Sacæ of the ancients. Two of the principal slokas, touching upon this important historical point, are here inserted in Tibetan, verbatim as they have been quoted from the ཙ་རྒྱུད rTsa-rgyud, by *Sureshamati*, in the same work from which the 13 dates for the death of Shákya have been taken. See *Sureshamati's* བསྟན་རྩིས, &c. ཀྱི བཅད, ཙ་བའི་རྒྱུད་ལས། བཅོམ་ལྡན་འདས་ཀྱིས།

༄༅། །ལོ་འདི་ནས་ནི་དྲུག་བརྒྱའི་ལོར། །དྲང་སྲོང་རྣམས་ཀྱི་སྨིན་དོན་ཏུ།
འཇམ་དབྱངས་མི་བདག་གྲགས་པ་ནི། །ཤམ་བྷ་ལ་ཞེས་བྱ་བར་འབྱུང་། །
འདི་ཡི་སྒྲོལ་མ་ཨུ་མོ་ཆེ། །སྲས་ནི་པད་འཛིན་འཇིག་རྟེན་དབང་།
བདག་གི་ཤཱཀྱའི་རིགས་བརྒྱུད་ལ། །བྱུང་ (or འབྱུང་) པ་ཟླ་བཟང་ཁྱོད་རིགས་ལའོ།

Literal Translation.

From this year, after 600 years, for the maturation of the hermits, (S. *Ris'his, or of religious persons,*) will be born, at *Shambhala*, h*Jam dvyangs mi* b*dag Gags-pa*, (a king, or lord of men,) called the *celebrated one (an incarnation of) Manyju Ghos'ha*, (he with a sweet voice.) The lady (Tib. *s*grol-ma; Sans. **Tárá**) of this (king) is (or will be called) the great goddess (Umá, i. e. an incarnation of that goddess,) his son or the young prince is (or will) (be an incarnation of) *Pad-*h*dsin* h*jig-rten dvang*, (S. *Padmapáni Lokéshvara,*) "the lord of the world, holding a lotus in his hand;" they will be born in my own *Shákya* race, and in your own nation, *Dázang!*

(5.) This is the first record of Padma Sambhava's incarnation, who, in the 8th century after Christ, was again born, in a miraculous manner, out of a lotus or water-lily, at *O'dheyana*, in the western part of India, as a celebrated *Guru*. Upon an invitation by *Khrisrong déhu tsan*, the king of Tibet, and a great patron of Buddhism, he visited that country in the beginning of the 9th century, and remained there for many years; he wrote several works, that are still extant under his name. His memory is greatly respected in the present day by the Tibetans, who call him *Urgyen Rinpochhé* (ཨུ་རྒྱན་རིན་པོ་ཆེ), and the most ancient religious sect in Tibet, after his name, is called *Urgyenpá* (ཨུ་རྒྱན་པ), followers of *Urgyen*.

(6.) This h*jam dvyangs*, (འཇམ་དབྱངས; S. *Manyju Ghos'ha*, "sweet voice,") is the same with h*jam-*d*pal*, (འཇམ་དཔལ; S. *Manyju Sri*, "the mild noble one.") He is a metaphysical personage, a pattern or beau-ideal of wisdom; also a spiritual son of *Shákya*.

(7.) k*Lu* s*grub*, (ཀླུ་སྒྲུབ, S. *Nágarjuna*, that forms or makes perfect the *Nágas* or the serpent race,) is a real personage, born 400 years after the death of Shákya, from Brahman parents, in the country of *Béta* or in *Bidarbha.* He turned Buddhist, and was educated in central India, in the *Nalenda* convent. He was a spiritual son of Manyju Sri, the God of Wisdom. The first philosophical system of Buddhism is attributed to him. He is respected as a second *r*Gyelva, (རྒྱལ་བ S. *Jina* ;) he is the *founder* or parent of the *Madhyamika* philosophy. There are many works, under his name, in the *Stan-gyur* upon several subjects.

(8.) For *Rigs-ldan Grags-pa,* (རིགས་ལྡན་གྲགས་པ,) see note 4.

(9.) *Thothori* is stated, in the *rGyel rabs gsal-vahi mé-long,* (རྒྱལ་རབས་གསལ་བའི་མེ་ལོང, "a clear mirror of royal pedigree," a historical work,) to have reigned 500 years after *gNya-khri tsan-po,* (གཉའ་ཁྲི་བཙན་པོ, the first king of Tibet, who originated from the *Shákya Litsabyi* race at *Vaisháli,* (Tib. Yangs-pa-chan, ཡངས་པ་ཅན, the ample city,) the modern Allahabad, or the ancient *Prayága.* He kept his residence at *Yambu lha,* (or b*la*) *sgang,* ཡམ་བུ་ལྷ (or བླ་སྒང་), where there are still some plastic images of the ancient kings with some other antiquities. Under his reign, there fell a chest from heaven, containing a small volume of a religious tract on Buddhism, (part of the Kah-gyur,) a holy shrine, and some other sacred things. No one could read the volume; but a voice was heard from heaven that after so many generations (in the 7th century) the contents should be made known. The king paid every respect to that heavenly gift, and, by its blissful influence, he lived 120 years.

(10.) The duration of the doctrine or religion established by *Shákya* is differently stated in different works of the sacred volumes. As for instance, 500, 1,000, 1,500, 2,000, 2,500, 3,000, and 5,000 years. The first (500) has been applied by some to the time of *Kaniska,* 400—500 after the death of *Shákya,* when the Buddhists had separated themselves into 18 sects, under four principal divisions, when there arose among them many disputes about various points, and when there was made a third compilation of the Buddhistic doctrine. The last (5,000 years) is according to the speculation of *Dans'hta Séna,* and other Indian Buddhistic writers, in the *Stan-gyur* volumes, in the 8th, 9th, &c. centuries. They calculated the duration of the Buddhistic religion thus:

1. འབྲས་བུའི་ བསྟན་པ or འབྲས་བུའི་དུས, h*Bras-buhi* b*stan-pa,* or h*Bras-buhi dus,* the time of the wonderful effects of the doctrine for immediately becoming perfect or possessed of supernatural powers. This period of 1,500 years commenced with the death of Shákya, and was again divided into three smaller ones, each of 500 years, according to the three different degrees of perfection. In the first period, upon hearing his doctrine, some became immediately possessed of superhuman powers, or overcame the enemy, became a d*Gra* b*Chom-pa,* དགྲ་བཅོམ་པ ; S. *Arhan.* In the second, many, though less perfect, proceeded unhindered in

their course to perfection, so as not to turn out of the right way, i. e. they became *phyir mihongva,* ཕྱིར་མི་འོང་བ S. *Anágámí,* that turns not out of his commenced race or course. In the third, though less perfect, yet there were many that entered into the stream, i. e. became r*Gyun-du zhugs-pa* རྒྱུན་དུ་ཞུགས་པ, S.. *Shrota panna,* one that has entered the stream (that will carry him through life to felicity).

2. སྒྲུབ་པའི་བསྟན་པ or སྒྲུབ་པའི་དུས, s*Grub-pahi* b*Stan-pa,* or s*Grub-pahi dus,* that period of the Buddhistic doctrine, in which yet many make great exertions to arrive at perfection. This period contains again 1,500 years, and is divided into three smaller ones, each of 500 years, according to the three diminishing degrees of diligent application. They are called ལྷག་མཐོང་ ཏིང་ངེ་འཛིན་དང་ ། ཚུལ་ཁྲིམས་ཀྱི་སྒོམ་པ, *lhag* m*thong, ting-gé* h*dsin dang, tshul khrims kyi* s*gom-pa,* the exercise or practice: 1, of high speculation; 2, of deep meditation; and 3, of good moral conduct.

3. ལུང་གི་དུས, *Lung-gi-dus,* i. e. that period of 1,500 years of the Buddhistic doctrine, in which the sacred volumes are yet read and explained, though the precepts which they contain are little followed. This period, according to the contents of those books, (read or studied in each respected period,) is sub-divided into the following three: 1, མངོན་པ ། 2. མདོ་སྡེ ། 3, འདུལ་བ་གསུམ་ལུང་གི་དུས, 1, m*Non-pa;* 2, m*Do, sdé;* 3, h*Dul-va, gsum Lung-gi dus,* i. e. 1, the period, in which the metaphysical works are studied; 2, in which the *Sútras* or common aphorisms; and 3, in which only books on the discipline of the religious men, and on the rites and ceremonies are read.

4. རྟགས་ཙམ་འཛིན་པའི་དུས, r*Tags tsam* h*dsin-pahi dus,* that period of 500 years, in which, though learning and good morals have declined, yet some signs of the Buddhistic religion are still to be found, as the dress of priests, holy shrines, relics, offerings, and pilgrimages to holy places.

(11.) This pretended king's arrival at *Shambhala,* in 622, has some coincidence with *Yezdejird,* the Persian king's taking refuge in the same country; for it is affirmed, that this prince, upon the fall of Seleucia, and the conquest of Persia by the Arabs, in 636 retired into *Transoxana* or *Ferghana.*

(12.) How these terms: *mé,* m*khah,* r*gya-mtsho* express the number of 403 years is explained in p. 155 of this Appendix. If we add these 403 years to 622, the first year of the Hegira, we have exactly the year 1025, whence with 1026 commences the first year of the cycle of 60 years of the Tibetans.

(13.) *Srong tsan Gambo* is the most celebrated king of the Tibetans, on account of his long and mild administration, his political wisdom, and of his having first laid the foundation of Buddhism in Tibet. In the

Mani-kabum, (མ་ཎིའི་བཀའ་འབུམ, *ma-n'i* b*kah* h*bum*, " a hundred thousand precious commandments,") a historical work attributed to him, there are detailed accounts respecting Buddhism, and its introduction into Tibet; the circumstances of his marriages with the two princesses, first of Nepal, and afterwards of China; and of the religious establishments made by those ladies, and by himself.

(14.) *Kongjo* or *Kongcho* is the name of that Chinese princess, whom *Srong tsan Gambo* had married. In the *Mani-kabum* it is told, that, when this Tibetan king sent his plenipotentiary (called b*Lon* m*Gar*, བློན་མགར) to China to demand the hand of that princess, he met the envoys of several foreign princes arrived there for the same purpose. The princess' father desired that she should be married to the king of *Magadha*, the religious king in India. Her mother preferred the *Tájik* (Persian) prince, the wealthy king of the West. Her brother commended the prince of the *Hors* (Turks); but she by her own accord wished to be married with *Qésar*, (གེ་སར, Gésar,) the warlike king of the North. The envoy of the Tibetan king at last succeeded in obtaining the princess by address.

(15.) This college (*Bihar* or *Vihar*) was built by that princess, whom *Srong tsan Gambo* had married from *Népal*. She on account of her being first married (or having first passed the lintel or threshold) pretended to have precedence before the Chinese princess. There were many disputes between them.

(16.) *Khri srong déhu tsan* was an excellent king; he made many useful regulations, and having invited into Tibet *Shanta raxita*; (in Tib. *Zhivah-htsho*, ཞི་བ་འཚོ,) but vulg. called *Bodhisato*, a learned man of *Bengal*, and upon the recommendation of this *Pandit*, also the great *Guru Padma Sambhava*, པད་འབྱུང vulg. *Padjung*; he permanently fixed the Buddhist religion by founding *Samyé*, (བསམ་ཡས, *b*sam-yas,) and other convents and colleges; by establishing a religious order with munificent endowments; and by making arrangements for the translation of Sanskrit works, by Indian *Pandits* and Tibetan *Lotsávás*, (interpreters or translators,) whom he caused to be fully instructed in Sanskrit. In the 8th and 9th centuries, under this king, and his sons, *Muné tsanpo* and *Mutik tsanpo*, and his grandsons, *Khri dé srong tsan*, *Khri-ral* or *Ralpathen*, this religion greatly flourished, till in the beginning of the 10th century, *Lang darma* oppressed, and endeavoured entirely to abolish it; for which reason he was murdered by a priest.

(17.) For the *Kála Chakra*, (Dus-*h*khor, དུས་འཁོར,) see note (3) also (4).

(18.) There are two periods of the propagation of Buddhism in Tibet, called the anterior and the posterior; that began with *Srong tsang Gambo*, in the 7th century, and lasted till the end of the 10th; this commenced with the eleventh century, and still continues. In the first period, there were no different religious sects. They who still keep the ancient rites and ceremonies, and have some peculiar manual or symbolical works of that age, are now called, in the Tibetan, *Nyigmapa*, (རྙིང་མ་པ,) a follower of the ancient Buddhistic religion, or *Urgyenpa*, a disciple of *Urgyen* or ***Padma-sambhava***, and they are very numerous, especially in those parts of Tibet that lie near to Népal and other parts of India. In the second (or posterior) period, in the 11th century, in the time of *Atisha*, (called by the Tibetans *Jovo* or *Chovo Atisha*, the lord *Atisha*,) a learned man of Bengal, by the endeavours of *Bromston* and some other zealous and learned Tibetan religious persons. Buddhism, that had been nearly abolished in the 10th century, commenced again to revive in Tibet. This celebrated *Pandit*, upon repeated invitations, at last visited that snowy country, going first to *Gugé* in *N̆ari*, (གུ་གེ་ in མངའ་རིས,) and afterwards to *Utsang*, where he remained till his death, in 1052. *Bromston*, his pupil, founded the *Rareng* (ར་སྒྲེང Ra-sgreng) monastery (still existing), and with him originated the Kadampa sect, from which afterwards issued that of *Gélukpa* by *Tsoṅkhapa*. About this time there arose several religious sects, in Tibet, for the names of which see p. 175 of the Grammar. And for the date of the foundation of several monasteries or convents, see the preceding Chronological Table.

(19.) The *Sa-skya* monastery and residence, in the province of ***Tsang*** (གཙང་), founded in 1071, is now also celebrated for its library of ancient works in Sanskrit and Tibetan. We will make hereafter no remarks on the birth or death of any religious person or ***Lama*** here recorded; or on the foundation of any convent or monastery; they will occur frequently in the following pages. It is sufficient to have given here their names in Tibetan and Roman character, with the corresponding Christian dates.

(20.) For this term, see note (10).

(21.) *Shákya Shrí*, a celebrated *Pandit* of *Cashmir*, who, in the beginning of the 13th century, about the time of Mahammed Gori's conquests, was in Central India; but afterwards retired to Tibet. He remained there, wrote several works, and assisted the Tibetans in the translation of Sanskrit books.

(22.) This is the celebrated Sa-skya Pandit, of whom there are many works. He, and his successor (a nephew) *Grogon phags-pa*, (འགྲོ་མགོན་འཕགས་པ,) were greatly patronized by the Emperors of the Mongol dynasty, especially by *Kublai Khan*, who granted the whole country of Tibet to *Phags-pa*.

(23.) *Tsonkhapa* (called also b*lo* b*zang grags-pahi* d*pal* བློ་བཟང་་གྲགས་པའི་དཔལ, S. *Sumati kírti shrí*) is greatly respected by the Tibetans and Mongols, especially by the *Gélukpa* sect, of which he is the founder. There are many of his works extant; the most celebrated is that of *Lam rim chhenmo*, (ལམ་རིམ་ཆེན་མོ,) "the large work on the gradual way to perfection." The great feast of general prayers, or supplication, established by him, is still yearly celebrated at *Lassa*, in the 15 first days of the new year, (commonly in February with the new-moon.) There are in the *Gáldan* monastery, founded by him, now about 2,000 religious persons, and to the chair still continue to succeed the most learned doctors, from the *Séra* or *Braspung* monasteries, under the title of m*khan-po*, (མཁན་པོ; S. *Upádhyáya*,) a principal or abbot.

(24.) d*Gé* h*dun-grub*, is a celebrated Lama, who founded the great convent of *Teshi lhun-po*, (བཀྲ་ཤིས་ལྷུན་པོ, b*kra-shis lhun-po*,) where now also there reside about 2,000 religious persons. He is the first of the Tibetan Lamas, to whom this title r*Gyelva* (རྒྱལ་བ, S. *Jina*) has been applied. The present great Lama of Lassa, *Tshul-khrims rgya-mtsho* (ཚུལ་ཁྲིམས་རྒྱ་མཚོ, "an ocean of morality") is the 10th among those r*Gyelvas* whom the Mongols and some Europeans call also *Dalai Lamas*.

(25.) d*Gé*-h*dun rgya-mtsho* is the second among those Lamas styled r*Gyelva*. The names of the others, down to the present Great Lama at Lassa, are as follows; 3, b*sod-nams-rgya mtsho*, (བསོད་ནམས་རྒྱ་མཚོ;) who upon an invitation by *Altun Khan*, a Mongol prince, visited him; 4, *Yon-tan rgya-mtsho*, (ཡོན་ཏན་རྒྱ་མཚོ,) 5, *Nag dvang blo bzang rgya-mtsho*, (ངག་དབང་བློ་བཟང་རྒྱ་མཚོ.) This is that Great Lama, who in 1640, founded the hierarchy of the Dalai Lamas, at Lassa, (four years before the conquest of China, by the Mantchus.) It was upon the solicitation of this ambitious man that a Mongol prince conquered Tibet, and afterwards made a present of it to him. The ancient palace of the kings of Tibet, upon the *Red Hill* or *mountain*, (*d*mar-po ri, དམར་པོ་རི,) an eminence near Lassa, was now rebuilt, increased with many buildings for a religious establishment, and converted into a residence of the r*Gyelva Rin-po chhé*, (རྒྱལ་བ་རིན་པོ་ཆེ; *His precious Majesty*,) and was called *Potala*, from the name of an ancient city, on an eminence, at the mouth of the Indus, (called in Tib. གྲུ་འཛིན, Gru *h*dsin, "a receiver of boats or ships, a harbour," which is a literal translation of the Sanskrit *Potala*, now called *Tata* or *Tatta*,) where was the residence of *Chenresi*, (སྤྱན་རས་གཟིགས་དབང་ཕྱུག; *spyan ras gzigs dvang phyug*, S. *Avalokitéshvara*,) the great patron saint of the Tibetans, and whence he is believed to have visited Tibet.

(26.) For his visit to China, see note 1. After the death of this Lama, under his pretended regenerations or new incarnations, Tibet has been visited by many calamities. The names of his successors are as follows: 6, *Rin-chhen Tshangs dvyangs rgya-mtsho*, (རིན་ཆེན་ཚངས་དབྱངས་རྒྱ་མཚོ;) 7, b*Lo bzang skal ldan rgyo-mtsho*, (བློ་བཟང་སྐལ་ལྡན་རྒྱ་མཚོ;) 8, b*Lo bzang hjam dpal rgya-mtsho*, (བློ་བཟང་འཇམ་དཔལ་རྒྱ་མཚོ;) 9, *Lung rtogs rgya-mtsho*, (ལུང་རྟོགས་རྒྱ་མཚོ;) 10, *Tshul khrims rgya-mtsho* (ཚུལ་ཁྲིམས་རྒྱ་མཚོ.)

Note. Their distinguishing names are those immediately set before *rgya-mtsho*; the r*gyelva*, b*lo-bzang*, and some others, are sometimes added, and sometimes omitted.

V.—EPOCH OF THE DEATH OF SHAKYA,

According to different authorities.

§ 255. Since in the Tibetan books there occur several passages containing predictions attributed to *Shákya*, respecting the years of the duration of his doctrine, and of its introduction into such and such a country; (for instance, that after 2,500 years from his death, it will be propagated in a country inhabited by red-faced men; which passage has been applied to the Tibetans, by a celebrated teacher in China, in the 8th century,) several Tibetan learned men have endeavoured, on different occasions, to fix the date of his birth and death. But there are so many discrepancies in the sacred volumes, and in the commentaries, that they cannot be reconciled.

I beg leave therefore to add here, in Tibetan and English, the various dates assigned for the death of *Shákya*, taken from a small work, consisting of 31 leaves, titled b*Stan-rtsis* h*dod-sbyin gter-bum*, (བསྟན་རྩིས་འདོད་སྦྱིན་གཏེར་བུམ, "*Reckoning or computation respecting the doctrine of the Buddhists*,") or "*Treasure-Vessel yielding whatever one wishes*," written by r*Ñog* h*Brug Lha-dvang* b*Logros*, (ངོག་འབྲུག་ལྷ་དབང་བློ་གྲོས,) or according to his Sanskrit name, *Suréshamati*, one of Padmakárpo's disciples. He wrote in the beginning of the 26th year of the tenth cycle of 60 years of the Tibetan era, (commencing with 1026 of the Christians,) which year is called *Nanda* in Sanskrit, and *d*Gah-va (དགའ་བ) in Tibetan, corresponding to 1591 of our era; this author computes the years elapsed from the death of Shákya, according to different authorities, as follows:

	Years elapsed till 1591, After J. C.		Years elapsed till 1591, After J. C.	Years before J. C.
༡ ཆོས་རྒྱལ་སྲོང་བཙན་སྒམ་པོའི་ལུགས་ལ། ལོ་བཞི་སྟོང་དང་བཅུ་གཉིས་སོང་། ...	༤༠༡༢	1. According to the followers of *Sron-btsang sgam-po*, the religious king, there have elapsed four thousand and twelve years, (1)	4012	2122
༢ ནེལ་པ་པཎ་ཌི་ཏའི་ལུགས་ལ། ལོ་སུམ་སྟོང་བདུན་བརྒྱ་སོ་བརྒྱད་སོང་། ...	༣༧༣༨	2. According to the followers of *Nelpa Pan'dita*, (2) there have elapsed three thousand seven hundred and thirty-eight years, ...	3738	2148

(Hereafter the number of past years in words, will be omitted in English.)

			Years before J. C.
༣ ས་སྐྱ་པཎྜི་ཏའི་ལུགས་ལ་སུམ་སྟོང་བདུན་བརྒྱ་ཉེར་ལྔ་ལོན་། ... ༣༧༢༥	3. According to the followers of *Sa-skya Pan'dita,* (3) there have elapsed,	... 3725	2135
༤ དབུས་པ་བློ་གསལ་ལུགས་ལ། སུམ་སྟོང་བདུན་བརྒྱ་ཉེར་དགུ་ལོན་། ... ༣༧༢༩	4. According to the followers of *Upa losal* (*dvus-pa* b*lo gsal,*) (4)	... 3729	2139
༥ དགེ་འདུན་འཕེལ་གྱི་ལུགས་ལ། ཉིས་སྟོང་དགུ་བརྒྱ་ཐམ་པ་ལོན་ ། ༢༩༠༠	5. According to the followers of d*Gé*-h*dun* h*phel,* (5)	... 2900	1310
༦ ཙན་དན་ཇོ་བོའི་ལོ་རྒྱུས་ལུགས་ལ། ཉིས་སྟོང་སུམ་བརྒྱ་ཞེ་གཉིས་ལོན་། ... ༢༣༤༢	6. According to the (fabulous) narration from the *Sandal Lord* (an image of Shákya made of that scented wood), (6)	... 2342	752
༧ གྲུབ་ཐོབ་ཨུ་རྒྱན་པའི་ལུགས་ལ། ཉིས་སྟོང་ཉིས་བརྒྱ་ཞེ་གསུམ་ལོན་། .. ༢༢༤༣	7. According to the followers of *U-rgyen-pa,* (the *Grub-thob ;* S. *Siddha,*) he that has arrived at perfection, (7)	... 2243	653
༨ ཤཱཀྱ་ཤྲཱི་དང་ནམ་བཟང་གཉིས་ཀྱི་ལུགས་ལ། ཉིས་སྟོང་ བརྒྱ་ སོ་དྲུག་ལོན་། ... ༢༡༣༦	8. According to the followers both of *Shákya Shri* and *Nam* b*zang,*	... 2136	546
༩ དུས་འཁོར་ པ། གཡུང་སྟོན། བུ་སྟོན། དཔལ་ལེགས་ དོན་གྲུབ། པད་མ་དཀར་པོའི་བཤད་པ་སྔ་མ་ལུགས་རྣམས་ལ་ཉིས་སྟོང་བཞི་བརྒྱ་བདུན་ཅུ་ཐམ་པ་ལོན་། .. ༢༤༧༠	9. According to the writers on the Kála Chakra system, as g*Yung ston, Bu-ston,* d*Pal-legs don-grub;* and as *Padmakárpo* formerly taught, (9)	.. 2470	880
༡༠ ཇོ་ནང་པ། ཆོས་ དགོན། རྣམ་རྒྱལ་གྲགས་བཟང་གསུམ་གྱི་ལུ་གས་ལ། ཉིས་སྟོང་བཞི་བརྒྱ་ཉེར་བདུན་ལོན་ ... ༢༤༢༧	10. According to the followers of these three : *Jo nang-pa, Chhos* m*Gon,* r*Nam-rgyel grags* b*zang,* (10)	.. 2427	837
༡༡ དཔལ་ལྡན་བླ་ མ་བསོད་ནམས་རྒྱལ་མཚན་ ལུགས་ལ། ཉིས་སྟོང་བརྒྱ་རེ་དྲུག་ལོན་། ... ༢༡༦༦	11. According to the followers of d*Pal*-l*dan* b*Lama* b*sod-nams* r*gyel-*m*tshan,* (11)	.. 2166	576

༡༢ ཕུག་པ་པ་ནོར་བཟང་རྒྱ་མཚོའི་ པད་ དཀར་ཞལ་ལུང་ལུགས་ལ། ཉིས་ སྟོང་བཞི་ བརྒྱ་དོན་བཞི་ལོང་། ... ༢༤༧༤	12. According to the followers of the *Pad-dkar zhal lung* work, written by *Phug-pa-pa nor bzang rgya-mtsho*, (12) ...	2474	884
༡༣ འབྲུག་པ་པད་མ་དཀར་པོའི་ བཤད་པ་ཕྱི་མ་དང་སུ་རེ་ཤ་མ་ཏིའི་ རང་ལུགས་ལ། ཉིས་སྟོང་དྲུག་བརྒྱ་ ལྔ་བཅུ་ལོང་། ... ༢༦༥༠	13. According to Padmakárpo's final decision, and as *Suréshamati* himself taught, (13) ...	2650	1060

To the above enumerated dates may be added that of s*Dé-srid sangs-rgyas* r*gya-mtsho*, as it has been stated before, in the Chronological Table, §. 254. Therefore,

༡༤ བོད་ཀྱི་ སྡེ་སྲིད་སངས་ རྒྱས་ རྒྱ་མཚོའི་ བསྟན་ བཅོས་བཻ ཌཱུརྱ་དཀར་པོའི་ ལུགས་ལ། རབ་ བྱུང་བཅུ་གཉིས་ པའི་མགོ་ མེ་ཡོས་ ཡན་ལ། ཉིས་ སྟོང་ལྔ་ བརྒྱ་དྲུག་ ཅུ་རྩ་བདུན་ལོང་། .. ༢༥༦༧	14. According to the *Bai'dúrya* d*kar-po* work, written by *Sangs-rgyas* r*gya-mtsho*, the regent of Tibet, in the beginning of the first year, called *Fire-hare*, of the 12th cycle of sixty years, (in the beginning of 1686 of the Christian æra,) there have elapsed two thousand five hundred and sixty-seven years, (14)	2567	882

It may be remarked, that all these dates differ from the epoch assumed for the death of Gotama by the Burmese, the Siamese, the Cingalese, and other nations professing the Buddhist faith. A comparison of these several authorities will be found in the Calcutta Oriental Magazine for 1825. They all agree in making the *nibban (nirvan)* occur in the year 544 B. C.; and yet from the several occurrences of the life of their saint, as quoted in their Chronological Tables, it is evident they allude to the same personage to whom the Chinese and some of the Tibetan authorities give the date 1027 B. C. It is impossible to reconcile the two in any way, and their discrepancy throws doubt on the real epoch of the life and writings of the author of one of the most extensively diffused religions on the face of the earth.

Notes (to the different æras of the death of Shákya).

(1.) This date is founded on the story of the wanderings of an image of *Shákya*, from one place to another, commencing with the abode of the gods, remaining in each for 500 years, till it was taken away from *Otantrapuri* (in Gangetic India) by the Turks, and carried afterwards to China, whence, in the 7th century, it was brought to Tibet, by *Kongcho*, a Chinese princess, married by *Srongtsan Gambo*; since which time, there were elapsed upwards of 800 years, till 1591, when *Suréshamati* wrote this treatise. See note 14 of the Chronological Table.

(2.) Nelpa Pandita. Not stated for what reasons.

(3.) This date is founded on a prediction by *Shákya*, that his doctrine would continue for 5,000 years, and would undergo such and such changes during certain periods (of 500 years each). See note 10, Chronological Table.

(4.) This reckons only four years more than the former.

(5.) This is founded on a calculation by some religious persons from *Li-yul*, who visited the seven convents founded by *Mésaktsom* (མེས་ཨག་ཚོམ) a Tibetan king, in the 8th century.

(6.) This date is founded on the story of the wanderings of an image of Sandal-wood of *Shákya*, according to Chinese records.

(7.) This is derived from a calculation made at *Samyé* (བསམ་ཡས) two days journey from Lassa, a large convent, by the Guru *Urgyen* (or Padma Sambhava), in the 8th or 9th century.

(8.) This is derived from a calculation, made at *Sol-nag thang po chhé* (སོལ་ནག་ཐང་པོ་ཆེ) a convent not far from Lassa, by *Pan' chhen Shákya Shri* of Cashmir, in the first half of the 13th century. See note 21, Chronological Table.

(9. 10, 11, 12.) These are founded on predictions by *Shákya* in the *Kála Chakra, Tantra*, (*Dus hkhor rgyud* (དུས་འཁོར་རྒྱུད) See note 4 Chronological Table.

(13.) This date is according to *Padma Carpo's* latest opinion; formerly he also supported the date founded on the Kála Chakra system.

(14.) This date is of great authority, from the celebrity and great research of that regent as a writer.

VI.—Introduction to the Lithographed Pages.

§ 256. That the learner of the Tibetan language may acquire by himself a full knowledge of the syllabic scheme, both in the large and small characters, and of the several kinds of letters used among the Tibetans, the following 40 lithographed pages have been added to this Grammar.

From p. 1 to 29, is contained a syllabic scheme of the Tibetan language, in four columns, being an alphabetical table of the consonants, combined respectively with the five vowels (a, i, u, é, o). In the first column stand the Tibetan capital characters, followed each by the intersyllabic point or sign. No. 2, contains the same expressed in Roman characters; but here, for brevity's sake, the dash, comma, or intersyllabic point (-) is omitted. No. 3, is the same in book-letter or small characters, together with the intersyllabic signs. No. 4, the same in running-hand, together with ditto.

Note 1, p. 6, No. 3, in the Tibetan character, there is a mistake, gu, phu, bu, mu, being written, instead of gyu, phyu, byu, myu, which the learner is requested to correct accordingly as those consonants have been written in their other respective syllables, or as they have been properly expressed in the running-hand, No. 4. Since every simple or compound consonant occurs five times, the student may, elsewhere, easily correct any small error in the shape of the letters. The asterisk or little star (*) added to some of the Tibetan capital characters, indicates that such syllables have not occurred in the Dictionary.

Note 2, for further information on this scheme, see the Grammar, p. 3, &c., the pronunciation of the Tibetan letters; and p. 12—18, the abstract of the orthography and orthoepy of the Tibetan language. The reason why, in the abstract (of the Grammar), p. 12—16, the general number of letters (preceding the vowel) in the whole scheme, amounts to 209, and here only to 208, is, that in the lithographed scheme, the རྨྱ, &c. *rmya*, &c. has been left out. But this is of little consequence, since this compound letter occurs only in two or three words.

Further, in p. 30, have been exhibited the initial signs, commas, and the intersyllabic points or marks, as they are used with the capitals; ditto with the small characters, p. 31—35, the *Bámyik*; p. 36, 37, the *Bruts'ha* characters, and the Tibetan numerical figures; and, lastly, p. 38—40, the *Lánts'ha* characters, (or pointed variety of the *Devanágari* alphabet

&c.) have been represented, that the learner may see how the Tibetans write the Sanskrit in their own characters, and may distinguish Tibetau and Sanskrit works accordingly.

For a collection of *Devanágari* alphabets, comprising all the varieties of this character, found in Tibet and Népal, see Mr. B. H. Hodgson's "Notices of the Languages, Literature, and Religion of the Bauddhas of Népal and Bhot," in the 16th vol. of the *Asiatic Researches*, p. 420.

The Tibetan alphabet itself, as has been noticed in other places, is stated to have been formed from the *Devanágari* prevalent in Central India in the seventh century. On comparing the forms of its letters with those of various ancient Sanskrit inscriptions, particularly that at Gya, translated by Mr. (now Sir Charles) Wilkins, and that on the column at Allahabad, translated by Captain Troyer and Dr. Mill, a striking similitude will be observed. There are also close analogies between the latter alphabet and the square form of the Palí character which is acknowledged to be the original of the Ceylonese, Burmese, Siamese, and other varieties now used in the south-eastern countries. The Palí is indeed called *Magadha*, or of Central India, whence the Bauddha religion and literature of all these countries was derived. I abstain from making any lengthened remarks on this subject here, but the circumstance noticed may help to fix the epoch of incriptions in this peculiar type of the *Devanágari* alphabet.

SYLLABIC SCHEME OF

དབུ་ཅན། [g vuchan]

CAPITAL LETTERS

I. *The thirty simple letters of the alphabet*

		N°1.						N° 2.				
1	1	ཀ་	ཀི་	ཀུ་	ཀེ་	ཀོ།	=	ka	ki	ku	ké	ko.
2	2	ཁ་	ཁི་	ཁུ་	ཁེ་	ཁོ།	=	kha	khi	khu	khé	kho.
3	3	ག་	གི་	གུ་	གེ་	གོ།	=	ga	gi	gu	gé	go.
4	4	ང་	ངི་	ངུ་	ངེ་	ངོ།	=	n̄ga	n̄gi	n̄gu	n̄gé	n̄go.
5	5	ཅ་	ཅི་	ཅུ་	ཅེ་	ཅོ།	=	cha	chi	chu	ché	cho.
6	6	ཆ་	ཆི་	ཆུ་	ཆེ་	ཆོ།	=	chha	chhi	chhu	chhé	chho.
7	7	ཇ་	ཇི་	ཇུ་	ཇེ་	ཇོ།	=	ja	ji	ju	jé	jo.
8	8	ཉ་	ཉི་	ཉུ་	ཉེ་	ཉོ།	=	nya	nyi	nyu	nyé	nyo.
9	9	ཏ་	ཏི་	ཏུ་	ཏེ་	ཏོ།	=	ta	ti	tu	té	to.
10	10	ཐ་	ཐི་	ཐུ་	ཐེ་	ཐོ།	=	tha	thi	thu	thé	tho.
11	11	ད་	དི་	དུ་	དེ་	དོ།	=	da	di	du	dé	do.
12	12	ན་	ནི་	ནུ་	ནེ་	ནོ།	=	na	ni	nu	né	no.

དབུ་མེད། [ḏ,vumed]

SMALL [*HEADLESS*] CHARACTERS

1. དཔེ་ཡིག [*ḏ,pé-yig*] འཁྱུག་ཡིག [*ẖ,khyug-yig*]

No 3. Manuscript letters for Books *No 4. Running hand*

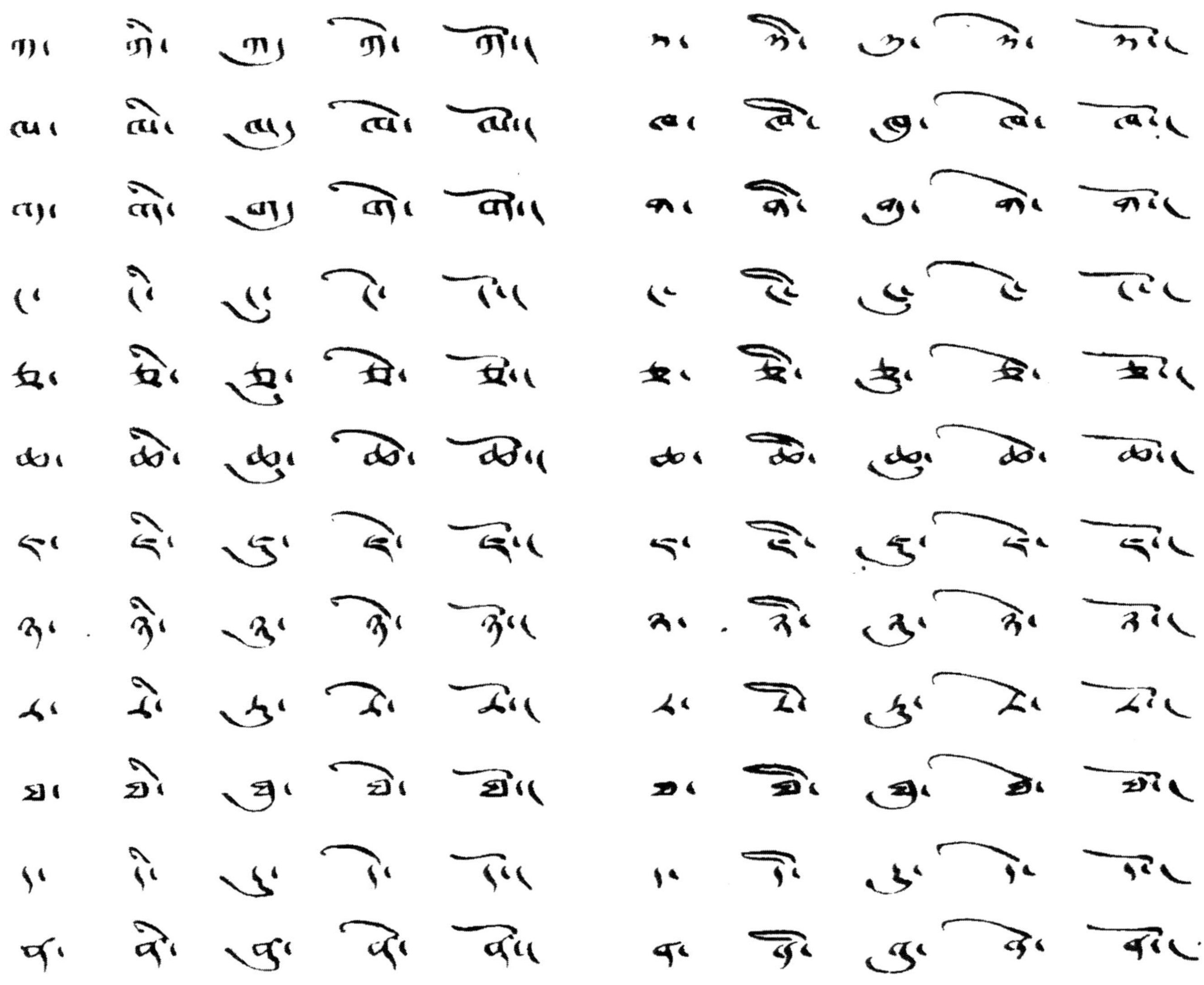

SYLLABIC SCHEME OF

Capital Letters.

13	13	པ་	པི་	པུ་	པེ་	པོ།	=	*pa*	*pi*	*pu*	*pé*	*po.*
14	14	ཕ་	ཕི་	ཕུ་	ཕེ་	ཕོ།	=	*pha*	*phi*	*phu*	*phé*	*pho.*
15	15	བ་	བི་	བུ་	བེ་	བོ།	=	*ba*	*bi*	*bu*	*bé*	*bo.*
16	16	མ་	མི་	མུ་	མེ་	མོ།	=	*ma*	*mi*	*mu*	*mé*	*mo.*
17	17	ཙ་	ཙི་	ཙུ་	ཙེ་	ཙོ།	=	*tsa*	*tsi*	*tsu*	*tsé*	*tso.*
18	18	ཚ་	ཚི་	ཚུ་	ཚེ་	ཚོ།	=	*tsha*	*tshi*	*tshu*	*tshé*	*tsho.*
19	19	ཛ་	ཛི་	ཛུ་	ཛེ་	ཛོ།	=	*dsa*	*dsi*	*dsu*	*dsé*	*dso.*
20	20	ཝ་	ཝི་	ཝུ་	ཝེ་	ཝོ།	=	*wa*	*wi*	*wu*	*wé*	*wo.*
21	21	ཞ་	ཞི་	ཞུ་	ཞེ་	ཞོ།	=	*zha*	*zhi*	*zhu*	*zhé*	*zho.*
22	22	ཟ་	ཟི་	ཟུ་	ཟེ་	ཟོ།	=	*za*	*zi*	*zu*	*zé*	*zo.*
23	23	འ་	འི་	འུ་	འེ་	འོ།	=	*ha*	*hi*	*hu*	*hé*	*ho.*
24	24	ཡ་	ཡི་	ཡུ་	ཡེ་	ཡོ།	=	*ya*	*yi*	*yu*	*yé*	*yo.*
25	25	ར་	རི་	རུ་	རེ་	རོ།	=	*ra*	*ri*	*ru*	*ré*	*ro.*
26	26	ལ་	ལི་	ལུ་	ལེ་	ལོ།	=	*la*	*li*	*lu*	*lé*	*lo.*
27	27	ཤ་	ཤི་	ཤུ་	ཤེ་	ཤོ།	=	*sha*	*shi*	*shu*	*shé*	*sho.*
28	28	ས་	སི་	སུ་	སེ་	སོ།	=	*sa*	*si*	*su*	*sé*	*so.*
29	29	ཧ་	ཧི་	ཧུ་	ཧེ་	ཧོ།	=	*ha*	*hi*	*hu*	*hé*	*ho.*
30	30	ཨ་	ཨི་	ཨུ་	ཨེ་	ཨོ།	=	*a*	*i*	*u*	*é*	*o.*

Small Characters.

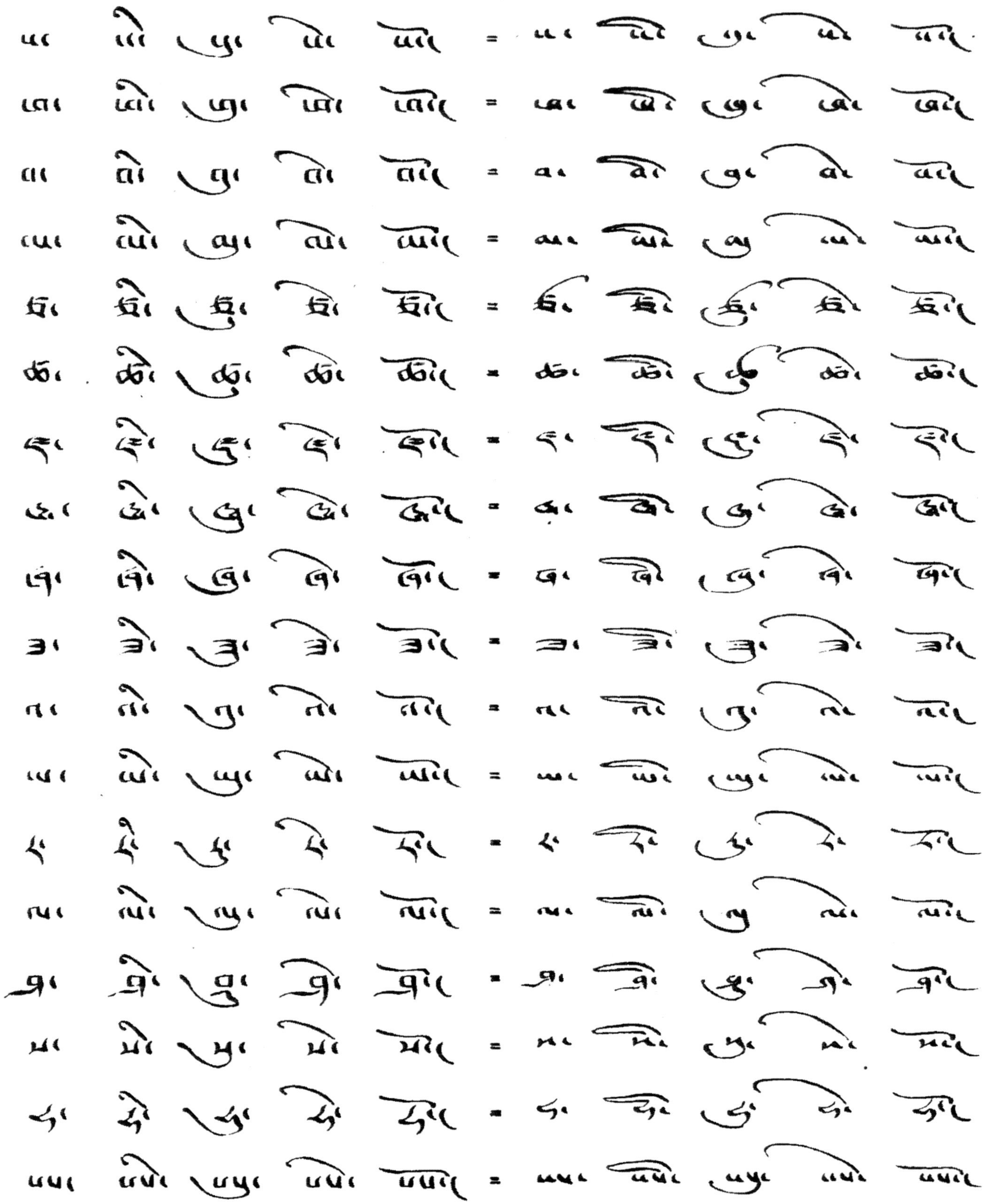

SYLLABIC SCHEME OF

Capital Letters.

II. The Seven Letters that

31	1	ཀྱ་	ཀྱི་	ཀྱུ་	ཀྱེ་	ཀྱོ་	।	=	kya	kyi	kyu	kyé	kyo.
32	2	ཁྱ་	ཁྱི་	ཁྱུ་	ཁྱེ་	ཁྱོ་	।	=	khya	khyi	khyu	khyé	khyo.
33	3	གྱ་	གྱི་	གྱུ་	གྱེ་	གྱོ་	।	=	gya	gyi	gyu	gyé	gyo.
34	4	པྱ་	....					=	pya				
35	5	ཕྱ་	ཕྱི་	ཕྱུ་	ཕྱེ་	ཕྱོ་	।	=	phya	phyi	phyu	phyé	phyo.
36	6	བྱ་	བྱི་	བྱུ་	བྱེ་	བྱོ་	।	=	bya	byi	byu	byé	byo.
37	7	མྱ་	མྱི་	མྱུ་	མྱེ་	མྱོ་	।	=	mya	myi	myu	myé	myo.

III. The fourteen Letters that

38	1	ཀྲ་	ཀྲི་	ཀྲུ་	ཀྲེ་	ཀྲོ་	।	=	kra	kri	kru	kré	kro.
39	2	ཁྲ་	ཁྲི་	ཁྲུ་	ཁྲེ་	ཁྲོ་	।	=	khra	khri	khru	khré	khro.
40	3	གྲ་	གྲི་	གྲུ་	གྲེ་	གྲོ་	।	=	gra	gri	gru	gré	gro.
41	4	ཏྲ་	ཏྲི་	ཏྲུ་	ཏྲེ་	ཏྲོ་	।	=	tra	tri	tru	tré	tro.
42	5	ཐྲ་	ཐྲི་	ཐྲུ་	ཐྲེ་	ཐྲོ་	।	=	thra	thri	thru	thré	thro.
43	6	དྲ་	དྲི་	དྲུ་	དྲེ་	དྲོ་	।	=	dra	dri	dru	dré	dro.
44	7	ནྲ་	....					=	nra				
45	8	པྲ་	པྲི་	པྲུ་	པྲེ་	པྲོ་	।	=	pra	pri	pru	pré	pro.
46	9	ཕྲ་	ཕྲི་	ཕྲུ་	ཕྲེ་	ཕྲོ་	।	=	phra	phri	phru	phré	phro.

Small Characters.

have a subjoined ཡ *(y, thus:* ྱ*)*

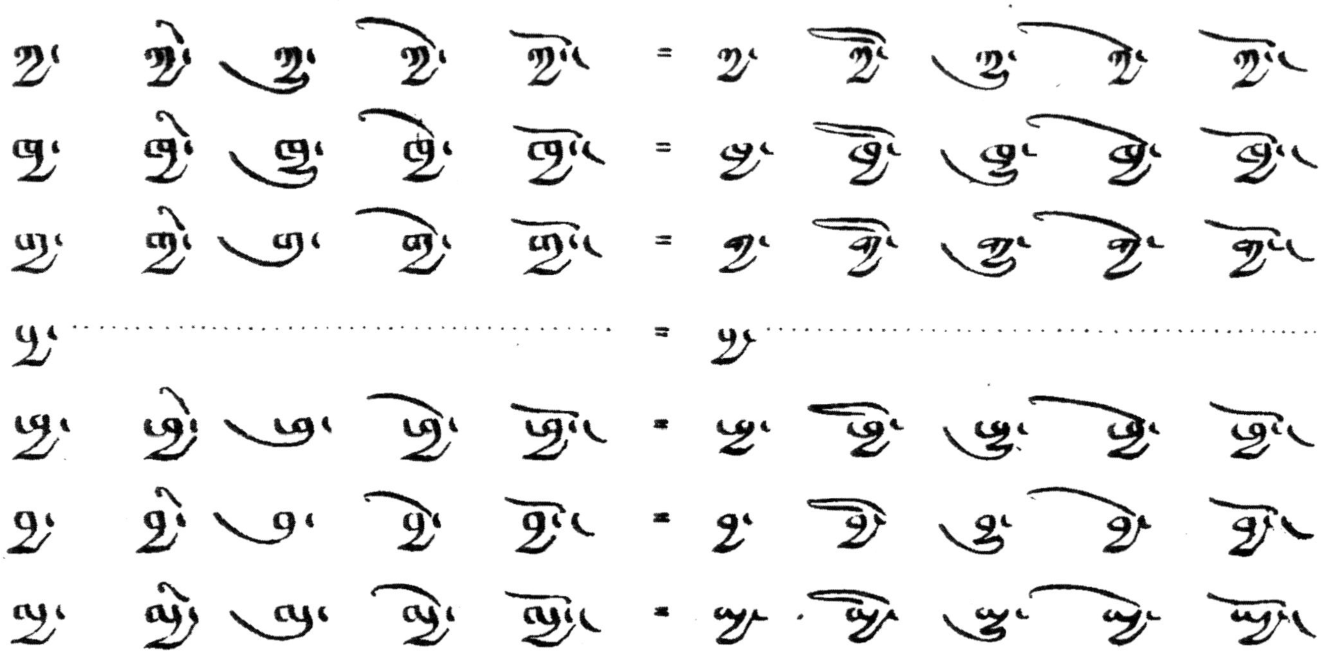

have a subjoined ར *(r, thus:* ྲ*)*

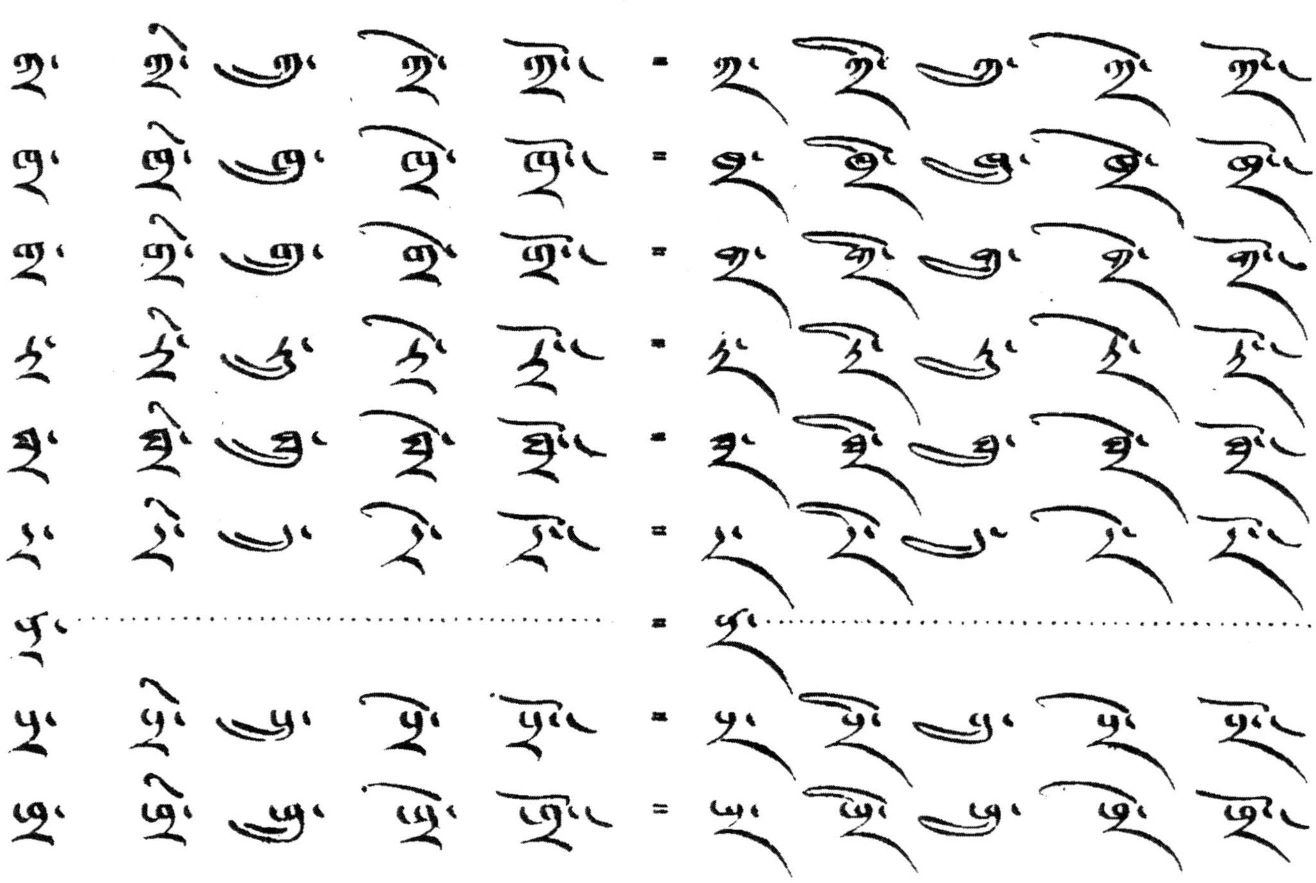

Capital Letters.

								=					
47	10	བྲ་	བྲི་	བྲུ་	བྲེ་	བྲོ།		=	*bra*	*bri*	*bru*	*bré*	*bro.*
48	11	མྲ་	....	....	....	....		=	*mra*	....	....	....	....
49	12	ཤྲ་	ཤྲི་	ཤྲུ་	ཤྲེ་	ཤྲོ།		=	*shra*	*shri*	*shru*	*shré*	*shro.*
50	13	སྲ་	སྲི་	སྲུ་	སྲེ་	སྲོ།		=	*sra*	*sri*	*sru*	*sré*	*sro.*
51	14	ཧྲ་	ཧྲི་	ཧྲུ་	ཧྲེ་	ཧྲོ།		=	*hra*	*hri*	*hru*	*hré*	*hro.*

IV. The Six Letters that

							=					
52	1	ཀླ་	ཀླི་	ཀླུ་	ཀླེ་	ཀློ།	=	*kla*	*kli*	*klu*	*klé*	*klo.*
53	2	གླ་	གླི་	གླུ་	གླེ་	གློ།	=	*gla*	*gli*	*glu*	*glé*	*glo.*
54	3	བླ་	བླི་	བླུ་	བླེ་	བློ།	=	*bla*	*bli*	*blu*	*blé*	*blo.*
55	4	ཟླ་	ཟླི་	ཟླུ་	ཟླེ་	ཟློ།	=	*zla*	*zli*	*zlu*	*zlé*	*zlo.*
56	5	རླ་	རླི་	རླུ་	རླེ་	རློ།	=	*rla*	*rli*	*rlu*	*rlé*	*rlo.*
57	6	སླ་	སླི་	སླུ་	སླེ་	སློ།	=	*sla*	*sli*	*slu*	*slé*	*slo.*
							=					

V. The Fifteen Letters

							=					
58	1	རྐ་	རྐི་	རྐུ་	རྐེ་	རྐོ།	=	*r,ka*	*r,ki*	*r,ku*	*r,ké*	*r,ko.*
59	2	རྐྱ་	རྐྱི་	རྐྱུ་	རྐྱེ་	རྐྱོ།	=	*r,kya*	*r,kyi*	*r,kyu*	*r,kyé*	*r,kyo.*
60	3	རྒ་	རྒི་	རྒུ་	རྒེ་	རྒོ།	=	*r,ga*	*r,gi*	*r,gu*	*r,gé*	*r,go.*

Small Characters.

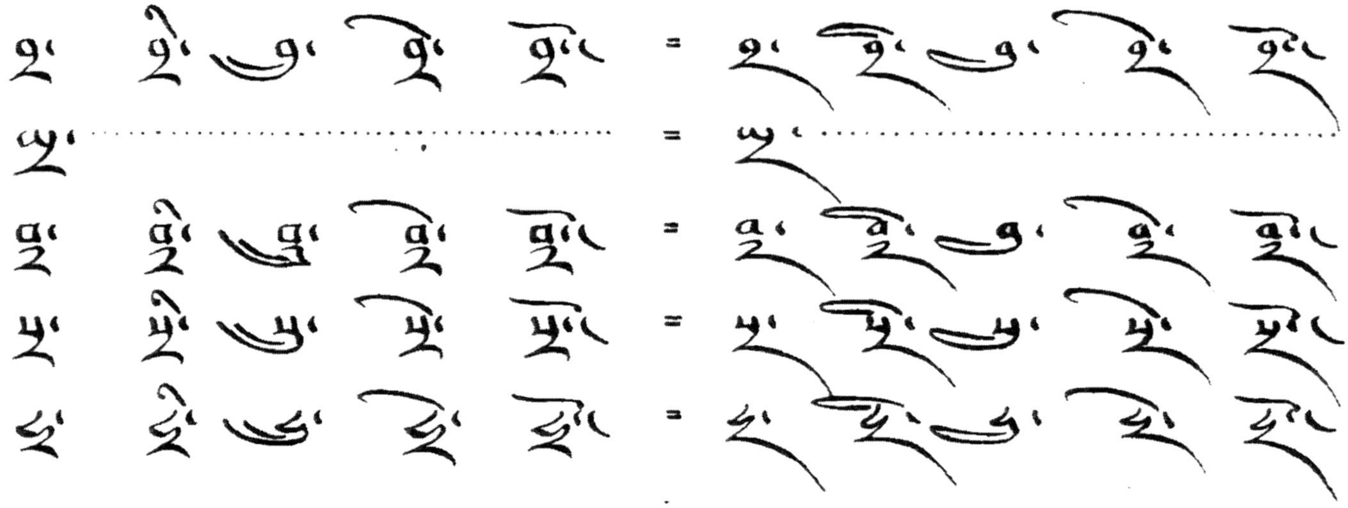

have ལ (*l.*) *subjoined.*

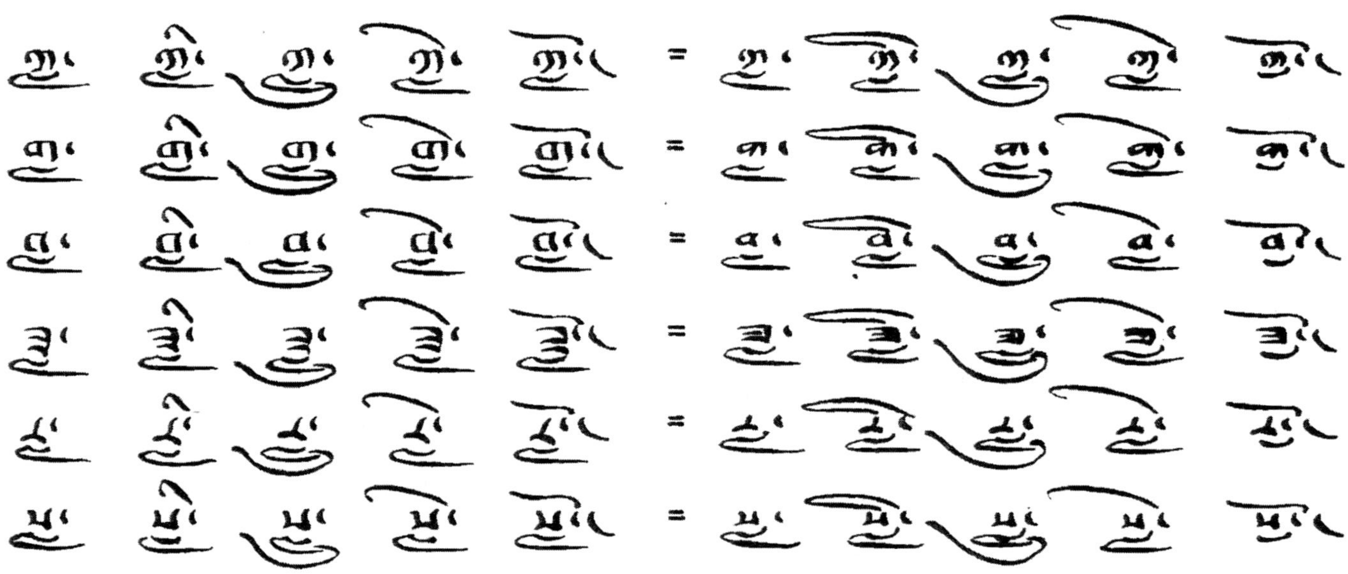

surmounted by ར (*r.*)

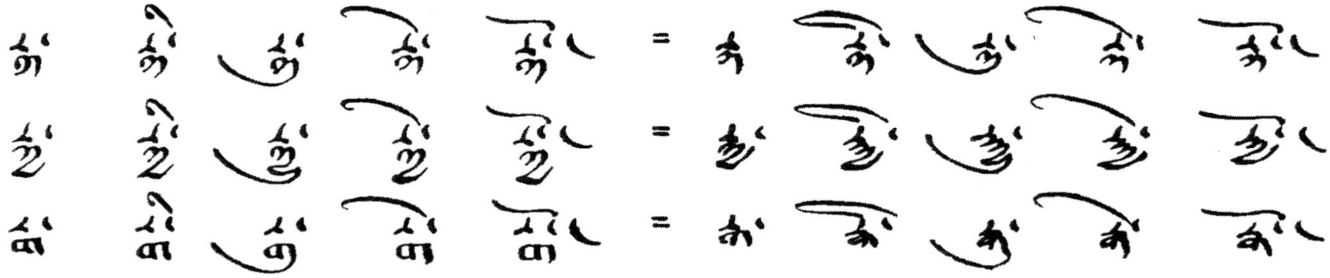

Capital Letters.

61	4	རྒྱ་	རྒྱི་	རྒྱུ་	རྒྱེ་	རྒྱོ་	།	=	r,gya	r,gyi	r,gyu	r,gyé	r,gyo.
62	5	རྔ་	རྔི་	རྔུ་	རྔེ་	རྔོ་	།	=	r,ña	r,ñi	r,ñu	r,ñé	r,ño.
63	6	རྗ་	རྗི་	རྗུ་	རྗེ་	རྗོ་	།	=	r,ja	r,ji	r,ju	r,jé	r,jo.
64	7	རྙ་	རྙི་	རྙུ་	རྙེ་	རྙོ་	།	=	r,nya	r,nyi	r,nyu	r,nyé	r,nyo.
65	8	རྟ་	རྟི་	རྟུ་	རྟེ་	རྟོ་	།	=	r,ta	r,ti	r,tu	r,té	r,to.
66	9	རྡ་	རྡི་	རྡུ་	རྡེ་	རྡོ་	།	=	r,da	r,di	r,du	r,dé	r,do.
67	10	རྣ་	རྣི་	རྣུ་	རྣེ་	རྣོ་	།	=	r,na	r,ni	r,nu	r,né	r,no.
68	11	རྦ་	རྦི་	རྦུ་	རྦེ་	རྦོ་	།	=	r,ba	r,bi	r,bu	r,bé	r,bo.
69	12	རྨ་	རྨི་	རྨུ་	རྨེ་	རྨོ་	།	=	r,ma	r,mi	r,mu	r,mé	r,mo.
70	13	རྩ་	རྩི་	རྩུ་	རྩེ་	རྩོ་	།	=	r,tsa	r,tsi	r,tsu	r,tsé	r,tso.
71	14	རྫ་	རྫི་	རྫུ་	རྫེ་	རྫོ་	།	=	r,dsa	r,dsi	r,dsu	r,dsé	r,dso.

VI. *The Ten Letters that*

72	1	ལྐ་	ལྐི་	ལྐུ་	ལྐེ་	ལྐོ་	།	=	l,ka	l,ki	l,ku	l,ké	l,ko.
73	2	ལྒ་	ལྒི་	ལྒུ་	ལྒེ་	ལྒོ་	།	=	l,ga	l,gi	l,gu	l,gé	l,go.
74	3	ལྔ་	ལྔི་	ལྔུ་	ལྔེ་	ལྔོ་	།	=	l,ña	l,ñi	l,ñu	l,ñé	l,ño.
75	4	ལྕ་	ལྕི་	ལྕུ་	ལྕེ་	ལྕོ་	།	=	l,cha	l,chi	l,chu	l,ché	l,cho.
76	5	ལྗ་	ལྗི་	ལྗུ་	ལྗེ་	ལྗོ་	།	=	l,ja	l,ji	l,ju	l,jé	l,jo.

Small Characters.

have a surmounting ལ (*l*) ——————————

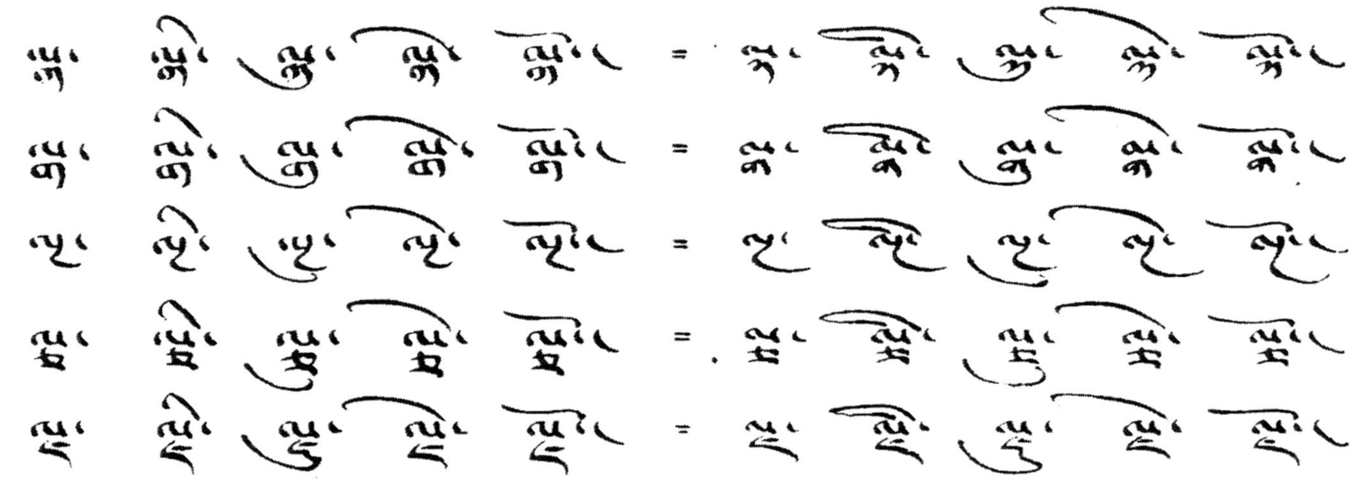

Capital Letters

77	6	ལྟ་	ལྟི་	ལྟུ་	ལྟེ་	ལྟོ་	=	l,ta	l,ti	l,tu	l,té	l,to.
78	7	ལྡ་	ལྡི་	ལྡུ་	ལྡེ་	ལྡོ་	=	l,da	l,di	l,du	l,dé	l,do.
79	8	ལྤ་	ལྤི་	ལྤུ་	ལྤེ་	ལྤོ་	=	l,pa	l,pi	l,pu	l,pé	l,po.
80	9	ལྦ་	ལྦི་	ལྦུ་	ལྦེ་	ལྦོ་	=	l,ba	l,bi	l,bu	l,bé	l,bo.
81	10	ལྷ་	ལྷི་	ལྷུ་	ལྷེ་	ལྷོ་	=	l,ha	l,hi	l,hu	l,hé	l,ho.

VII. The Twenty-two Letters

82	1	སྐ་	སྐི་	སྐུ་	སྐེ་	སྐོ་	=	s,ka	s,ki	s,ku	s,ké	s,ko.
83	2	སྐྱ་	སྐྱི་	སྐྱུ་	སྐྱེ་	སྐྱོ་	=	s,kya	s,kyi	s,kyu	s,kyé	s,kyo.
84	3	སྐྲ་	སྐྲི་	སྐྲུ་	སྐྲེ་	སྐྲོ་	=	s,kra	s,kri	s,kru	s,kré	s,kro.
85	4	སྒ་	སྒི་	སྒུ་	སྒེ་	སྒོ་	=	s,ga	s,gi	s,gu	s,gé	s,go.
86	5	སྒྱ་	སྒྱི་	སྒྱུ་	སྒྱེ་	སྒྱོ་	=	s,gya	s,gyi	s,gyu	s,gyé	s,gyo.
87	6	སྒྲ་	སྒྲི་	སྒྲུ་	སྒྲེ་	སྒྲོ་	=	s,gra	s,gri	s,gru	s,gré	s,gro.
88	7	སྔ་	སྔི་	སྔུ་	སྔེ་	སྔོ་	=	s,ña	s,ñi	s,ñu	s,ñé	s,ño.
89	8	སྙ་	སྙི་	སྙུ་	སྙེ་	སྙོ་	=	s,nya	s,nyi	s,nyu	snyé	s,nyo.
90	9	སྟ་	སྟི་	སྟུ་	སྟེ་	སྟོ་	=	s,ta	s,ti	s,tu	s,té	s,to.
91	10	སྡ་	སྡི་	སྡུ་	སྡེ་	སྡོ་	=	s,da	s,di	s,du	s,dé	s,do.

Small Characters

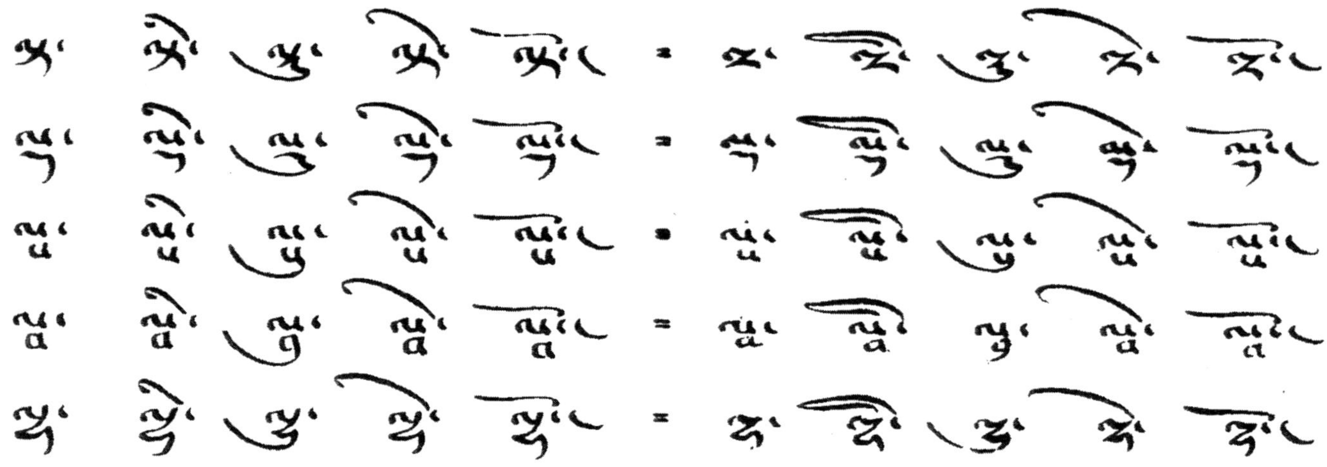

with a surmounting ས (*s*)

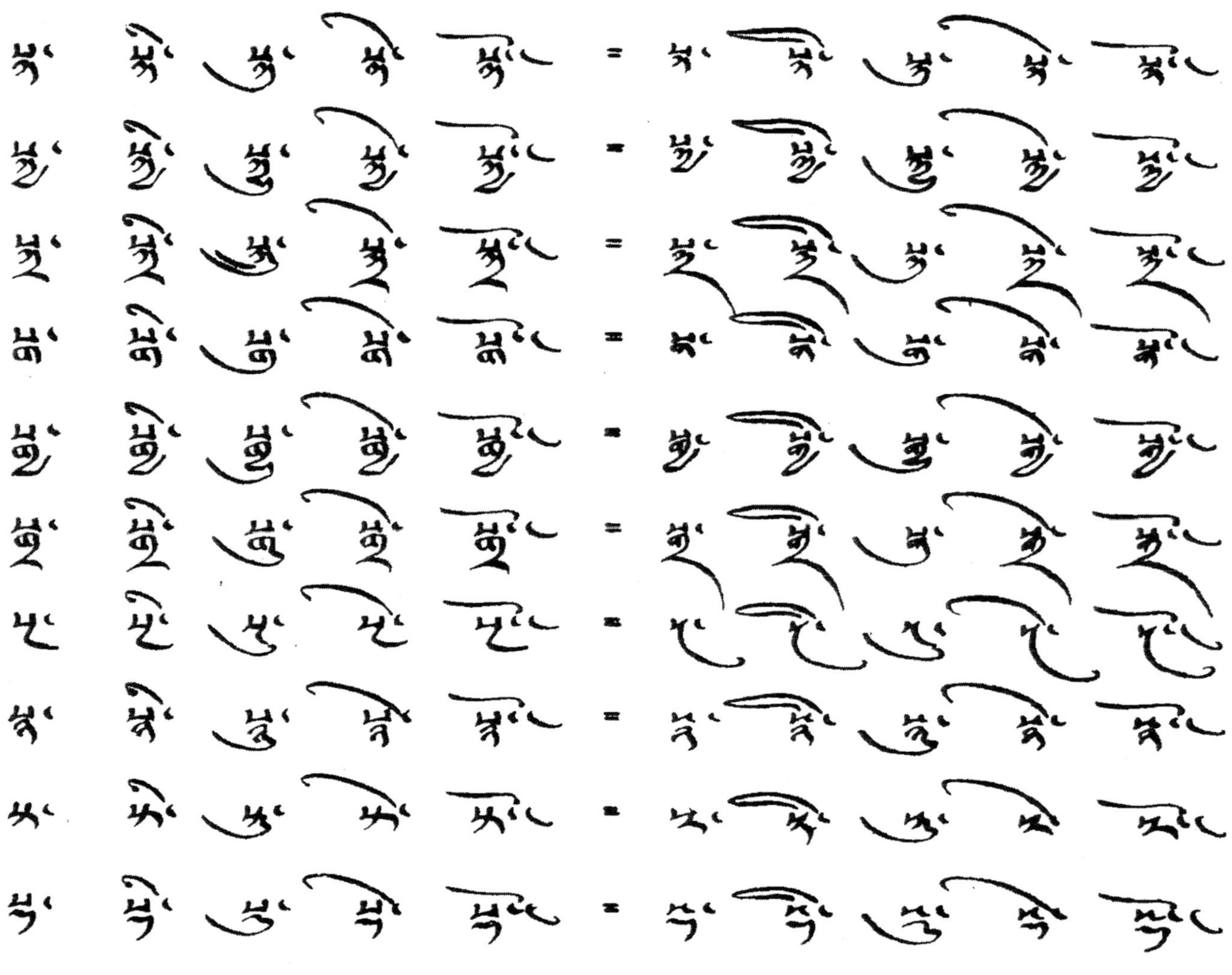

SYLLABIC SCHEME OF

Capital Letters

92	11	སྣ་	སྣི་	སྣུ་	སྣེ་	སྣོ།	=	s,na	s,ni	s,nu	s,ne	s,no.
93	12	སྣྲ་	སྣྲི་	སྣྲུ་	སྣྲེ་	སྣྲོ།	=	s,nra	s,nri	s,nru	s,nre	s,nro.
94	13	སྤ་	སྤི་	སྤུ་	སྤེ་	སྤོ།	=	s,pa	s,pi	s,pu	s,pe	s,po.
95	14	སྤྱ་	སྤྱི་	སྤྱུ་	སྤྱེ་	སྤྱོ།	=	s,pya	s,pyi	s,pyu	s,pye	s,pyo.
96	15	སྤྲ་	སྤྲི་	སྤྲུ་	སྤྲེ་	སྤྲོ།	=	s,pra	s,pri	s,pru	s,pre	s,pro.
97	16	སྦ་	སྦི་	སྦུ་	སྦེ་	སྦོ།	=	s,ba	s,bi	s,bu	s,be	s,bo.
98	17	སྦྱ་	སྦྱི་	སྦྱུ་	སྦྱེ་	སྦྱོ།	=	s,bya	s,byi	s,byu	s,bye	s,byo.
99	18	སྦྲ་	སྦྲི་	སྦྲུ་	སྦྲེ་	སྦྲོ།	=	s,bra	s,bri	s,bru	s,bre	s,bro.
100	19	སྨ་	སྨི་	སྨུ་	སྨེ་	སྨོ།	=	s,ma	s,mi	s,mu	s,me	s,mo.
101	20	སྨྱ་	སྨྱི་	སྨྱུ་	སྨྱེ་	སྨྱོ།	=	s,mya	s,myi	s,myu	s,mye	s,myo.
102	21	སྨྲ་	སྨྲི་	སྨྲུ་	སྨྲེ་	སྨྲོ།	=	s,mra	s,mri	s,mru	s,mre	s,mro.
103	22	སྩ་	སྩི་	སྩུ་	སྩེ་	སྩོ།	=	s,tsa	s,tsi	s,tsu	s,tse	s,tso.

VIII. *The Eleven simple Letters*

104	1	གཅའ་	གཅི་	གཅུ་	གཅེ་	གཅོ།	=	g,chah	g,chi	g,chu	g,che	g,cho.
105	2	གཉའ་	གཉི་	གཉུ་	གཉེ་	གཉོ།	=	g,nyah	g,nyi	g,nyu	g,nye	g,nyo.

Small Characters

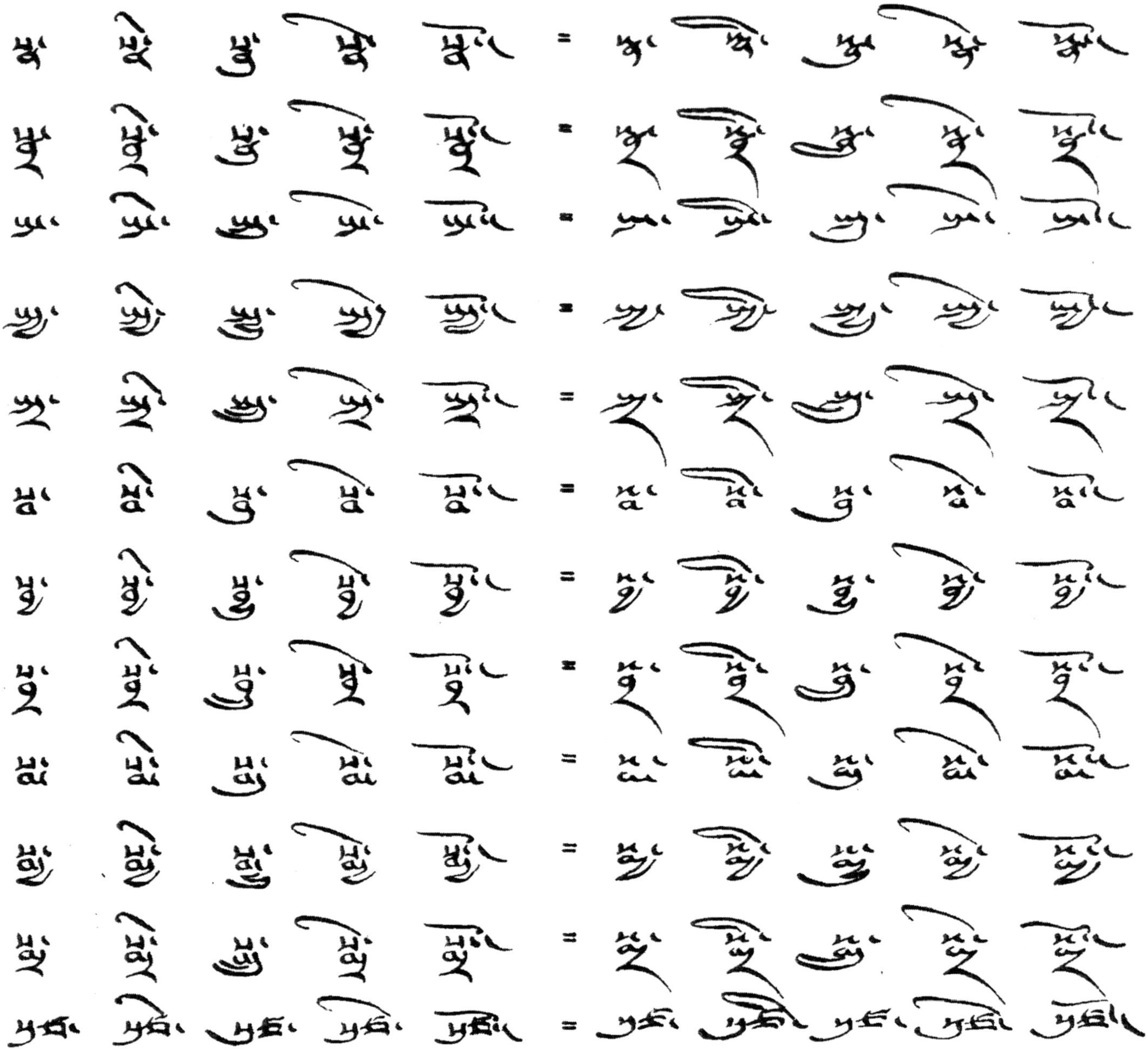

with ག, (*g*) *as a prefix* ________________

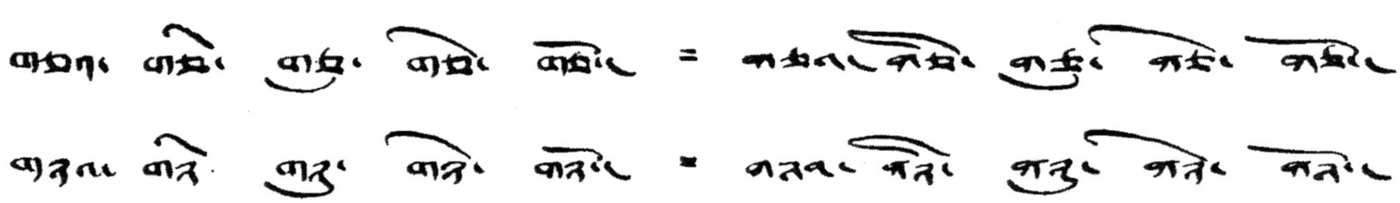

Capital Letters

106	3	གཏའ་	གཏི་	གཏུ་	གཏེ་	གཏོ།	=	g,tah	g,ti	g,tu	g,té	g,to.
107	4	གདའ་	གདི་	གདུ་	གདེ་	གདོ།	=	g,dah	g,di	g,du	g,dé	g,do.
108	5	གནའ་	གནི་	གནུ་	གནེ་	གནོ།	=	g,nah	g,ni	g,nu	g,né	g,no.
109	6	གཙའ་	གཙི་	གཙུ་	གཙེ་	གཙོ།	=	g,tsah	g,tsi	g,tsu	g,tsé	g.tso.
110.	7	གཞའ་	གཞི་	གཞུ་	གཞེ་	གཞོ།	=	g,zhah	g,zhi	g,zhu	g,zhé	g,zho.
111	8	གཟའ་	གཟི་	གཟུ་	གཟེ་	གཟོ།	=	g,zah	g,zi	g,zu	gzé	g,zo.
112	9	གཡའ་	གཡི་	གཡུ་	གཡེ་	གཡོ།	=	g,yah	gyi	gyu	gyé	g,yo.
113	10	གཤའ་	གཤི་	གཤུ་	གཤེ་	གཤོ།	=	g,shah	g,shi	g,shu	g,shé	g,sho.
114	11	གསའ་	གསི་	གསུ་	གསེ་	གསོ།	=	g,sah	g,si	g,su	g,sé	g,so.

IX. *The Fifteen Simple and*

115	1	དཀའ་	དཀི་	དཀུ་	དཀེ་	དཀོ།	=	d,kah	d,ki	d,ku	d,ké	d,ko.
116	2	དཀྱ་	དཀྱི་	དཀྱུ་	དཀྱེ་	དཀྱོ།	=	d,kya	d,kyi	d,kyu	dkyé	d,kyo.
117	3	དཀྲ་	དཀྲི་	དཀྲུ་	དཀྲེ་	དཀྲོ།	=	d,kra	d,kri	d,kru	d,kré	d,kro.
118	4	དགའ་	དགི་	དགུ་	དགེ་	དགོ།	=	d,gah	d,gi	d,gu	d,gé	d,go.
119	5	དགྱ་	དགྱི་	དགྱུ་	དགྱེ་	དགྱོ།		d,gya	dgyi	d,gyu	dgyé	d,gyo.

Small Characters

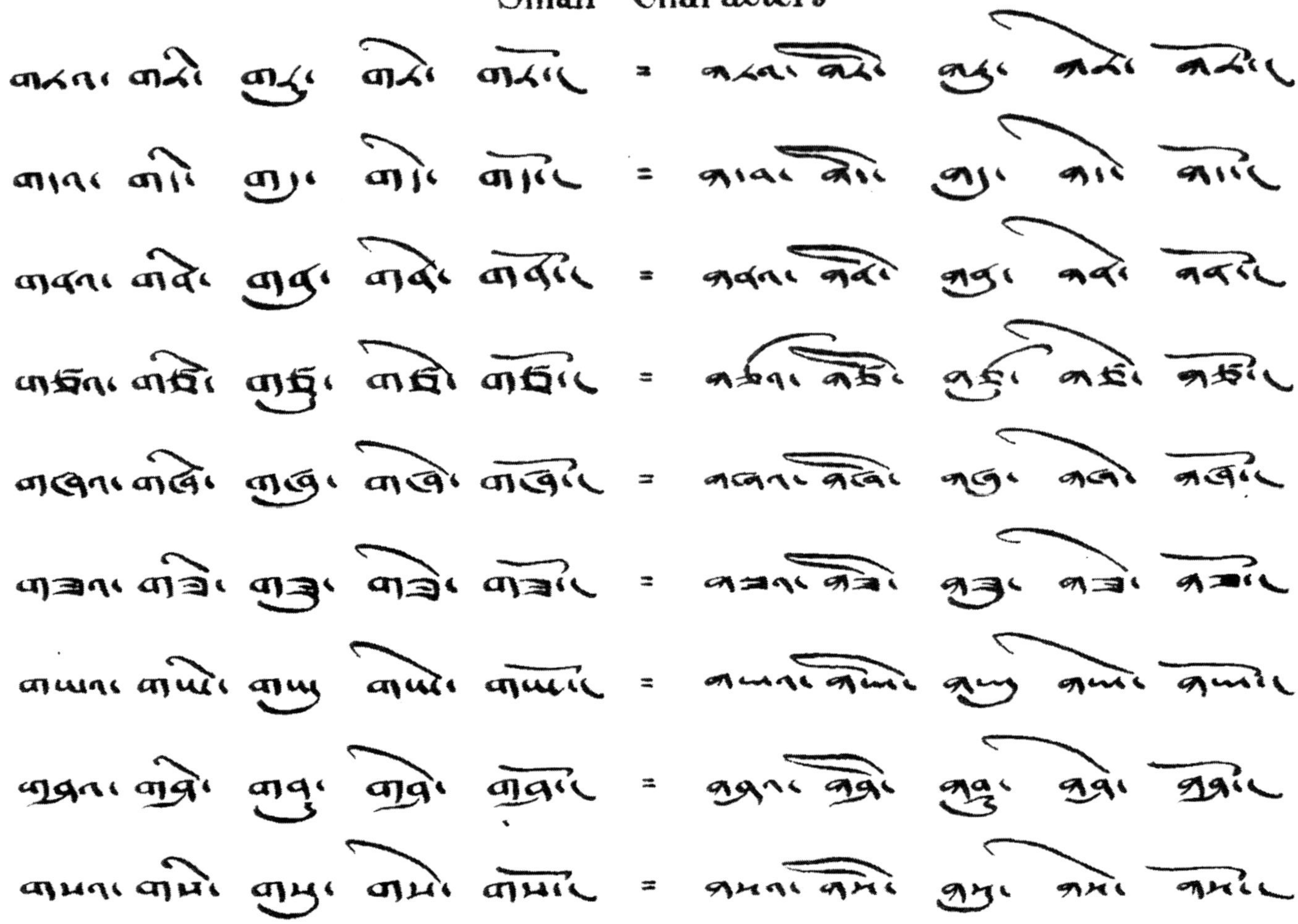

double Letters preceded by a ད *(d)*

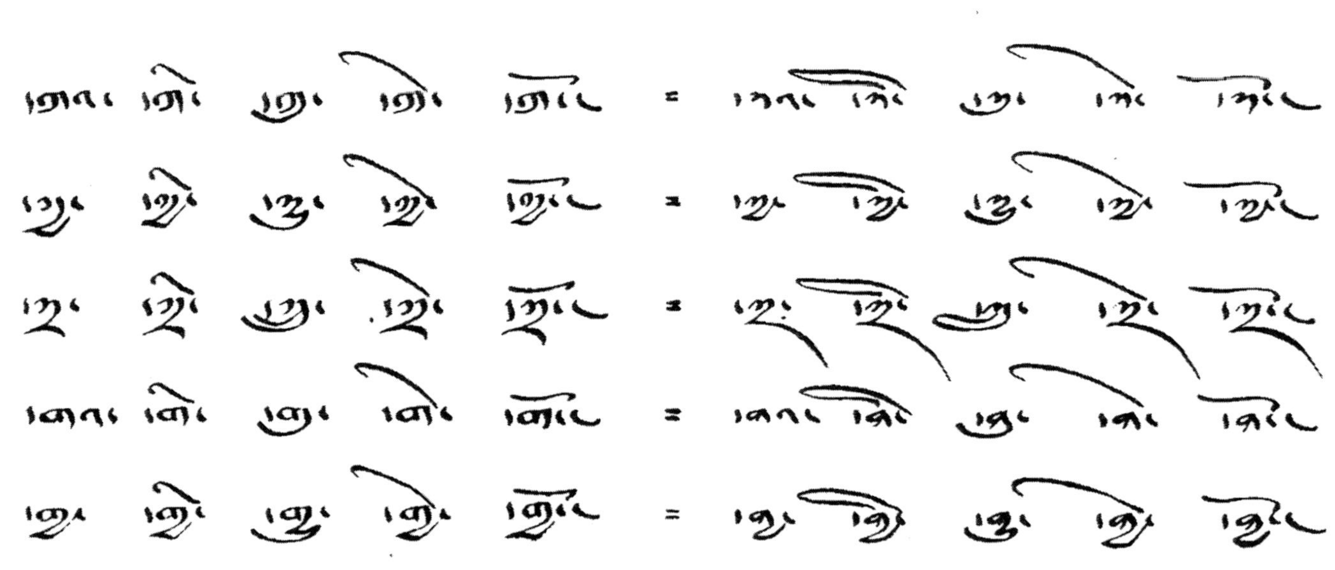

SYLLABIC SCHEME OF

Capital Letters.

120	6	དགྲ་	དགྲི་	དགྲུ་	དགྲེ་	དགྲོ།	=	*d,gra*	*d,gri*	*d,gru*	*d,gré*	*d,gro.*
121	7	དངའ་	དངི་	དངུ་	དངེ་	དངོ།	=	*d,ñah*	*d,ñi*	*d,ñu*	*d,ñé*	*d,ño.*
122	8	དཔའ་	དཔི་	དཔུ་	དཔེ་	དཔོ།	=	*d,pah*	*d,pi*	*d,pu*	*d,pé*	*d,po.*
123	9	དཔྱ་	དཔྱི་	དཔྱུ་	དཔྱེ་	དཔྱོ།	=	*d,pya*	*d,pyi*	*d,pyu*	*d,pyé*	*d,pya*
124	10	དཔྲ་	དཔྲི་	དཔྲུ་	དཔྲེ་	དཔྲོ།	=	*d,pra*	*d,pri*	*d,pru*	*d,pré*	*d,pro.*
125	11	དབའ་	དབི་	དབུ་	དབེ་	དབོ།	=	*d,vah*	*d,vi*	*d,vu*	*d,vé*	*d,vo.*
126	12	དབྱ་	དབྱི་	དབྱུ་	དབྱེ་	དབྱོ།	=	*d,vya*	*d,vyi*	*d,vyu*	*d,vyé*	*d,vyo.*
127	13	དབྲ་	དབྲི་	དབྲུ་	དབྲེ་	དབྲོ།	=	*d,vra*	*d,vri*	*d,vru*	*d,vré*	*d,vro.*
128	14	དམའ་	དམི་	དམུ་	དམེ་	དམོ།	=	*d,mah*	*d,mi*	*d,mu*	*d,mé*	*d,mo.*
129	15	དམྱ་	དམྱི་	དམྱུ་	དམྱེ་	དམྱོ།		*d,mya*	*d,myi*	*d,myu*	*d,myé*	*d,myo.*

X. *The Forty five simple, double and*

130	1	བཀའ་	བཀི་	བཀུ་	བཀེ་	བཀོ།	=	*b,kah*	*b,ki*	*b,ku*	*b,ké*	*b,ko.*
131	2	བཀྱ་	བཀྱི་	བཀྱུ་	བཀྱེ་	བཀྱོ།	=	*b,kya*	*b,kyi*	*b,kyu*	*b,kyé*	*b,kyo.*
132	3	བཀྲ་	བཀྲི་	བཀྲུ་	བཀྲེ་	བཀྲོ།	=	*b,kra*	*b,kri*	*b,kru*	*b,kré*	*b,kro.*
133	4	བཀླ་	བཀླི་	བཀླུ་	བཀླེ་	བཀློ།	=	*b,kla*	*b,kli*	*b,klu*	*b,klé*	*b,klo.*

Small Characters.

triple Letters that take ཀ *(b) as a prefix.* ———————————

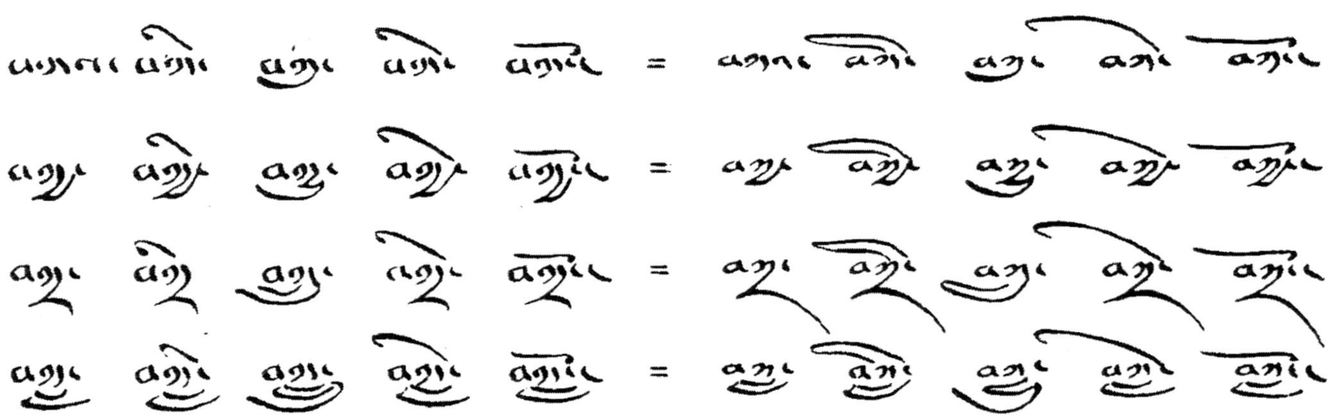

SYLLABIC SCHEME OF

Capital Letters.

134 5 བརྐ་ བརྐི་ བརྐུ་ བརྐེ་ བརྐོ། = b,rka b,rki b,rku br,ké br,ko.

135 6 བརྐྱ་ བརྐྱི་ བརྐྱུ་ བརྐྱེ་ བརྐྱོ། = br,kya br,kyi br,kyu br,kyé br,kyo.

136 7 བསྐ་ བསྐི་ བསྐུ་ བསྐེ་ བསྐོ། = bs,ka bs,ky bs,ku bs,ké bs,ko.

137 8 བསྐྱ་ བསྐྱི་ བསྐྱུ་ བསྐྱེ་ བསྐྱོ། = bs,kya bs,kyi bs,kyu bs,kyé bs,kyo.

138 9 བསྐྲ་ བསྐྲི་ བསྐྲུ་ བསྐྲེ་ བསྐྲོ། = bs,kra bs,kri bs,kru bs,kré bs,kro.

139 10 བགའ་ བགི་ བགུ་ བགེ་ བགོ། = b,gah b,gi b,gu b,gé b,go.

140 11 བགྱ་ བགྱི་ བགྱུ་ བགྱེ་ བགྱོ། = b,gya b,gyi b,gyu b,gyé b,gyo.

141 12 བགྲ་ བགྲི་ བགྲུ་ བགྲེ་ བགྲོ། = b,gra b,gri b,gru b,gré b,gra

142 13 བརྒ་ བརྒི་ བརྒུ་ བརྒེ་ བརྒོ། = br,ga br,gi br,gu br,gé br,go.

143 14 བརྒྱ་ བརྒྱི་ བརྒྱུ་ བརྒྱེ་ བརྒྱོ། = br,gya br,gyi br,gyu br,gyé br,gyo.

144 15 བསྒ་ བསྒི་ བསྒུ་ བསྒེ་ བསྒོ། = bs,ga bs,gi bs,gu bs,gé bs,go.

145 16 བསྒྱ་ བསྒྱི་ བསྒྱུ་ བསྒྱེ་ བསྒྱོ། = bs,gya bs,gyi bs,gyu bs,gyé bs,gyo.

146 17 བསྒྲ་ བསྒྲི་ བསྒྲུ་ བསྒྲེ་ བསྒྲོ། = bs,gra bs,gri bs,gru bs,gré bs,gro.

147 18 བརྔ་ བརྔི་ བརྔུ་ བརྔེ་ བརྔོ། = br,n̄a br,n̄i br,n̄u br,n̄é br,n̄o.

148 19 བསྔ་ བསྔི་ བསྔུ་ བསྔེ་ བསྔོ། = bs,n̄a bs,n̄i bs,n̄u bs,n̄é bs,n̄o.

149 20 བཅའ་ བཅི་ བཅུ་ བཅེ་ བཅོ། = b,chah b,chi b,chu b,ché b,cho.

Small Characters.

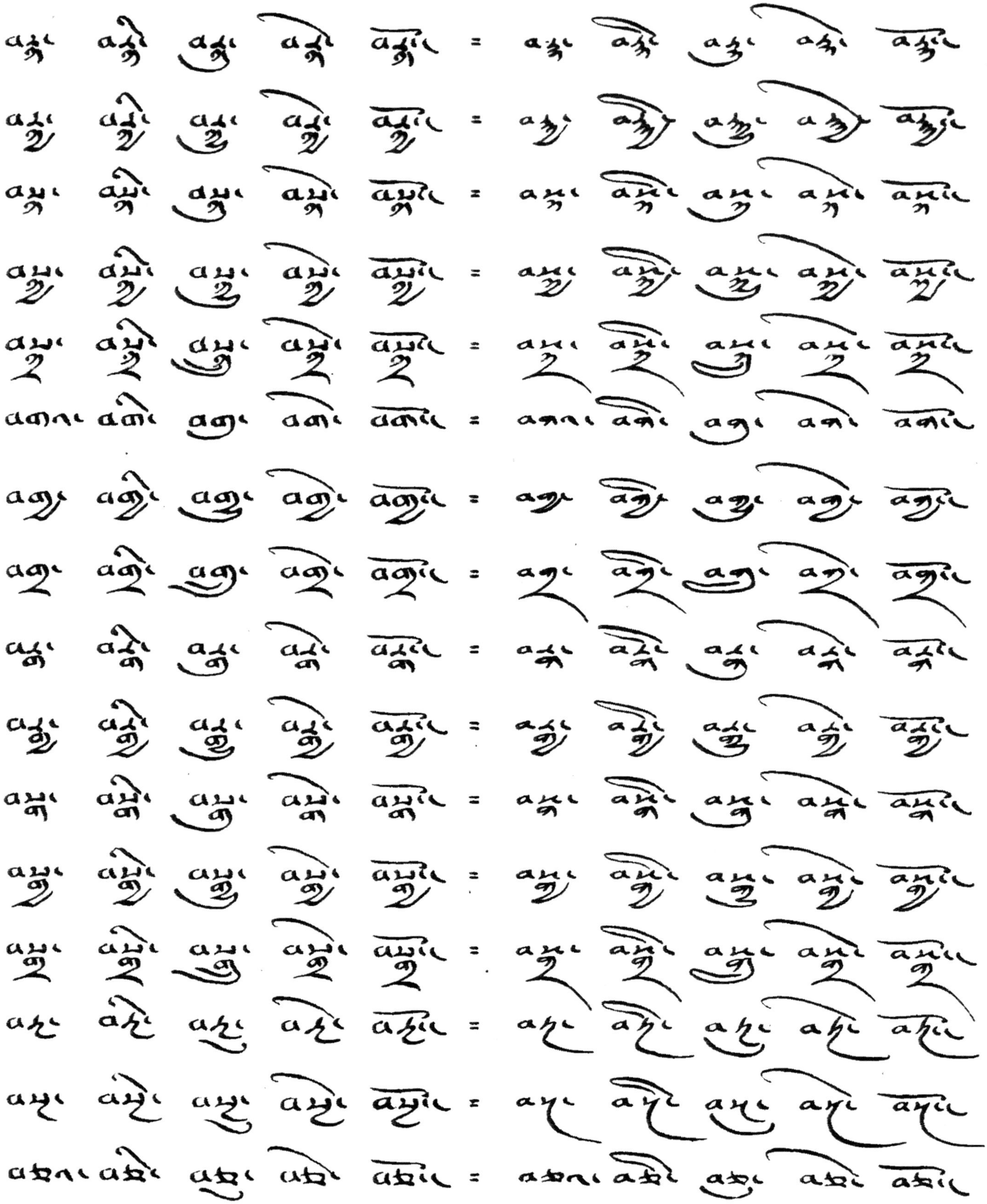

SYLLABIC SCHEME OF

Capital Letters

150	21	བརྗ་	བརྗི་	བརྗུ་	བརྗེ་	བརྗོ།	=	br,ju	br,ji	br,ju	br,jé	br,jo.
151	22	བརྙ་	བརྙི་	བརྙུ་	བརྙེ་	བརྙོ།	=	br,nya	br,nyi	br,nyu	br,nyé	br,nyo
152	23	བསྙ་	བསྙི་	བསྙུ་	བསྙེ་	བསྙོ།	=	bs,nya	bs,nyi	bs,nyu	bs,nyé	bs,nyo
153	24	བཏའ་	བཏི་	བཏུ་	བཏེ་	བཏོ།	=	b,tah	b,ti	b,tu	b,té	b,to.
154	25	བརྟ་	བརྟི་	བརྟུ་	བརྟེ་	བརྟོ།	=	br,ta	br,ti	br,tu	br,té	br,to.
155	26	བལྟ་	བལྟི་	བལྟུ་	བལྟེ་	བལྟོ།	=	bl,ta	bl,ti	bl,tu	bl,té	bl,to.
156	27	བསྟ་	བསྟི་	བསྟུ་	བསྟེ་	བསྟོ།	=	bs,ta	bs,ti	bs,tu	bs,té	bs,to.
157	28	བདའ་	བདི་	བདུ་	བདེ་	བདོ།	=	b,dah	b,di	b,du	b,dé	b,do.
158	29	བརྡ་	བརྡི་	བརྡུ་	བརྡེ་	བརྡོ།	=	br,da	br,di	br,du	br,dé	br,do.
159	30	བལྡ་	བལྡི་	བལྡུ་	བལྡེ་	བལྡོ།	=	bl,da	bl,di	bl,du	bl,dé	bl,do.
160	31	བསྡ་	བསྡི་	བསྡུ་	བསྡེ་	བསྡོ།	=	bs,da	bs,di	bs,du	bs,dé	bs,do
161	32	བརྣ་	བརྣི་	བརྣུ་	བརྣེ་	བརྣོ།	=	br,na	br,ni	br,nu	br,né	br,no.
162	33	བསྣ་	བསྣི་	བསྣུ་	བསྣེ་	བསྣོ།	=	bs,na	bs,ni	bs,nu	bs,né	bs,no.
163	34	བཙའ་	བཙི་	བཙུ་	བཙེ་	བཙོ།	=	b,tsah	b,tsi	b,tsu	b,tsé	b,tso.
164	35	བརྩ་	བརྩི་	བརྩུ་	བརྩེ་	བརྩོ།	=	br,tsa	br,tsi	br,tsu	b,-tsé	br,tso.
165	36	བསྩ་	བསྩི་	བསྩུ་	བསྩེ་	བསྩོ།	=	bs,tsa	bs,tsi	bs,tsu	bs,tsé	bs,tso.

Small Character

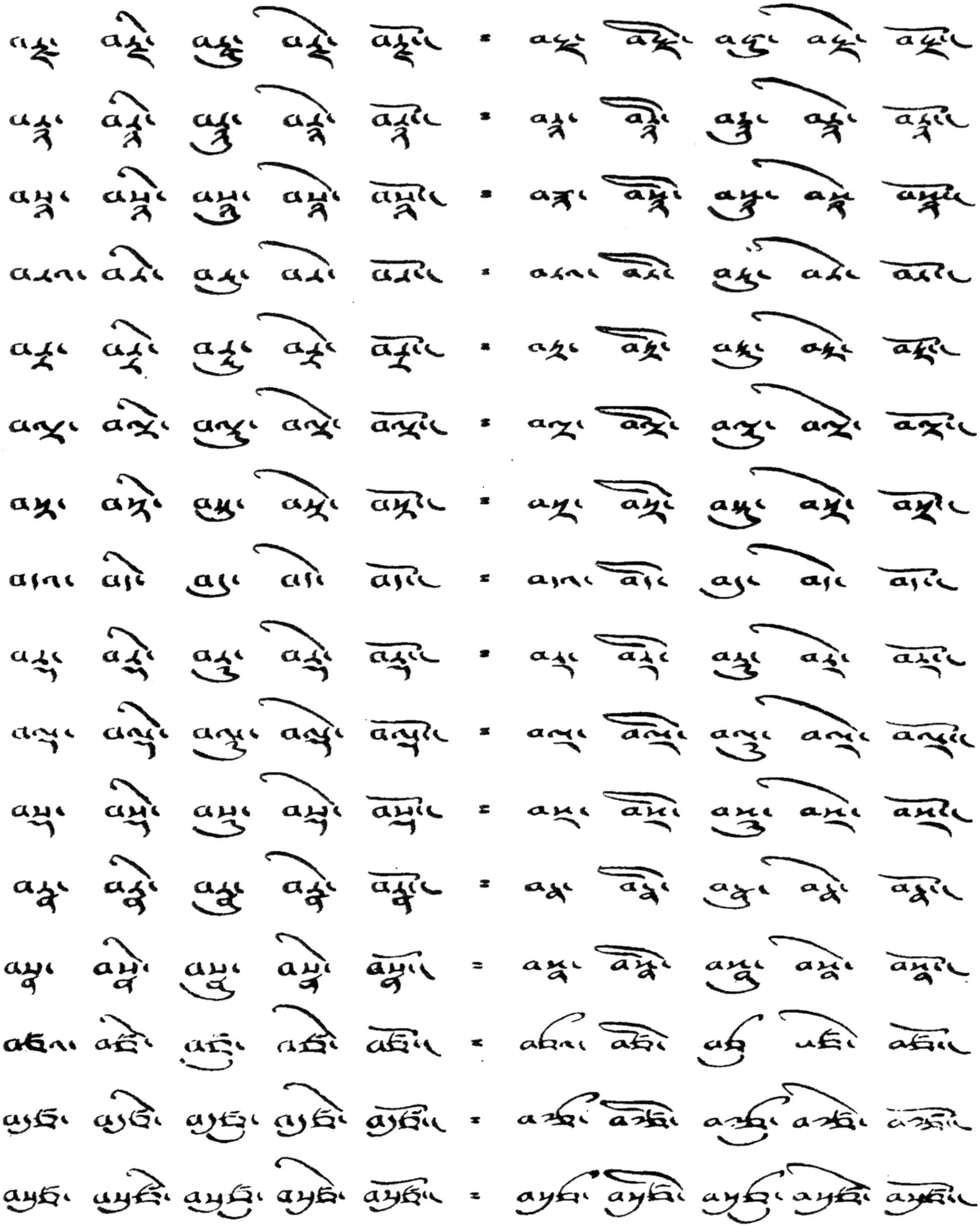

Capital Letters.

166	37	བརྫ་	བརྫི་	བརྫུ་	བརྫེ་	བརྫོ།	=	br,dsa	br,dsi	br,dsu	br,dsé	br,dso.
167	38	བཞའ་	བཞི་	བཞུ་	བཞེ་	བཞོ།	=	b,zhah	b,zhi	b,zhu	b,zhé	b,zho.
168	39	བཟའ་	བཟི་	བཟུ་	བཟེ་	བཟོ།	=	b,zah	b,zi	b,zu	b,zé	b,zo.
169	40	བཟླ་	བཟླི་	བཟླུ་	བཟླེ་	བཟློ།	=	bz,la	bz,li	bz,lu	bz,lé	bz,lo.
170	41	བརླ་	བརླི་	བརླུ་	བརླེ་	བརློ།	=	br,la	br,li	br,lu	br,lé	br,lo.
171	42	བཤའ་	བཤི་	བཤུ་	བཤེ་	བཤོ།	=	b,shah	b,shi	b,shu	b,shé	b,sho.
172	43	བསའ་	བསི་	བསུ་	བསེ་	བསོ།	=	b,sah	b,si	b,su	b,sé	b,so.
173	44	བསྲ་	བསྲི་	བསྲུ་	བསྲེ་	བསྲོ།	=	b,sra	b,sri	b,sru	b,sré	b,sro.
174	45	བསླ་	བསླི་	བསླུ་	བསླེ་	བསློ།	=	bs,la	bs,li	bs,lu	bs,lé	bs,lo.

XI. *The Fifteen simple and double*

175	1	མཁའ་	མཁི་	མཁུ་	མཁེ་	མཁོ།	=	m,khah	m,khi	m,khu	m,khé	m,kho.
176	2	མཁྱ་	མཁྱི་	མཁྱུ་	མཁྱེ་	མཁྱོ།	=	m,khya	m,khyi	m,khyu	m,khyé	m,khyo.
177	3	མཁྲ་	མཁྲི་	མཁྲུ་	མཁྲེ་	མཁྲོ།	=	m,khra	m,khri	m,khru	m,khré	m,khra
178	4	མགའ་	མགི་	མགུ་	མགེ་	མགོ།	=	m,gah	m,gi	m,gu	m,gé	m,go.
179	5	མགྱ་	མགྱི་	མགྱུ་	མགྱེ་	མགྱོ།	=	m,gya	m,gyi	m,gyu	m,gyé	m,gyo.

Small Characters

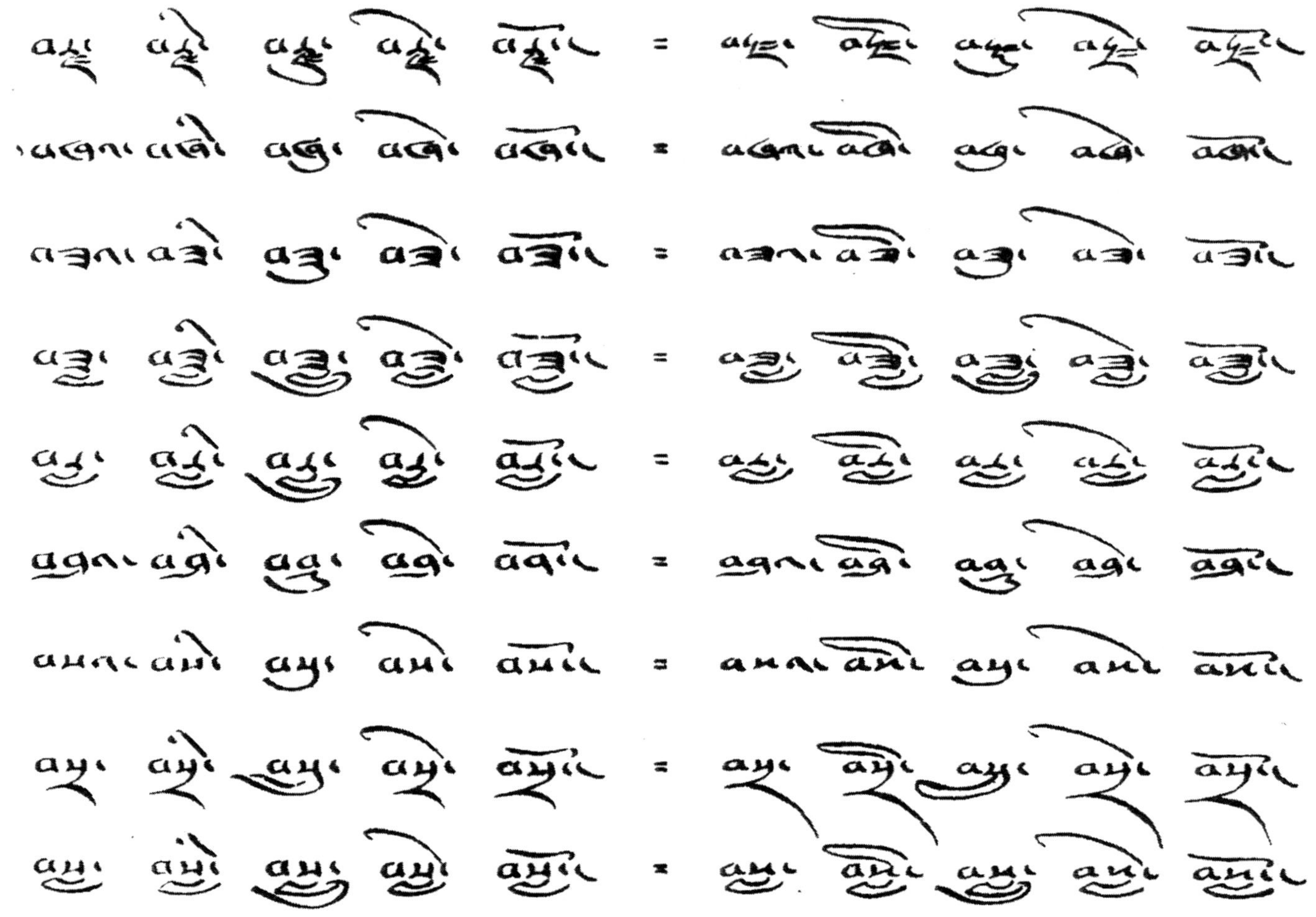

Letters that have མ *(m) as a Prefix.*

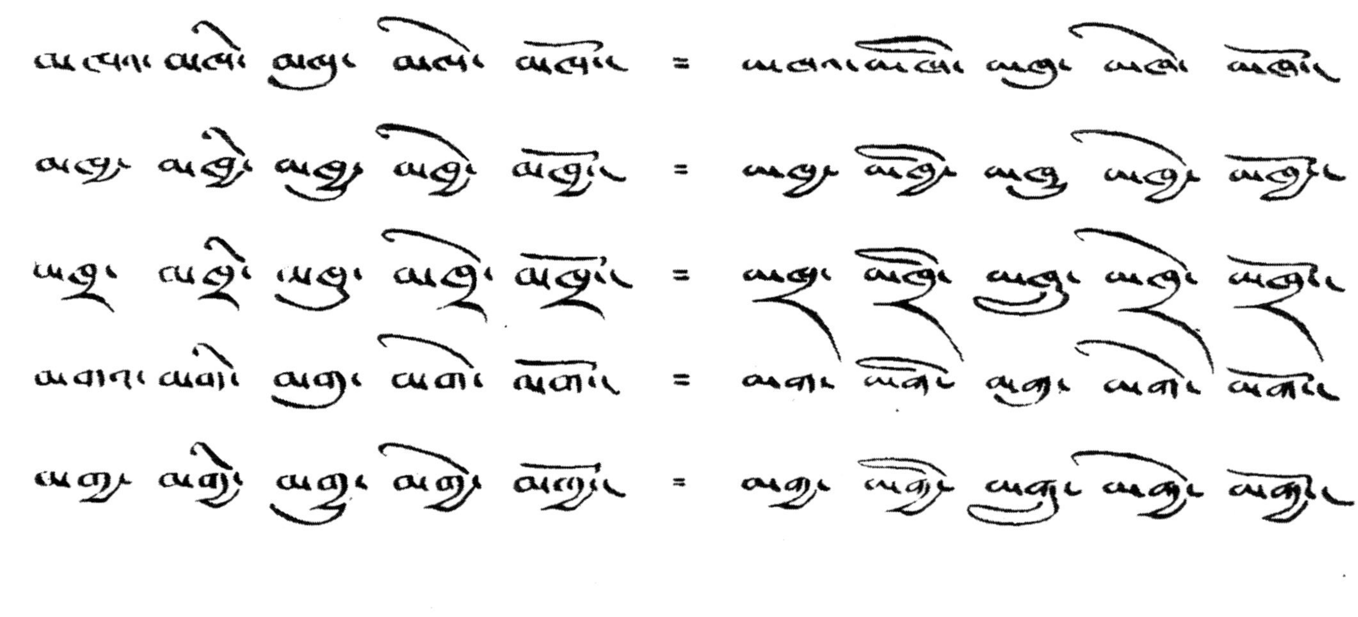

SYLLABIC SCHEME OF

Capital Letters

180	6	མགྲ་	མགྲི་	མགྲུ་	མགྲེ་	མགྲོ།	=	m,gra	m,gri	m,gru	m,gré	m,gro.
181	7	མངའ་	མངི་	མངུ་	མངེ་	མངོ།	=	m,n̄ah	m,n̄i	m,n̄u	m,n̄é	m,n̄o.
182	8	མཆའ་	མཆི་	མཆུ་	མཆེ་	མཆོ།	=	m,chhah	m,chhi	m,chhu	m,chhé	m,chho
183	9	མཇའ་	མཇི་	མཇུ་	མཇེ་	མཇོ།	=	m,jah	m,ji	m,ju	m,jé	m,jo
184	10	མཉའ་	མཉི་	མཉུ་	མཉེ་	མཉོ།	=	m,nyah	m,nyi	m,nyu	m,nyé	m,nyo.
185	11	མཐའ་	མཐི་	མཐུ་	མཐེ་	མཐོ།	=	m,tha	m,thi	m,thu	m,thé	m,tha
186	12	མདའ་	མདི་	མདུ་	མདེ་	མདོ།	=	m,dah	m,di	m,du	m,dé	m,do.
187	13	མནའ་	མནི་	མནུ་	མནེ་	མནོ།	=	m,nah	m,ni	m,nu	m,né	m,no.
188	14	མཚའ་	མཚི་	མཚུ་	མཚེ་	མཚོ།	=	m,tshah	m,tshi	m,tshu	m,tshé	m,tsha
189	15	མཛའ་	མཛི་	མཛུ་	མཛེ་	མཛོ།	=	m,dsah	m,dsi	m,dsu	m,dsé	m,dso

XII. *The Nineteen simple and double*

190	1	འཁའ་	འཁི་	འཁུ་	འཁེ་	འཁོ།	=	h,khah	h,khi	h,khu	h,khé	h,kho.
191	2	འཁྱ་	འཁྱི་	འཁྱུ་	འཁྱེ་	འཁྱོ།	=	h,khya	h,khyi	h,khyu	h,khyé	h,kho.
192	3	འཁྲ་	འཁྲི་	འཁྲུ་	འཁྲེ་	འཁྲོ།	=	h,khra	h,khri	h,khru	h,khré	h,khro.
193	4	འགའ་	འགི་	འགུ་	འགེ་	འགོ།	=	h,gah	h,gi	h,gu	h,gé	h,go.

Small Characters

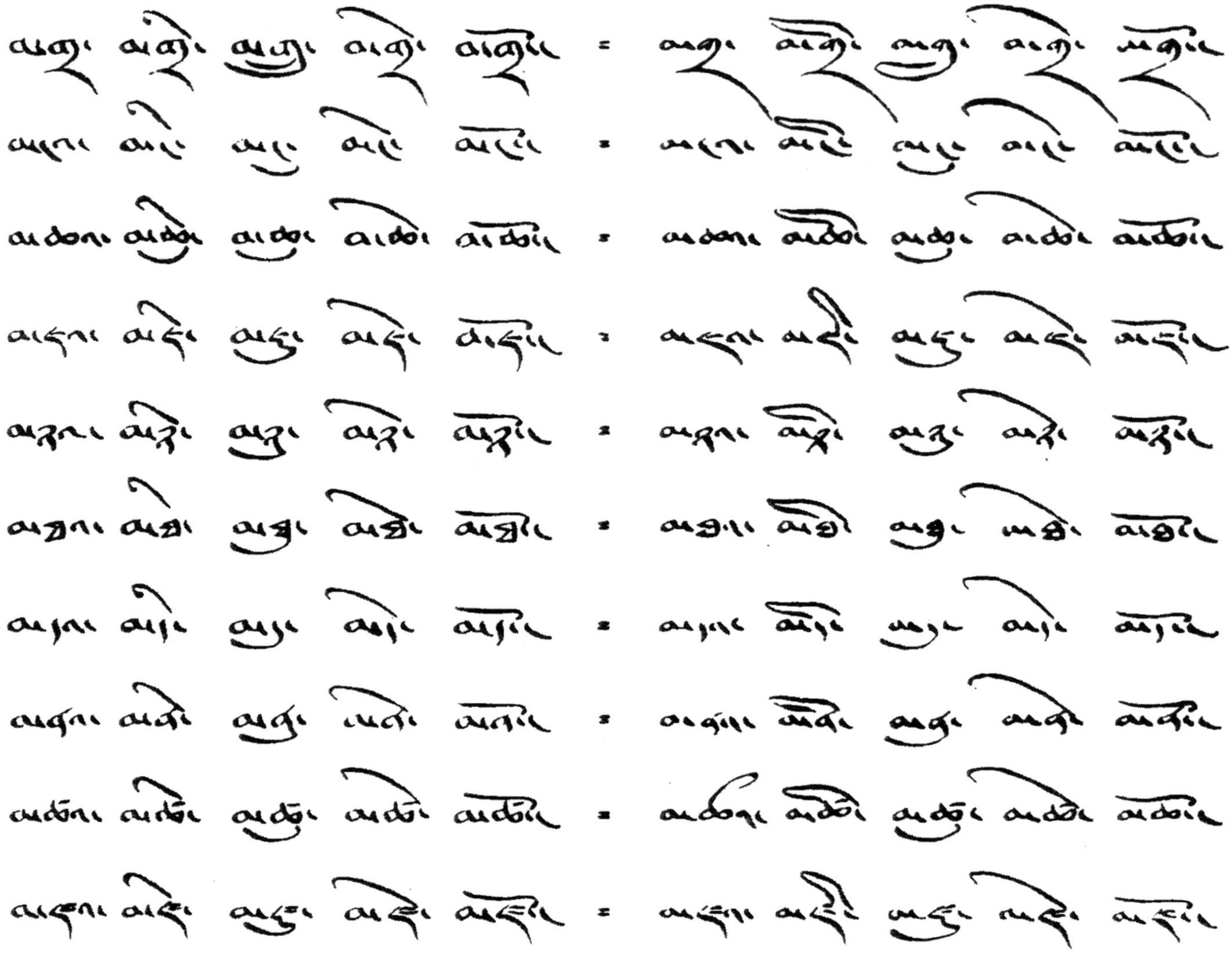

Letters that take འ *(h) as a prefix.*

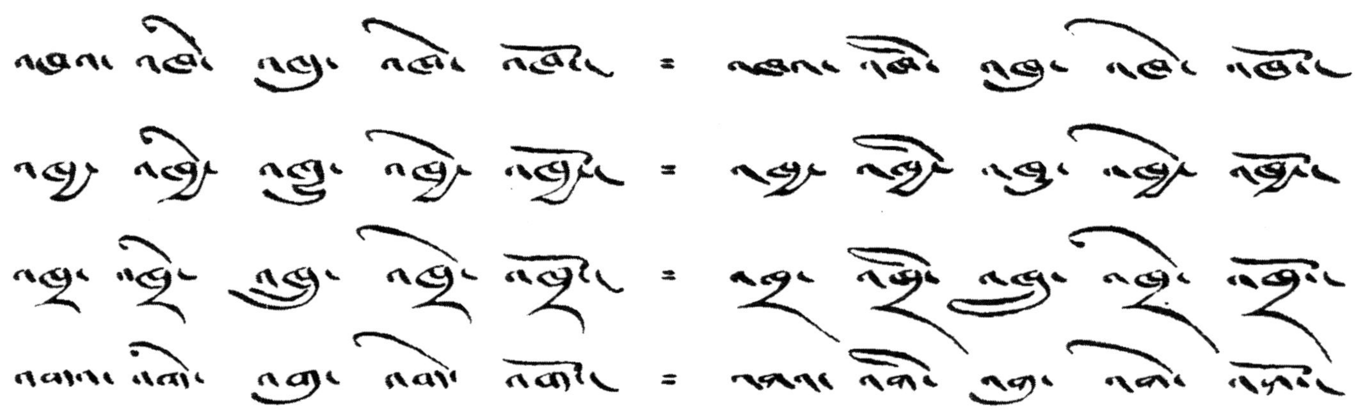

SYLLABIC SCHEME OF

Capital Letters.

194 5 འགྱ་ འགྱི་ འགྱུ་ འགྱེ་ འགྱོ། = h,gya h,gyi h,gyu h,gyé h,gyo.

195 6 འགྲ་ འགྲི་ འགྲུ་ འགྲེ་ འགྲོ། = h,gra h,gri h,gru h,gré h,gro.

196 7 འཆའ་ འཆི་ འཆུ་ འཆེ་ འཆོ། = h,chhah h,chhi h,chhu h,chhé h,chho.

197 8 འཇའ་ འཇི་ འཇུ་ འཇེ་ འཇོ། = h,jah h,ji h,ju h,jé h,jo.

198 9 འཐའ་ འཐི་ འཐུ་ འཐེ་ འཐོ། = h,thah h,thi h,thu h,thé h,tho.

199 10 འདའ་ འདི་ འདུ་ འདེ་ འདོ། = h,dah h,di h,du h,dé h,do.

200 11 འདྲ་ འདྲི་ འདྲུ་ འདྲེ་ འདྲོ། = h,dra h,dri h,dru h,dré h,dro.

201 12 འཕའ་ འཕི་ འཕུ་ འཕེ་ འཕོ། = h,phah h,phi h,phu h,phé h,pho

202 13 འཕྱ་ འཕྱི་ འཕྱུ་ འཕྱེ་ འཕྱོ། = h,phya h,phyi h,phyu h,phyé h,phyo.

203 14 འཕྲ་ འཕྲི་ འཕྲུ་ འཕྲེ་ འཕྲོ། = h,phra h,phri h,phru h,phré h,phro.

204 15 འབའ་ འབི་ འབུ་ འབེ་ འབོ། = h,bah h,bi h,bu h,bé h,bo.

205 16 འབྱ་ འབྱི་ འབྱུ་ འབྱེ་ འབྱོ། = h,bya h,byi h,byu h,byé h,byo.

206 17 འབྲ་ འབྲི་ འབྲུ་ འབྲེ་ འབྲོ། = h,bra h,bri h,bru h,bré h,bro.

207 18 འཚའ་ འཚི་ འཚུ་ འཚེ་ འཚོ། = h,tshah h,tshi h,tshu h,tshé h,tsho.

208 19 འཛའ་ འཛི་ འཛུ་ འཛེ་ འཛོ། = h,dsah h,dsi h,dsu h,dsé h,dso.

Small Characters.

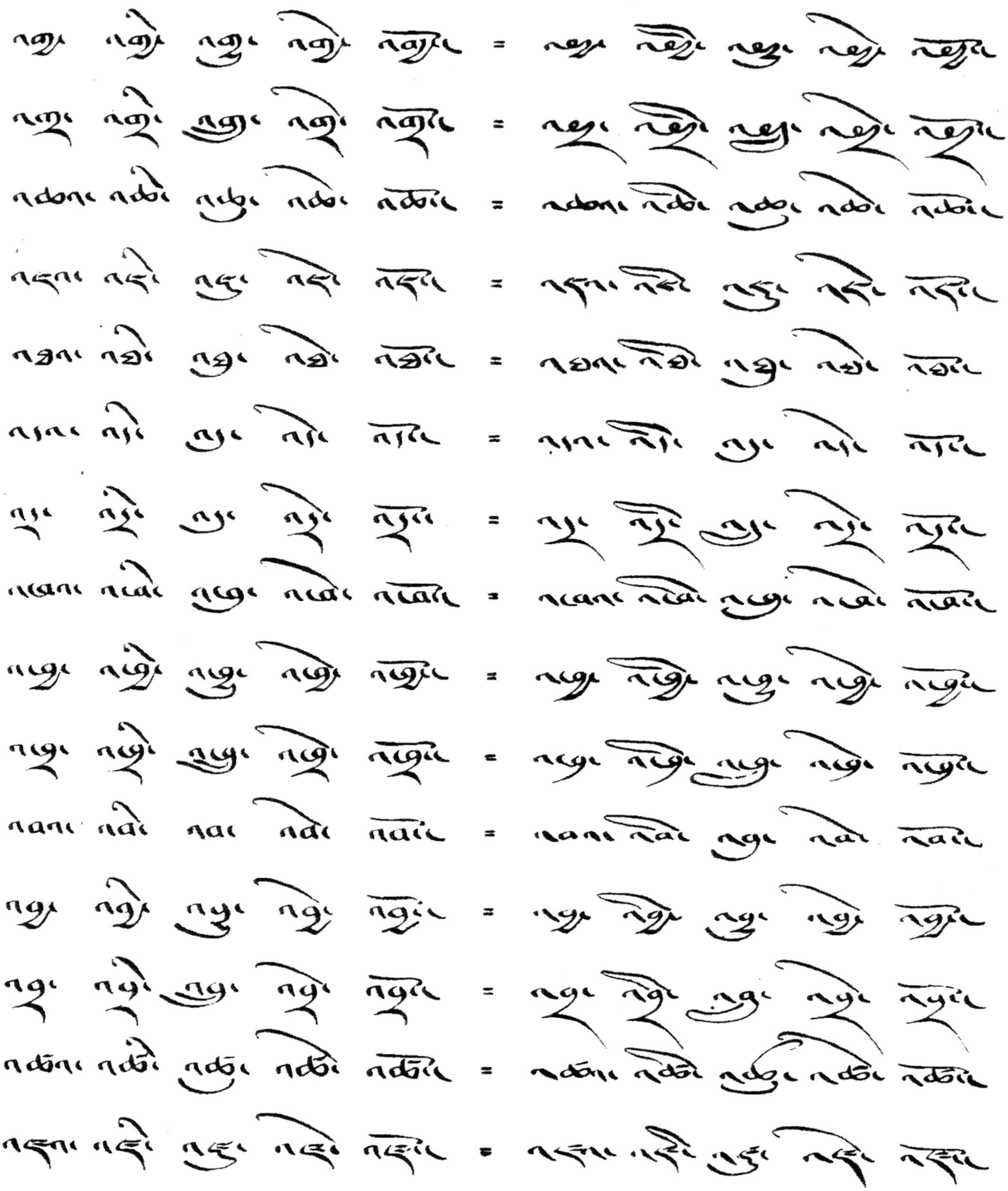

SYLLABIC SCHEME OF

XIII. Letters that follow the vowel either inherent or expressed, or that close a syllable.

		Capital Letters.		
209	1	ག།	=	*q or g.*
210	2	གས།	=	*qs or gs.*
211	3	ང།	=	*n̄g.*
212	4	ངས།	=	*n̄gs.*
213	5	ད།	=	*t̲ or d.*
214	6	ན།	=	*n.*
215	7	ནད།	=	*nt̲ or nd.*
216	8	བ།	=	*p̲ or b.*
217	9	བས།	=	*p̲s or bs.*
218	10	མ།	=	*m.*
219	11	མས།	=	*ms.*
220	12	འ།	=	*h.*
221	13	ར།	=	*r.*
222	14	རད།	=	*rt̲ or rd.*
223	15	ལ།	=	*l.*
224	16	ལད།	=	*lt̲ or ld.*
225	17	ས།	=	*s.*

Small Characters.

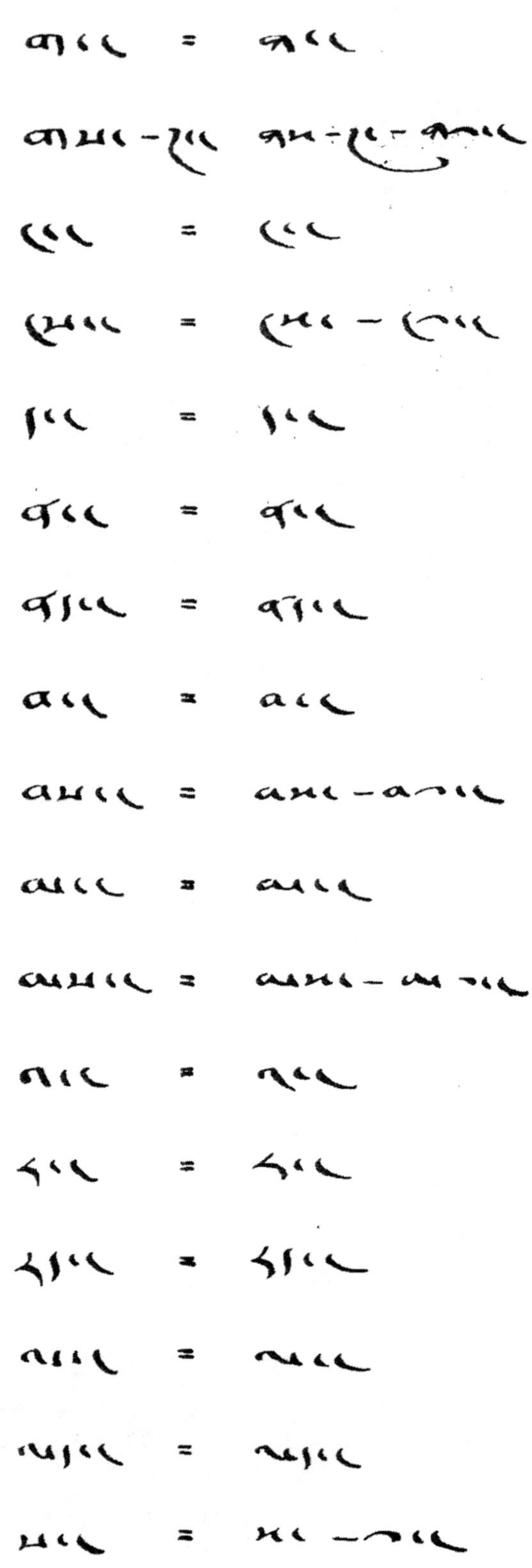

THE TIBETAN LANGUAGE.

Initial Signs, commas, and intersyllabic points, used

with the Capitals — *with the small Characters.*

1 ༄༅༅།། ༄། །།

2 ༄༅༅། །

3 ༄༅། །

4 ༄༔

5 ༄༅༅། །

མགོ་ཡིག་རྒྱས་པའི་རྣམ་གྲངས་སོ། །

6 

མགོ་ཡིག་བསྡུས་པའི་རྣམ་གྲངས་སོ།།

7 ༀ༔ ༔

ཨོ་རྒྱན་པདྨའི་གཏེར་ཡིག་གི་མགོ་ཡིག་གོ།

8 ། ། ། །བཞི་བཤད།

9 ། །གཉིས་བཤད།

10 ། ཚེག་བཤད།

11 ༏༏ ༏༏ཚེག་བཤད་ཀྱི་བཞི་བཤད།

12 ༐༐ ༐༐ ༐ ༐ ༐

13 ༏༏ ༏༏

14 ༏ ༏ཚེག་བཤད་ཀྱི་གཉིས་བཤད།

15 ༏ ཚེག་བཤད་ཀྱི་རྐྱང་བཤད།

16 ༔ ༔ ཨོ་རྒྱན་པདྨའི་གཏེར་ཡིག་གི་བཤད།

17 ་ ་ ་ ཚེག་རྒྱས་འབྲིང་བསྡུས་གསུམ།

18, 19, 20, 21, 22, 23, 24

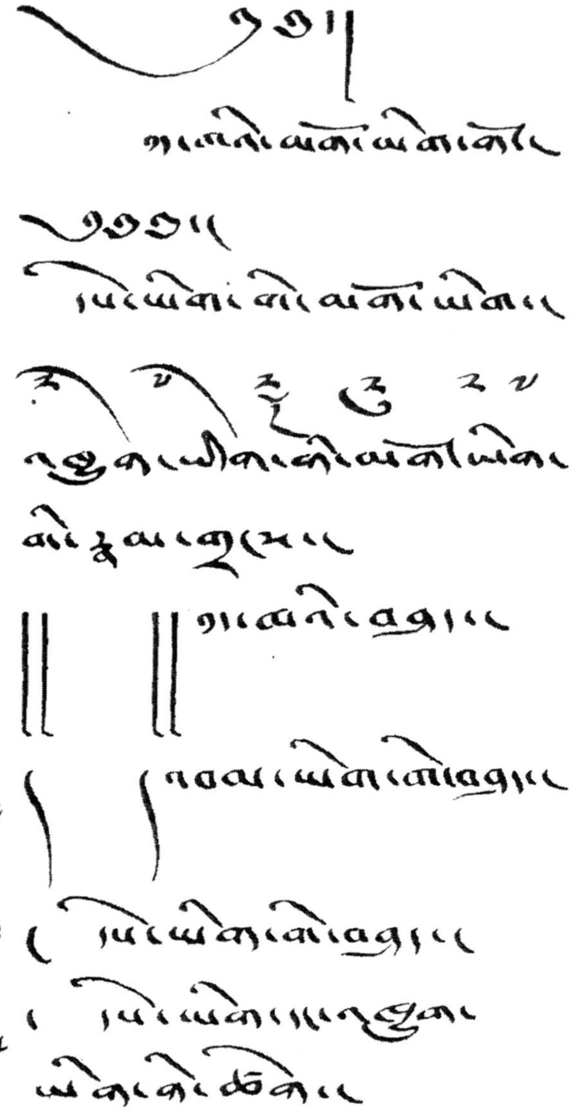

Note – The N.os 1.2.3.4.5 show the initial signs, in a book written in large characters.

N.o 6 those of minor divisions.

" 7 initial signs, in books attributed to Urgyen Padma Guru.

" 8,9,10 design: 4, 2 and 1 commas or points.

" 11–15 are pointed commas equivalent to the former (N.os 8,9,10)

" 16 the comma of Urgyen Padma's books &c.

" 17 denote the large, middle, and small intersyllabic points.

" 18,19,20 denote the initial signs, used before the alphabet (when teaching to write) in books written in small characters, in running hand.

" 21 four commas placed before the alphabet.

" 22 the 2 commas of the Bamyik.

" 23 the comma in book-letter.

" 24 the intersyllabic point of the book-letter & running hand.

TIBETAN ALPHABET

in the Bámyik (འབམ་ཡིག) Character

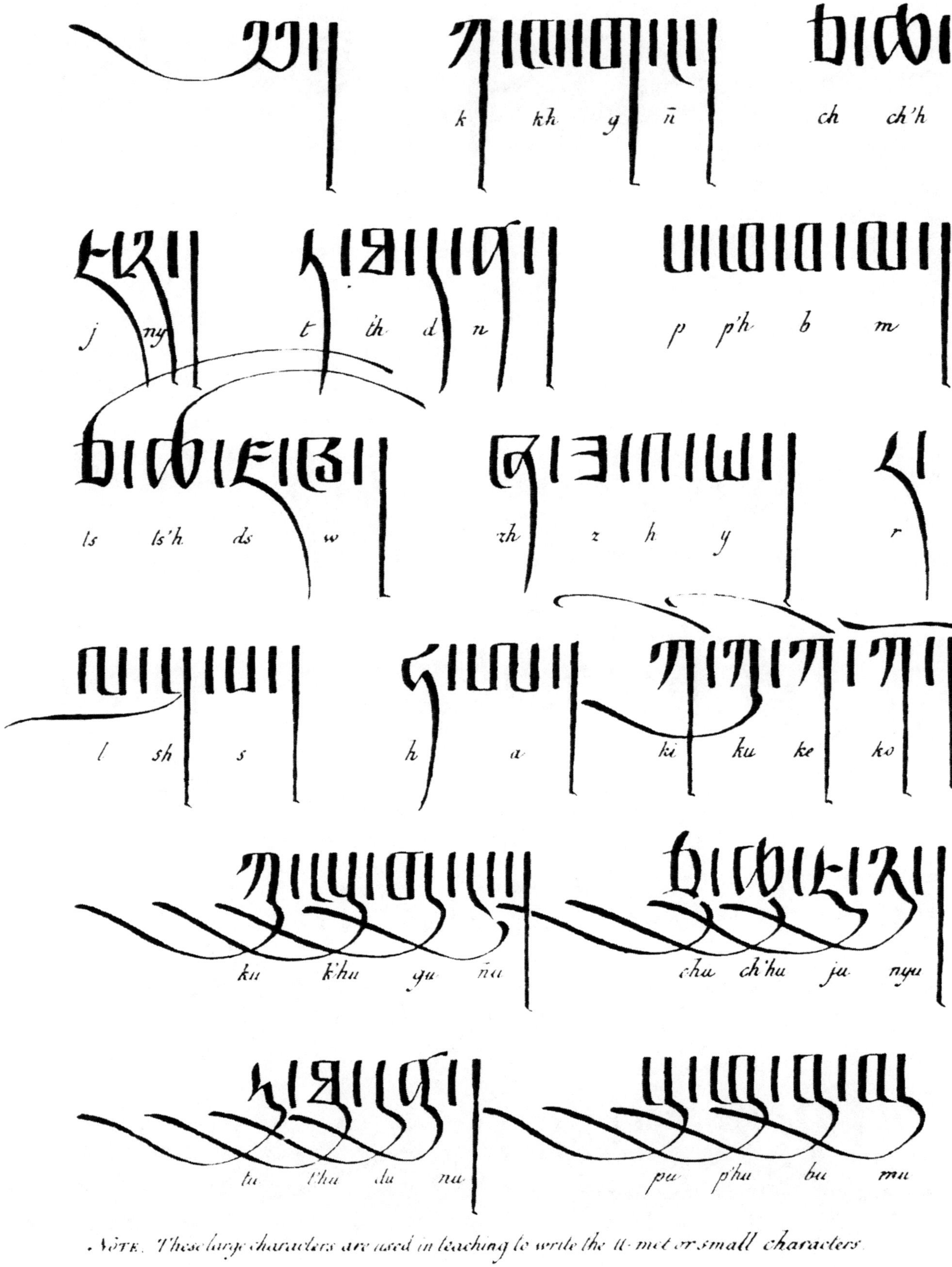

Note. These large characters are used in teaching to write the U-met or small characters.

TIBETAN ALPHABET

in the Bámyik (འབམ་ཡིག) Character

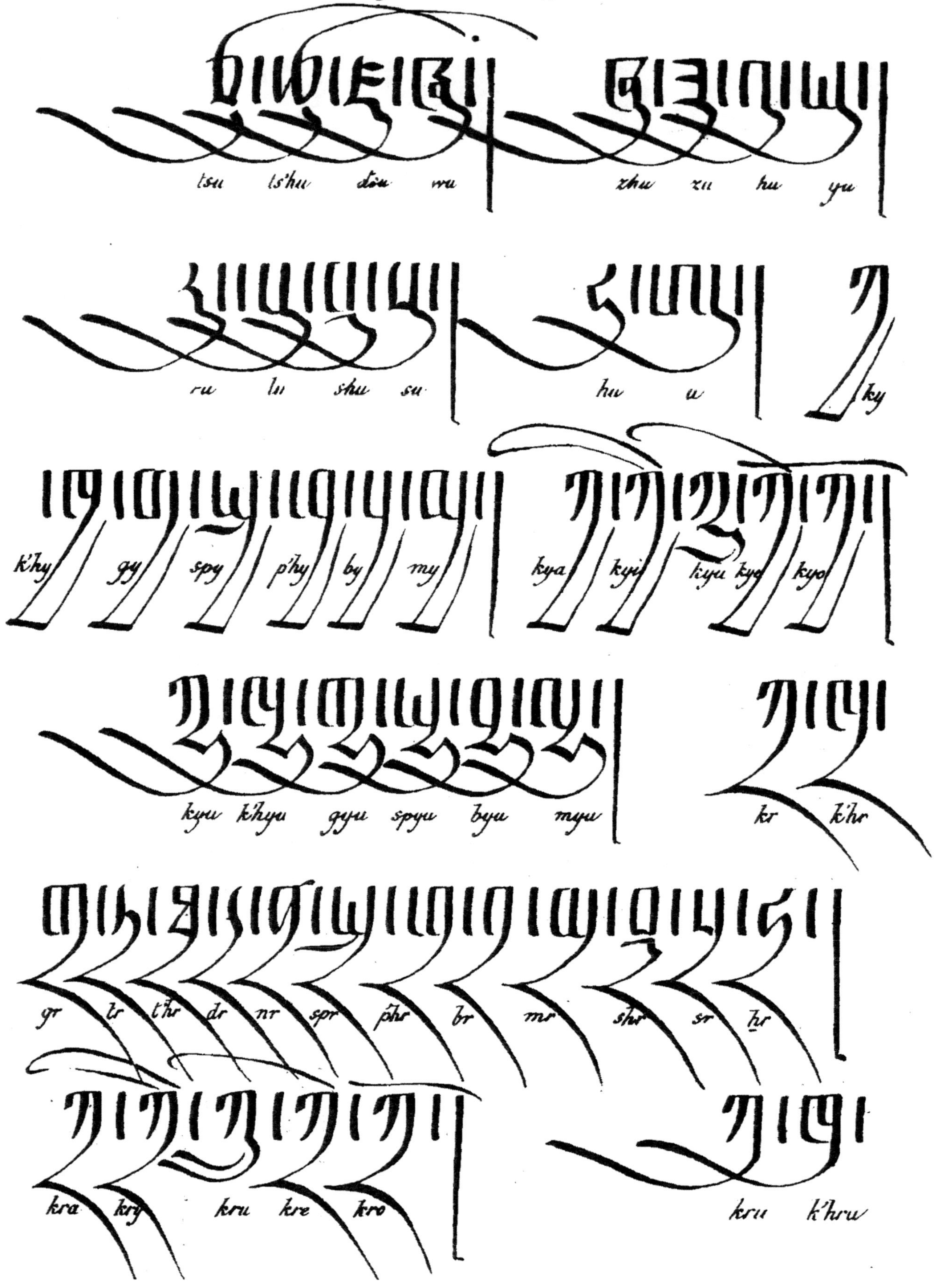

TIBETAN ALPHABET

in the Bámyik (འབམ་ཡིག) Character

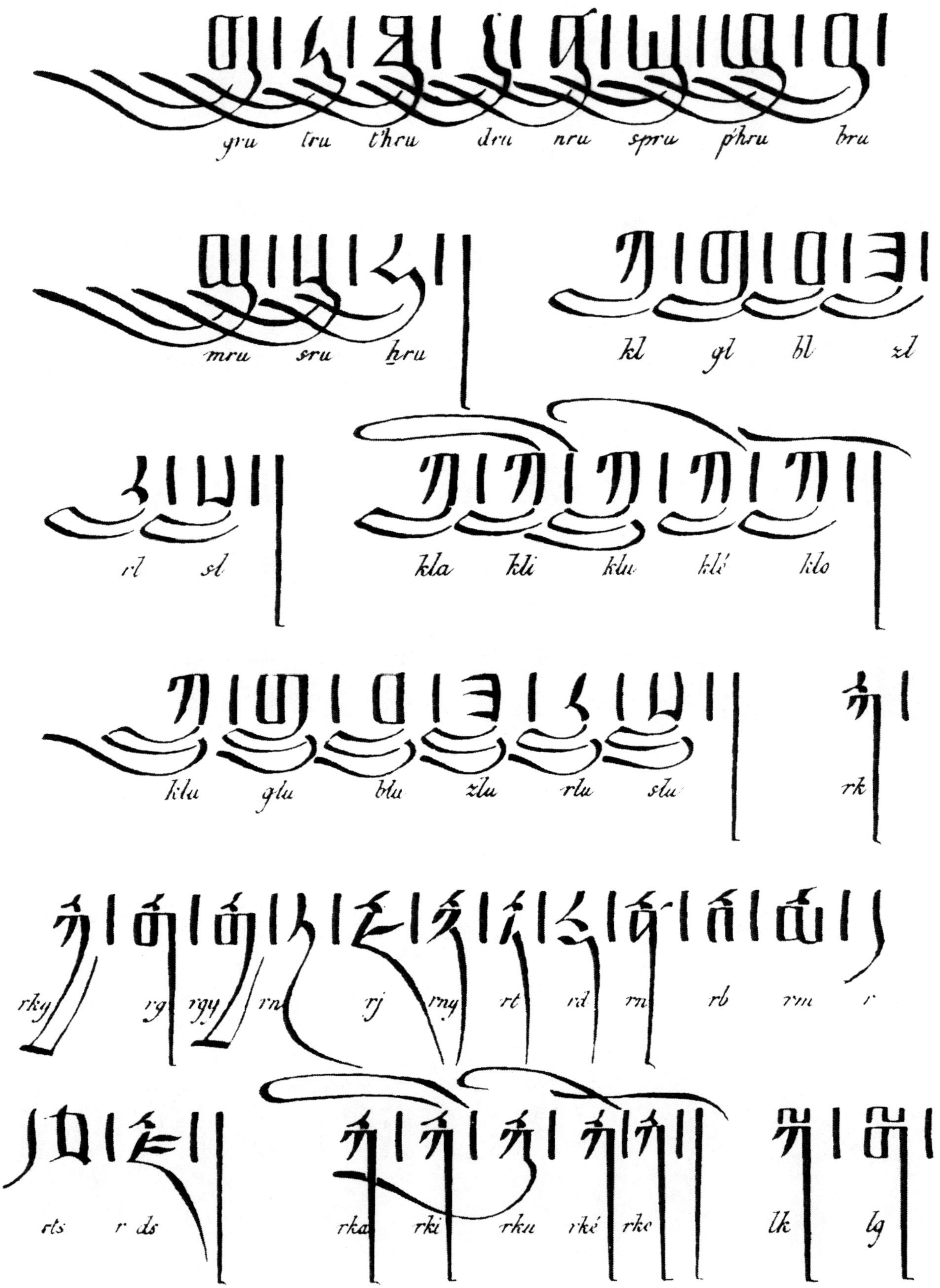

TIBETAN ALPHABET

in the Bámyik (འབམ་ཡིག) Character

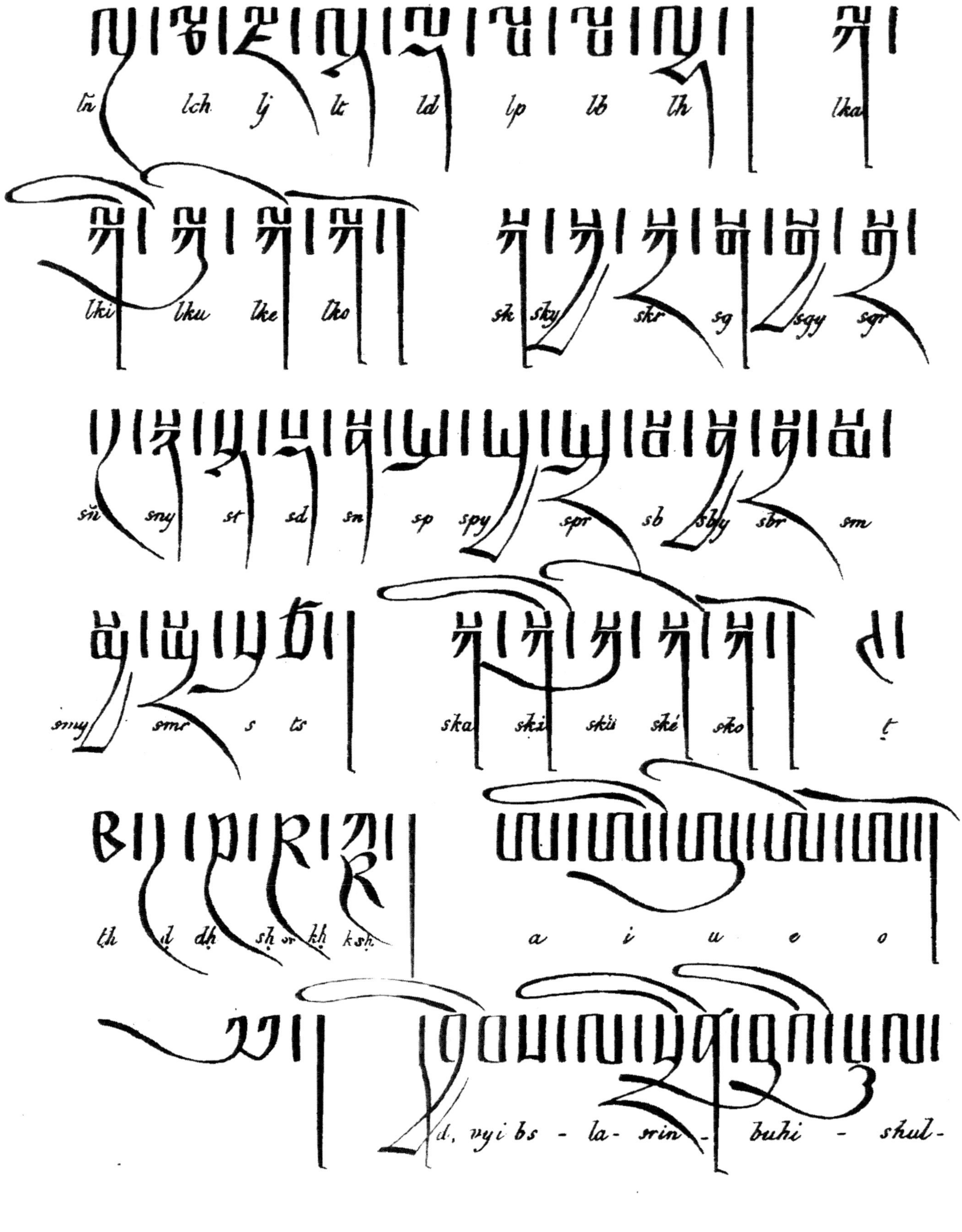

TIBETAN ALPHABET

in the Bámyik (འབམ་ཡིག) Character

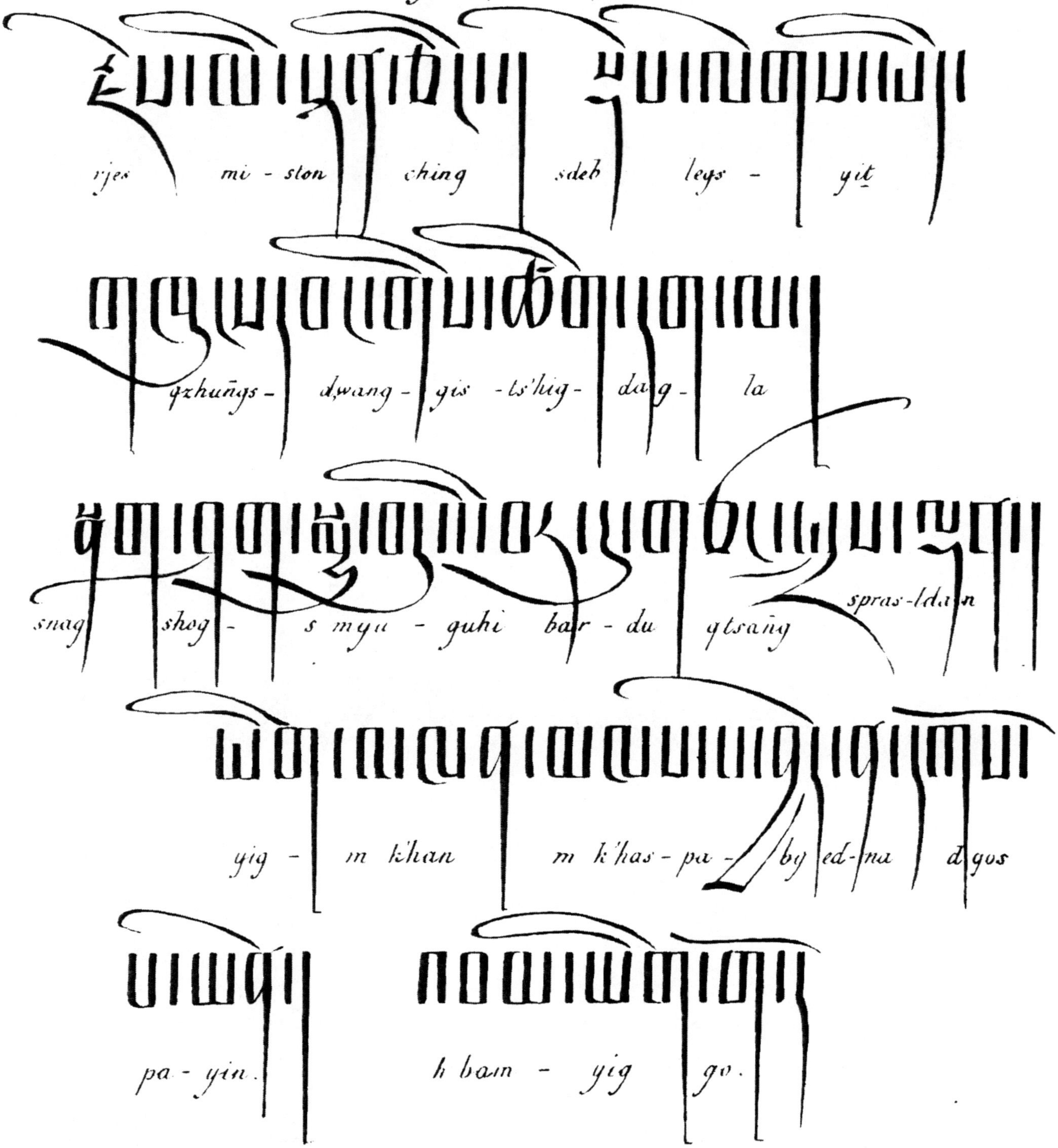

TIBETAN ALPHABET

in the Bruts'ha (འབྲུ་ཚ) Character

The Bruts'ha form of the Tibetan alphabet is distinguished, like the German or old English character, by the angular shape of the letters. It is used as an agreeable variety in ornamental writing.

k kh g ṅ, ch chh j ny, t th d n, p ph b m,

ts ts'h ds wav, zh z h y, r l sh s h' a.

ka ki ku ké ko, ku khu gu ṅu, chu chhu ju nyu, tu thu du nu,

pu phu bu mu, tsu ts'hu dsu wu, zhu zu hu yu, ru lu shu su,

h'u u, ky khy gy spy phy by my, kya kyi kyu kyé kyo,

kyu khyu gyu spyu phyu byu myu, kr khr gr tr thr dr nr pr phr br mr

shr sr h'r, kra kri kru kré kro, kru khru gru tru thru dru nru spru phru

bru mru shru sru h'ru, kl gl bl zl rl sl, kla kli klu klé klo,

rk rky rg rgy rñ rny rt rd rn rb rm rts rds, rka rki rku rké rko.

TIBETAN ALPHABET

in the Bruts'ha () Character

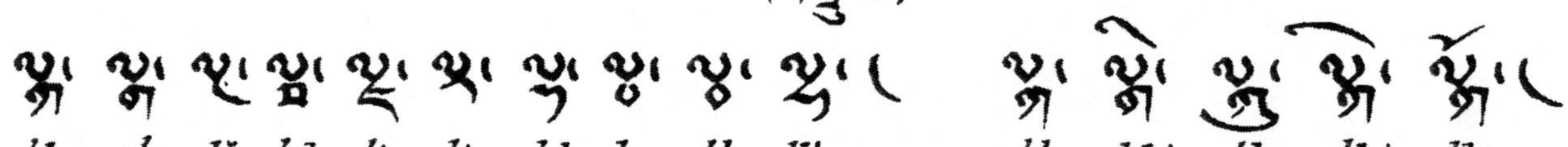

bk lg lṅ lch lj lt ld lp lb lh'. l̦ka l̦ki l̦ku l̦ké l̦ko

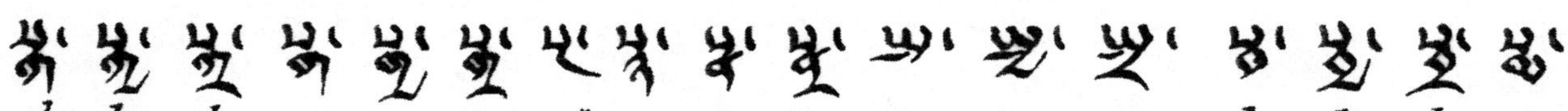

sk sky skr sg sgy sgr sṅ sny sn snr sp spy spr sb sby sbr sm

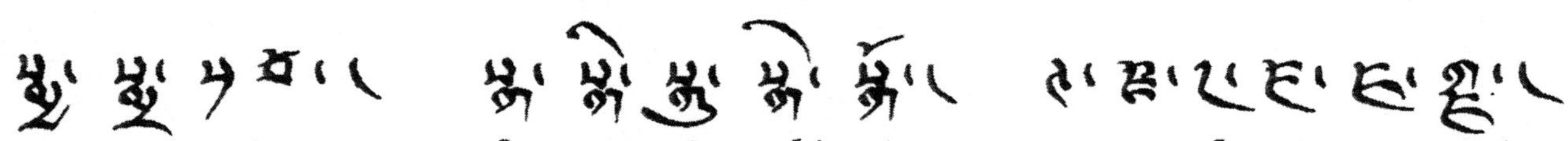

smy smr sts. șka șki șku șké șko. ṭ ṭh ḍ ḍh ṇ kṣh.

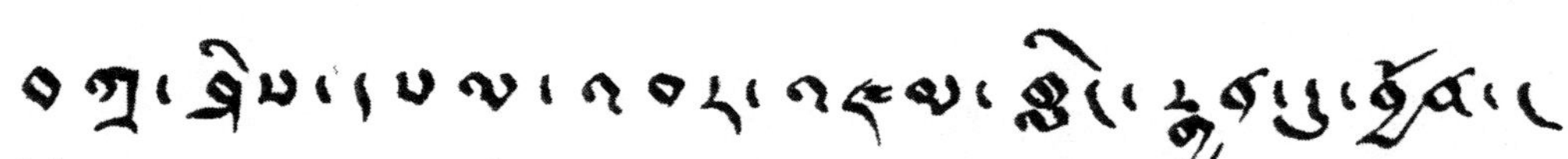

b,kra shis d,pal h,bar h,j am g,ling r,gyan-du byon.

Tibetan Numerals

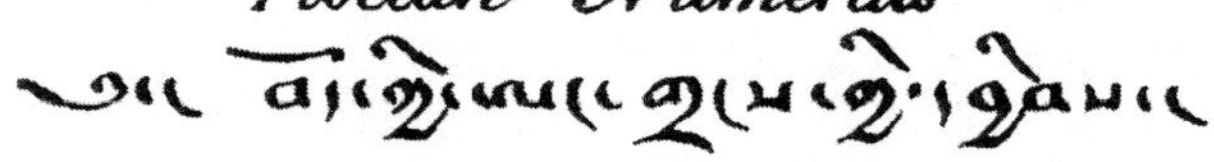

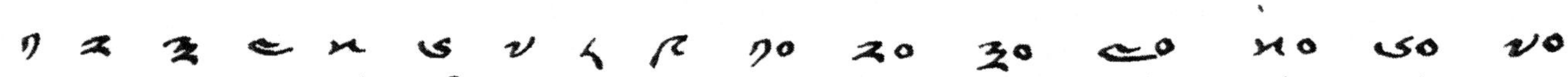

1 2 3 4 5 6 7 8 9 10 20 30 40 50 60 70

80 90 100 1000 10000 11 22 33 44 55

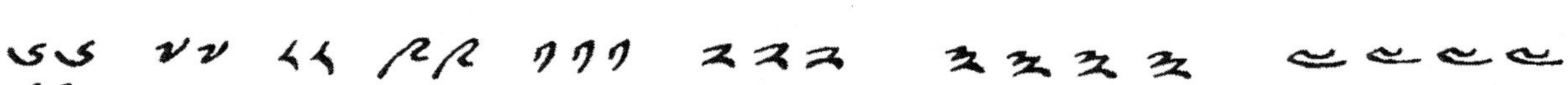

66 77 88 99 111 222 3333 4444.

LÁNTSHA CHARACTERS

or POINTED VARIETY of the DEVANAGARI alphabet used by the Buddhists in India and Tibet.

VOWELS

ཉ།	ཨ	ཨཱ	ཨི	ཨཱི	ཨུ	ཨཱུ	རྀ	རཱྀ	ལྀ	ལཱྀ	ཨེ	ཨཻ	ཨོ	ཨཽ	ཨཾ	ཨཿ
	ă	*ā*	*ĭ*	*ī*	*ŭ*	*ū*	*rĭ*	*rī*	*lĭ*	*lī*	*ē*	*ai*	*ō*	*au*	*ang*	*ah*

CONSONANTS

ཀ	ཁ	ག	གྷ	ང།	ཙ	ཚ	ཛ	ཛྷ	ཉ།	ཊ	ཋ	ཌ	ཌྷ
k	*kh*	*g*	*gh*	*ng*	*ts*	*ts'h*	*ds*	*ds'h*	*ny*	*ṭ*	*ṭh*	*ḍ*	*ḍh*

ཎ།	ཏ	ཐ	ད	དྷ	ན།	པ	ཕ	བ	བྷ	མ།
ṇ	*t*	*th*	*d*	*dh*	*n*	*p*	*ph*	*b*	*bh*	*m*

ཡ	ར	ལ	ཝ།	ཤ	ཥ	ས	ཧ།	ཀྵ།
y	*r*	*l*	*v or w*	*sh*	*sh*	*s*	*h*	*ks'h*

Combination of vowel signs with the first class of consonants

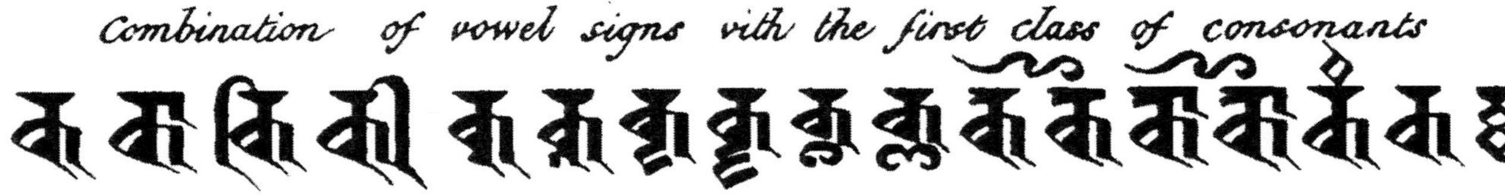

ཀ	ཀཱ	ཀི	ཀཱི	ཀུ	ཀཱུ	ཀྲྀ	ཀྲཱྀ	ཀླྀ	ཀླཱྀ	ཀེ	ཀཻ	ཀོ	ཀཽ	ཀཾ	ཀཿ
kă	*kā*	*kĭ*	*kī*	*kŭ*	*kū*	*krĭ*	*krī*	*klĭ*	*klī*	*kē*	*kai*	*kō*	*kau*	*kang*	*kah*

LÁNTS'HA CHARACTERS

ཁ ཁཱ ཁི ཁཱི ཁུ ཁཱུ ཁྲྀ ཁྲཱྀ ཁླྀ ཁླཱྀ ཁེ ཁཻ ཁོ ཁཽ ཁཾ ཁཿ

khă khā khĭ khī khŭ khū khrĭ khrī khlĭ khlī khē khai khō khau khang khah

ག གཱ གི གཱི གུ གཱུ གྲྀ གྲཱྀ གླྀ གླཱྀ གེ གཻ གོ གཽ གཾ གཿ

gă gā gĭ gī gŭ gū grĭ grī glĭ glī gē gai gō gau gang gah

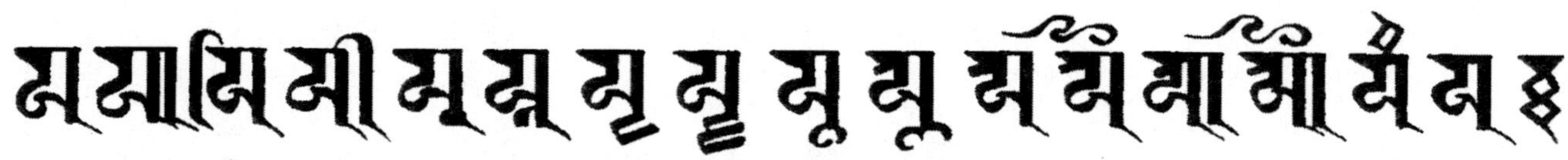

གྷ གྷཱ གྷི གྷཱི གྷུ གྷཱུ གྷྲྀ གྷྲཱྀ གྷླྀ གྷླཱྀ གྷེ གྷཻ གྷོ གྷཽ གྷཾ གྷཿ

ghă ghā ghĭ ghī ghŭ ghū ghrĭ ghrī ghlĭ ghlī ghē ghai ghō ghau ghang ghah

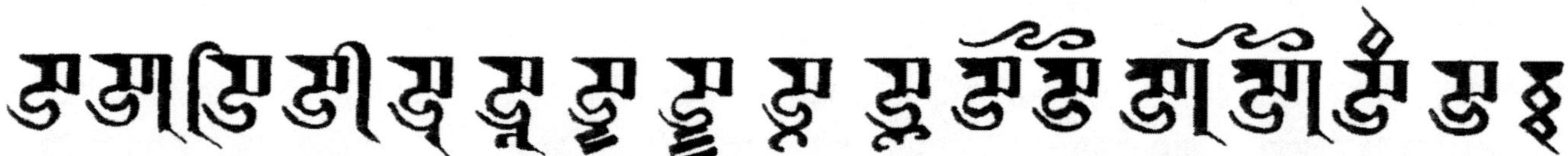

ང ངཱ ངི ངཱི ངུ ངཱུ ངྲྀ ངྲཱྀ ངླྀ ངླཱྀ ངེ ངཻ ངོ ངཽ ངཾ ངཿ

gnă gnā gnĭ gnī gnŭ gnū gnrĭ gnrī gnlĭ gnlī gnē gnai gnō gnau gnang gnah

and so on with the six other classes of Consonants

Consonants with the subjoined y, r, l and v or w.

ཀྱ ཀྲ ཀླ ཀྭ།

ky kr kl kw

ཁྱ ཁྲ ཁླ ཁྭ།

khy khr khl khw

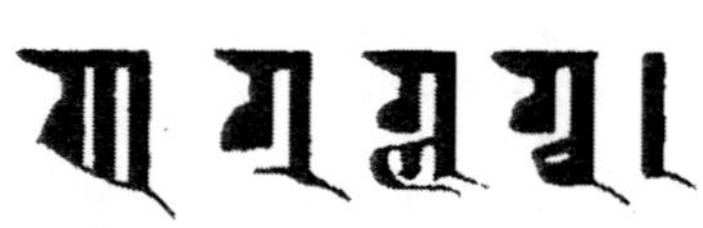

གྱ གྲ གླ གྭ།

gy gr gl gw

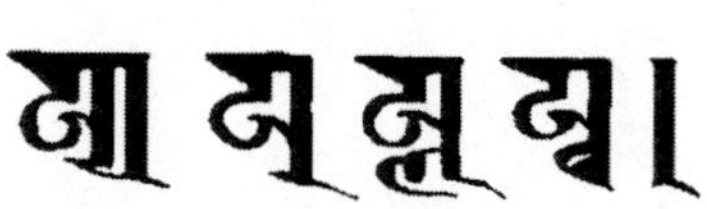

གྷྱ གྷྲ གྷླ གྷྭ།

ghy ghr ghl ghw

ངྱ ངྲ ངླ ངྭ།

ngy ngr ngl ngw

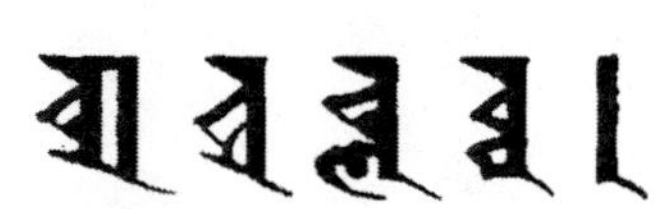

ཙྱ ཙྲ ཙླ ཙྭ།

tsy tsr tsl tsw
or
chy &c.

ts'hy ts'hr ts'hl ts'hu   dsy dsr dsl dsw   ds'hy ds'hr ds'hl ds'hw   nyy nyr nyw
chhy &c   jy &c   jhy &c
and so on with the rest of the alphabet

How the nasal ° (ṅ) is expressed before its respective classes.

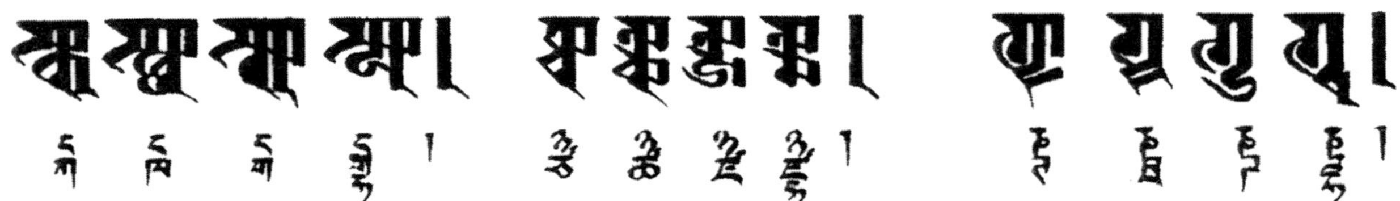

ṅk ṅkh ṅg ṅgh   nyts nyts'h nyds nyds'h   ṇṭ ṇṭh ṇḍ ṇḍh

nt nth nd ndh   mp mph mb mbh

Reduplicated Consonants

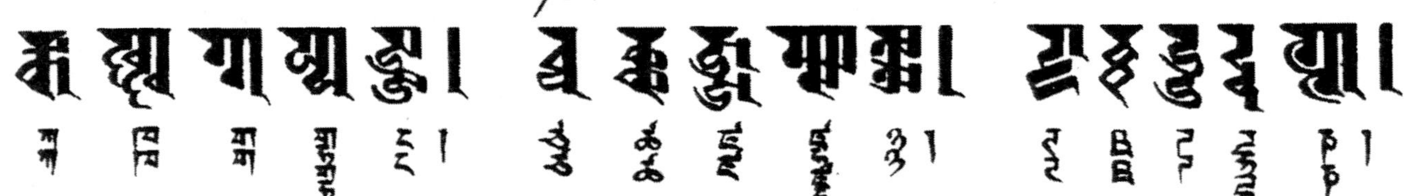

kk khkh gg ghgh ṅṅ   tsts ts'hts'h dsds ds'hds'h nyny   ṭṭ ṭhṭh ḍḍ ḍhḍh ṇṇ

kwa or kova   khwa or khova   pova phova pova phova   rb rm rk rg

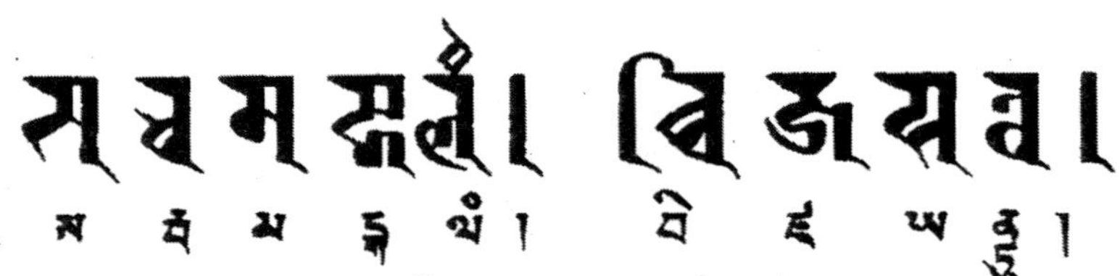

sar va mangalam vi ja yantu.

FINIS